Application of Machine Learning and Data Mining

Application of Machine Learning and Data Mining

Editors

Mingbo Zhao
Haijun Zhang
Zhou Wu

Basel • Beijing • Wuhan • Barcelona • Belgrade • Novi Sad • Cluj • Manchester

Editors

Mingbo Zhao
College of Information and
Science Technology
Donghua University
Shanghai
China

Haijun Zhang
Department of Computer
Science
Harbin Institute of
Technology
Shenzhen
China

Zhou Wu
School of Automation
Chongqing University
Chongqing
China

Editorial Office
MDPI AG
Grosspeteranlage 5
4052 Basel, Switzerland

This is a reprint of articles from the Special Issue published online in the open access journal *Mathematics* (ISSN 2227-7390) (available at: https://www.mdpi.com/journal/mathematics/special_issues/RF9D2426MO).

For citation purposes, cite each article independently as indicated on the article page online and as indicated below:

Lastname, A.A.; Lastname, B.B. Article Title. *Journal Name* **Year**, *Volume Number*, Page Range.

ISBN 978-3-7258-1925-6 (Hbk)
ISBN 978-3-7258-1926-3 (PDF)
doi.org/10.3390/books978-3-7258-1926-3

© 2024 by the authors. Articles in this book are Open Access and distributed under the Creative Commons Attribution (CC BY) license. The book as a whole is distributed by MDPI under the terms and conditions of the Creative Commons Attribution-NonCommercial-NoDerivs (CC BY-NC-ND) license.

Contents

About the Editors vii

Preface ix

Houqiang Yu, Yian Liang and Yinghua Xie
Predicting Scientific Breakthroughs Based on Structural Dynamic of Citation Cascades
Reprinted from: *Mathematics* 2024, *12*, 1741, doi:10.3390/math12111741 1

Shengye Jin, Zhengyu Zhu, Junli Liu and Shouqi Cao
Driving Style Recognition Method Based on Risk Field and Masked Learning Techniques
Reprinted from: *Mathematics* 2024, *12*, 1363, doi:10.3390/math12091363 19

Jingjing Cao, Zhipeng Wen, Liang Huang, Jinshan Dai and Hu Qin
EFE-LSTM: A Feature Extension, Fusion and Extraction Approach Using Long Short-Term Memory for Navigation Aids State Recognition
Reprinted from: *Mathematics* 2024, *12*, 1048, doi:10.3390/math12071048 34

Ahmad Al-Buenain, Mohamed Haouari and Jithu Reji Jacob
Predicting Fan Attendance at Mega Sports Events—A Machine Learning Approach: A Case Study of the FIFA World Cup Qatar 2022
Reprinted from: *Mathematics* 2024, *12*, 926, doi:10.3390/math12060926 54

Fuyong Zhang, Kuan Li and Ziliang Ren
Improving Adversarial Robustness of Ensemble Classifiers by Diversified Feature Selection and Stochastic Aggregation
Reprinted from: *Mathematics* 2024, *12*, 834, doi:10.3390/math12060834 77

Yiyang Wang, Dehao Xu, Xianpeng Li and Wei Wang
Prediction Model of Ammonia Nitrogen Concentration in Aquaculture Based on Improved AdaBoost and LSTM
Reprinted from: *Mathematics* 2024, *12*, 627, doi:10.3390/math12050627 98

Baochuan Liu, Li Zhang, Zhenwei Liu and Jing Jiang
Developer Assignment Method for Software Defects Based on Related Issue Prediction
Reprinted from: *Mathematics* 2024, *12*, 425, doi:10.3390/math12030425 116

Jiachuan Shi, Dingrui Zhi and Rao Fu
Research on a Non-Intrusive Load Recognition Algorithm Based on High-Frequency Signal Decomposition with Improved VI Trajectory and Background Color Coding
Reprinted from: *Mathematics* 2024, *12*, 30, doi:10.3390/math12010030 140

Xiumin Li, Wanyan Lin, Hao Yi, Lei Wang and Jiawei Chen
A Visually Inspired Computational Model for Recognition of Optic Flow
Reprinted from: *Mathematics* 2023, *11*, 4777, doi:10.3390/math11234777 160

Samson Ademola Adegoke, Yanxia Sun and Zenghui Wang
Minimization of Active Power Loss Using Enhanced Particle Swarm Optimization
Reprinted from: *Mathematics* 2023, *11*, 3660, doi:10.3390/math11173660 173

Nan Zhao and Chun Feng
Research on Multi-AGV Task Allocation in Train Unit Maintenance Workshop
Reprinted from: *Mathematics* 2023, *11*, 3509, doi:10.3390/math11163509 190

Juhyung Park, Sungtae Kim and Beakcheol Jang
Analysis of Psychological Factors Influencing Mathematical Achievement and Machine Learning Classification
Reprinted from: *Mathematics* **2023**, *11*, 3380, doi:10.3390/math11153380 . . . . **208**

Xue-song Tang, Luchao Jiang, Kuangrong Hao, Tong Wang and Xiaoyan Liu
A Moth–Flame Optimized Echo State Network and Triplet Feature Extractor for Epilepsy Electro-Encephalography Signals
Reprinted from: *Mathematics* **2023**, *11*, 1438, doi:10.3390/math11061438 . . . . **221**

Fines Miyoba, Egbert Mujuni, Musa Ndiaye, Hastings M. Libati and Adnan M. Abu-Mahfouz
Sustainable Rail/Road Unimodal Transportation of Bulk Cargo in Zambia: A Review of Algorithm-Based Optimization Techniques
Reprinted from: *Mathematics* **2024**, *12*, 348, doi:10.3390/math12020348 . . . . **237**

About the Editors

Mingbo Zhao

Mingbo Zhao is currently a full professor at Donghua University, Shanghai, P.R. China. He has authored or co-authored over 100 technical papers published in prestigious international journals and at conferences including TII, TIE, Pattern Recognition, Neural Networks, etc., with over 4000 Google Scholar citations and an H-index of 33. His current research interests include machine learning, deep learning and computer vision, fault diagnosis, and medical diagnosis. He currently serves as an associate editor (AE) for IEEE Trans on Consumer Electronics and The International Journal of Pattern Recognition and Artificial Intelligence. He is also serving/has served as the Area Chair of ACM Multimedia 2021/2022/2023 and as an SPC member of AAAI 2022/2023/2024/2025. He is now a Senior Member of the IEEE and CCF.

Haijun Zhang

Haijun Zhang received his B.Eng. and master's degrees from Northeastern University, Shenyang, China, in 2004 and 2007, respectively, and his Ph.D. from the Department of Electronic Engineering, City University of Hong Kong, Hong Kong, in 2010. He worked as a Postdoctoral Research Fellow with the Department of Electrical and Computer Engineering, University of Windsor, Windsor, ON, Canada, from 2010 to 2011. Since 2012, he has been with the Shenzhen Graduate School, Harbin Institute of Technology, China, where he is currently a Professor of Computer Science. His current research interests include data mining, machine learning, fashion intelligence, and service computing. He is a senior member of the IEEE and serves as an associate editor for IEEE Trans. on Consumer Electronics.

Zhou Wu

Zhou Wu is a full professor at the School of Automation, Chongqing University, China. His research interests include renewable energy systems, demand-side management, and green building technology. He has been working in these areas for decades and has set up many collaborations with institutions in South Africa and Hong Kong. He has published more than 30 peer-reviewed papers in Applied Energy, Energy, Solar Energy, and other related journals. He is a senior member of the IEEE. He serves as an associate editor for IEEE Trans. on Consumer Electronics, IEEE/CAA Journal of Automatica Sinica, and The International Journal of Computer Science and Mathematics.

Preface

Machine learning and data mining are intertwined fields that leverage mathematical principles to extract valuable insights from data. Machine learning involves developing algorithms that improve through experience, enabling machines to learn from data without explicit human intervention. This field aims to create intelligent systems that automate complex tasks and provide smart solutions. In contrast, data mining focuses on discovering new, accurate, and useful patterns to inform decision-making, serving as a tool for humans to analyze vast datasets. Both fields rely heavily on mathematical foundations, including statistics, linear algebra, calculus, graph theory, and optimization, which are essential for analyzing data, optimizing models, and understanding relationships within datasets.

Recent decades have seen a dramatic rise in the application of machine learning and data mining. Recent technologies, e.g., the Internet of Things (IoTs), neural networks, deep learning, and smart things, have brought new developments in machine learning and data mining to areas such as healthcare, manufacturing, automobiles, and agriculture. One important breakthrough in artificial intelligence techniques is deep learning, which includes a large family of neural computing methods, e.g., convolutional neural networks (CNNs), generative adversarial networks (GANs), and transformers, that employ deep architectures composed of multiple non-linear transformations to model high-level abstractions of raw data. Recent studies have shown that deep neural networks significantly improve the performance of learning tasks such as object detection, image classification, and segmentation. As a consequence, many advanced real-world applications have developed increasingly close relations with machine learning and data mining technologies.

The following book contains 14 articles accepted and published in the Special Issue "Mathematics and Computer Science, 2024" of the MDPI journal Mathematics. The included articles cover a wide range of topics related to the theory and applications of Machine Learning and Data Mining, as well as their extensions and generalizations. These topics include, but are not limited to, supervised, unsupervised, and self-learning methods; large-scale data mining; applicable neural networks and artificial intelligence; neural network-based industrial applications; neural models for natural language processing; deep learning for health informatics and biomedical engineering; graph convolutional neural networks and their applications; deep reinforcement learning and its applications; deep sparse and low-rank representation; and computer vision and pattern recognition techniques.

As the Guest Editor of this Special Issue, I am grateful to the authors for their quality contributions, to the reviewers for their valuable comments that contributed to the improvement of the submitted works, and to the administrative staff of MDPI Publications for their support in completing this project. Special thanks are due to Ms. Rebecca Xue, the Managing Editor of the Special Issue, for her excellent collaboration and valuable assistance.

Mingbo Zhao, Haijun Zhang, and Zhou Wu
Editors

Article

Predicting Scientific Breakthroughs Based on Structural Dynamic of Citation Cascades

Houqiang Yu, Yian Liang and Yinghua Xie *

School of Information Management, Sun Yat-sen University, Guangzhou 510006, China; yuhq8@mail.sysu.edu.cn (H.Y.); liangyan3@mail2.sysu.edu.cn (Y.L.)
* Correspondence: xieyh53@mail2.sysu.edu.cn; Tel.: +86-150-0359-9289

Abstract: Predicting breakthrough papers holds great significance; however, prior studies encountered challenges in this task, indicating a need for substantial improvement. We propose that the failure to capture the dynamic structural-evolutionary features of citation networks is one of the major reasons. To overcome this limitation, this paper introduces a new method for constructing citation cascades of focus papers, allowing the creation of a time-series-like set of citation cascades. Then, through a thorough review, three types of structural indicators in these citation networks that could reflect breakthroughs are identified, including certain basic topological metrics, PageRank values, and the von Neumann graph entropy. Based on the time-series-like set of citation cascades, the dynamic trajectories of these indicators are calculated and employed as predictors. Using the Nobel Prize-winning papers as a landmark dataset, our prediction method yields approximately a 7% improvement in the ROC-AUC score compared to static-based prior methods. Additionally, our method advances in achieving earlier predictions than other previous methods. The main contribution of this paper is proposing a novel method for creating citation cascades in chronological order and confirming the significance of predicting breakthroughs from a dynamic structural perspective.

Keywords: predictions; breakthroughs; networks; structure; dynamics

MSC: 05C82; 68T20

Citation: Yu, H.; Liang, Y.; Xie, Y. Predicting Scientific Breakthroughs Based on Structural Dynamic of Citation Cascades. *Mathematics* **2024**, *12*, 1741. https://doi.org/10.3390/math12111741

Academic Editors: Mingbo Zhao, Haijun Zhang and Zhou Wu

Received: 7 May 2024
Revised: 29 May 2024
Accepted: 31 May 2024
Published: 3 June 2024

Copyright: © 2024 by the authors. Licensee MDPI, Basel, Switzerland. This article is an open access article distributed under the terms and conditions of the Creative Commons Attribution (CC BY) license (https://creativecommons.org/licenses/by/4.0/).

1. Introduction

Scientific breakthroughs often imply the new emergence and growth of science or society [1]. Many recent studies have focused on capturing the characteristics of breakthroughs and trying to predict them. One of the characteristics drawn from classical and widely acknowledged theories exhibits potential power in predictions: breakthrough discoveries often lead to dramatic changes in knowledge evolution [2]. Certain theories, like the theory of disruptive innovation [3], Kuhn's concept of paradigm shift [4], and other classical theories, all share this perspective.

In this perspective, the variation in the knowledge structure represents one important dimension of the so-called "dramatic changes", which is accessible and easy to quantify compared to other dimensions. In recent years, this idea has attracted great interest, and several works of literature have been designed based on it. They benefit from the advancement of complex network technology, which allows them to model the knowledge evolution structure. Among them, there is one kind of complex network, the citation cascades [5], showing power in breakthrough predictions. Citation cascades refer to a type of citation structure that involves the constitution of a series of subsequent citing events initiated by a focus paper (more details are in the reference [6]). Using the citing cascades, Min et al. [2] predicted the Nobel Prize-winning papers based on their topological metrics and achieved a performance that exceeded prior methods. Theoretically, they also confirmed that the variation in knowledge structure indicated scientific breakthroughs.

However, despite numerous methods proposed to predict scientific breakthroughs, accurately predicting them remains very hard, as confirmed consistently [2,7,8]. They claim that it is challenging to identify scientific breakthroughs, with predicting them being even more difficult. The aforementioned prediction, based on the basic topological metrics of citation cascades by Min et al. [2], only achieved less than 70% of the highest AUC score, indicating great room for improvement and a long distance to go before practical application. Through a literature review, we conclude that the static nature of prior methods, which are based mostly on a particular snapshot of the structure of knowledge evolution, impedes the prediction performance, while intuitively, the "dramatic change in knowledge structure" exhibits a strong dynamic nature.

We argue that the dynamic structure of knowledge evolution can reveal further information beyond static topological metrics, enhancing the prediction of breakthrough papers. One possibility, for example, is that different structural features may exhibit distinct characteristics at earlier and later stages of knowledge evolution. Nevertheless, capturing information about the dynamic evolution of citation cascades poses a challenge. This is closely related to the construction methods of citation cascades (more details in Sections 2.2 and 3.3). Due to the explosive growth potential of citation cascade networks, certain restrictions are necessary. Previous studies limit the time span of citation cascades (for example, restricting the cascades within 2, 3, or 4 years after the focus paper's publication year), and though it is effective to some extent, this also poses difficulties in capturing the dynamic properties of citation cascades. Hence, we aim to adjust the construction method of cascade citations to capture their dynamic nature for predicting scientific breakthroughs.

In this paper, we modify the construction of citation cascades. Under this construction method, the citation cascades grow the edges in a chronological order and have a limited number of edges. By considering the citation cascades at various growth stages, a series of snapshots is generated. Then, specific structure metrics of these snapshots are calculated, thereby leading to time-series-like data, and they serve as the raw predictors. In the experiment of this study, the structure metrics involve the basic topological metrics, PageRank values, and the von Neumann graph entropy. Finally, we extract certain features as predictors from this time-series-like data and utilize them to predict scientific breakthroughs.

In summary, we aim to quantify the dynamic evolution of knowledge structure to predict scientific breakthroughs, with citation cascades as the agents. Using the Nobel Prize-winning papers as a landmark dataset of scientific breakthroughs, prediction experiments are performed; it is anticipated that our method surpasses the static approach and achieves a higher prediction performance.

In Section 2, we provide a brief overview of scientific breakthroughs, predicting breakthroughs, and citation cascades. Section 3 illustrates our forecasting method and modeling process. Section 4 shows the prediction performance and compares our method with previous approaches. The final Section 5 addresses our contributions, implications, and future directions.

2. Background
2.1. Definition and Prediction of Breakthroughs
2.1.1. Scientific Breakthroughs

Scientific breakthroughs do not have a widely accepted definition. Some studies in recent years have defined them as scientific advancements that can override and significantly expand existing knowledge and even create new fields [9]. Many studies that predict or identify breakthroughs often root in this idea.

A breakthrough drives new growth [10]. And scientific breakthroughs are more transformative, triggering new growth in wide ranges and involving academic, social, and economic aspects. Therefore, forecasting and nurturing scientific breakthroughs are crucial. Especially in the post-epidemic era, the COVID-19 pandemic not only threatens human health but also profoundly changes the socioeconomic structure [11]. Scientific breakthroughs hold more significance. They are the key to offering novel solutions to some global challenges, drawing new growth points to stimulate economics, and providing the potential to address development disparities.

Some scholars categorize scientific breakthroughs into different types. For instance, the well-known cha-cha-cha theory [12]. It argues that scientific breakthroughs can be divided into three types: "solving obvious but previously unsolvable problems", "addressing some accidental but crucial problems", and "some discoveries challenge or cannot be explained by existing knowledge". While the types of scientific breakthroughs are well explored, where and when they occur remains unclear. Some studies have identified correlations with scientific breakthroughs, such as diverse knowledge [13] and scientists' characteristics [14], but none of these can predict them. For example, in datasets with artificially constructed control groups, atypical combination index is not able to differentiate Nobel Prize-winning papers [15]. It is challenging to pinpoint when and where a scientific breakthrough happens in a vast dataset instead of with artificially constructed control groups. In short, predicting scientific breakthroughs is a challenging task. In the following section, we will also highlight this point.

2.1.2. Predicting Breakthroughs

In this section, the primary methods for identifying or predicting scientific breakthroughs are outlined.

From the perspective of knowledge structure variation to predict scientific breakthroughs, there are various methods. The most famous one is the Disruption Index [16,17], which has been featured in papers published in some reputed journals like Nature or Science several times [18,19]. Figure 1 illustrates its basic idea and computation method. This method evaluates the breakthrough of a focus paper by checking if the citing papers (of the focus paper) cite the focus paper's references. There are numerous variations of this method, including adjustments to the detailed calculation process and integrated knowledge entities in it [7,20]. However, all these methods have significant difficulty predicting scientific breakthroughs effectively. The Disruptive Index fails to differentiate Nobel Prize-winning papers, and its enhanced methodology also struggles with this task [7,21].

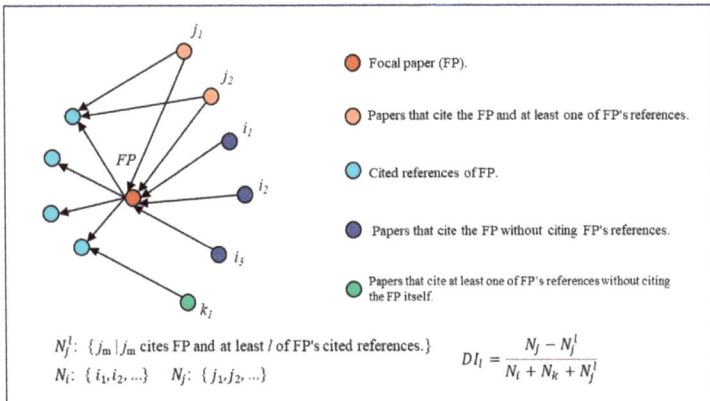

Figure 1. The basic idea and calculation of the Disruption Index. Note: After constructing the citation structure, DI_l in the lower right corner is the value of the Disruptive Index. Generally speaking, l is equal to 1, and Bormann et al. [20] expanded this index and extended the l to any value.

Another approach based on knowledge structure variation utilizes the citation cascades as an agent for scientific evolution. The topological indicators of them are employed to predict breakthroughs, and they achieve promising outcomes [2,8]. However, only certain topological indicators are effective in predicting, including the average clustering coefficient, average degree, maximum closeness centrality, and number of components. They discover that papers with distinct characteristics of the above indicators indicate breakthroughs, which may suggest that breakthrough findings lead to greater knowledge structure variation. These effective indicators also hold theoretical significance. In the citation structure, the node's degree indicates its influence on knowledge diffusion [22], and the closeness centrality reflects the effectiveness of knowledge dissemination [23], among other factors. However, the highest AUC scores in their papers on breakthrough predictions are only 69% in economics science and 67.5% in natural science, indicating the great challenge of predicting them. One of the reasons may be that they rely solely on static characteristics; they only use some topological metrics of citation cascades within a specific fixed time (a snapshot).

Other algorithms based on knowledge structure perspectives have also been proposed, in addition to the Disruption Index and the topological metrics of citation cascades. PageRank is a classical algorithm that measures the importance of a node and is commonly utilized in the information retrieval field [24]. Some literature has also used it to identify breakthrough patents, suggesting that an important node in a citation network may indicate a breakthrough [25].

However, these above indicators may remain limited. Other indicators may still be worth considering, especially those from complex network techniques. Entropy, for instance. Entropy is a crucial concept for complex networks, representing a wealth of information. The structure entropy of a graph can serve as an indicator of the complexity of a network. We believe that it is related to the "dramatic change" brought about by scientific breakthroughs. Therefore, we incorporate the von Neumann graph entropy [26] into our experiment.

Besides the method based on structure information, there are also many other dimensional methods. These approaches include expert-manual selection, content-based identification, and citation-count-based methods. (1) Manual selection is an effective but relatively inefficient method, yet it remains important [27]. Some examples are the selection of breakthroughs by the Science journal, the MIT press, and others. (2) At the content-based identification level, studies often analyze the topic distribution of focus papers using a topic model and assess their breakthroughs by examining the extent to which they cover previous and subsequent topics [28,29]. In the field of business, breakthrough patents are those that significantly differ from previous patents but are similar to subsequent patents [30]. Alternatively, keyword networks can be created, and their entropy is used to detect the surge in topic evolution [27]. Those that led to sudden topic evolution may be breakthroughs. (3) Citation count is often used as a proxy for breakthroughs [31], particularly in defining patent breakthroughs [32]. However, it exhibits obvious shortcomings. For example, review papers have higher citation counts but lack breakthroughs. Some studies point out its limitations: it may lead to bias [1], and it is proven to be challenging to identify scientific breakthroughs [2].

2.2. Citation Cascades

From the perspective of forecasting breakthroughs through the structure variation features, proxying knowledge structure is a challenging task. Citation behavior, or citation structure, is a crucial tool for analyzing the evolution of knowledge. Citation behavior is often viewed as a form of knowledge diffusion [33]. Then, these citations interact, forming a network-like citation structure. These network structures provide a strong foundation for modeling knowledge structures and creating advanced models to predict and improve organizational outcomes [34]. Since the whole citation network, being a huge complex graph, is challenging to use directly. The variational methods based on it are more practical. Among them, citation cascades have become a prominent one in recent years [5,6,35]. It is utilized for various tasks such as technology forecasting [2], agent knowledge structure [36] or intelligence structure [37], impact evaluation [38], scientific evaluation [39], topic detection or hot spot prediction [6], and cascade information exploration in social media [40]. A typical example of citation cascades is illustrated in Figure 2B.

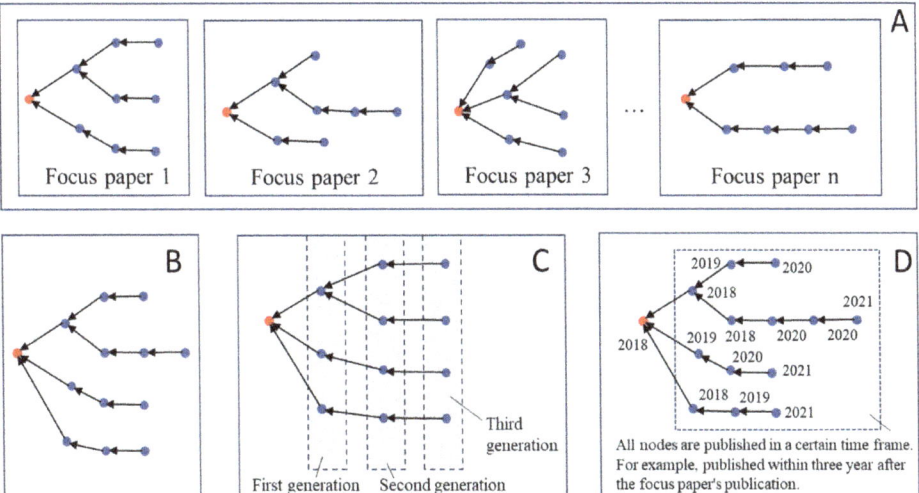

Figure 2. Notation and construction methods of citation cascades. Note: In (**A**), each focal document in our approach has a corresponding citation cascade. (**B**) illustrates an example of citation cascade networks. (**C**,**D**) show two previous methods of creating cascading citations.

We specifically explain the citation cascades, as they are a feasible and promising tool for forecasting scientific breakthroughs [5]. Citation cascades are created from a focus paper to represent the knowledge flow it initiates. Initially, the generation of citations is defined as "the collection of papers that cite a focus paper either directly (first generation) or indirectly (through a path in the citation graph originating from a citing paper and ending at the focus paper)" [41]. Min et al. develop this idea and use it to predict breakthroughs [2]. It is notable that each focus paper spans its citation cascade networks, which occur individually, as depicted in Figure 2A. They utilize the basic topological metrics of these citation cascades to predict which focus paper is a scientific breakthrough.

However, as mentioned in Section 1, the growth of citation cascade networks is inherently explosive. For a simple example, if each generation has 20 citations, there will be millions of citations with only five generations. Therefore, certain restrictions are typically necessary when using them. Create citation cascades with a limited number of generations, and in Figure 2C, three generations are selected. However, this approach remains limited by the highly uneven distribution of the number of papers in the citation cascades. Min et al. address this issue by restricting their growth time, such as limiting them to 2–4 years after the publication of the focus paper. An example can be seen in Figure 2D. While this approach is effective in some cases, it is static and struggles to capture the dynamic nature of knowledge structures. Additionally, this approach may lead to an uneven distribution of citation sizes among papers: some papers may experience rapid growth in the cascades, while others, known as "sleeping beauty literature" [42], may remain dormant for a long time. Hence, we adjust the structure of cascading citations to reflect their dynamic nature, as detailed in Section 3.3.

The citation structure not only involves the citation cascades but also includes various forms like main path analysis [43], the max-min method to identify core nodes in the network [44,45], and others. These technologies, especially their combination with intelligence algorithms like deep learning and machine learning, are potential methods for future studies.

3. Methodology

3.1. Overviews of the Research Processs

The following paragraphs describe the methodology used in this study. The basic process is illustrated in Figure 3, and further details are presented in the following Sections (Sections 3.2–3.6).

(1) The dataset of Nobel Prize-winning papers is chosen as a landmark of scientific breakthroughs. (More details are shown in Section 3.2).
(2) Find a control group for the breakthrough dataset, representing the non-breakthrough papers. (More details are shown in Section 3.2).
(3) Construct citation cascade networks for each paper using our method. After that, a series of snapshots of the cascade networks is generated. (More details are shown in Section 3.3).
(4) Calculate specific structural indicators for these series of citation cascade network snapshots. The indicators include the number of nodes, average clustering coefficient, average degree, maximum closeness centrality, number of components, PageRank value of the focus paper, mean value and variance of PageRank, and the von Neumann graph entropy. In this step, the series data for these metrics is then generated. (More details are shown in Sections 3.4 and 3.5).
(5) Feature selections: extract certain features from the series data. (More details are shown in Section 3.5).
(6) Finally, the extracted features are utilized to forecast scientific breakthroughs using machine learning algorithms. (More details are shown in Section 3.5).

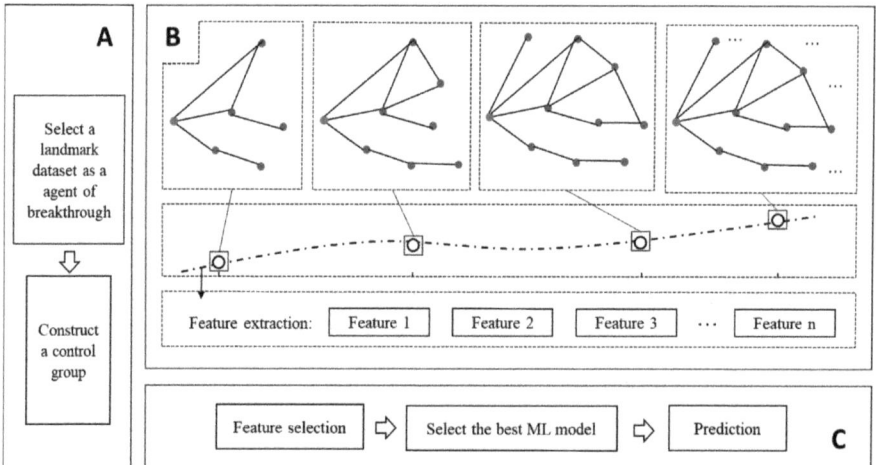

Figure 3. Overview of the process. Note: The process of our study follows the sequence (**A**) → (**B**) → (**C**). (**A**) illustrates the process of constructing the dataset. (**B**) provides a basic description of our dynamic approach. The red dot represents the focus paper, and the blue dots represent papers that directly or indirectly cite the focus papers. As the number of edges expands, we capture lots of snapshots of the citation cascade. For each one, we calculate specific structural metrics (e.g., the average cluster coefficient). As a result, time-series-like data is generated. Afterward, extract features from these sequences, which then serve as predictors. (**C**) illustrates the final machine learning process.

3.2. Landmark Dataset

With increased attention to scientific breakthroughs, landmark datasets have been created. Among them, the most widely used and acknowledged are the Nobel Prize-winning papers. The Nobel Prize signifies broad recognition within the academic community, often acknowledging the scientists who discover breakthrough findings. Though the Nobel Prize is awarded to individual scientists, it is primarily based on one or a few specific paper(s) by those winners. Hence, scholars have manually identified a dataset of Nobel Prize-winning papers [46], which is published in Scientific Data. According to this work, we compile a dataset of Nobel Prize-winning papers published after 1960, totaling 648 papers.

In the work of [46], the prize-winning papers are determined by the laureate's speech. In general, winning papers are cited as references in the lectures. The paper that meets all the following criteria is considered a Nobel Prize-winning paper: (1) has at least one author with the same name as a Nobel Prize winner; (2) is published in the same period as the winning paper; (3) has consistent institution and co-author information with the award-winning paper; and (4) has a subject consistent with the motivation of the Nobel Prize.

To enable a prediction, it is necessary to establish a suitable control group. Based on previous research, certain variables need to be controlled [2,7]. According to previous literature, the citation count, team size (the number of authors of a paper), publication year, and academic discipline all influence breakthroughs and should be involved. Then, we ensure that the breakthrough and non-breakthrough paper groups have similar citation counts, which differ by 20% or less, are authored by the same number of individuals, published in the same year, and belong to the same discipline. Only one paper is randomly selected from the control papers that meet these criteria, thereby creating a one-to-one paired dataset.

The Matthew effect is significant, as Nobel Prize-winning papers tend to receive a high number of citations. Therefore, we ensure that the citation cascade networks for each Nobel Prize-winning paper have a shorter span than the prize year. Those who do not meet this criterion are excluded, and then 335 papers remain.

The metadata and citation data of papers in this study are sourced from the SciSciNet [47] and OpenAlex databases [48]. These databases are built on the well-known MAG (Microsoft academic graph) database, and their quality has also been checked by several studies.

3.3. Construction of Citation Cascades

As discussed earlier, constructing a citation cascade network for modeling scientific evolution is challenging due to its explosive nature. Previous studies have restricted cascading citation networks to 2–4 years after the focus paper publication. However, this approach leads to a static nature, making it hard to capture their dynamic structure characteristics for prediction.

To tackle the aforementioned issues, we suggest a new approach to constructing citation cascade networks. This method creates cascade citations by controlling the number of edges and selecting a fixed number (threshold) of edges in a chronological sequence. See Figure 4 for details. Firstly, we obtain the citation time for each citation, and all the citations are then sorted chronologically. Then, a threshold is set, and a fixed number of edges with the earliest citation time are chosen to build the citation cascade network. These processes can be executed using a graph traversal algorithm. With this construction method, it is possible to ensure an equal number of edges for each paper's citation cascades. Most importantly, this method is able to capture citation cascade networks at different temporal snapshots. For instance, the snapshots of a cascade network have thresholds for the number of edges at 100, 200, 500, and 1000.

In our study, we set the maximum number of edges threshold at 1000. Starting with the 100 edges, every 10th edge increases, creating a snapshot until reaching 1000 edges. So, in total, this process yields 90 snapshots of the citation cascade networks. In the following sections, certain structure features of these snapshots are computed, then forming the time-series-like predictors.

The construction of cascade networks for the entire dataset, including the Nobel Prize-winning papers dataset and its control group, consists of 327,245 papers and 752,849 citations.

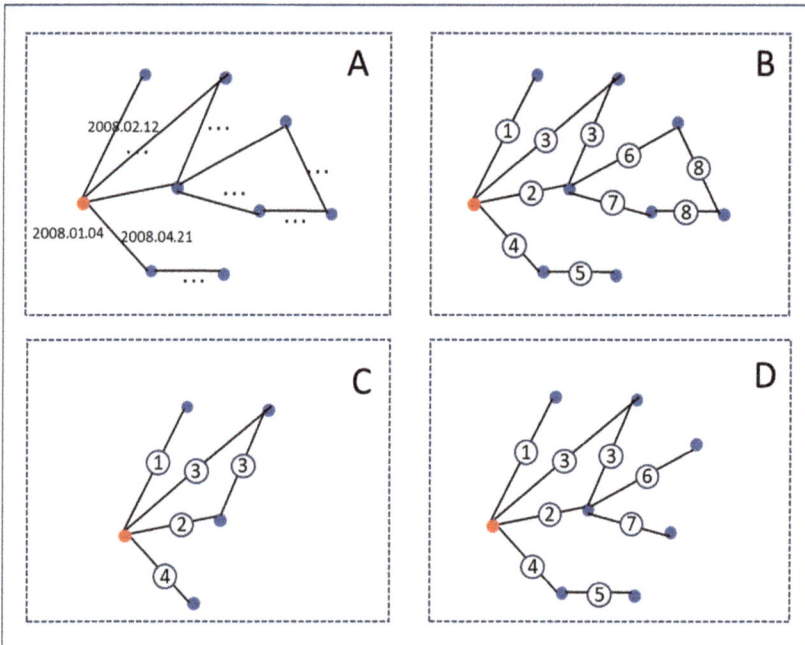

Figure 4. The new approach proposed in this study to constructing citation cascade networks for capturing dynamic structural information. Note: (**A**) shows that the citation time of each citation is recorded. A chronological order is added to each citation based on the citation time, with "2" indicating the second citation in the chronological sequence, as shown in (**B**). Finally, a threshold (the maximum number of edges) is selected. (**C**) shows the result of setting the threshold at 4, and (**D**) illustrates a network with a maximum of 7 edges. In our experiments, the threshold is indeed set at 1000.

Formally, the pseudocode creating the citation cascades in chronological order is provided in Algorithm 1.

Algorithm 1. Create citation cascade network.

Input: P_f (Focus paper).
Output: Citation cascade in chronological order.
1: $P_{PotentialPapers} \leftarrow \varnothing$
2: $P_{SelectedPapers} \leftarrow \varnothing$
3: $Index \leftarrow 0$
4: $Threshould \leftarrow 1000$
5: Add all papers that cite to $P_{PotentialPapers}$
6: **while** $Index < 1000$ and $P_{PotentialPapers} \neq \varnothing$ **do**
7:    Select paper P_{Index} with thee arliest citation date from $P_{PotentialPaper}$
8:    Add P_{Index} to $P_{SelectedPapers}$
9:    Remove P_{Index} from $P_{PotentialPapers}$
10:   Add all papers that cite P_{Index} to $P_{PotentialPaper}$
11:   $Index \leftarrow Index + 1$
12: **end while**
13: **return** $P_{SelectedPapers}$

In Algorithm 1, start by initializing the input focus papers. Create empty sets for the potential paper set and the selected paper set, and set the index to zero. Define a threshold of 1000 and include all papers citing the focus paper in the potential paper set. If the index is below 1000 and there are papers in the potential paper set, choose the paper with the earliest citation date, add it to the selected paper set, and remove it from the potential paper set. Add all articles citing this paper to the potential paper set and increment the index value by one. Finally, return the selected papers, which constitute the citation cascades.

3.4. Predictors

In this step, we calculate various metrics for each snapshot (cascade networks generated from every 10 edges increased), including the number of nodes, average clustering coefficient, average degree, maximum closeness centrality, number of components, PageRank value of the focus paper, average of PageRank values, variance of PageRank values, and the von Neumann graph entropy. The calculation of von Neumann graph entropy is detailed in a paper [49]. For each network structural metric abovementioned, time-series-like data are generated.

There are numerous mature algorithms available for extracting features from time-series data. Python's tsfresh package [50] is one of them, and we extract features of the metrics time series using it. For the time series of indicators mentioned, a total of 1602 features were extracted.

3.4.1. Topological Indicators

The formal calculations of certain topological indicators used above are explained in this section.

Average degree:
$$AVD = \frac{1}{N}\sum_{i=1}^{N} k_i \qquad (1)$$

Average clustering coefficient:
$$ACC = \frac{1}{N}\sum_{i=1}^{N} C_i \qquad (2)$$

Maximum closeness centrality:
$$MCC = CC_c^{max} = max\left(\frac{1}{\sum_{j \neq i} d(i,j)}\right) \qquad (3)$$

where the C_i is defined as:
$$C_i = \frac{2E_i}{k_i(k_i - 1)} \qquad (4)$$

Number of components (NOC): the number of connected components in a network.

In the Formulas (1)–(4), E_i is the actual number of edges between the neighbors of node (i), k_i is the degree of node (i) like the number of neighbor nodes directly connected to node (i), N is the number of nodes of the network, C_i is the clustering coefficient of node (i), and $d(i, j)$ denotes the shortest path between node (i) and node (j).

3.4.2. PageRank Indicator

The calculation of the PageRank value is defined by the Formula (5).
$$P(i) = \frac{1-d}{N} + d\sum_{j \in M(i)} \frac{P(j)}{L(j)} \qquad (5)$$

In Formula (5), $P(i)$ is the PageRank value of the node (i), d is the damping factor (usually takes the value 0.85), N is the total number of pages in the network, $M(i)$ is the set of all pages pointing to page (i), $P(j)$ is the PageRank value of page (j), and $L(j)$ is the number of outgoing links on page (j).

3.4.3. Graph Entropy Indicator

This section introduces some detail on the calculation of the von-Neumann graph entropy. Given a first unweighted graph $G = (V, E, A)$, where A is the symmetric adjacency matrix. The degree matrix is defined as $D = \text{diag}(d_1, \ldots, d_n)$, and its Laplacian matrix is $L = D - A$. Its eigenvalues λ_i are called the Laplacian spectrum. Here, $H_{vn}(G)$ is the von Neumann graph entropy.

$$H_{vn}(G) = -\sum_{i=1}^{n}\left(\frac{\lambda_i}{\text{vol}(G)} \log \frac{\lambda_i}{\text{vol}(G)}\right) \quad (6)$$

The volume of the graph is:

$$\text{vol}(G) = \sum_{i=1}^{n} \lambda_i = \text{trace}(L) \quad (7)$$

However, the time complexity of computing the von-Neumann graph entropy directly is relatively high, which is $O(n^3)$. The approximation is necessary. It is worth noting that Chen et al. have proposed an approximation method called FINGER [35], which reduces the cubic complexity to a linear complexity concerning the number of nodes and edges. The pseudocode is displayed in Algorithm 2.

Algorithm 2. Approximate Von-Neumann Graph Entropy (VNGE).

Input: *Adjacency matrix A.*
Output: *Approximate von Neumann graph entropy H_{vn}.*

1: $A \leftarrow$ adjacency matrix of a graph with node number and sparsity
2: $d \leftarrow$ sum of elements in each row of A
3: $c \leftarrow 1/\sum bd$
4: $W \leftarrow$ edge weights from non $-$ zero elements of A
5: approx $\leftarrow 1 - c^2 \left(\sum bd^2 + \sum bW^2\right)$
6: $L \leftarrow UnnormalizedLaplacian(A)$
7: $\lambda_{max} \leftarrow$ largest eigen value of L
8: $H_{vn} \leftarrow -approx \times \log_2(\lambda_{max})$
9: **return** H_{vn}

In Algorithm 2, the input is the adjacency matrix of the graph representation. The sum of elements in each row of the adjacency matrix is calculated and stored to create a vector. The inverse of the sum of these values is calculated to derive a constant. The edge weights of all non-zero elements in the adjacency matrix are then extracted. Use the extracted weights and the previously calculated vector to determine an intermediate approximation. Then, calculate the maximum eigenvalue of unnormalized Laplacian matrix. Finally, utilize the prior approximation and the maximum eigenvalue to compute the approximate von-Neumann graph entropy.

3.5. Forecasting Process

Due to the large number of features generated by our method, feature selection is required. Then, we utilize grid search to choose the top N variables and sequentially place variables to determine the optimal variable group and prediction impact. The N ranges from 1 to 100 with the step of 1 (i.e., 1, 2, 3, ..., 100) and from 100 to 1600 with the step of 100 (i.e., 100, 150, ..., 1600).

Indeed, we attempt various methods for feature selection engineering. Various methods, including the single filter method, RFE (Recursive Feature Elimination) and RFECV (Recursive Feature Elimination with Cross-Validation) [51], the shadow search method [52], and the filter combined with sequential modeling, are included. Finally, the used method (filter combined with sequential modeling) is found to be optimal.

The performance is assessed through two-repetitions and five-fold cross-validation (outer resampling), with the average ROC-AUC serving as the evaluation metric. The prediction performance using various representative classification models, including Random

Forest, Logistic Regression, SVM (Support Vector Machine), LDA (Linear Discriminant Analysis), and Naive Bayes, is all considered. The best classification model is selected, and parameter tuning is conducted.

Here, we provide some brief introductions for each model. The random forest algorithm is an ensemble learning method using multiple decision trees to enhance classification and regression accuracy by averaging their results [53]. Logistic regression is a statistical model used for binary classification that estimates the probability of an input belonging to a specific category. SVM is a supervised learning model that finds the optimal hyperplane for classifying data into different categories in higher-dimensional space [54]. LDA is a dimensionality reduction technique used for classification by finding the linear combination of features that best separates classes. Naive Bayes is a probabilistic classifier based on Bayes' theorem, assuming independence between predictors, suitable for large datasets and text classification.

3.6. Benchmark Indicators

In order to compare with the prior approaches, the static methods are selected for comparison. As mentioned in Section 2, certain static methods have been developed in prior studies. Here, we use the following indicators as benchmarks: The prediction process for these benchmark indicators follows the same procedure as described in Section 3.4, but without the need for feature selection.

(1) The static topological indicators of citation cascade networks. We select the topological metrics, including the number of nodes, average degree, maximum closeness centrality, number of components, and average clustering coefficient of the cascade networks, with a number of edges set at 1000 as a benchmark.

(2) The static PageRank indicators. The PageRank-based metrics (the PageRank value of the focus paper, average of PageRank values, and variance of PageRank values) are benchmarks, with the number of edges at 1000.

(3) The Disruptive Index. The Disruptive Index is a widely recognized metric for measuring disruption. The specific principles and calculation details can be found in Section 2 and the corresponding references.

(4) The (aggregated) static method, the union of static indicators in (1), (2), and (3).

The descriptions and calculation method of indicator (3), the Disruption Index, can be seen in Section 2.1.2 and especially in Figure 1. For Indicators (2) and (3), their descriptions and calculation methods are provided in Sections 3.4.1–3.4.3.

4. Results

4.1. Descriptive Analysis

Figure 5 presents the trajectories of various metrics of the network as the number of edges expands. These trajectories in breakthrough and non-breakthrough papers show significant differences. In terms of certain metrics, including the average clustering coefficient and the variance of PageRank value, the gap between breakthrough and non-breakthrough papers is evident in the early stage of citation network growth, while for others, it is more pronounced in the later stages. This highlights the importance of tracking the dynamic trajectories of these multiple structural metrics, which offers more predictive insights than static networks.

The average time required to span a citation cascade network within 1000 edges is depicted in Figure 6. Figure 6B illustrates the distribution of the time needed in our empirical study, and the peak is typically less than 6 years. Figure 6A shows the relationship between the time needed for spanning citation cascades and the papers' publication year. It is evident that, as time progresses, the speed of spanning cascade citations increases significantly, with the span time dropping to about 2 years around 2010. The above analysis shows that this network construction method allows for early prediction of breakthrough papers. In the future, it will be earlier due to the faster growth of cascades.

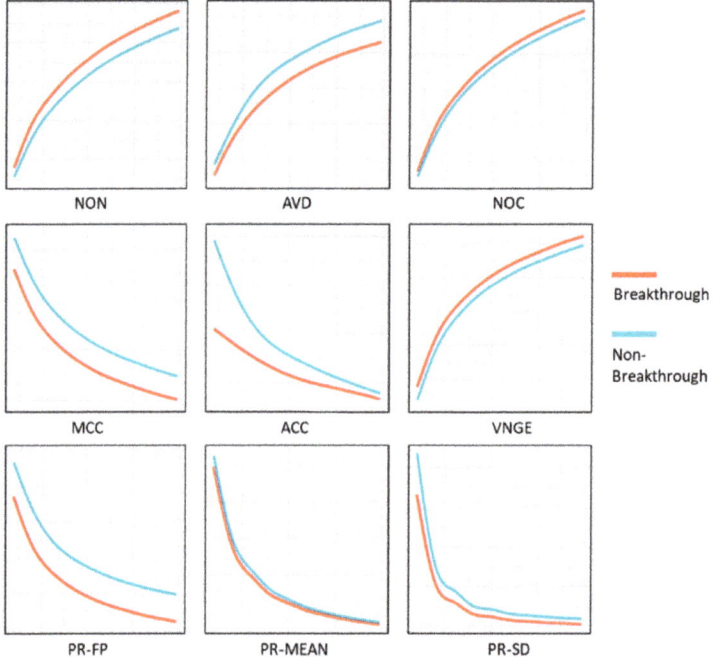

Figure 5. The tendency of the indicators used when the number of edges increases. Note: This graph illustrates the "time-series" distribution of the selected structural indicators. The x-axis represents the number of edges (increasing to the right), and the y-axis represents the magnitude of the values. Below is an explanation of the notation. NON: the number of nodes. AVD: the average degree. NOC: the number of components. MCC: the maximum closeness centrality. ACC: the average clustering coefficient. VNGE: the von Neumann graph entropy. PR-FP: the PageRank value of the focus paper. PR-MEAN: the average of PageRank values. PR-SD: the variance of PageRank values.

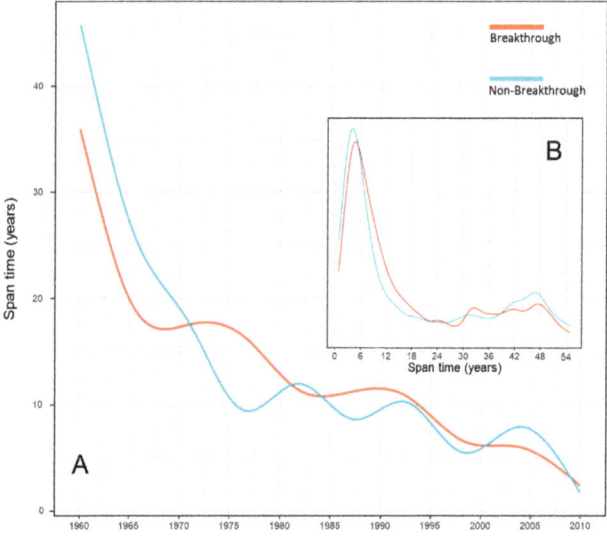

Figure 6. The span of time across publication years and its distribution.

4.2. Prediction Results

We make the prediction based on the process outlined in Chapter 3. The optimal model is random forests, and the ROC-AUC score for our method is 73.9%. And Tables 1 and 2 below display the additional prediction results using our method. Our study also demonstrates the challenge of predicting breakthrough papers or Nobel Prize-winning papers. For further analysis, the following section shows the performance of our method compared to other metrics. Learning curves are also offered in Figure 7. It can be seen that, although there is overfitting, as the sample size increases, the AUC value of the test set converges with that of the training set.

Table 1. Confusion matrix and evaluation metrics.

	Pred-Ture	Pred-False
Truth-True	436	216
Truth-False	226	462

Note: The confusion matrix presented here is the sum of predictions made using the two-repeat, five-fold strategy (10 times in total).

Table 2. Certain evaluation metrics.

Metrics	ROC-AUC (%)	ACCURACY (%)	F1-SCORE (%)	RECALL (%)
Score	73.9	67.01	66.38	66.32

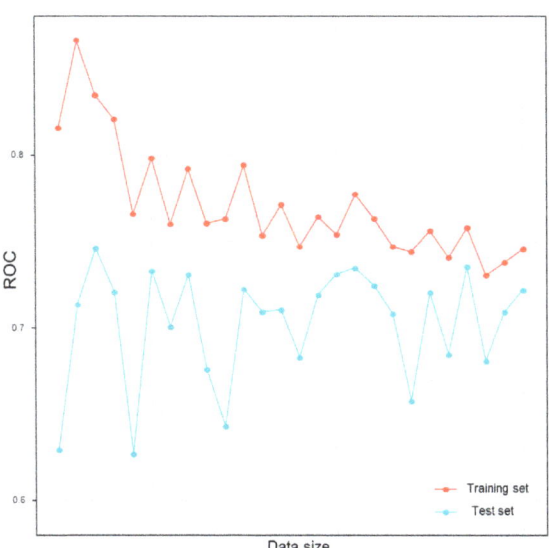

Figure 7. The learning curves.

4.3. Comparisons

To emphasize the improvement of our proposed approach, we compare it with the prior static method within the same prediction process (Section 3.5). The comparison results (ROC curves) of the selected benchmark indicators (Section 3.6) are displayed in Figure 8, and the detailed ROC scores are shown in Table 3. Our dynamic method shows superior results, achieving an improvement of about 7%. This suggests that the dynamic evolutionary-structure information from the citation cascade networks enhances the prediction of scientific breakthroughs.

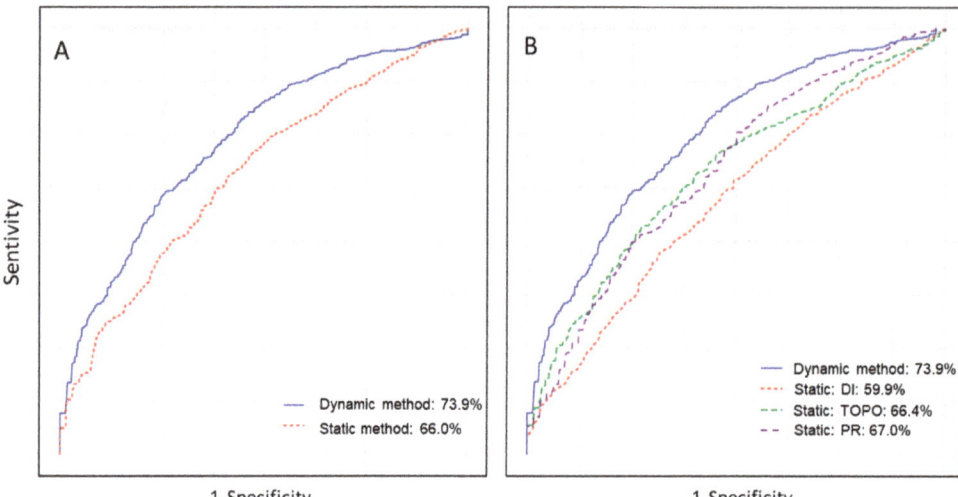

Figure 8. The ROC curves of the benchmark indicators. Note: (**A**) shows the dynamic method against the static method. The static method denotes the union of the three static methods in (**B**) and the (4) benchmark in Section 3.6. (**B**) shows the dynamic method against each static method. "DI" denotes the disruption index, the (3) benchmark in Section 3.6. "Topo" denotes the prediction using the basic topological metrics of citation cascade networks, the (1) benchmark in Section 3.6. "PR" denotes PageRank-based metrics, the (2) benchmark in Section 3.6. For presentation, the 95% confidence interval (CI) is not displayed in the figure.

Table 3. ROC scores of benchmark indicators.

Benchmarks	ROC-AUC	Improvement (%)
Dynamic method	73.9%	\
Static method	66.0%	+7.9%
Static: DI (Disruption Index)	59.9%	+14.0%
Static: TOPO (Topological indicator of cascades)	66.4%	+7.5%
Static: PR (PageRank)	67.0%	+6.9%

Note: The notation of the benchmark indicators can be seen in the legend of Figure 8. Improvement indicates the degree to which our method can outperform previous indicators.

The ROC curve is located on a two-dimensional coordinate axis, where the x-axis represents FPR (Fault Positive Rate) and the y-axis represents TPR (True Positive Rate). The area under the ROC curve (AUC) is a common metric used to measure the performance of classification algorithms in machine learning. The algorithm's performance improves as the value approaches 1.

The previous static methods achieved an overall ROC score of around 66–67%. Despite combining indicators from various prior static methods, their effectiveness did not significantly improve. The combining may have even slightly made the predictions less accurate, possibly due to the covariance between these variables. Additionally, the prediction in our study is made using the method of Min et al., yielding similar results (ROC scores between 65% and 70%).

5. Discussions and Conclusions

5.1. Main Contributions

Our main work has utilized the dynamic structural information of citation cascade networks instead of the (prior) static methods to enhance the performance of predicting scientific breakthroughs. Two main contributions are detailed below:

(1) We have enhanced the static approach to the dynamic method by measuring the dynamic structure evolution of citation cascade networks. The method has been validated and yields an evident improvement using a landmark dataset (Nobel Prize-winning papers).

(2) This study proposes a new method for constructing citation cascade networks to capture the network's dynamic information. Although citation cascade networks play a crucial role in predicting scientific breakthroughs, the practical construction of them poses a challenging issue. Previous construction methods have impeded the measurement of their dynamic nature.

(3) Additionally, our method of constructing a cascade citation network (Section 4.1) allows for earlier prediction of breakthrough papers than before. Furthermore, the growth rate of cascade citation networks is accelerating over time, thereby reaching earlier predictions in the future. It is recognized that early prediction holds special importance [55].

5.2. Implications

This study differs from previous studies by basing our predictions on citation cascade networks' dynamic structure information instead of the static information used in previous studies. Our ability to achieve this change relies on the proposed construction method of citation cascade networks. We also highlight the benefits of citation cascades as a proxy for scientific evolution. It offers a cost-effective modeling method to capture dynamic scientific evolution information.

At the theoretical level, we further expand relevant theories. Scientific breakthroughs lead to significant changes in the knowledge structure, which varies across different stages of knowledge evolution. Or, the structure of intelligence and knowledge diffusion evolves differently over time. Intuitively (Section 4.1), we reveal the distinct information provided by different indicators during the early and late stages of knowledge evolution. In the early stages, indicators like the average cluster coefficient and the variance of the PageRank values are better at differentiating breakthrough from non-breakthrough papers, while indicators such as the average degree, the PageRank value of the focus paper, the maximum closeness centrality, and others are more predictive in later stages.

This paper highlights the importance of understanding and predicting breakthroughs from a dynamic perspective. As mentioned in Section 1, though scientific breakthroughs often lead to changes in the structure of knowledge, most previous approaches have mainly viewed this concept statically. Our study indicates that the temporal-like characteristics of knowledge structure evolution offer valuable insights into predicting scientific breakthroughs. Thus, considering scientific breakthroughs dynamically is promising.

Despite significant efforts to improve prediction performance, identifying scientific breakthroughs remains challenging, and prediction performance is not yet at a level ready for practical applications. However, our method has significant potential for enhancement and solidifies the foundation for future practical applications of breakthrough predictions. (1) The threshold for maximum edges can be increased beyond 1000. More edges and a bigger cascade may provide more predictive power. (2) More indicators of cascade networks, especially the technique in complex networks, are valuable to be developed, measuring more information that reflects breakthroughs. (3) Additionally, our method for constructing cascaded networks ensure low computational costs in practice by controlling the number of edges, thus avoiding the need to compute excessively large networks.

Despite promising improvements and the potential for enhancement in our method, predicting scientific breakthroughs remains a challenging task. Our predictions, including those from previous literature, are mainly based on a dataset with an artificially created control group. Hence, it is more challenging (of course, and more valuable) to pinpoint the exact moment and place of a scientific breakthrough in the extensive literature.

5.3. Limitations and Future Directions

(1) Although we have utilized the dynamic structure information from citation cascade networks to predict scientific breakthroughs, relying solely on structural information may have limitations. Other-dimensional information, particularly dynamic factors, also has the potential to predict breakthroughs. In the future, measuring the dynamic evolution of other information is a potential direction.

(2) Citation cascade networks, while effective for modeling, may introduce additional noise. It is acknowledged that some citations may not accurately reflect scientific knowledge. In the future, enhancing the cascade citation networks to accurately identify scientific flows or developing a more efficient complex network are possible improvements. For instance, in the background, we highlight modeling solutions like main path analysis and max-min core document identification.

(3) The opaque nature of extracting features in time series impedes our understanding of scientific breakthrough generations and their characterization. Understanding that is helpful for developing policies that facilitate the implementation of breakthrough catalysts. In the future, it is essential to design specific algorithms to understand scientific breakthroughs.

5.4. Conclusions

Previous methods for predicting scientific breakthroughs have encountered great challenges. Most of them have utilized many static methods, while information regarding dynamic evolution is overlooked. We propose a dynamic method that captures the structural information of the cascade citation and achieves an improvement compared to the prior static methods. We revise the construction method of citation cascade networks to enable the measurement of their dynamic structural characteristics. Certain topological indicators, PageRank values, and the von-Neumann graph entropy of a series of cascade network snapshots are computed, forming the time-series-like predictors. The prediction results indicate that our dynamic method offers better prediction performance. This highlights the validity of the dynamic perspective on scientific breakthrough predictions; in the future, enhanced modelling on dynamic knowledge structure evolution and more complex network indicators are promising.

Author Contributions: Conceptualization, H.Y., Y.L. and Y.X.; investigation, Y.X.; methodology, H.Y.; data curation, Y.L.; formal analysis, Y.L.; writing—original draft, Y.L.; writing—review and editing, H.Y. and Y.X. All authors have read and agreed to the published version of the manuscript.

Funding: This article is supported by National Natural Science Foundation of China (No. 72274227), Humanity and Social Science Foundation of Ministry of Education of China (No. 22YJA870016), and Guangzhou Special Program for Basic and Applied Basic Research Projects (2024A04J4306).

Data Availability Statement: The data are sourced from the following databases/datasets: SciSciNet dataset (https://www.nature.com/articles/s41597-023-02198-9, accessed on 1 October 2023), MAG dataset (https://zenodo.org/records/2628216, accessed on 12 September 2023), and OpenAlex database (https://docs.openalex.org/, accessed on 26 August 2023). The raw data supporting the conclusions of this article will be made available by the authors on request.

Conflicts of Interest: The authors declare that they have no known competing financial interests or personal relationships that could have appeared to influence the work reported in this paper.

References

1. Wuestman, M.; Hoekman, J.; Frenken, K. A typology of scientific breakthroughs. *Quant. Sci. Stud.* **2020**, *1*, 1203–1222. [CrossRef]
2. Min, C.; Bu, Y.; Sun, J. Predicting scientific breakthroughs based on knowledge structure variations. *Technol. Forecast. Soc. Chang.* **2021**, *164*, 120502. [CrossRef]
3. Ramdorai, A.; Herstatt, C.; Ramdorai, A.; Herstatt, C. Disruptive innovations theory. In *Frugal Innovation in Healthcare: How Targeting Low-Income Markets Leads to Disruptive Innovation*; Springer: Berlin/Heidelberg, Germany, 2015; pp. 27–38.
4. Kuhn, T.S. *The Structure of Scientific Revolutions*; University of Chicago Press: Chicago, IL, USA, 1997; Volume 962.
5. Min, C.; Sun, J.; Ding, Y. Quantifying the evolution of citation cascades. *Proc. Assoc. Inf. Sci. Technol.* **2017**, *54*, 761–763. [CrossRef]

6. Min, C.; Chen, Q.; Yan, E.; Bu, Y.; Sun, J. Citation cascade and the evolution of topic relevance. *J. Assoc. Inf. Sci. Technol.* **2021**, *72*, 110–127. [CrossRef]
7. Wang, S.; Ma, Y.; Mao, J.; Bai, Y.; Liang, Z.; Li, G. Quantifying scientific breakthroughs by a novel disruption indicator based on knowledge entities. *J. Assoc. Inf. Sci. Technol.* **2023**, *74*, 150–167. [CrossRef]
8. Min, C.; Bu, Y.; Wu, D.; Ding, Y.; Zhang, Y. Identifying citation patterns of scientific breakthroughs: A perspective of dynamic citation process. *Inf. Process. Manag.* **2021**, *58*, 102428. [CrossRef]
9. Li, X.; Wen, Y.; Jiang, J.; Daim, T.; Huang, L. Identifying potential breakthrough research: A machine learning method using scientific papers and Twitter data. *Technol. Forecast. Soc. Chang.* **2022**, *184*, 122042. [CrossRef]
10. Alberts, B. Science breakthroughs. *Science* **2011**, *334*, 1604. [CrossRef]
11. Taques, F.H. Challenges in the post-covid-19 world. *Socioecon. Anal.* **2024**, *2*, 1–5. [CrossRef]
12. Koshland Jr, D.E. The cha-cha-cha theory of scientific discovery. *Science* **2007**, *317*, 761–762. [CrossRef]
13. Hage, J.; Mote, J. Transformational organizations and a burst of scientific breakthroughs: The Institut Pasteur and biomedicine, 1889–1919. *Soc. Sci. Hist.* **2010**, *34*, 13–46. [CrossRef]
14. Grumet, G.W. Insubordination and genius: Galileo, Darwin, Pasteur, Einstein, and Pauling. *Psychol. Rep.* **2008**, *102*, 819–847. [CrossRef] [PubMed]
15. Wang, J.; Veugelers, R.; Stephan, P. Bias against novelty in science: A cautionary tale for users of bibliometric indicators. *Res. Policy* **2017**, *46*, 1416–1436. [CrossRef]
16. Wu, L.; Wang, D.; Evans, J.A. Large teams develop and small teams disrupt science and technology. *Nature* **2019**, *566*, 378–382. [CrossRef]
17. Funk, R.J.; Owen-Smith, J. A dynamic network measure of technological change. *Manag. Sci.* **2017**, *63*, 791–817. [CrossRef]
18. Park, M.; Leahey, E.; Funk, R.J. Papers and patents are becoming less disruptive over time. *Nature* **2023**, *613*, 138–144. [CrossRef]
19. Lin, Y.; Frey, C.B.; Wu, L. Remote collaboration fuses fewer breakthrough ideas. *Nature* **2023**, *623*, 987–991. [CrossRef] [PubMed]
20. Bornmann, L.; Devarakonda, S.; Tekles, A.; Chacko, G. Are disruption index indicators convergently valid? The comparison of several indicator variants with assessments by peers. *Quant. Sci. Stud.* **2020**, *1*, 1242–1259. [CrossRef]
21. Wei, C.; Zhao, Z.; Shi, D.; Li, J. Nobel-Prize-winning papers are significantly more highly-cited but not more disruptive than non-prize-winning counterparts. In *iConference 2020 Proceedings*; iSchools: Westford, MA, USA, 2020.
22. Sizemore, A.E.; Karuza, E.A.; Giusti, C.; Bassett, D.S. Knowledge gaps in the early growth of semantic feature networks. *Nat. Hum. Behav.* **2018**, *2*, 682–692. [CrossRef]
23. Albert, R.; Barabási, A.-L. Statistical mechanics of complex networks. *Rev. Mod. Phys.* **2002**, *74*, 47. [CrossRef]
24. Berkhin, P. A survey on PageRank computing. *Internet Math.* **2005**, *2*, 73–120. [CrossRef]
25. Mukherjee, S.; Romero, D.M.; Jones, B.; Uzzi, B. The nearly universal link between the age of past knowledge and tomorrow's breakthroughs in science and technology: The hotspot. *Sci. Adv.* **2017**, *3*, e1601315. [CrossRef]
26. Han, L.; Escolano, F.; Hancock, E.R.; Wilson, R.C. Graph characterizations from von Neumann entropy. *Pattern Recognit. Lett.* **2012**, *33*, 1958–1967. [CrossRef]
27. Xu, H.; Luo, R.; Winnink, J.; Wang, C.; Elahi, E. A methodology for identifying breakthrough topics using structural entropy. *Inf. Process. Manag.* **2022**, *59*, 102862. [CrossRef]
28. Savov, P.; Jatowt, A.; Nielek, R. Identifying breakthrough scientific papers. *Inf. Process. Manag.* **2020**, *57*, 102168. [CrossRef]
29. Jia, W.; Xie, Y.; Zhao, Y.; Yao, K.; Shi, H.; Chong, D. Research on disruptive technology recognition of China's electronic information and communication industry based on patent influence. *J. Glob. Inf. Manag. (JGIM)* **2021**, *29*, 148–165. [CrossRef]
30. Kelly, B.; Papanikolaou, D.; Seru, A.; Taddy, M. Measuring technological innovation over the long run. *Am. Econ. Rev. Insights* **2021**, *3*, 303–320. [CrossRef]
31. Yan, E. Disciplinary knowledge production and diffusion in science. *J. Assoc. Inf. Sci. Technol.* **2016**, *67*, 2223–2245. [CrossRef]
32. Datta, A.A.; Srivastava, S. (Re) conceptualizing technological breakthrough innovation: A systematic review of the literature and proposed framework. *Technol. Forecast. Soc. Chang.* **2023**, *194*, 122740. [CrossRef]
33. Sun, Y.; Latora, V. The evolution of knowledge within and across fields in modern physics. *Sci. Rep.* **2020**, *10*, 12097. [CrossRef]
34. Satarova, B.; Siddiqui, H.; Raza, H.; Abbasi, N.; Kydyrkozha, S. A Systematic Review of "The Performance of Knowledge Organizations and Modelling Human Action". *Socioecon. Anal* **2023**, *1*, 56–77. [CrossRef]
35. Chen, P.-Y.; Wu, L.; Liu, S.; Rajapakse, I. Fast incremental von neumann graph entropy computation: Theory, algorithm, and applications. In Proceedings of the International Conference on Machine Learning, Long Beach, CA, USA, 10–15 June 2019.
36. Lv, Y.; Ding, Y.; Song, M.; Duan, Z. Topology-driven trend analysis for drug discovery. *J. Informetr.* **2018**, *12*, 893–905. [CrossRef]
37. Yang, J.; Liu, Z. The effect of citation behaviour on knowledge diffusion and intellectual structure. *J. Informetr.* **2022**, *16*, 101225. [CrossRef]
38. Bu, Y.; Waltman, L.; Huang, Y. A multidimensional framework for characterizing the citation impact of scientific publications. *Quant. Sci. Stud.* **2021**, *2*, 155–183. [CrossRef]
39. Nepomuceno, T.C.C.; Piubello Orsini, L.; de Carvalho, V.D.H.; Poleto, T.; Leardini, C. The core of healthcare efficiency: A comprehensive bibliometric review on frontier analysis of hospitals. *Healthcare* **2022**, *10*, 1316. [CrossRef] [PubMed]
40. Hou, J.; Yang, X.; Zhang, Y. The effect of social media knowledge cascade: An analysis of scientific papers diffusion. *Scientometrics* **2023**, *128*, 5169–5195. [CrossRef]

41. Rousseau, R. The Gozinto theorem: Using citations to determine influences on a scientific publication. *Scientometrics* **1987**, *11*, 217–229. [CrossRef]
42. Van Raan, A.F. Sleeping beauties in science. *Scientometrics* **2004**, *59*, 467–472. [CrossRef]
43. Yu, D.; Yan, Z. Combining machine learning and main path analysis to identify research front: From the perspective of science-technology linkage. *Scientometrics* **2022**, *127*, 4251–4274. [CrossRef]
44. Nepomuceno, T.C.C.; de Carvalho, V.D.H.; Nepomuceno, K.T.C.; Costa, A.P.C. Exploring knowledge benchmarking using time-series directional distance functions and bibliometrics. *Expert Syst.* **2023**, *40*, e12967. [CrossRef]
45. Van Eck, N.; Waltman, L. Software survey: VOSviewer, a computer program for bibliometric mapping. *Scientometrics* **2010**, *84*, 523–538. [CrossRef] [PubMed]
46. Li, J.; Yin, Y.; Fortunato, S.; Wang, D. A dataset of publication records for Nobel laureates. *Sci. Data* **2019**, *6*, 33. [CrossRef] [PubMed]
47. Lin, Z.; Yin, Y.; Liu, L.; Wang, D. SciSciNet: A large-scale open data lake for the science of science research. *Sci. Data* **2023**, *10*, 315. [CrossRef] [PubMed]
48. Priem, J.; Piwowar, H.; Orr, R. OpenAlex: A fully-open index of scholarly works, authors, venues, institutions, and concepts. *arXiv* **2022**, arXiv:2205.01833.
49. Liu, X.; Fu, L.; Wang, X.; Zhou, C. On the similarity between von Neumann graph entropy and structural information: Interpretation, computation, and applications. *IEEE Trans. Inf. Theory* **2022**, *68*, 2182–2202. [CrossRef]
50. Christ, M.; Braun, N.; Neuffer, J.; Kempa-Liehr, A.W. Time series feature extraction on basis of scalable hypothesis tests (tsfresh–a python package). *Neurocomputing* **2018**, *307*, 72–77. [CrossRef]
51. Guyon, I.; Weston, J.; Barnhill, S.; Vapnik, V. Gene selection for cancer classification using support vector machines. *Mach. Learn.* **2002**, *46*, 389–422. [CrossRef]
52. Kursa, M.B.; Rudnicki, W.R. Feature selection with the Boruta package. *J. Stat. Softw.* **2010**, *36*, 1–13. [CrossRef]
53. Breiman, L. Random forests. *Mach. Learn.* **2001**, *45*, 5–32. [CrossRef]
54. Cortes, C.; Vapnik, V. Support-vector networks. *Mach. Learn.* **1995**, *20*, 273–297. [CrossRef]
55. Li, X.; Ma, X.; Feng, Y. Early identification of breakthrough research from sleeping beauties using machine learning. *J. Informetr.* **2024**, *18*, 101517. [CrossRef]

Disclaimer/Publisher's Note: The statements, opinions and data contained in all publications are solely those of the individual author(s) and contributor(s) and not of MDPI and/or the editor(s). MDPI and/or the editor(s) disclaim responsibility for any injury to people or property resulting from any ideas, methods, instructions or products referred to in the content.

Article

Driving Style Recognition Method Based on Risk Field and Masked Learning Techniques

Shengye Jin, Zhengyu Zhu, Junli Liu and Shouqi Cao *

College of Engineering Science and Technology, Shanghai Ocean University, Shanghai 201306, China; m210801333@st.shou.edu.cn (S.J.); m220851459@st.shou.edu.cn (Z.Z.); m210811370@st.shou.edu.cn (J.L.)
* Correspondence: sqcao@shou.edu.cn

Abstract: With the increasing demand for road traffic safety assessment, global concerns about road safety have been rising. This is particularly evident with the widespread adoption of V2X (Vehicle-to-Everything) technology, where people are more intensively focused on how to leverage advanced technological means to effectively address challenges in traffic safety. Through the research of driving style recognition technology, accurate assessment of driving behavior and the provision of personalized safety prompts and warnings have become crucial for preventing traffic accidents. This paper proposes a risk field construction technique based on environmental data collected by in-vehicle sensors. This paper introduces a driving style recognition algorithm utilizing risk field visualization and mask learning technologies. The research results indicate that, compared to traditional classical models, the improved algorithm performs excellently in terms of accuracy, stability, and robustness, enhancing the accuracy of driving style recognition and enabling a more effective evaluation of road safety.

Keywords: driving style recognition; driving risk field; mask learning; environmental data; safety tips and warnings; vehicle-to-everything

MSC: 68T07

1. Introduction

With the continuous growth of urban traffic congestion and the increasing number of vehicles, traffic accidents have become a serious societal issue. In this context, V2X (Vehicle-to-Everything) technology, as a key component of intelligent transportation systems, offers new solutions to enhance traffic safety, playing a crucial role in improving road safety [1]. V2X technology enables vehicles to communicate wirelessly, sharing information such as location, speed, and direction, fostering real-time connectivity among vehicles, and facilitating information exchange with infrastructure, pedestrians, and other traffic participants. Despite the potential of V2X technology to enhance communication and coordination among vehicles, preventing traffic accidents still poses challenges. One reason is the behavioral differences among drivers, and existing technologies have not fully leveraged V2X data to address this issue effectively. Research on driving style recognition plays a vital role in improving road safety assessment and preventing traffic accidents. Through the study of driving style recognition, a more accurate assessment of a driver's driving habits and style can be achieved, leading to personalized safety prompts and warnings and ultimately reducing the occurrence of traffic accidents.

Driver style recognition methods are primarily categorized into unsupervised learning, semi-supervised learning, and supervised learning. Unsupervised learning [2–6] and semi-supervised learning [7–9] methods require a smaller amount of data but face challenges in obtaining reliable sample features within limited data. In situations where data are sufficiently abundant, researchers opt for supervised learning for driver style

Citation: Jin, S.; Zhu, Z.; Liu, J.; Cao, S. Driving Style Recognition Method Based on Risk Field and Masked Learning Techniques. *Mathematics* 2024, 12, 1363. https://doi.org/10.3390/math12091363

Academic Editor: Marjan Mernik

Received: 3 April 2024
Revised: 26 April 2024
Accepted: 29 April 2024
Published: 30 April 2024

Copyright: © 2024 by the authors. Licensee MDPI, Basel, Switzerland. This article is an open access article distributed under the terms and conditions of the Creative Commons Attribution (CC BY) license (https:// creativecommons.org/licenses/by/ 4.0/).

recognition [10–16]. This approach achieves high accuracy but demands high requirements for both the quantity and quality of training data.

Researchers have seldom considered the variations in environmental data in the algorithms for discriminating driving styles. However, it is evident that driving styles that involve the same operations differ across different environments. With advancements in sensor technology and the gradual proliferation of V2X (Vehicle-to-Everything) technology, smart vehicles now acquire a more diverse and extensive set of driving data. Consequently, there is a growing body of research related to assessing environmental conditions. The concept of a driving risk field serves as a model for evaluating driving risks on roads. By modeling a driving risk field, one can assess environmental risks and gather relevant variable information about the current environmental conditions. Through real-time monitoring and analysis of driving risks, this model allows for the assessment of real-time risks [17–25] in driving environments and the planning of feasible paths [21]. It also facilitates the prediction of potential risks under different road and traffic conditions.

In comparison to traditional machine learning methods, contrastive learning, as a form of self-supervised learning, has gained widespread research and application in fields such as computer vision and natural language processing. It is characterized by high data efficiency, strong generalization capabilities, and robust resistance to interference, achieving results that approach or even surpass the performance of supervised learning [26–28]. Mask learning, as a branch of contrastive learning, can handle more complex data features and exhibits superior performance compared to traditional contrastive learning methods. Currently, mask learning has demonstrated outstanding performance in the fields of image recognition and video recognition [29,30].

This study aims to explore a new approach for comprehensively assessing driving styles through changes in driving risk. We believe that the evaluation of driving styles should not be solely based on characteristics observed at a single moment but should instead delve into the trends of driving risk variations over a period of time. For instance, a driver who transitions suddenly from a prolonged period of low-risk driving to a high-risk state may indicate a temporary lapse of attention, reflecting a more aggressive driving tendency. Similarly, a consistent high-risk driving state may reveal a lower sensitivity to risk perception, manifesting as an impulsive driving pattern.

Furthermore, we recognize the pivotal role of environmental factors in driving risk variations and have thus introduced the concept of driving risk fields to address the oversights in earlier research. By further refining the driving risk field model, we strive to comprehensively consider various factors that influence driving risk, including vehicle dynamics, road environmental factors, and individual driver braking behavior characteristics. This enhancement not only enriches the dataset for prediction models but also significantly enhances the dimensionality and precision of the data.

To address the challenges of processing high-dimensional data, we have adopted a driving style recognition model similar to the MAE architecture, which efficiently extracts features from high-dimensional data, demonstrating significant advantages in handling such data. Compared to traditional methods, this model exhibits more stable performance when dealing with complex data, effectively overcoming the limitations of traditional methods in handling high-dimensional data with decreasing performance.

In summary, this study aims to achieve accurate identification of driving styles by improving the driving risk field model and combining advanced feature extraction and recognition techniques, thereby providing stronger technical support for road traffic safety.

2. Method

2.1. Design of Driving Risk Field Model

The driving risk field is divided into the "Vehicle Driving Risk Field" and the "Road Boundary Risk Field Model". The former assesses the risks generated during the vehicle's travel, while the latter evaluates the risks associated with road boundaries (including solid and broken lines).

In the past, research on driving risk fields has exhibited several notable shortcomings. Firstly, these studies have failed to adequately consider the braking reaction characteristics of drivers when operating a vehicle, which is a crucial factor in real-world driving scenarios. Secondly, some risk value functions exhibit excessively large differences over similar distances, potentially leading to inaccurate assessments of driving risks. Additionally, when road participants change, the computational burden of existing models often becomes significant, compromising their efficiency in practical applications.

To address these issues, we propose utilizing the sigmoid function to optimize the model. By incorporating the sigmoid function, we aim to more accurately capture the braking reaction characteristics of drivers, thereby enhancing the model's precision. Based on this, we introduce a novel vehicle driving risk field model that incorporates the braking reaction time. The braking reaction time, defined as the duration from when a driver detects the need to brake to the point when their foot reaches the brake pedal, serves as a critical metric for assessing driving safety. By comprehensively considering the braking reaction time and other relevant factors, our model offers a more comprehensive assessment of driving risks, providing effective support for road traffic safety.

Some studies have suggested [20] that from the perspective of physical fields, vehicles driving on roads are subject to a virtual "force" due to the presence of driving risks. Under the influence of this force, vehicles adjust their motion state to ensure driving safety, which is very similar to the phenomenon of particles being affected by forces in physical fields. Following this consideration, Tian et al. [20], drawing inspiration from the Yukawa potential [31] for field construction, formulated the driving risk field model in the form of an exponential function, integrating both physical attributes and kinematic states. When the vehicle heading angle is 0°, the driving risk assessment formula constructed by Tian et al. is shown in Formula (1).

$$E_i = \lambda_1 M_{eq-i} e^{\frac{\lambda_2 m_j \Delta v}{|k|}} \cdot e^{-\beta a \cos\theta} \cdot \frac{k}{|k|} \quad (1)$$

In this context, E_i represents the driving risk generated by object i towards its surroundings, v_i denotes the speed magnitude of object i, λ_1, λ_2, and β are coefficients to be determined, θ is the angle between the distance vector from the vehicle's centroid to a certain point around the vehicle and the positive direction of the x-axis, Δv represents the speed difference, a is the acceleration of the vehicle, m_{eq-i} is the equivalent mass of object i, m_j is the mass of object j, k is the distance vector from the vehicle's centroid to a point around the vehicle, and $|k|$ is the scalar distance from the vehicle's centroid to that specific point.

The definition of equivalent mass is crucial for assessing the potential hazards encountered during vehicle operation. It takes into account both the mass and speed of a vehicle to quantify the risk it poses to other road users. Put simply, the greater the mass and speed of a vehicle, the larger its equivalent mass becomes, thus increasing the potential driving risk. This viewpoint is strongly supported by multiple studies, including the findings of the World Bank and the World Health Organization's report on "Road Safety Countermeasures in Developing Countries" published in 2004. The report points out that in developing countries, there is a significant correlation between the number of traffic accidents, the number of injured individuals, and the number of fatalities, and the average road speed, exhibiting a relationship of the second, third, and fourth power, respectively.

Building on this theoretical foundation, Wu and their colleagues [17,32] conducted further research on the impact of speed on driving risk, utilizing a polynomial incorporating speed power function terms to represent this effect. By leveraging accident data from highways, they fitted relevant parameters and derived an empirical formula (Formula (2)) for vehicle equivalent mass. By substituting this empirical formula into the calculation formula for vehicle equivalent mass, the original formula (Formula (1)) was transformed into a new formula (Formula (3)). This transformation not only enhances the accuracy of risk assessments but also provides a more scientific and effective tool for our subsequent research.

$$M_{eq-i} = 1.566 m_i v_i^{6.687} \times 10^{-14} + 0.3345 \tag{2}$$

$$E_i = \left(1.566 m_i v_i^{6.687} \times 10^{-14} + 0.3345\right) \lambda_1 e^{\frac{\lambda_2 m_j \Delta v}{|k|}} \cdot e^{-\beta a \cos\theta} \cdot \frac{k}{|k|} \tag{3}$$

Let $A = e^{\frac{\lambda_2 m_j \Delta v}{|k|}}$ and $B = e^{-\beta a \cos\theta}$. The formula is then transformed into Formula (4).

$$E_i = \lambda_1 m_{eq-i} A \cdot B \cdot \frac{k}{|k|} \tag{4}$$

The function A serves to assess the level of risk based on the Time-to-Collision (TTC) model [20], while the function B is designed to evaluate the risk distribution under different angles. According to Formula (1), it is evident that function A is an exponential function, indicating that, when Δv remains constant, the rate of change is also an exponential function. Over the domain [0, +inf], the derivative of this function is consistently less than 0, but the absolute value of its rate of change gradually decreases.

However, scientific studies indicate that drivers have a reaction time when encountering danger. During this braking reaction time, drivers are in an unconscious state and are unable to actively perform braking, steering, or other operations. Therefore, during this period, the risk should be higher, and the rate of change in risk should be smaller. After exceeding the reaction time, it can be assumed that drivers have the ability and initiate a response, at which point the rate of change in risk should reach its maximum and gradually decrease. Therefore, to align with the operational characteristics of drivers, and based on relevant research and experiments, the sigmoid function is chosen as the core function for part A. The formula for function A is then modified to meet driver behavior, as shown in Formula (5).

$$A = c_1 \times sigmoid\left(-c_2\left(|k| - c_{reaction}\, v - \frac{v^2}{2 a_{max}}\right)\right) \tag{5}$$

where c_1, c_2, and $c_{reaction}$ are constants. c_1 is a threshold constant, a positive constant such that the threshold of A is constrained within the range $(0, c_1)$; c_2 is another positive constant controlling the horizontal shape of the sigmoid function, with larger values of c_2 leading to a quicker saturation of A; $c_{reaction}$ is a positive constant representing the driver's braking reaction time. $|k|$ is the distance from the experimental point to the current vehicle's center of mass; v is the speed of the vehicle itself; and a_{max} is the maximum acceleration of the vehicle. Ultimately, the Vehicle Driving Risk Field Model is obtained, as shown in Formula (6).

$$E_i = \lambda_1 m_{eq-i} c_1 \times sigmoid\left(-c_2\left(|k| - c_{reaction}\, v - \frac{v^2}{2 a_{max}}\right)\right) e^{\beta a \cos\theta} \cdot \frac{k}{|k|} \tag{6}$$

The Road Boundary Risk Field refers to a collection of potential hazards or adverse factors associated with the road edge. It describes various risks that may occur along the road boundary, such as traffic accidents, conflicts between pedestrians and vehicles, visibility issues, and more. It assists decision makers in understanding potential risk factors, optimizing road design and traffic planning, and implementing preventive measures to reduce the occurrence of traffic accidents.

Based on research on the Road Boundary Risk Field [17,20], the formula for the road risk field used is depicted in Formula (7).

$$E = c_3 e^{\frac{-\beta^2}{2\gamma^2}} \tag{7}$$

where c_3 is a positive constant used to control the maximum field strength; s is the perpendicular distance from a point to the lane line; and γ is a positive constant used to control the decay rate of the field strength from the boundary line to the center, with a larger γ resulting in slower decay.

2.2. Driving Style Recognition Based on Mask Learning Technology

The masked autoencoder (MAE) [29] is a self-supervised learning method used in computer vision. It is based on the Vision Transformer (ViT) architecture, known for its strong scalability and simplicity. The MAE method trains by randomly masking parts of input images and reconstructing the missing pixels. Today, MAE is also applied to process temporal images, with VideoMAE [30] being an extension that views images as individuals within temporal data, making it suitable for handling video data. Similarly, each frame of a risk field can be considered as an image, and the temporal data of the risk field can be likened to video data, enabling relevant feature extraction.

In this research, we have developed a driving style recognition process grounded in the MAE philosophy with the goal of effectively classifying driving risk styles. The classification aims to categorize driving styles into "Aggressive", "Moderate", and "Conservative". This procedure is principally divided into two phases: the pre-training phase and the downstream training phase. Figure 1 illustrates the training process and network architecture.

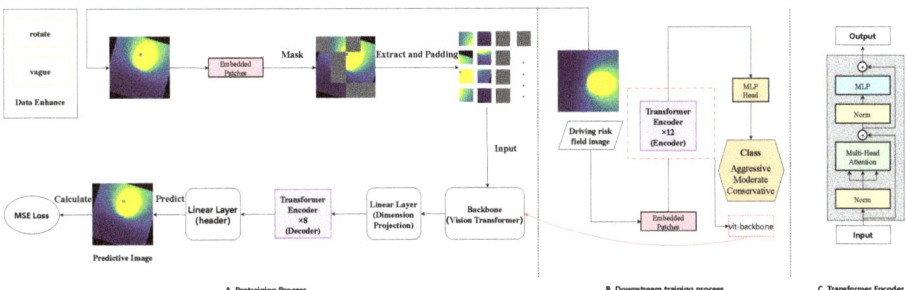

Figure 1. The overall training process and structure of masked autoencoder.

As indicated on the left side of Figure 1, in the pre-training phase, we initially apply data augmentation techniques such as rotation and blurring to the input images to enhance the model's generalization abilities. Once augmented, we mask certain regions of the image to replicate the visual system's handling of incomplete information. Then, segments from the unmasked image are extracted and processed through the backbone network. We chose the Vit-Base as our backbone network, which employs the self-attention mechanism from Transformers, particularly suited for image-centric tasks. The processed image segments are then passed on to the Header network, a densely connected neural network consisting of multiple dense layers. Each dense layer features neurons tightly interconnected, with each neuron connecting to all neurons from the preceding layer. The Header network is tasked with predicting the content of the masked portions of the image. During this process, the mean square error (MSE) loss between the prediction and the actual image is computed to guide the model's self-optimization in future iterations. Additionally, in our research on driving style recognition, we recognize that the data augmentation approach differs from that of traditional image recognition. Traditional image recognition mainly focuses on detecting the presence of relevant semantics within the image and emphasizes the extraction of image contour features; on the other hand, driving style recognition is less sensitive to the extraction of image contour features but more attentive to the variation differences between adjacent risk field intensity images and certain statistical parameters. Therefore, data augmentation strategies from traditional image recognition cannot be entirely applicable, and we opt for only those data augmentation strategies that marginally impact semantics. The final determined data augmentation strategy is the application of random rotation and blurring to temporal images. Rotation itself does not affect semantics, so each data augmentation instance includes a random rotation, and the range of random rotation is between −10 degrees and 10 degrees; blurring is randomly applied with a minimal probability and range during the data augmentation process.

As shown on the right side of Figure 1, we have selected the ViT-Base architecture as our backbone network due to its exemplary performance in processing visual information. The "Embedded Patch" module divides the input image into 16x16 patches and adds positional encoding to these feature vectors. Afterward, these patches are transformed into a series of lower-dimensional vectors through a linear layer to be fed into the Transformer model. Subsequently, a series of self-attention layers process each vector within the sequence, with each layer capable of establishing intricate dependencies between different patches. The entire network also employs residual connections and layer normalization to refine the process, which aids in preventing gradient vanishing issues in deep networks while also expediting the training procedure. This entire process, through the cohesion of pre-training and downstream training, fortifies the model's capability in identifying driving risks. This comprehensive training methodology not only enhances the model's efficiency in recognizing complex driving risk images but also, through an in-depth combination of self-supervised and supervised learning, is set to improve driving style recognition performance.

3. Experiment

3.1. Experimental Design

The experiment utilized a dataset constructed by X. Liu et al. [13]. This dataset was acquired through Liu's self-built vehicle data collection platform, capturing natural driving trajectories such as straight driving and lane changes on roads. The data were collected on highways and urban roads in Shanghai, covering various regions of the city and amassing over 1000 km of travel data. The dataset includes diverse road conditions and spans different time periods throughout the day.

For the experiment, representative left lane change and right lane change data were selected from the dataset. Figure 2 illustrates the trajectory routes of lane change data. In these sets, each line of a different color represents a different lane change trajectory. It is notable that the starting point of each lane change trajectory is located in the very center of the lane, while the end point is the last trajectory point where the vehicle stops after completing the lane change. In establishing the coordinate system, we used the starting point of each lane change trajectory as the origin of coordinates. The forward direction of the lane is defined as the positive direction of the x-axis, and rotating the positive direction of the x-axis counterclockwise by 90 degrees yields the positive direction of the y-axis. Such a definition constructs a global Cartesian coordinate system, enabling us to describe more accurately the position and movement of the vehicles on the road. Additionally, in the data collection experiment, the width of each lane was 4.4 m.

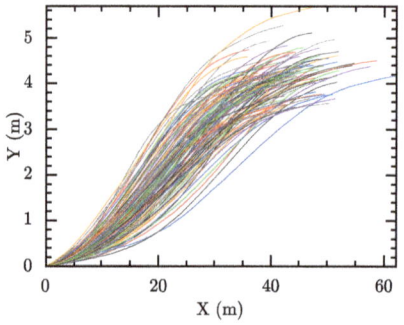 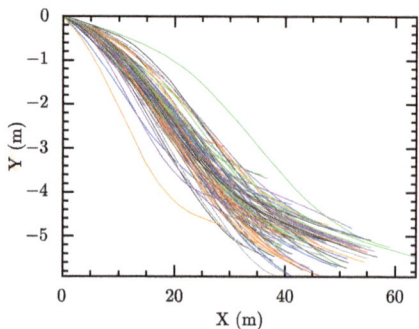

Figure 2. Visualization of lane change data.

Table 1 illustrates the basic attributes of the dataset. In this context, the *lon_speed* field represents longitudinal speed, and the *lat_speed* field represents lateral speed, both measured in meters per second. The *lon_acc* field corresponds to longitudinal acceleration, the *lat_acc* field corresponds to lateral acceleration, and both are measured in meters per second squared. The *Angleheadingrate* field represents the yaw rate.

Table 1. Basic properties of the dataset.

	lon_speed	*lat_speed*	*lon_acc*	*lat_acc*	*Angleheadingrate*
mean	9.610189	1.153941	−0.189604	−0.001717	0.050463
std	1.233309	0.436482	0.535301	0.588758	3.525656
min	6.495732	−0.099031	−4.649437	−2.236996	−9.725
25%	8.669245	0.786684	−0.531937	−0.498131	−3.004
50%	9.476567	1.168756	−0.222171	−0.048021	−0.018
75%	10.347681	1.496506	0.132453	0.543476	3.317
max	13.376584	2.453871	3.579057	1.606629	9.001

The experiment will utilize the aforementioned dataset and, after further preprocessing, generate a new dataset for driver style recognition. We will compare the use of different data extraction modules and prediction networks, examining the differences across various models.

3.1.1. Data Preprocessing

The original dataset has a sampling frequency of 100 Hz, recording data every 0.01 s. Following previous research [13], this experiment uses data collected every 0.3 s as input to discern driving styles. For every 30 raw data entries, 30 images of driving risk fields are generated. The data preprocessing workflow is as shown in Figure 3. Subsequently, the images of driving risk fields are fed into the model for driving style discrimination. Figure 4 illustrates the variation pattern of field strength when both the road boundary risk field and vehicle risk field coexist under different parameters. The field strength generated by both types of fields is vector-based. Directly adding these vectors does not assess the overall level of risk but only the combined field strength of the experimental object in multiple fields. Therefore, a vector modulus superposition method is employed to assess the risk level at a specific point.

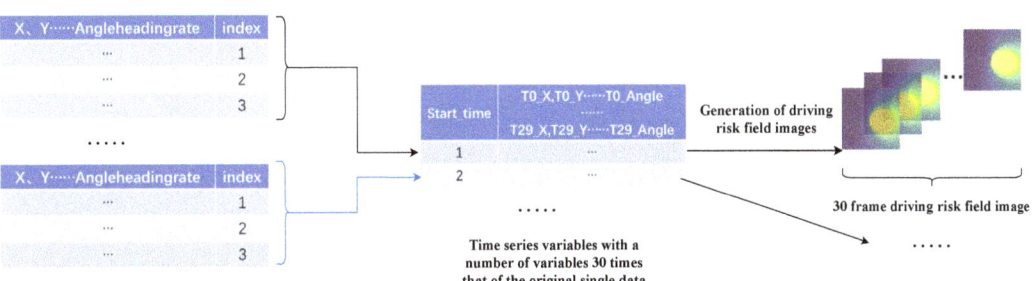

Figure 3. Data preprocessing process.

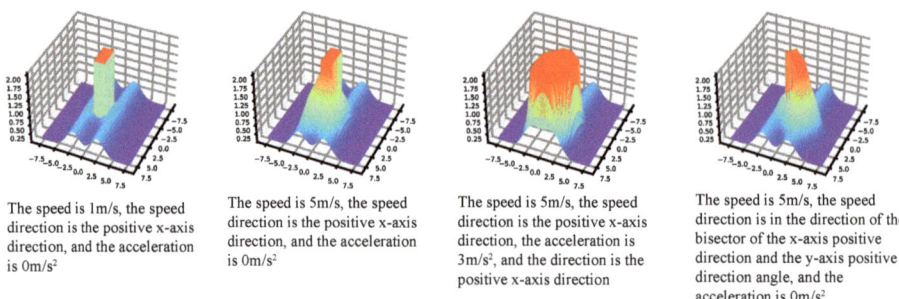

| The speed is 1m/s, the speed direction is the positive x-axis direction, and the acceleration is 0m/s^2 | The speed is 5m/s, the speed direction is the positive x-axis direction, and the acceleration is 0m/s^2 | The speed is 5m/s, the speed direction is the positive x-axis direction, the acceleration is 3m/s^2, and the direction is the positive x-axis direction | The speed is 5m/s, the speed direction is in the direction of the bisector of the x-axis positive direction and the y-axis positive direction angle, and the acceleration is 0m/s^2 |

Figure 4. Field strength images of road boundary risk field and vehicle risk field coexisting under different parameters.

After obtaining the driving risk images, the dataset is labeled for driving style. Referring to the labeling method proposed by X. Liu et al. [13], relevant statistical properties are computed. A Gaussian Mixture Model is used for pre-labeling, with a cluster count of 3. The three driving styles are categorized as aggressive, moderate, and conservative. We posit that data points with a confidence level greater than 90% have a distinct driving style classification. Conversely, other data points exhibit some classification ambiguity, yet the labels themselves are accurate. Therefore, data points with confidence levels below 90% can be utilized to assess robustness. The experiment selects data points with confidence levels exceeding 90% for each driving style as their labels. For these data points, 20% are used as the training set, 80% as the validation set, and the remaining points with confidence levels below 90% are designated as the test set. The experiment will conduct relevant tests on this dataset.

3.1.2. Comparative Experiment

We will prove the effectiveness of the models under the MAE framework through comparative experiments, and the model comparison framework is illustrated in Figure 5.

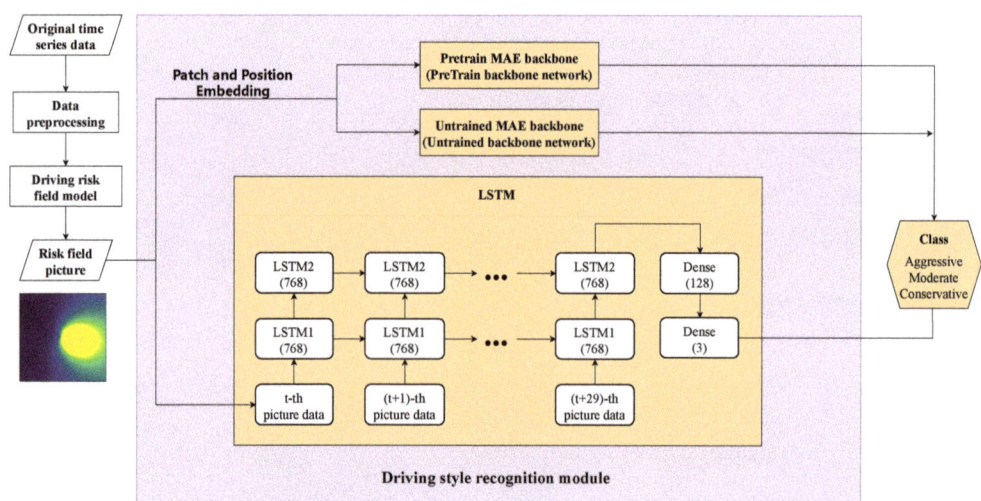

Figure 5. Model comparison framework.

Three models are designed for comparison: MAE-Pretrain, MAE-Untrained (ViT), and LSTM. The ViT model and LSTM model each have advantages in image feature extraction and temporal feature extraction, making them classic benchmark models. Additionally, since MAE, as a training framework, shares the same backbone network and ViT-base network structure, the MAE-Untrained model is equivalent to the ViT-base model. Comparing MAE-Pretrain and MAE-Untrained is essentially comparing the effectiveness of the pre-trained structure of MAE. Long Short-Term Memory (LSTM) [33] is a variant of recurrent neural networks (RNNs) and is a classic model in extracting temporal data features. Moreover, X. Liu et al. proposed using LSTM for driver style recognition [13], demonstrating the effectiveness of LSTM in extracting features from temporal variables.

3.2. Experimental Parameters

As part of the upstream task training, the MAE-Pretrain model employs a masking rate of 70% to enhance the model's generalization capabilities. The Decoder network architecture utilizes the TransformerEncoder structure, repeated eight times, with an embed_dim of 512. Correspondingly, the Encoder network architecture is also based on the TransformerEncoder, repeated twelve times, and has an embed_dim set to 768. In the upstream task, the header section comprises a single linear layer with 768 neurons, whose primary function is to transform the output of the Decoder network into an image, fulfilling the output requirements of the target task.

When transitioning to the downstream task, the backbone network directly adopts the model obtained from the upstream task training to ensure the effectiveness of knowledge transfer. The head network consists of two LinearLayers, with the number of neurons in the first and second layers being 768 and 3, respectively. This design facilitates the extraction and refinement of feature information. The loss function chosen is the cross-entropy function, suitable for classification tasks.

The MAE-Untrained model, on the other hand, has not undergone the pre-training phase. Therefore, its network structure and loss function remain consistent with the MAE-Pretrain model in downstream tasks, maintaining fairness in comparisons. Additionally, in the context of LSTM models, a two-layer stacked LSTM model with a hidden layer feature count of 768 is employed, and the cross-entropy function is selected as the loss function.

The experiment was conducted using the Ubuntu 20.04 system and the NVIDIA A4000 graphics card for training. During the pre-training phase of MAE-Pretrain, the AdamW optimizer was used, employing a cosine annealing schedule for learning rate adjustment, and a total of 200 epochs were trained. For both the MAE-Pretrain and MAE-Untrained downstream tasks, the AdamW optimizer was utilized, employing a cosine annealing with restarts scheduler for learning rate adjustment. Full fine-tuning was applied as the training method for these downstream tasks, with each task trained for a total of 200 epochs. Additionally, an LSTM model was trained separately using the SGD optimizer, also adopting a cosine annealing with restarts scheduler for learning rate adjustment, and underwent 200 epochs of training.

3.3. Result Analysis

The processing and analysis of experimental data demonstrate the accuracy, stability, and robustness of the MAE-based model. In the experiments assessing generalization under different conditions, both models exhibit excellent performance, accurately discerning driving styles.

Figure 6 illustrates the accuracy and loss variations during the training process of different models under two operating conditions. Figure 6a,c depict the data changes during left lane change conditions, while Figure 6b,d show the data changes during right lane change conditions. Whether in left lane change or right lane change conditions, the accuracy of the MAE-Pretrain model is consistently higher than that of the MAE-Untrained and LSTM models at any given moment. Based on the statistical data presented in Table 2 and an integrated analysis of the statistical characteristics of left-turn and right-turn conditions, it can be observed that the accuracy characteristics are noteworthy. The MAE-Pretrain model has an average accuracy of around 97%, with peak accuracy consistently exceeding

98%. In comparison to the other two classical models, its accuracy is significantly improved. Moreover, the accuracy curves of the MAE-Pretrain model and the LSTM model fluctuate more smoothly in both conditions, with the MAE-Pretrain model exhibiting greater stability than the LSTM model. In contrast, the fluctuation of the MAE-Untrained model is pronounced. Combining the relevant statistical data from Tables 2 and 3, it is evident that the range and variance of the MAE-Pretrain model are significantly smaller than the other two models. Additionally, its average accuracy surpasses the other two models, indicating better training stability.

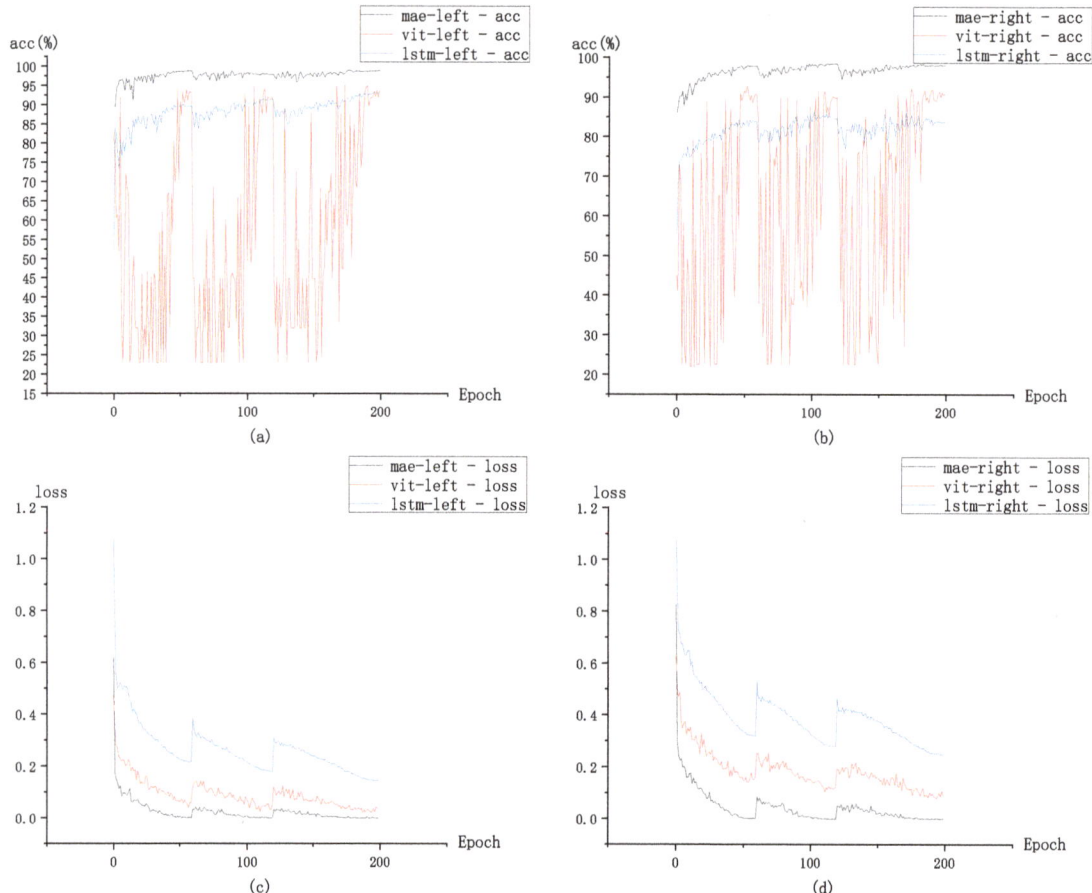

Figure 6. Accuracy and loss changes during downstream task training under left and right lane changing conditions. (**a**) Accuracy variation graphs of the three models under left lane change conditions, (**b**) Accuracy variation graphs of the three models under right lane change conditions, (**c**) Loss variation graphs of the three models under left lane change conditions, (**d**) Loss variation graphs of the three models under right lane change conditions.

Table 2. Statistical data on accuracy during downstream task training process.

	MAE	ViT	LSTM		MAE	ViT	LSTM
count	200	200	200	count	200	200	200
mean	97.64517	56.54148	88.47549	mean	96.58314	63.51776	81.86565
std	1.33474	25.01102	4.08483	std	2.04889	24.80087	3.34323
min	89.54546	23.08712	52.67578	min	86.17064	22.00397	55.38651
25%	97.36269	32.08334	87.33887	25%	96.14584	39.7123	80.29914
50%	97.95455	49.89584	89.24805	50%	97.10318	70.1885	82.56579
75%	98.4375	82.06439	90.60059	75%	97.89683	88.69544	83.8456
max	98.97727	95.17046	93.20313	max	98.47223	92.93651	86.51316
	Left				Right		

Table 3. Statistical data on losses during downstream task training.

	MAE	ViT	LSTM		MAE	ViT	LSTM
count	200	200	200	count	200	200	200
mean	0.02443	0.09204	0.26841	mean	0.04367	0.18668	0.39453
std	0.05108	0.05989	0.10822	std	0.07612	0.08009	0.11427
min	1.00E-06	0.0219	0.14414	min	0.00001	0.07958	0.24852
25%	0.00269	0.0219	0.20878	25%	0.00373	0.1404	0.31935
50%	0.01306	0.07677	0.25021	50%	0.02319	0.17134	0.37981
75%	0.02795	0.11113	0.29671	75%	0.0526	0.2116	0.437
max	0.61776	0.471	1.07257	max	0.82601	0.63153	1.07428
	Left				Right		

To further evaluate the effectiveness of the experiments, testing was conducted on additional data with confidence levels below 90%, i.e., the trained models were applied to a new dataset for testing. Table 4 illustrates the difference in accuracy between the validation set and the test set under different methods.

Table 4. The difference in accuracy between the validation set and the test set under different methods.

	MAE	ViT	LSTM		MAE	ViT	LSTM
Val-acc	98.97727	95.17046	93.20313	Val-acc	98.47223	92.93651	86.51316
Test-acc	90.2789	84.9561	78.7145	Test-acc	88.9945	81.5197	80.27
	Left				Right		

The MAE model achieved the highest accuracy on all three sets, especially on the test set, which had a significantly larger data quantity than the training and validation sets. This implies that, in scenarios with a small amount of high-confidence data as input, the robustness of the MAE-based driving style recognition model is significantly stronger than that of other models.

In conclusion, by taking into account Figure 6 and Tables 2–4, we can deduce the advantages of the MAE model in comparison to other models, as outlined in Table 5.

Table 5. Performance improvement comparison of MAE model relative to ViT and LSTM models.

	ViT	LSTM
Accuracy (Training Set)	At least 3% improvement	At least 5% improvement
Stability	Significantly improved	Improved
Accuracy (Test Set)	At least 5% improvement	At least 8% improvement

Regarding the superior accuracy, stability, and robustness of the MAE-Pretrain model in comparison, we have the following hypotheses: The effectiveness of the MAE-Pretrain model in accuracy, stability, and robustness stems from its superior feature extraction performance in the upstream task. The reason for this superiority lies in the high similarity between the pre-training task under the mask mode and the downstream task in driving style recognition.

The MAE-Pretrain and MAE-Untrained models have identical network structures, with the only difference being their involvement in upstream task training, indicating the crucial role of the upstream task in improving accuracy. Generally, in the full fine-tune training mode, when the similarity between the upstream and downstream tasks is high, i.e., when the two tasks require similar features, the effect is better. Based on this experience, it can indirectly suggest that the reconstruction features extracted from the upstream tasks of the two methods in this paper, i.e., driving risk field visualization and MAE temporal image reconstruction, are closely related and effective for driving style discrimination.

From another perspective, both image-based models achieved higher maximum accuracy than the LSTM model, indicating that after visualizing the driving risk field, features can be better extracted through image-based methods.

As the features extracted from the upstream task have high similarity to the target features required by the downstream task, the MAE-Pretrain model experiences minor changes to the backbone network during downstream task training, leading to relatively small variations in loss and accuracy. In contrast, the MAE-Untrained model, without pre-training, needs continuous learning and adjustment to find the extremum of the loss function, resulting in larger fluctuations.

Furthermore, in discussing the architecture of this paper, Figure 1A illustrates the upstream task. Within this task, the Encoder module plays a crucial role in extracting the inherent features from the sequential image series. The quality of this feature extraction directly impacts the capabilities of the downstream task. On the other hand, the Decoder module utilizes a relatively simple feature reconstruction network to reconstruct image information. Figure 1B depicts the downstream task, which relies heavily on the Encoder module from the upstream task. If the Encoder module is able to extract features effectively, it will significantly enhance the training speed, accuracy, and overall performance of the downstream task.

4. Conclusions

In this research, we present a cutting-edge methodology for risk evaluation and driving style identification, designed to navigate the complexities of driving environments. Utilizing a method that constructs driving risk field images based on braking reaction times, and coupled with an autoencoder-based driving style recognition algorithm that leverages masked learning for data feature enhancement, our approach not only offers a fresh perspective in visualizing risk fields but also fully exploits the potential of masked learning for data augmentation, refining the risk discrimination process.

Regarding performance evaluation, the model demonstrates at least a 3% increase in accuracy over the ViT and at least a 5% increase over LSTM networks on the training dataset. In terms of stability, it shows marked improvements compared to both ViT and LSTM. Most notably, on the testing dataset, the model's accuracy outperforms ViT by at least 5% and LSTM by at least 8%.

In summary, the model proposed in this paper not only introduces innovation in the construction of driving risk field imagery but also exhibits significant advantages in data feature extraction. Empirical evidence confirms its superior performance in accuracy, stability, and robustness, promising to offer an effective technological solution for driving safety evaluation and personalized driving style recognition.

The main contributions of this paper are as follows:

1. An innovative method for constructing a driving risk field based on braking reaction time is proposed. This method breaks through the limitations of existing research by more comprehensively considering the actual reaction characteristics of drivers during the driving process, thus improving the accuracy and reliability of driving risk assessment.
2. The concept of converting the driving risk field into image representation is creatively proposed, and the idea of masked autoencoder is utilized for feature extraction. This innovation provides a more effective means of feature extraction for the pre-trainer, thereby contributing to the enhancement of subsequent driving style recognition performance.
3. A multi-stage training approach is adopted, which effectively reduces the influence of subjective factors on transfer tasks while addressing the common clustering bias issues in traditional unsupervised clustering algorithms. The application of this method improves accuracy and stability, providing more reliable technical support for the practical application of driving risk style recognition.
4. In response to the problem of decreasing effectiveness of traditional time-series algorithms in handling high-dimensional data, this paper innovatively adopts algorithms from the field of computer vision to address this issue, providing a new perspective for driving style recognition.

Further research:

We will enrich the data augmentation techniques used in the upstream task stage, considering factors such as the driver's position in the main driving seat within the vehicle. We will explore generating similar paths and evaluate driving style recognition by comparing the driving styles of generated paths with the original paths.

Author Contributions: Conceptualization, S.C.; methodology, S.J.; software, S.J. and J.L.; validation, Z.Z. and J.L.; investigation, Z.Z.; writing—original draft preparation, S.J.; writing—review and editing, S.J. and Z.Z.; visualization, Z.Z. and J.L.; supervision, S.C.; project administration, S.C. All authors have read and agreed to the published version of the manuscript.

Funding: This research received no external funding.

Institutional Review Board Statement: Not applicable.

Informed Consent Statement: Not applicable.

Data Availability Statement: The data presented in this study are available on request from the corresponding author due to privacy and confidentiality agreements.

Conflicts of Interest: The authors declare no conflicts of interest.

References

1. Ghosal, A.; Conti, M. Security Issues and Challenges in V2X: A Survey. *Comput. Netw.* **2020**, *169*, 107093. [CrossRef]
2. Xing, Y.; Lv, C.; Wang, H.; Cao, D.; Velenis, E.; Wang, F.Y. Driver Activity Recognition for Intelligent Vehicles: A Deep Learning Approach. *IEEE Trans. Veh. Technol.* **2019**, *68*, 5379–5390. [CrossRef]
3. de Zepeda, M.; Meng, F.; Su, J.; Zeng, X.J.; Wang, Q. Dynamic Clustering Analysis for Driving Styles Identification. *Eng. Appl. Artif. Intell.* **2021**, *97*, 104096. [CrossRef]
4. Ma, Y.; Li, W.; Tang, K.; Zhang, Z.; Chen, S. Driving Style Recognition and Comparisons among Driving Tasks Based on Driver Behavior in the Online Car-Hailing Industry. *Accid. Anal. Prev.* **2021**, *154*, 106096. [CrossRef] [PubMed]

5. Li, X.S.; Cui, X.T.; Ren, Y.Y.; Zheng, X.L. Unsupervised Driving Style Analysis Based on Driving Maneuver Intensity. *IEEE Access* **2022**, *10*, 48160–48178. [CrossRef]
6. Li, Y.; Zhang, H.; Wang, Q.; Wang, Z.; Yao, X. Study on Driver Behavior Pattern in Merging Area under Naturalistic Driving Conditions. *J. Adv. Transp.* **2024**, *2024*, e7766164. [CrossRef]
7. Wang, W.; Xi, J.; Chong, A.; Li, L. Driving Style Classification Using a Semisupervised Support Vector Machine. *IEEE Trans. Hum. Mach. Syst.* **2017**, *47*, 650–660. [CrossRef]
8. Liu, W.; Deng, K.; Zhang, X.; Cheng, Y.; Zheng, Z.; Jiang, F.; Peng, J. A Semi-Supervised Tri-CatBoost Method for Driving Style Recognition. *Symmetry* **2020**, *12*, 336. [CrossRef]
9. Zhang, W. A Semi-Supervised Learning Method for Multi-Condition Driving Style Recognition. Master's Thesis, Jilin University, Changchun, China, 2022. [CrossRef]
10. Silva, I.; Eugenio Naranjo, J. A Systematic Methodology to Evaluate Prediction Models for Driving Style Classification. *Sensors* **2020**, *20*, 1692. [CrossRef]
11. Guo, Y.; Wang, X.; Huang, Y.; Xu, L. Collaborative Driving Style Classification Method Enabled by Majority Voting Ensemble Learning for Enhancing Classification Performance. *PLoS ONE* **2021**, *16*, e0254047. [CrossRef]
12. Kim, D.; Shon, H.; Kweon, N.; Choi, S.; Yang, C.; Huh, K. Driving Style-Based Conditional Variational Autoencoder for Prediction of Ego Vehicle Trajectory. *IEEE Access* **2021**, *9*, 169348–169356. [CrossRef]
13. Liu, X.; Wang, Y.; Zhou, Z.; Nam, K.; Wei, C.; Yin, C. Trajectory Prediction of Preceding Target Vehicles Based on Lane Crossing and Final Points Generation Model Considering Driving Styles. *IEEE Trans. Veh. Technol.* **2021**, *70*, 8720–8730. [CrossRef]
14. Jia, L.; Yang, D.; Ren, Y.; Qian, C.; Feng, Q.; Sun, B. A Dynamic Driving-Style Analysis Method Based on Drivers' Interaction with Surrounding Vehicles. *J. Transp. Saf. Secur.* **2024**, *0*, 1–24. [CrossRef]
15. Zhang, S.; Shao, X.; Wang, J. Research on Lane-Changing Decision Model with Driving Style Based on XGBoost. In Proceedings of the Third International Conference on Intelligent Traffic Systems and Smart City (ITSSC 2023), Xi'an, China, 10–12 November 2023; SPIE: Cergy-Pontoise, France, 2023; Volume 12989, pp. 95–100. [CrossRef]
16. Wang, K.; Qu, D.; Yang, Y.; Dai, S.; Wang, T. Risk-Quantification Method for Car-Following Behavior Considering Driving-Style Propensity. *Appl. Sci.* **2024**, *14*, 1746. [CrossRef]
17. Wang, J.; Wu, J.; Li, Y. Concept, Principles, and Modeling of Driving Risk Field Based on Human-Vehicle-Road Coordination. *China J. Highw. Transp.* **2016**, *29*, 105–114. [CrossRef]
18. Mullakkal-Babu, F.A.; Wang, M.; He, X. Probabilistic Field Approach for Motorway Driving Risk Assessment. *Transp. Res. Part C Emerg. Technol.* **2020**, *118*, 102716. [CrossRef]
19. Xiong, J.; Shi, J.; Wan, H. Construction of Integrated Human-Vehicle-Road Risk Field Model and Driving Style Evaluation. *J. Transp. Syst. Eng. Inf. Technol.* **2021**, *21*, 105–114. [CrossRef]
20. Tian, Y.; Pei, H.; Yan, S.; Zhang, Y. Extension and Application of Driving Risk Field Model under Vehicle-Road Coordination Environment. *J. Tsinghua Univ. (Sci. Technol.)* **2022**, *62*, 447–457. [CrossRef]
21. Luo, J.; Li, S.; Li, H.; Xia, F. Intelligent Network Vehicle Driving Risk Field Modeling and Path Planning for Autonomous Obstacle Avoidance. *J. Mech. Eng. Sci.* **2022**, *236*, 8621–8634. [CrossRef]
22. Tan, H.; Lu, G.; Liu, M. Risk Field Model of Driving and Its Application in Modeling Car-Following Behavior. *IEEE Trans. Intell. Transp. Syst.* **2022**, *23*, 11605–11620. [CrossRef]
23. Chen, C.; Lan, Z.; Zhan, G.; Lyu, Y.; Nie, B.; Li, S.E. Quantifying the Individual Differences of Drivers' Risk Perception via Potential Damage Risk Model. *IEEE Trans. Intell. Transp. Syst.* **2024**, Early Access. [CrossRef]
24. Zhong, N.; Gupta, M.K.; Kochan, O.; Cheng, X. Evaluating the Efficacy of Real-Time Connected Vehicle Basic Safety Messages in Mitigating Aberrant Driving Behaviour and Risk of Vehicle Crashes: Preliminary Insights from Highway Scenarios. *Elektron. Elektrotechnika* **2024**, *30*, 56–67. [CrossRef]
25. Xiong, X.; Zhang, S.; Chen, Y. Review of Intelligent Vehicle Driving Risk Assessment in Multi-Vehicle Interaction Scenarios. *World Electr. Veh. J.* **2023**, *14*, 348. [CrossRef]
26. He, K.; Fan, H.; Wu, Y.; Xie, S.; Girshick, R. Momentum Contrast for Unsupervised Visual Representation Learning. *arXiv* **2020**, arXiv:1911.05722. [CrossRef]
27. Chen, T.; Kornblith, S.; Norouzi, M.; Hinton, G. A Simple Framework for Contrastive Learning of Visual Representations. *arXiv* **2020**, arXiv:2002.05709. [CrossRef]
28. Chen, X.; He, K. Exploring Simple Siamese Representation Learning. *arXiv* **2020**, arXiv:2011.10566. [CrossRef]
29. He, K.; Chen, X.; Xie, S.; Li, Y.; Dollár, P.; Girshick, R. Masked Autoencoders Are Scalable Vision Learners. *arXiv* **2021**, arXiv:2111.06377. [CrossRef]
30. Tong, Z.; Song, Y.; Wang, J.; Wang, L. VideoMAE: Masked Autoencoders Are Data-Efficient Learners for Self-Supervised Video Pre-Training. *arXiv* **2022**, arXiv:2203.12602. [CrossRef]
31. Khrapak, S.; Ivlev, A.; Morfill, G.; Zhdanov, S.; Thomas, H. Scattering in the Attractive Yukawa Potential: Application to the Ion-Drag Force in Complex Plasmas. *IEEE Trans. Plasma Sci.* **2004**, *32*, 555–560. [CrossRef]

32. Wu, J. Research on Driving Risk Assessment Method Considering Human Vehicle Road Factors. Master's Thesis, Tsinghua University, Beijing, China, 2017.
33. Hochreiter, S.; Schmidhuber, J. Long Short-Term Memory. *Neural Comput.* **1997**, *9*, 1735–1780. [CrossRef]

Disclaimer/Publisher's Note: The statements, opinions and data contained in all publications are solely those of the individual author(s) and contributor(s) and not of MDPI and/or the editor(s). MDPI and/or the editor(s) disclaim responsibility for any injury to people or property resulting from any ideas, methods, instructions or products referred to in the content.

Article

EFE-LSTM: A Feature Extension, Fusion and Extraction Approach Using Long Short-Term Memory for Navigation Aids State Recognition

Jingjing Cao [1,2], Zhipeng Wen [1], Liang Huang [2,3,4], Jinshan Dai [1,*] and Hu Qin [5]

1 School of Transportation and Logistics Engineering, Wuhan University of Technology, Wuhan 430063, China; bettycao@whut.edu.cn (J.C.); zpwen6@163.com (Z.W.)
2 State Key Laboratory of Maritime Technology and Safety, Wuhan University of Technology, Wuhan 430063, China; leung.huang@whut.edu.cn
3 National Engineering Research Center for Water Transport Safety, Wuhan University of Technology, Wuhan 430063, China
4 Intelligent Transportation Systems Research Center, Wuhan University of Technology, Wuhan 430063, China
5 School of Management, Huazhong University of Science and Technology, Wuhan 430063, China; tigerqin@hust.edu.cn
* Correspondence: jinshan.dai@whut.edu.cn; Tel.: +86-1862-714-7823

Abstract: Navigation aids play a crucial role in guiding ship navigation and marking safe water areas. Therefore, ensuring the accurate and efficient recognition of a navigation aid's state is critical for maritime safety. To address the issue of sparse features in navigation aid data, this paper proposes an approach that involves three distinct processes: the extension of rank entropy space, the fusion of multi-domain features, and the extraction of hidden features (EFE). Based on these processes, this paper introduces a new LSTM model termed EFE-LSTM. Specifically, in the feature extension module, we introduce a rank entropy operator for space extension. This method effectively captures uncertainty in data distribution and the interrelationships among features. The feature fusion module introduces new features in the time domain, frequency domain, and time–frequency domain, capturing the dynamic features of signals across multiple dimensions. Finally, in the feature extraction module, we employ the BiLSTM model to capture the hidden abstract features of navigational signals, enabling the model to more effectively differentiate between various navigation aids states. Extensive experimental results on four real-world navigation aid datasets indicate that the proposed model outperforms other benchmark algorithms, achieving the highest accuracy among all state recognition models at 92.32%.

Keywords: navigation aids; state recognition; extended space; multi-domain features; hidden feature extraction; maritime safety

MSC: 68T01

1. Introduction

Navigation aids are specialized floating devices used extensively in maritime navigation to assist with navigation and waterway positioning. Their primary functions include indicating the position, direction, and boundaries of navigable channels as well as providing warnings of obstacles or hazardous areas in the water, such as reefs, shoals, or other navigation impediments. These devices are typically equipped with distinctive identifying features, such as unique shapes, colors, patterns, and markers, to ensure recognition under various visual conditions. Moreover, certain aids to navigation are equipped with lights, reflectors, or sound signals to enhance visibility and identifiability in conditions of reduced visibility. As integral components of maritime traffic, navigation aids play an indispensable role in maintaining navigation safety, fostering effective waterway management, and ensuring the smooth and efficient flow of maritime traffic [1].

In the traditional maintenance and management of navigation aids, the predominant approach has long been reliant on periodic manual inspections. However, due to the scattered distribution of navigation aids, this inspection process is both time-consuming and labor-intensive. With the rapid development of communication technology, various countries have adopted the approach of installing sensors on traditional navigation aids [2]. By regularly collecting sensor data and conducting continuous monitoring, the subjectivity bias associated with manual monitoring has been successfully mitigated, and the accuracy of monitoring has been significantly enhanced. The recognition of navigation aid states is typically achieved by collecting sensor data related to the aids which encompass information on their positions, movements, and lighting apparatuses [3]. Specific models are then employed to accurately discern whether the aids are operating normally or exhibiting anomalies. Considering that navigation aid devices are commonly deployed in complex and dynamic natural environments such as rivers and oceans, acquiring key environmental features like water flow velocity, water level, maritime traffic volume, sunlight intensity, and river surface wind force [3] poses considerable challenges. Currently, the feature data collected by navigation aid sensors mainly include latitude, longitude, current, voltage, and offset distance. The magnitude of these datasets, compounded by the absence or indistinctness of pivotal information, introduces complexities in the effective interpretation and analysis of data. Consequently, the development of models capable of efficiently and accurately recognizing states of navigation aid in the presence of sparse features remains an unresolved challenge for researchers in this field.

Given the limited research on navigation aids, which primarily focuses on aspects such as the development of navigation aids [4–6], risk assessments of navigation aids [7,8], and the impact of navigation aids on maritime transportation [9,10], we have opted to conduct a review of the literature on status recognition in fields such as transportation. Although the research subjects of these papers are not navigation aids, we believe that the findings are applicable to a certain extent and can be generalized to the field of navigation aids to some degree. Alharbi et al. [11] proposed an integrated model that combines long short-term memory (LSTM) and convolutional neural networks (CNNs) for the precise classification of electrocardiogram signals. The objective is to enhance the efficiency of cardiovascular disease prevention and medical care. Mustaqeem et al. [12] proposed a hierarchical convolutional LSTM network to enhance the accuracy of speech emotion recognition. By employing deep feature extraction and optimizing using the center loss function, the model achieved high recognition rates on prominent datasets. Chen et al. [13] addressed the dependency on fault state monitoring data in fault detection by modifying bidirectional long short-term memory (BiLSTM). The modification involved excluding the input corresponding to a predicted outputted data point. Dong et al. [14] proposed a mixed-truth-value CNN framework, TKRNet, which effectively addresses the counting challenges in navigation aid state recognition through coarse-to-fine density maps and an adaptive Top-k relation module. An et al. [15], based on the principles of calculus and in conjunction with LSTM networks and a novel loss function, significantly enhanced the accuracy and efficiency of state recognition under time-varying operating conditions. Alotaibi et al. [16] developed a model that integrates LSTM with attention mechanisms to enhance the accuracy of electromyographic signal recognition. By effectively incorporating the advantages of time series analysis and focused attention, the experiment yielded a high average accuracy of 91.5%. These scholarly works collectively underscore the superior efficacy of LSTM models in the domain of state recognition, thereby providing a compelling foundation for this study to further investigate and extend upon the capabilities of LSTM-based methodologies.

Wang et al. [17] introduced an innovative CNN-LSTM architecture for equipment health monitoring, demonstrating the feasibility of state recognition in raw datasets without the necessity for extensive feature engineering. Building upon this foundation, our research extends these methodologies by enhancing feature learning to improve recognition accuracy, thereby addressing gaps not yet fully explored [17]. Zhao et al. [18] utilized a BiLSTM network to analyze data from smartphone sensors, such as accelerometers and gyroscopes, circumventing the limitations of sole reliance on GPS data. However, given the complex environmental conditions of buoys, which preclude the acquisition of diverse sensor data, our study employs advanced feature processing techniques to enhance feature representation, thereby improving state recognition accuracy under conditions of limited feature availability. Mekruksavanich et al. [19] demonstrated the capability of deep learning frameworks to process complex time series data and extract meaningful features, inspiring our application of deep learning, particularly LSTM techniques, to extract intricate features from limited sensor data for more precise state recognition. Our work not only inherits methodologies from these studies but also innovatively expands upon them to meet the unique requirements of buoy state recognition, aiming to facilitate more accurate state recognition under conditions of feature sparsity through feature extension. However, when confronted with specific sparse datasets, relying solely on raw data may not accurately identify the working state of a device.

Some researchers attempt to improve state recognition accuracy by integrating data from sensors such as smartphones. Wang et al. [20] significantly enhanced the accuracy and efficiency of transportation mode detection through the multimodal sensors of smartphones. Wang et al. [21] presented a traffic mode detection method based on low-power sensors in smartphones and LSTM. The utilization of these sensors resulted in the successful achievement of a 96.9% recognition rate for traffic modes. Drosouli et al. [22] successfully elevated the accuracy of traffic mode detection by applying an optimized LSTM model to multimodal sensor data from smartphones. Wang et al. [20] further leveraged data from smartphone sensors to construct a neural network model, significantly improving the accuracy of identifying different traffic states. Shi et al. [23] constructed a gait recognition LSTM network based on multimodal wearable inertial sensor data with features automatically extracted. Nevertheless, the methods proposed in these studies still face limitations in obtaining data, and the correlation with device states is not sufficiently prominent.

Some studies focus on processing raw features to obtain a more comprehensive dataset. In [24], the researchers propose an Extended Space Forest (ESF) method for decision tree construction, enhancing the performance of ensemble algorithms by introducing original features and their random combinations into the training set. Dhibi et al. [25] innovatively combined multiple learning models and kernel principal component analysis for feature extraction and selection, significantly enhancing the accuracy and decision efficiency of diagnosis. Wen et al. [3] enhanced the accuracy of navigation aids status recognition by generating additional features through the use of Extended Space Forests and integrating temporal domain feature fusion to capture the dynamic changes and temporal correlations of data, achieving a maximum precision of 84.17%. Sun et al. [26] proposed an end-to-end intelligent bearing-fault-diagnosis method that combines 1D convolutional neural networks (1DCNNs) and LSTM networks, eliminating the need for manual feature extraction. This approach avoids errors caused by reliance on expert experience and incomplete information, achieving an average fault identification accuracy of 99.95%. Malik et al. [27] carried out training by utilizing an extended feature space generated through an analysis of the original feature space, incorporating the original features, supervised randomized features, and unsupervised randomized features. Xu et al. [28] employed a combination of multiscale rotation reconstruction and subspace-enhanced features in a mixed space-enhancement process, effectively enhancing the method's performance through various feature combination strategies. Wang et al. [29] refined features by comparing the overall contributions of each feature to the construction of classification regression trees in a cross-validation framework. This process aids the model in better capturing latent relationships within the data. Nonetheless, acquiring data from sensors and obtaining deep features containing more information from a limited set of features still present a certain level of complexity. Thus, the research methods employed in the literature mentioned above have certain limitations.

This research paper elaborates on a new LSTM-based model that is based on rank entropy extended space, along with multi-domain feature fusion and hidden feature extraction techniques, to achieve highly accurate classifications of navigation aid states. The core innovation of this model lies in the introduction of a space-extending operator called "rank entropy". This operator not only provides a different framework for quantifying and comparing the uncertainty of various features in the dataset but also facilitates an insightful understanding of complex data structures. Additionally, the model designs a unique multi-domain feature fusion method which captures and analyzes the inter-dependencies of signals in the time and frequency domains. This module comprehensively and precisely reflects dynamic changes in navigation aid states. Finally, through the application of hidden feature extraction techniques, the model further explores and extracts abstract representations from the data, enhancing the recognition and understanding of multi-level features related to navigation aid states. The integration of these three different modules allows the model to fully leverage and enrich the features of the dataset, resulting in considerable accuracy in navigation aid state recognition.

The main contributions of this paper are as follows:

- This study represents the first introduction of a new feature-processing framework in the field of maritime safety, with a specific focus on navigation aids under complex conditions. By employing advanced feature-processing techniques, our approach accurately captures relationships among features and comprehensively considers the impact of multidimensional characteristics, leading to a more precise identification of the operational status of navigation aids.
- We propose three independent feature-processing modules. The feature expansion module utilizes the rank entropy operator to capture associations between features. The feature fusion module integrates features from the time domain, frequency domain, and time–frequency domain, capturing the correlation of signals in both the time and frequency domains, providing a more comprehensive reflection of the dynamic evolution of navigation aids states. The feature extraction module, through the BiLSTM model, better captures the abstract representation of navigation aids signals.
- We conducted a comprehensive comparison of our model with deep learning network models such as LSTM, BiLSTM, 1DCNN, and LSTM-CNN. Through experimental validation on four actual navigation aids datasets collected by the Guangzhou Maritime Safety Administration, the results indicate that our proposed model significantly surpasses current leading methods in terms of performance. This provides strong support for research and practical applications in the field of maritime navigation.

The remaining sections of this research paper are organized as follows: Section 2 provides a detailed exposition of the three feature-processing methods proposed in this paper. Section 3 details the experimental results, and Section 4 summarizes the study and discusses its limitations.

2. Materials and Methods

This chapter provides a detailed introduction to the proposed EFE-LSTM model framework, depicted in Figure 1.

The model consists of three main modules: a feature extension module, a feature fusion module, and a feature extraction module. Firstly, in the feature extension module, the rank entropy operator is introduced, integrating the concept of entropy into the extended space algorithm. This operator effectively captures the uncertainty of data distribution and complex relationships between features, greatly enhancing the model's ability to handle and understand high-dimensional, complex data. Next, in the feature fusion module, we conduct in-depth feature fusion from three different dimensions: the time domain, frequency domain, and time–frequency domain. The core advantage of this stage lies in the ability to comprehensively consider the relevant characteristics of signals in the time and frequency domains, comprehensively revealing dynamic changes in the navigation state. This multidimensional fusion not only improves the accuracy of recognizing the time patterns and spectral features of navigation signals but also significantly enhances the uniqueness and expressiveness of the model's features. In the feature extraction module, we employ the BiLSTM model to extract hidden features. The bidirectional modeling capability of the BiLSTM model demonstrates outstanding performance in capturing the spatiotemporal correlations of time series data. Through this step, the model can more accurately grasp the abstract features of navigation signals, thereby effectively distinguishing subtle differences between various navigation aid states. Finally, after finely processing the original features through the three aforementioned modules, the LSTM base model is employed for navigation state recognition.

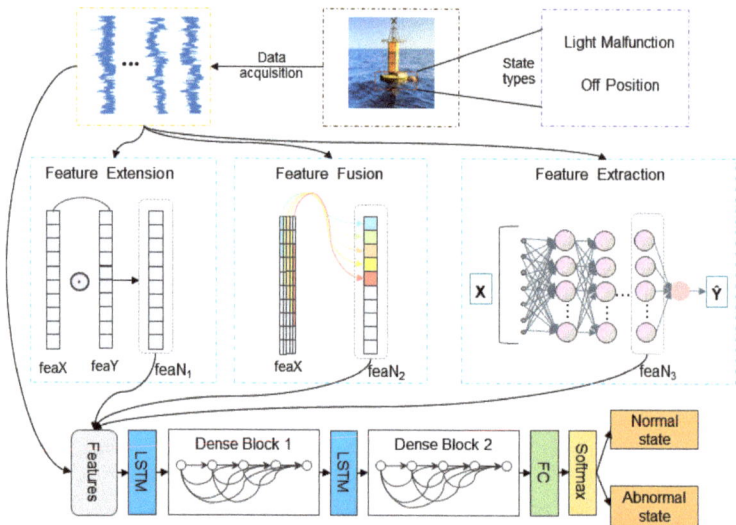

Figure 1. The framework of the EFE-LSTM model.

2.1. Feature Extension Module

The Extended Space Forest (ESF) [24] method marks a progressive strategy in building decision trees, incorporating an innovative training tactic that employs both the existing features and those created via random combinations. This approach of feature amalgamation not only broadens the diversity of data portrayal but also elevates data collection quality. The ESF algorithm exhibits exceptional performance in classification predictions, surpassing traditional approaches, particularly in situations with datasets containing a limited number of features.

The core concept of this module rests on the generation of new features through the application of a series of simple yet effective feature-generating operators (such as sum, diff, multiply, and tanh_multiply) on randomly paired sets of original features. The detailed procedure for this method is outlined in Table 1, where feaX and feaY denote any two features from the original dataset. To eliminate bias arising from predetermined feature ordering, the algorithm initially randomizes the arrangement of all features, subsequently selecting pairs from this randomized set for operation to create new features. With n original features, the theoretical maximum number of feature pairs that can be generated is $n*(n-1)/2$, which could potentially lead to duplicate features. Consequently, this study opts to generate only $n/2$ new features at a time, and through a process repeated twice, it effectively generates a total of n new features. The process flow of the ESF algorithm is illustrated in Figure 2.

Entropy plays a pivotal role in information theory, in which it serves as a metric for quantifying the uncertainty and information content associated with random variables. Within the domain of state recognition, the field of feature engineering strives to identify features that exhibit enhanced discriminative capabilities across distinct categories. The incorporation of entropy values is primarily geared toward cultivating a profound comprehension of the information interdependencies among features, thereby increasing feature distinctiveness and consequently optimizing model performance.

Table 1. Feature-generating operators.

Operator Name	Equation
Sum	$NewFea = feaX + feaY$
Diff	$NewFea = feaX - feaY$
Multiply	$NewFea = feaX \times feaY$
Tanh_multiply	$NewFea = tanh(feaX \times feaY)$

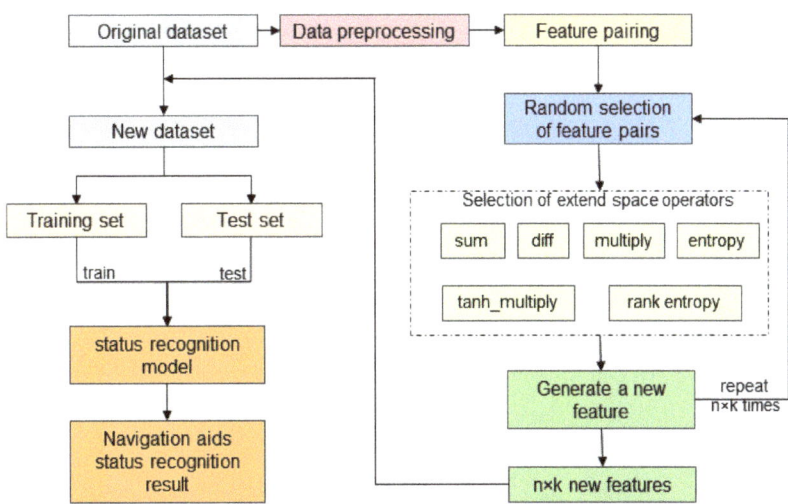

Figure 2. ESF algorithm flowchart.

To begin, we calculate the entropy value for each feature and normalize it to serve as a coefficient for the original feature. This step is designed to introduce information interplay among features, leveraging the entropy value to precisely evaluate each feature's significance. Features with high entropy, indicative of a wealth of information, are accorded great weight, while features with low entropy, indicating a dearth of information, receive a correspondingly reduced weight. This augmentation significantly bolsters the model's capacity to acquire data, especially in complex datasets in which the interrelationship between features assumes heightened significance. The process for generating new features is as follows:

$$NewFea = w_1 \cdot x_1 + w_2 \cdot x_2. \tag{1}$$

Here, x_1 and x_2 represent any two original features, and w_1 and w_2 represent the entropy values of the corresponding x_1 and x_2.

To broaden our analytical scope, we develop a method for determining the relative ranking of each sample's features and design a new operator named rank entropy. Its fundamental principle unfolds as follows: initially, we employ an exponential function to map each feature value of every sample to the realm of probability, ensuring that data points with lower rankings receive higher probabilities. Specifically, for the ith sample ($i = 1, 2, 3, \ldots, m$), the probability mapping process for the jth ($j = 1, 2, 3, \ldots, n$) feature value can be elucidated through the ensuing equation, where x_{ij} represent the jth feature value of the ith sample., and r_{ij} denotes the rank of x_{ij} within the feature values, ranging from 1 to n. The parameter λ is a modifiable factor that regulates the steepness of the probability distribution. Through the computation of Equation (2), we derive the probability distribution $p(x_{ij})$ among the features.

$$p(x_{ij}) = e^{-\lambda \cdot r_{ij} \cdot x_{ij}}. \tag{2}$$

Subsequently, we substitute these probability values into Equation (3) to calculate the feature entropy $H(x_i)$, where x_i denotes the ith sample vector. By calculating the entropy value of each sample for the jth feature, a new feature $feaN_1 = [H(x_1), H(x_2), ..., H(x_m)]^T$ can be obtained.

$$H(x_i) = -\sum_{j=1}^{n} p(x_{ij}) \log(p(x_{ij})). \tag{3}$$

In comparison to traditional extended space operators such as sum, diff, etc., this operator enables us to calculate the rank entropy value between any two features. This rank entropy value can be perceived as a new feature, serving to more accurately capture the interrelations between features, thereby enhancing model performance and the precision of data analysis.

2.2. Feature Fusion Module

This module focuses on introducing the time domain, frequency domain, and time–frequency domain features adopted in this study, along with their corresponding computational formulas.

(1) Time domain features: The temporal features employed in this study include the following: the mean value F_{t1}, variance F_{t2}, mean square value F_{t3}, root mean square value F_{t4}, maximum value F_{t5}, minimum value F_{t6}, peak value F_{t7}, peak-to-peak value F_{t8}, and root amplitude F_{t9}. Additionally, dimensionless indicators include skewness F_{t10}, kurtosis F_{t11}, a waveform indicator F_{t12}, a peak indicator F_{t13}, an impulse indicator F_{t14}, a clearance indicator F_{t15}, a skewness indicator F_{t16}, and a kurtosis indicator F_{t17} [30].

(2) Frequency domain features: The frequency domain describes the relationship between the frequency and amplitude of a signal, usually with frequency as the independent variable and amplitude as the dependent variable. By employing a Fourier transform, the time-domain signal is mapped to the frequency domain. Subsequently, based on the frequency distribution characteristics and trends of the signal, the navigation state or fault conditions of the beacon can be determined. Frequency domain analyses include methods such as spectrum analysis, energy spectrum analysis, and envelope analysis. A basic introduction to these methods is provided below.

(1) Spectral analysis: A spectrum analysis usually provides more intuitive feature information than time-domain waveforms. For a time-domain signal $x(t)$, its spectrum $X(f)$ can be obtained through the Fourier transform:

$$X(f) = \int_{-\infty}^{\infty} x(t) e^{-j2\pi ft} dt. \tag{4}$$

Here, $X(f)$ is the frequency domain representation, f is the frequency, and $x(t)$ is the original time-domain signal.

(2) Energy spectral analysis: The energy spectrum is the magnitude squared of the signal's Fourier transform, representing the distribution of energy across different frequencies. The energy spectrum $E(f)$ of a signal $x(t)$ can be expressed as follows:

$$E(f) = |X(f)|^2. \tag{5}$$

where $|X(f)|$ is the magnitude of the Fourier transform $X(f)$ of the signal $x(t)$.

(3) Envelope analysis: An envelope analysis extracts low-frequency signals from high-frequency signals. From a time-domain perspective, it is equivalent to extracting the envelope trajectory of a time-domain waveform. First, the analytic signal $x_a(t)$ of the signal $x(t)$ can be obtained via the Hilbert transform:

$$x_a(t) = x(t) + j\hat{x}(t). \quad (6)$$

where $\hat{x}(t)$ is the Hilbert transform of $x(t)$. The envelope $E(t)$ can then be determined by calculating the magnitude of the analytic signal:

$$E(t) = |x_a(t)| = \sqrt{x(t)^2 + \hat{x}(t)^2}. \quad (7)$$

(3) Time–frequency domain features: Time–frequency analysis methods provide a more comprehensive description of the relationship between frequency, energy, and time for non-stationary signals. Classical methods for analyzing non-stationary signals include the short-time Fourier transform (STFT) [31] and wavelet decomposition [32], both of which serve as important tools in the analysis of non-stationary signals. These methods can effectively illustrate variations in the frequency and energy of a signal at different time points. The STFT is suited for signals whose frequency content changes gradually over time, whereas wavelet decomposition is more appropriate for signals with sharp transitions or localized features.

(1) Short-time Fourier transform: The STFT operates by sliding a window across the signal and performing a Fourier transform on the signal within this window. This approach reveals the frequency content of the signal at various time instances. The formula for STFT is expressed as follows:

$$STFT\{x(t)\}(\tau,\omega) = \int x(t)w(t-\tau)e^{-j\omega t}dt. \quad (8)$$

Here, $x(t)$ represents the original signal, $w(t-\tau)$ denotes the window function centered at τ, and ω is the frequency variable.

(2) Wavelet decomposition: Wavelet decomposition involves analyzing the signal using a series of wavelet functions derived by scaling and translating a mother wavelet. This method provides insights into the signal's characteristics at different scales (frequencies) and locations (times). The wavelet decomposition is formulated as follows:

$$W_x(a,b) = \int x(t)\frac{1}{\sqrt{a}}\psi\left(\frac{t-b}{a}\right)dt. \quad (9)$$

In this equation, $x(t)$ is the original signal, $\psi(t)$ is the mother wavelet function, a is the scaling parameter, and b is the translation parameter.

Multi-domain feature fusion is a data-processing process aimed at enhancing the feature representation of time series datasets. The key steps of this process are as follows:

(a) For each feature column, we employ a time window with a length of n to slide over each sampling data point, including the current sampling point and its adjacent two sampling points.
(b) Calculate specific time domain or frequency domain features, such as the standard deviation, spectral analysis short-time Fourier transform, etc.
(c) Finally, add the calculated new features to the original feature columns to extend the feature set.

This process enables us to capture local features of time series data while integrating time domain, frequency domain, and time–frequency domain information, thereby improving the diversity and information density of data features. The process of multi-domain feature fusion is depicted in Figure 3.

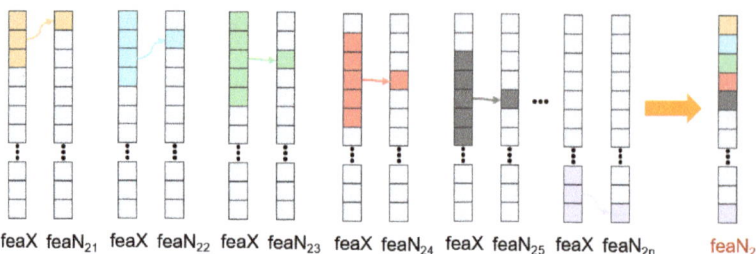

Figure 3. The process of the feature fusion module.

2.3. Feature Extraction Module

This paper constructs a BiLSTM architecture, as depicted in Figure 4. Utilizing it as a feature converter, the input navigation data are mapped to a new feature space to more effectively express the temporal dependencies within the data. The network comprises an input layer, two LSTM layers, two fully connected layers (FCs), and an output layer.

The input layer is responsible for receiving input sequences $X_{i-1}, X_i, X_{i+1}, \ldots$ in which each X represents a different time step of the input feature vector. The first LSTM layer processes the input sequence in the forward direction, with each unit containing a Constant Error Carousel (CEC) for storing and forgetting information as the memory component and a hidden state h representing the network's short-term memory. The second LSTM layer, similar to the first, processes the sequence in the reverse direction, enabling the network to utilize information from future time steps during training [33]. The subsequent two fully connected layers (FCs) are dense layers, with each neuron connected to all neurons in the preceding layer, facilitating the nonlinear transformation of learned features. The ReLU activation function applied after each FC layer introduces nonlinearity, assisting the network in learning complex data patterns. The output layer provides the final outputs $Y_{i-1}, Y_i, Y_{i+1}, \ldots$, corresponding to the predictions of the input sequence after being processed by the network.

Finally, the hidden features extracted from the first fully connected layer are labeled as $feaN_3$. The deep temporal features learned by the BiLSTM reveal critical information about the navigation state, such as variations, periodicities, or anomalous behaviors in the navigation signals, which are not directly evident in the original features. Combining these hidden features with the original features provides a rich feature set for classifier training, enhancing the model's recognition accuracy and robustness.

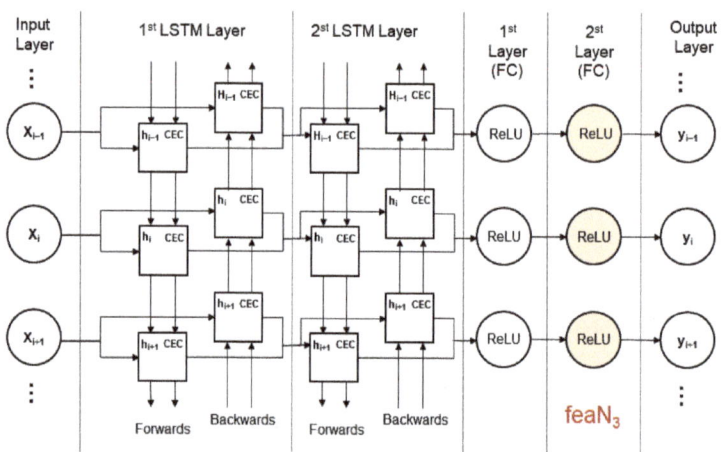

Figure 4. The architectural diagram of the feature extraction network.

2.4. LSTM

The long short-term memory (LSTM) neural network, a specialized variant of recurrent neural networks, demonstrates outstanding performance in sequence modeling and processing, rendering it a crucial algorithm in the realm of deep learning. In recent years, significant progress has been made in LSTM research, particularly in the domain of state recognition [34–37]. Conventional recurrent neural networks are plagued by issues such as gradient vanishing and exploding, rendering them unsuitable for effective long-sequence modeling. In contrast, LSTM networks incorporate temporal memory units, enabling the adept assimilation of dependencies across varying temporal scales within time series data. Consequently, LSTM exhibits notable efficacy in handling and forecasting events characterized by intervals and delays in time series data. Within the LSTM hidden layer, the computational process of an individual neuron encompasses updating cell states and calculating output values. Internally, each neuron is equipped with three gating functions: the forget gate, input gate, and output gate. These gating functions judiciously regulate input values, memory states, and output values. The structural configuration of a neuron is delineated in Figure 5, with the mathematical formulations for the forget gate, input gate, and output gate denoted, respectively.

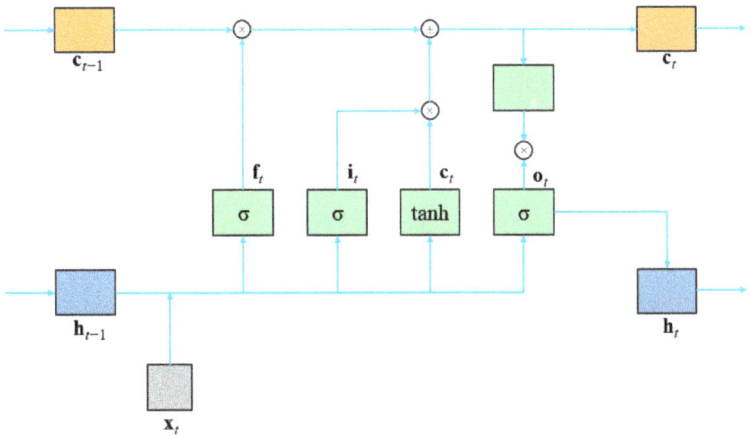

Figure 5. The hidden layer structure of LSTM.

$$f_t = \sigma\left(W_f h_{t-1} + W_f x_t + b_f\right). \tag{10}$$

$$i_t = \sigma(W_i h_{t-1} + W_i x_t + b_i). \tag{11}$$

$$o_t = \sigma(W_o h_{t-1} + W_o x_t + b_o). \tag{12}$$

In these equations, h_{t-1} represents the hidden state from the previous time step, and *sigma* denotes the sigmoid function. f_t, i_t, and o_t denote the computed results of the forget gate, input gate, and output gate states, respectively. W_f, W_i, and W_o are the weight matrices corresponding to the forget gate, input gate, and output gate, respectively. b_f, b_i, and b_o represent the bias terms associated with the forget gate, input gate, and output gate. The final output of the LSTM is jointly determined by the output gate and the cell state.

$\tilde{C}_t$ represents the candidate value vector, and the product of the input value and the candidate value vector is utilized to update the cell state. The computational process is delineated as follows. Here, W_c represents the weight matrix of the input unit state, b_c is the bias term associated with the input unit state, and *tanh* denotes the activation function. The forget gate regulates the extent to which information is discarded from the current cell state. o_t represents the output value of the neuron, and h_t signifies the hidden state at the current time step.

$$\tilde{C}_t = \tanh(W_c h_{t-1} + W_c x_t + b_c). \tag{13}$$

$$C_t = f_t C_{t-1} + i\tilde{C}_t. \tag{14}$$

$$h_t = o_t \tanh(C_t). \tag{15}$$

$$f(x) = \frac{1}{1 + e^{-x}}. \tag{16}$$

$$f(x) = \tanh(x). \tag{17}$$

2.5. Hyperparameter Optimization

The Adam optimizer was utilized in this study to minimize the cross-entropy loss function, with a learning rate set to 0.001. To alleviate overfitting and expedite model convergence, dropout and batch normalization techniques were applied [38–40]. The dropout rate was set to 0.3, and the batch size was set to 100. Detailed architecture specifications of the LSTM model can be found in Table 2.

Table 2. LSTM model summary

Layer (Type)	Output Shape	Param
lstm_1 (LSTM)	(None, 256)	268,288
dense_3 (Dense))	(None, 256)	65,792
activation_3 (Activation)	(None, 256)	0
dropout_2 (Dropout)	(None, 256)	0
batch_normalization_2 (Batch Normalization)	(None, 256)	1024
dense_4 (Dense)	(None, 64)	16,448
activation_4 (Activation)	(None, 64)	0
dropout_3 (Dropout)	(None, 64)	0
batch_normalization_3 (Batch Normalization)	(None, 64)	256
dense_5 (Dense)	(None, 2)	130
activation_5 (Activation)	(None, 2)	0

3. Data Source Description and Analysis of Results

This section aims to validate the effectiveness of the algorithm proposed in this paper through comprehensive experiments. Firstly, we conducted an experimental analysis using four different datasets from the Guangzhou Maritime Bureau. We comprehensively compared and evaluated the navigation aid state recognition results of our proposed EFE-LSTM algorithm combined with a classic LSTM algorithm [41] and an LSTM model with three modules. Subsequently, to verify the stability and reliability of the experimental results, we compared our EFE-LSTM algorithm with other algorithms such as BiLSTM, 1DCNN and LSTM_CNN. To mitigate the impact of random factors on the experimental results, we conducted five repetitions of the experiments and recorded the average results.

3.1. Data Description and Preprocessing

Ensuring diversity in datasets is crucial when evaluating the performance of the navigation aid state recognition model. The data employed in this study originate from the historical records of four navigation buoys managed by the Guangzhou Maritime Bureau. It's pertinent to note that within the context of this study, the term "navigation aids" refers explicitly to buoys. These datasets encompass various features of the buoys, including longitude, latitude, voltage, current, and offset distance. Specifically, Figure 6 illustrates the geographical coordinates of the four buoys, namely, Beihai Port Buoy No. 19 (Beihai No. 19), Huizhou Port Buoy No. 5 (Huizhou No. 5), Houjiang Waterway Buoy No. 3 (Houjiang No. 3), and Guang'ao Port Area Buoy No. 1 (Guang'ao No. 1), with coordinates as follows: 109°5′36.48″ N, 21°29′54.45″ E; 114°38′39.87″ N, 22°36′52.49″ E; 116°57′31.23″ N, 23°28′12.92″ E; and 116°46′8.87″ N, 23°9′52.56″ E. A detailed description of each dataset is provided in Table 3. The diversity and richness of these datasets hold significant implications for assessing the performance of the navigation buoy state recognition model.

In order to guarantee the model's robustness and accuracy, this paper employs a range of meticulous data preprocessing techniques. Using historical record table data for Beihai No. 19 as a case study, the dataset spans from 9 September 2019 to 11 July 2023. A portion of the data is displayed in Table 4.

Firstly, we conducted rigorous data cleaning to eliminate samples with abnormal values or errors, which is crucial for reducing interference factors in the dataset. Secondly, when dealing with missing data, this paper adopted a mean imputation strategy to maintain data integrity and availability as much as possible. Next, to enhance the stability of model training and accelerate the convergence speed, we normalized the dataset. This step involved mapping different feature data into a standardized numerical range, effectively reducing biases caused by varying feature scales during the model training process. The normalization formula is presented below:

$$x' = \frac{x - x_{\min}}{x_{\max} - x_{\min}} \tag{18}$$

Here, x represents the original data, x' represents the normalized data, and $x_{\min}$ and $x_{\max}$ represent the minimum and maximum values within the feature vector, respectively.

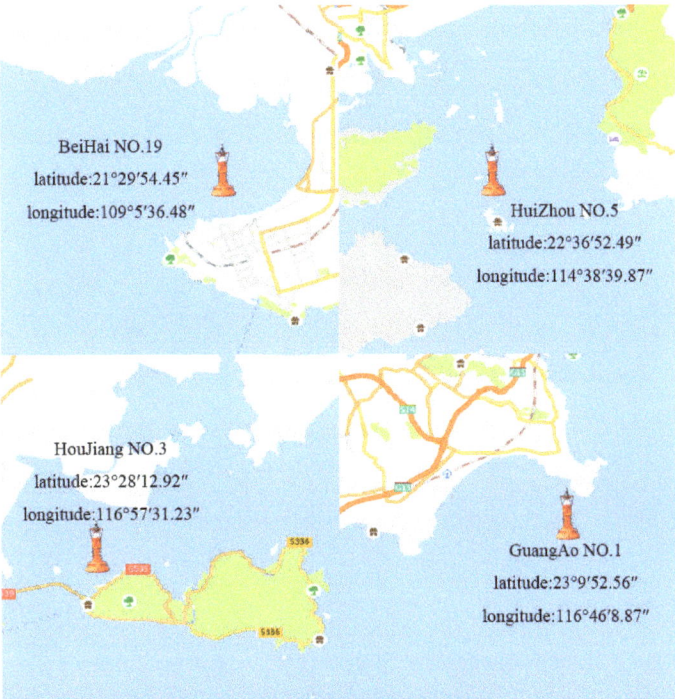

Figure 6. Schematic diagram of the position of the light buoy.

Table 3. The description of each dataset.

Dataset ID	Dataset Name	Sample Quantity	Feature Quantity
1	Beihai No. 19	26,727	5
2	Huizhou No. 5	5152	5
3	Houjiang No. 3	4891	5
4	Guang'ao No. 1	17,016	5

Table 4. Partial data of Yangjiang Port navigation aid dataset.

Acquisition Time	Latitude	Longitude	Voltage	Current	Offset Distance
9 September 2019 15:04:36	21.48142333	109.08951500	12.3	0	9.7579337793
9 September 2019 15:30:43	21.48151500	109.47328333	12.3	0	8.4548264142
9 September 2019 17:30:46	21.48174833	109.08964500	12.3	0	10.062118750
...	...	...	...	...	...
11 July 2023 13:38:13	21.49850000	109.09360500	13.700	0	13.305813355
11 July 2023 13:48:59	21.49850000	109.09360500	13.700	0.35	9.8824060802
11 July 2023 14:00:47	21.49850500	109.09360500	13.700	0.36	9.6478582663

3.2. Model Evaluation Metrics

When it comes to identifying the state of a navigation aid, there is a significant imbalance in sample categories. If we only use accuracy as the sole evaluation criterion, models that tend to classify unknown samples as majority classes (normal labels) will be considered to have better performance. To avoid this issue, we chose to use several other evaluation criteria, including accuracy, precision, recall, and F1 score, when measuring the performance of the model. The F1 score is a calculation definition that takes into account both precision and recall, providing us with a more comprehensive measure of the model's performance [42].

$$Accuracy = \frac{TP + TN}{TP + FP + TN + FN} \tag{19}$$

$$Precision = \frac{TP}{TP + FP} \tag{20}$$

$$Recall = \frac{TP}{TP + FN} \tag{21}$$

$$F1 = 2 \times \frac{Precision \times Recall}{Precision + Recall} \tag{22}$$

3.3. Assessment Results

3.3.1. Experimental Comparison of Extended Space Operators

In a paper by Amasyali, M.F. et al. [24], the concept of extended space was introduced for the first time. However, although traditional extension methods provided a larger feature space for data, they failed to fully exploit the information within the original features. To address this issue, our research innovatively introduces the concept of entropy and proposes a novel rank entropy for feature extraction. This rank entropy not only considers the distribution characteristics of the data but also comprehensively captures the complexity and uncertainty of features within the framework of information theory. The experimental results, as presented in Table 5, validate the effectiveness and superiority of our method in feature extraction.

Table 5. Comparison of performance among different extended space operators.

Operator	Mean Accuracy	Mean Recall	Mean Precision	Mean F1
/	60.53%	<u>74.87%</u>	60.53%	53.59%
Sum	61.03%	71.86%	61.02%	55.39%
Diff	<u>63.10%</u>	74.44%	<u>63.09%</u>	58.22%
Multiply	62.65%	74.10%	62.65%	57.59%
Tanh_multiply	62.99%	73.89%	62.97%	<u>58.31%</u>
Entropy	62.06%	73.31%	62.05%	56.80%
Rank entropy (Proposed)	**71.63%**	**78.66%**	**71.62%**	**69.68%**

Note: Bold numbers represent the best performance among each evaluation metric. Underlined numbers indicate the second-best performance.

In Table 5, "/" denotes direct model training using the original dataset, while "sum", "diff", "multiply", and "tanh_multiply" represent traditional extended space operators; "entropy" signifies the direct introduction of entropy as a coefficient, and "rank entropy" is the ranking entropy proposed in this paper. All results in the table represent outcomes averaged across the four datasets. The optimal results are highlighted in bold, while the second-best results are underscored.

As illustrated in Table 5, upon the introduction of the extended space operators, an overall improvement in the model's performance was observed. Among the traditional extended space operators, the "diff" operator exhibited the best performance across four evaluation metrics. Specifically, compared to the direct use of the original dataset, the "diff" operator significantly improved both the average accuracy and average precision by 2.57% and 2.56%, respectively. In terms of the average F1 score, the improvement reached 4.63% when using the "diff" operator compared to the original features. Despite a slight decrease of 0.43% in the average recall rate, considering all four metrics together, the use of the "diff" operator for extended space still shows significant advantages. This indicates that traditional extended space operators effectively enhance the overall performance of the model while maintaining balance.

Furthermore, the direct introduction of the concept of entropy does not lead to a significant performance improvement. Although the "entropy" operator exhibits improvements across all metrics compared to the original model, the improvement is relatively modest. In this context, the proposed "rank entropy" operator stands out. Compared to the traditional extended space operator "diff", "rank entropy" achieves a significant enhancement in all evaluation metrics. Specifically, relative to "diff", "rank entropy" improves the average accuracy, recall, precision, and F1 score by approximately 8.53%, 4.22%, 8.53%, and 11.46%, respectively. This indicates that the "rank entropy" operator successfully introduces a more effective feature extraction mechanism, significantly improving the model's ability to identify navigation aid states. All subsequent experiments in the following text are based on the proposed "rank entropy" operator introduced in this paper.

3.3.2. Select Multi-Domain Features

Through the multi-domain feature fusion method proposed in this paper, the original dataset's 5 features were extended to 260. An analysis of the features revealed inconsistent correlations between different features and relatively high similarity among some feature values. A PCA was employed for dimensionality reduction, allowing for the elimination of insignificant principal components while retaining maximal data variance. According to the analysis results, the cumulative variance of the first 30 principal components reached 90%, with the remaining components contributing insignificantly to the total variance. Consequently, analyzing these principal components is sufficient for achieving a dimensionality reduction, ensuring the preservation of essential data information. The specific retention states of feature vectors are delineated in Table 6. Following the PCA-based dimensionality reduction, the overall relationships within the dataset are preserved, critical data information is retained, and a substantial reduction in computational load is achieved during the feature extraction process.

Table 6. Preserved features.

Domain	Reserved Features
Time domain	root amplitude variance skewness indicator kurtosis indicator
Frequency domain	spectral analysis
Time–frequency domain	wavelet decomposition

3.3.3. Comparison with Other Feature Extraction Models

In this study, we designed and compared multiple deep-learning models to extract effective hidden features from navigation aid state data. Specifically, we developed four different model architectures: the LSTM model [43], BiLSTM model [44], 1DCNN model [45], and LSTM-CNN model [46], each comprising two respective feature extraction layers and two fully connected layers. All models use the output of the first fully connected layer as the extracted hidden features. The "/" in Table 7 represents direct utilization of raw features without extraction.

As is evident from Table 7, BiLSTM demonstrates significant advantages over other models in multiple key performance indicators. Specifically, BiLSTM achieves an accuracy of 68.35% and an F1 score of 65.51%, reflecting its outstanding performance in overall prediction accuracy and true positive identification. Moreover, BiLSTM exhibits impressive performance in recall and precision, reaching 74.85% and 68.35%, respectively, highlighting its efficient performance in true positive identification and prediction accuracy. These data unequivocally indicate the exceptional performance of BiLSTM in the complex task of extracting features from time-series data.

Table 7. Comparison with other feature extraction models.

Model	Mean Accuracy	Mean Recall	Mean Precision	Mean F1
/	60.53%	**74.87%**	60.53%	53.59%
LSTM	62.60%	73.45%	62.60%	57.02%
1DCNN	66.86%	74.48%	66.87%	63.15%
LSTM_CNN	67.10%	73.87%	67.11%	63.97%
BiLSTM	**68.35%**	74.85%	**68.35%**	**65.51%**

Note: Bold numbers represent the best performance among each evaluation metric.

3.3.4. Comparison of Performance among Different Modules

Next, a detailed comparative analysis of the performance of the standard LSTM, rank entropy LSTM (RE-LSTM), multi-domain feature fusion LSTM (MD-LSTM), and hidden feature extraction LSTM (HF-LSTM) models and the LSTM model incorporating rank entropy extension, multi-domain feature fusion, and hidden feature extraction (EFE-LSTM) was conducted across various datasets, as shown in Figure 7.

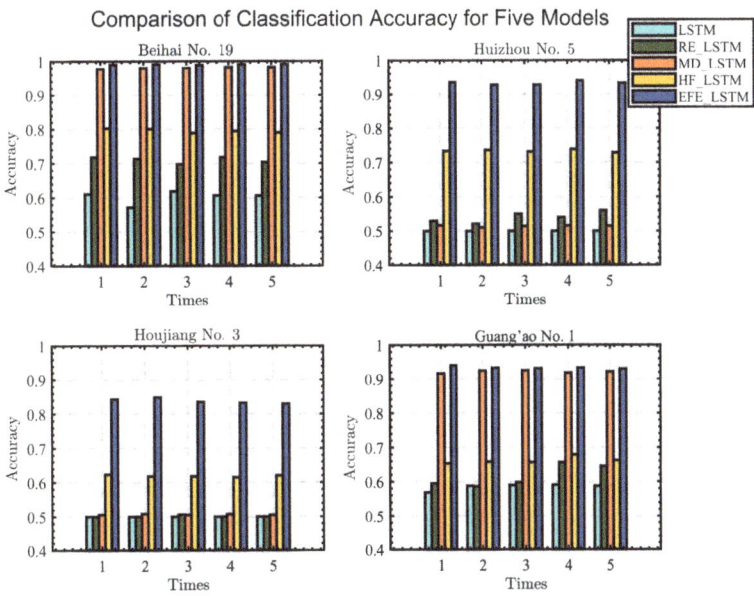

Figure 7. Comparison of classification accuracies of five models.

Firstly, the introduction of rank entropy results in increases in accuracy for LSTM on the BeiHai and GuangAo datasets by approximately 0.13 and 0.07, respectively, compared to the standard LSTM. This highlights its effectiveness in capturing the importance of sequence elements, emphasizing its crucial role in enhancing the model's understanding of inherent relationships within the data. Secondly, introducing the multi-domain feature fusion module provides a noticeable improvement in model performance. On the BeiHai, HuiZhou, and GuangAo datasets, TF-LSTM shows an accuracy increase of approximately 0.4 to 0.5 relative to the standard LSTM. This suggests that by fusing multi-domain features, the model can more comprehensively capture changes in the temporal dimension, enhancing its adaptability in the context of complex and variable data backgrounds. Thirdly, the introduction of the hidden feature extraction module leads to a slight increase in accuracy for LSTM on the BeiHai and GuangAo datasets relative to the standard LSTM, with an improvement of about 0.2 to 0.3. On the HuiZhou dataset, the improvement for HF-LSTM is more pronounced at around 0.2. This demonstrates that the hidden feature extraction module has a significant positive effect on capturing abstract features within the data.

Finally, the EFE-LSTM model, integrating the rank entropy, multi-domain feature fusion, and hidden feature extraction modules, demonstrates outstanding performance across all datasets. The EFE-LSTM model achieves an accuracy increase of approximately 0.4 on the BeiHai dataset relative to the standard LSTM, while the improvements on the HuiZhou and GuangAo datasets are more significant, ranging from 0.4 to 0.5. This further validates that by integrating different feature fusion modules, our model can more comprehensively and accurately capture key features in multidimensional time data. This provides an effective and comprehensive modeling approach for multidimensional time data classification tasks, as demonstrated by experimental validation. Even without relying on a complex network structure, the proposed method achieves highly accurate navigation state recognition, highlighting the robust performance and practical value of this approach.

3.3.5. Comparison of Performance among Different Models

Finally, this paper provides a comprehensive comparison of different models in the navigation aid state recognition task, as depicted in Table 8. Compared to 1DCNN, EFE-

LSTM demonstrates more stable and significant improvements in accuracy. Across various datasets, EFE-LSTM's accuracy increases by approximately 0.12 to 0.28 relative to 1DCNN. In comparison to LSTM-CNN, EFE-LSTM exhibits a more noticeable improvement in accuracy. Across multiple datasets, EFE-LSTM's accuracy increases by about 0.05 to 0.16 compared to LSTM-CNN. When compared to BiLSTM, EFE-LSTM consistently shows higher accuracy across multiple datasets, with an improvement ranging from 0.28 to 0.41. Relative to TCN, EFE-LSTM also achieves higher accuracy, with an improvement ranging from 0.16 to 0.27.

In summary, EFE-LSTM outperforms models such as 1DCNN, LSTM-CNN, BiLSTM, and TCN in multidimensional time data classification tasks. Its performance improvement is not only remarkable across various datasets but also demonstrates significant advantages in capturing time series information and handling complex associations in comparisons with different models.

Table 8. Performance metrics for different methods on four datasets.

Method	Confusion Matrix		Mean Accuracy	Mean Precision	Mean Recall	Mean F1
	Beihai No. 19					
LSTM	961.8	48.4	0.6511	0.7505	0.6507	0.6134
	656.6	353.6				
BiLSTM	907.8	102.4	0.6602	0.7124	0.6606	0.6352
	584.2	426				
1DCNN	947.2	63	0.7821	0.8125	0.7821	0.7767
	377.2	633				
LSTM-CNN	971.8	38.4	0.7614	0.8119	0.7614	0.7514
	443.6	566.6				
EFE-LSTM	1004.2	6	0.9922	0.9921	0.9922	0.9922
	9.8	1000.4				
	Huizhou No. 5					
Method	Confusion Matrix		Mean Accuracy	Mean Precision	Mean Recall	Mean F1
LSTM	185	14	0.7010	0.7547	0.7008	0.6841
	105	94				
BiLSTM	164.8	34.2	0.7020	0.7173	0.7022	0.6969
	84.4	114.6				
1DCNN	180.6	18.4	0.7231	0.7584	0.7233	0.7133
	91.8	107.2				
LSTM-CNN	181.2	17.8	0.7085	0.7497	0.7087	0.6959
	98.2	100.8				
EFE-LSTM	189.4	9.6	0.9191	0.9212	0.9191	0.9189
	22.6	176.4				
	Houjiang No. 3					
Method	Confusion Matrix		Mean Accuracy	Mean Precision	Mean Recall	Mean F1
LSTM	175.4	8.8	0.5994	0.7013	0.5996	0.5418
	138.8	45.4				
BiLSTM	177.2	7	0.5874	0.7001	0.5875	0.5199
	145	39.2				
1DCNN	173.6	10.6	0.5993	0.6890	0.5995	0.5456
	137	47.2				
LSTM-CNN	171.6	12.6	0.5988	0.6788	0.5995	0.5456
	135.2	49				
EFE-LSTM	166	18.2	0.8334	0.8404	0.8339	0.8325
	43.2	141				

Table 8. *Cont.*

Method	Confusion Matrix		Guang'ao No. 1			
			Mean Accuracy	Mean Precision	Mean Recall	Mean F1
LSTM	598.4	21.2	0.5734	0.6913	0.5734	0.4956
	507.4	112.2				
BiLSTM	584.2	35.4	0.5689	0.6636	0.5699	0.4978
	498.8	120.8				
1DCNN	577.6	42	0.6067	0.6876	0.6074	0.5599
	445.4	174.2				
LSTM-CNN	598.2	21.4	0.5778	0.6947	0.5778	0.5030
	501.8	117.8				
EFE-LSTM	588.4	31.2	0.9385	0.9387	0.9387	0.9385
	45	574.6				

Note: The gray background in the confusion matrix cells highlights true positives and true negatives.

4. Conclusions

This paper introduces the EFE-LSTM model, which achieves significant progress in the recognition of navigation beacon states through the integration of entropy space extension, multi-domain feature fusion, and hidden feature extraction. Its primary advantage lies in extending the feature space through rank entropy, allowing for a more nuanced understanding of complex signal patterns by capturing uncertainty in data distribution. Additionally, the model integrates time and frequency domain features, providing a multidimensional and comprehensive representation of the data, which is crucial for accurately capturing the dynamic evolution of navigation beacon states. Finally, extracting hidden features from the data to capture abstract representations of beacon signals further enhances the modeling capability for navigation beacon states. Compared to traditional models, the proposed EFE-LSTM model achieved average accuracy rates of 99.22%, 91.91%, 83.34%, and 93.85% on four datasets, respectively. This represents an improvement of over 20% in accuracy compared to the best-performing model in traditional models for navigational beacon state recognition, highlighting its robustness in handling complex multidimensional temporal data.

Future research should focus on enhancing the real-time performance of the model and further optimizing computational efficiency to ensure that the model maintains excellent performance when processing large datasets. Additionally, exploring a variety of feature extension methods to enhance the model's generalizability will be an important research direction. Moreover, constructing more complex deep learning models to delve deeper into the intrinsic connections among data could also improve the accuracy of status recognition.

Author Contributions: J.C.: conceptualization, methodology, and formal analysis. Z.W.: methodology, software, validation, and writing—original draft preparation. L.H.: investigation, resources, data curation, and funding acquisition. J.D.: visualization, supervision, project administration. H.Q.: writing—review and editing. All authors have read and agreed to the published version of the manuscript.

Funding: This project was supported by the National Key Research and Development Program of China (No. 2021YFB2600300).

Data Availability Statement: Dataset available on request from the authors.

Conflicts of Interest: The authors declare no conflicts of interest.

References

1. Redondo, R.; Atienza, R.; Pecharroman, L.; Pires, L. Aids to navigation improvement to optimize ship navigation. In *Smart Rivers*; Springer: Berlin/Heidelberg, Germany, 2022; pp. 803–813.
2. Sang, L.; Hong, S. Development of navigational aids telemetry and telecontrol system in south China sea. *Navig. China* **2020**, *43*, 35–40.

3. Wen, Z.; Cao, J.; Huang, L.; Li, D.; Sun, L.; Huang, X. Enhancing Navigation Aids Status Recognition Based on Extended Space Forest and Time Domain Features Fusion. In Proceedings of the 2023 IEEE International Symposium on Product Compliance Engineering—Asia (ISPCE-ASIA), Shanghai, China, 3–5 November 2023; pp. 1–6.
4. Muhammad Irsyad Hasbullah, N.A.O.; Salleh, N.H.M. A systematic review and meta-analysis on the development of aids to navigation. *Aust. J. Marit. Ocean. Aff.* **2023**, *15*, 247–267. [CrossRef]
5. Cho, M.; Choi, H.R.; Kwak, C. A study on the navigation aids management based on IoT. *Int. J. Control Autom.* **2015**, *8*, 193–204. [CrossRef]
6. Cho, M.; Choi, H.; Kwak, C. A Study on the method of IoT-based navigation aids management. *Adv. Sci. Technol. Lett.* **2015**, *98*, 55–58.
7. Ostroumov, I.; Kuzmenko, N. Risk analysis of positioning by navigational aids. In Proceedings of the 2019 Signal Processing Symposium (SPSympo), Krakow, Poland, 17–19 September 2019; IEEE: Piscataway, NJ, USA, 2019; pp. 92–95.
8. Ostroumov, I.; Kuzmenko, N. Risk assessment of mid-air collision based on positioning performance by navigational aids. In Proceedings of the 2020 IEEE 6th International Conference on Methods and Systems of Navigation and Motion Control (MSNMC), Kyiv, Ukraine, 20–23 October 2020; IEEE: Piscataway, NJ, USA, 2020; pp. 34–37.
9. Wu, F.; Qu, Y. The positive impact of intelligent aids to navigation on maritime transportation. In Proceedings of the Seventh International Conference on Traffic Engineering and Transportation System (ICTETS 2023), Dalian, China, 22–24 September 2023; SPIE: Washington, DC, USA, 2024; Volume 13064, pp. 959–966.
10. Liang, Y. Route planning of aids to navigation inspection based on intelligent unmanned ship. In Proceedings of the 2021 4th International Symposium on Traffic Transportation and Civil Architecture (ISTTCA), Suzhou, China, 12–14 November 2021; IEEE: Piscataway, NJ, USA, 2021; pp. 95–98.
11. Alharbi, N.S.; Jahanshahi, H.; Yao, Q.; Bekiros, S.; Moroz, I. Enhanced classification of heartbeat electrocardiogram signals using a long short-term memory–convolutional neural network ensemble: Paving the way for preventive healthcare. *Mathematics* **2023**, *11*, 3942. [CrossRef]
12. Mustaqeem; Kwon, S. CLSTM: Deep feature-based speech emotion recognition using the hierarchical ConvLSTM network. *Mathematics* **2020**, *8*, 2133. [CrossRef]
13. Chen, Y.; Niu, G.; Li, Y.; Li, Y. A modified bidirectional long short-term memory neural network for rail vehicle suspension fault detection. *Veh. Syst. Dyn.* **2023**, *61*, 3136–3160. [CrossRef]
14. Dong, L.; Zhang, H.; Yang, K.; Zhou, D.; Shi, J.; Ma, J. Crowd counting by using Top-k relations: A mixed ground-truth CNN framework. *IEEE Trans. Consum. Electron.* **2022**, *68*, 307–316. [CrossRef]
15. An, Z.; Li, S.; Wang, J.; Jiang, X. A novel bearing intelligent fault diagnosis framework under time-varying working conditions using recurrent neural network. *ISA Trans.* **2020**, *100*, 155–170. [CrossRef]
16. Alotaibi, N.D.; Jahanshahi, H.; Yao, Q.; Mou, J.; Bekiros, S. An ensemble of long short-term memory networks with an attention mechanism for upper limb electromyography signal classification. *Mathematics* **2023**, *11*, 4004. [CrossRef]
17. Wang, H.; Fu, S.; Peng, B.; Wang, N.; Gao, H. Equipment health condition recognition and prediction based on CNN-LSTM deep learning. In Proceedings of the International Conference on Maintenance Engineering, Online, 15–17 April 2020; Springer: Berlin/Heidelberg, Germany, 2020; pp. 830–842.
18. Zhao, H.; Hou, C.; Alrobassy, H.; Zeng, X. Recognition of transportation state by smartphone sensors using deep BiLSTM neural network. *J. Comput. Netw. Commun.* **2019**, *2019*, 830–842.
19. Mekruksavanich, S.; Jitpattanakul, A. Lstm networks using smartphone data for sensor-based human activity recognition in smart homes. *Sensors* **2021**, *21*, 1636. [CrossRef] [PubMed]
20. Wang, C.; Luo, H.; Zhao, F.; Qin, Y. Combining residual and LSTM recurrent networks for transportation mode detection using multimodal sensors integrated in smartphones. *IEEE Trans. Intell. Transp. Syst.* **2020**, *22*, 5473–5485. [CrossRef]
21. Wang, H.; Luo, H.; Zhao, F.; Qin, Y.; Zhao, Z.; Chen, Y. Detecting Transportation Modes with Low-Power-Consumption Sensors Using Recurrent Neural Network; IEEE: Piscataway, NJ, USA, 2018; pp. 1098–1105.
22. Drosouli, I.; Voulodimos, A.; Miaoulis, G.; Mastorocostas, P.; Ghazanfarpour, D. Transportation mode detection using an optimized long short-term memory model on multimodal sensor data. *Entropy* **2021**, *23*, 1457. [CrossRef] [PubMed]
23. Shi, L.; Liu, Z.; Zhou, K.; Shi, Y.; Jing, X. Novel deep learning network for gait recognition using multimodal inertial sensors. *Sensors* **2023**, *23*, 849. [CrossRef] [PubMed]
24. Amasyali, M.F.; Ersoy, O.K. Classifier ensembles with the extended space forest. *IEEE Trans. Knowl. Data Eng.* **2013**, *26*, 549–562. [CrossRef]
25. Dhibi, K.; Mansouri, M.; Bouzrara, K.; Nounou, H.; Nounou, M. An enhanced ensemble learning-based fault detection and diagnosis for grid-connected PV systems. *IEEE Access* **2021**, *9*, 155622–155633. [CrossRef]
26. Sun, H.; Zhao, S. Fault diagnosis for bearing based on 1DCNN and LSTM. *Shock Vib.* **2021**, *2021*, 1–17. [CrossRef]
27. Malik, A.K.; Ganaie, M.; Tanveer, M.; Suganthan, P.N. Extended features based random vector functional link network for classification problem. *IEEE Trans. Comput. Soc. Syst.* **2022**. [CrossRef]
28. Xu, Y.; Yu, Z.; Cao, W.; Chen, C.P. A novel classifier ensemble method based on subspace enhancement for high-dimensional data classification. *IEEE Trans. Knowl. Data Eng.* **2021**, *35*, 16–30. [CrossRef]
29. Wang, Y.; Wang, S.; Sima, X.; Song, Y.; Cui, S.; Wang, D. Expanded feature space-based gradient boosting ensemble learning for risk prediction of type 2 diabetes complications. *Appl. Soft Comput.* **2023**, *144*, 110451. [CrossRef]

30. Duan, Y.; Cao, X.; Zhao, J.; Xu, X. Health indicator construction and status assessment of rotating machinery by spatiotemporal fusion of multi-domain mixed features. *Measurement* **2022**, *205*, 112170. [CrossRef]
31. Boashash, B. *Time-Frequency Signal Analysis and Processing: A Comprehensive Reference*; Academic Press: Cambridge, MA, USA, 2015.
32. Mallat, S.G. A theory for multiresolution signal decomposition: The wavelet representation. *IEEE Trans. Pattern Anal. Mach. Intell.* **1989**, *11*, 674–693. [CrossRef]
33. Abduljabbar, R.L.; Dia, H.; Tsai, P.W. Development and evaluation of bidirectional LSTM freeway traffic forecasting models using simulation data. *Sci. Rep.* **2021**, *11*, 23899. [CrossRef]
34. Xia, K.; Huang, J.; Wang, H. LSTM-CNN architecture for human activity recognition. *IEEE Access* **2020**, *8*, 56855–56866. [CrossRef]
35. Khan, P.; Reddy, B.S.K.; Pandey, A.; Kumar, S.; Youssef, M. Differential channel-state-information-based human activity recognition in IoT networks. *IEEE Internet Things J.* **2020**, *7*, 11290–11302. [CrossRef]
36. Du, X.; Ma, C.; Zhang, G.; Li, J.; Lai, Y.K.; Zhao, G.; Deng, X.; Liu, Y.J.; Wang, H. An efficient LSTM network for emotion recognition from multichannel EEG signals. *IEEE Trans. Affect. Comput.* **2020**, *13*, 1528–1540. [CrossRef]
37. Xiao, H.; Sotelo, M.A.; Ma, Y.; Cao, B.; Zhou, Y.; Xu, Y.; Wang, R.; Li, Z. An improved LSTM model for behavior recognition of intelligent vehicles. *IEEE Access* **2020**, *8*, 101514–101527. [CrossRef]
38. Kingma, D.P.; Ba, J. Adam: A method for stochastic optimization. *arXiv* **2014**, arXiv:1412.6980.
39. Srivastava, N.; Hinton, G.; Krizhevsky, A.; Sutskever, I.; Salakhutdinov, R. Dropout: A simple way to prevent neural networks from overfitting. *J. Mach. Learn. Res.* **2014**, *15*, 1929–1958.
40. Ioffe, S.; Szegedy, C. Batch normalization: Accelerating deep network training by reducing internal covariate shift. In Proceedings of the International Conference on Machine Learning, Lille, France, 7–9 July 2015; Volume 37, pp. 448–456.
41. Dogan, G.; Ford, M.; James, S. Predicting ocean-wave conditions using buoy data supplied to a hybrid RNN-LSTM neural network and machine learning models. In Proceedings of the 2021 IEEE International Conference on Machine Learning and Applied Network Technologies (ICMLANT), Soyapango, El Salvador, 16–17 December 2021; pp. 1–6.
42. Powers, D.M.W. Evaluation: From precision, recall and F-measure to ROC, informedness, markedness and correlation. *arXiv* **2020**, arXiv:2010.16061.
43. Sherstinsky, A. Fundamentals of recurrent neural network (RNN) and long short-term memory (LSTM) network. *Phys. D Nonlinear Phenom.* **2020**, *404*, 132306. [CrossRef]
44. Woźniak, M.; Wieczorek, M.; Siłka, J. BiLSTM deep neural network model for imbalanced medical data of IoT systems. *Future Gener. Comput. Syst.* **2023**, *141*, 489–499. [CrossRef]
45. Huang, S.; Tang, J.; Dai, J.; Wang, Y. Signal status recognition based on 1DCNN and its feature extraction mechanism analysis. *Sensors* **2019**, *19*, 2018. [CrossRef]
46. Kim, T.; Kim, H.Y. Forecasting stock prices with a feature fusion LSTM-CNN model using different representations of the same data. *PLoS ONE* **2019**, *14*, e0212320. [CrossRef]

Disclaimer/Publisher's Note: The statements, opinions and data contained in all publications are solely those of the individual author(s) and contributor(s) and not of MDPI and/or the editor(s). MDPI and/or the editor(s) disclaim responsibility for any injury to people or property resulting from any ideas, methods, instructions or products referred to in the content.

Article

Predicting Fan Attendance at Mega Sports Events—A Machine Learning Approach: A Case Study of the FIFA World Cup Qatar 2022

Ahmad Al-Buenain [1,*], Mohamed Haouari [1] and Jithu Reji Jacob [2]

[1] Mechanical and Industrial Engineering Department, College of Engineering, Qatar University, Doha 2713, Qatar; mohamed.haouari@qu.edu.qa
[2] Computer Science and Engineering Department, College of Science and Technology, Cochin University, Kalamassery 682022, India; mf1407364@qu.edu.qa
* Correspondence: aa1304017@qu.edu.qa

Abstract: Mega sports events generate significant media coverage and have a considerable economic impact on the host cities. Organizing such events is a complex task that requires extensive planning. The success of these events hinges on the attendees' satisfaction. Therefore, accurately predicting the number of fans from each country is essential for the organizers to optimize planning and ensure a positive experience. This study aims to introduce a new application for machine learning in order to accurately predict the number of attendees. The model is developed using attendance data from the FIFA World Cup (FWC) Russia 2018 to forecast the FWC Qatar 2022 attendance. Stochastic gradient descent (SGD) was found to be the top-performing algorithm, achieving an R^2 metric of 0.633 in an Auto-Sklearn experiment that considered a total of 2523 models. After a thorough analysis of the result, it was found that team qualification has the highest impact on attendance. Other factors such as distance, number of expatriates in the host country, and socio-geopolitical factors have a considerable influence on visitor counts. Although the model produces good results, with ML it is always recommended to have more data inputs. Therefore, using previous tournament data has the potential to increase the accuracy of the results.

Keywords: mega sports events; FIFA World Cup; machine learning; attendee prediction; stochastic gradient descent

MSC: 68T07

1. Introduction

Mega sports events bring together the world's top athletes to compete in international competitions and represent their countries at the highest level of sports. Examples of such events include the Olympic Games and the FIFA World Cup (FWC). These events receive significant media coverage and can bring economic benefits and enhance the host country's global profile [1]. However, hosting a mega-sport is a challenging undertaking that requires significant planning, resources, and investment [2]. The success of these events is often determined by the number of fans who attend and their satisfaction level [3]. Therefore, accurately predicting the number of fans expected to attend from each country is crucial for the host nation. This can help optimize the planning process and ensure a positive experience for both fans and players.

Over the years, attendance at FWC tournaments has steadily increased. In this regard, from 1930 to 1950, average FWC attendance ranged from fewer than 10,000 to around 25,000 [4]. By the 1970s and 1980s, average attendance had increased from around 40,000 to 50,000 and reached an all-time high of almost 60,000 in the 1990s and early 2000s [4]. Overall, total attendance has grown dramatically, from under 500,000 in 1930 to over 2 million at the

Citation: Al-Buenain, A.; Haouari, M.; Jacob, J.R. Predicting Fan Attendance at Mega Sports Events—A Machine Learning Approach: A Case Study of the FIFA World Cup Qatar 2022. *Mathematics* **2024**, *12*, 926. https://doi.org/10.3390/math12060926

Academic Editors: Mingbo Zhao, Haijun Zhang and Zhou Wu

Received: 21 February 2024
Revised: 10 March 2024
Accepted: 16 March 2024
Published: 21 March 2024

Copyright: © 2024 by the authors. Licensee MDPI, Basel, Switzerland. This article is an open access article distributed under the terms and conditions of the Creative Commons Attribution (CC BY) license (https://creativecommons.org/licenses/by/4.0/).

World Cup held in Russia in 2018 and Qatar in 2022. The rising number of spectators is due in large part to the growth of the global economy and the rise of the middle class in many countries, making it affordable for more people to attend these events [5]. Additionally, improvements in transportation and communication technology have made it easier for people to travel and follow their teams [5]. Despite the COVID-19 pandemic fears, the 2022 World Cup in Qatar saw a relatively high attendance, with 3,404,252 fans [6].

Ref. [7] highlights that planning an FWC event usually involves identifying a suitable location and facilities to host the event, securing funding and managing the budget, coordinating transportation, housing, and other logistics for athletes, officials, and fans, and ensuring the safety and security of all participants and attendees. For example, the planning process for the 2018 FWC in Russia first took into consideration the expected numbers of fans from different countries [8]. The Russian government then collaborated with local and international transportation providers to ensure that fans from all over the world could easily and safely travel to and from the tournament venues.

Additionally, Russia secured enough hotel rooms and other types of accommodations to host all fans [8]. Furthermore, the local organizing committee provided fans with multilingual support and information to assist them in navigating the tournament and the host city. They also made certain that a wide range of food and beverage options were available to meet the diverse dietary needs and preferences of fans from different cultures [8]. Overall, the 2018 FWC provided a positive and memorable experience for all participants and attendees, regardless of their cultural backgrounds [9]. This is attributable to good planning for the expected number of fans from all over the world. However, there is still room for improvement in fan prediction models, which is what this study aims to address.

In recent years, the significance of big data and predictive analytics has soared [10]. Organizations now handle vast volumes of data due to the proliferation of digital devices and the increased availability of big data. Predictive analytics, a subset of data analytics, involves using historical data, machine learning algorithms, and statistical models to predict future events or outcomes [11]. Widely applied across industries, predictive analytics drives data-driven decision-making to improve business outcomes [11]. By employing prediction models, organizations effectively utilize predictive analytics to inform their decisions.

On the other hand, prediction models use historical data to forecast events. Trained on historical data comprising inputs and outputs, these models generate predictions based on new inputs [12]. They aim to estimate outcomes based on inputs, enabling accurate predictions to guide decision-making and anticipate future trends [12]. Designed using various statistical techniques and tools, the accuracy of prediction models relies on data quality, availability, choice of model, and validation methods [13]. Thus, prediction models are valuable for enhancing decision-making and anticipating trends.

To achieve the expected economic benefits, nations that host mega sports events strive to maximize fan attendance and their level of satisfaction [14]. However, predicting fan attendance at these events is a complex task due to various factors that can impact the number of attendees. Specifically, for the FWC, fan attendance can be influenced by factors such as team qualification, football popularity in the host nation, event location, and travel and accommodation costs, to quote just a few.

Accurate prediction of fan attendance is crucial for optimizing FWC planning and resource utilization. Understanding these factors allows organizers to enhance the overall fan experience and maximize the event's impact. This study utilizes various prediction models to develop the optimal fan attendance prediction model, including linear regression, logistic regression, decision trees, random forests, gradient boosting, and neural networks [15]. The choice of prediction model depends on the data type and prediction goals [15]. Some models are suitable for linear relationships, while others handle non-linear relationships or data with many variables [16].

Recent advancements in predictive analytics and data science have significantly impacted the development of models that forecast fan attendance at mega sporting events [17,18].

The integration of various innovative methodologies and technologies is pushing the boundaries of existing research, offering new insights and approaches, as follows.

1. Advanced machine learning and AI applications: The application of cutting-edge machine learning and AI technologies has marked a significant shift in predictive analytics. These technologies facilitate nuanced analysis and forecasting, offering a more dynamic understanding of fan behavior [19].
2. Exploitation of big data: The exponential growth in data generation and the strategic utilization of big data analytics have enabled researchers to harness diverse datasets, providing a multifaceted view of fan engagement and preferences [20].
3. Adoption of real-time data analytics: Leveraging real-time data has become crucial for timely and relevant insights, enabling stakeholders to make informed decisions rapidly as event dynamics unfold [21].
4. Focus on personalization and fan engagement: Emphasizing personalization, researchers are exploring how targeted strategies can enhance fan experiences, thereby potentially increasing attendance and satisfaction [22].
5. Comprehensive economic and social impact assessments: The economic and social ramifications of mega sports events are being examined in greater detail, providing a holistic view of their impact and informing better planning and execution strategies [23].
6. Sustainability and ethical frameworks: The integration of sustainability and ethics into predictive analytics underscores the field's progression toward responsible and conscientious research practices [24].
7. Interdisciplinary research approaches: The convergence of various fields, including economics, psychology, and data science, is enriching the research landscape, fostering a deeper and more comprehensive understanding of fan attendance dynamics [25].

In recent research, the importance of integrating domain knowledge in machine learning applications for sports predictions has been emphasized, particularly in soccer [26]. One study highlights the nuanced ways domain expertise can enhance the predictive accuracy of machine learning models and tailoring algorithms to better understand and anticipate the outcomes of soccer matches. Furthermore, ref. [27] provide an innovative perspective by analyzing a soccer team's adaptive behaviors through an entropy-based framework. This approach offers a deeper insight into the dynamics and variability of team performance, suggesting that a team's ability to adapt and vary its strategies is crucial for success. These findings underscore the potential of combining advanced data analysis techniques with expert insights to refine predictive models in sports analytics.

1.1. Paper's Objective

Specifically, the primary objective of this study is to introduce a novel application for machine learning, enabling accurate predictions of fan attendance at the FIFA World Cup. The machine learning model takes into consideration a wide range of factors that can significantly influence the number of fans attending the tournament. By leveraging data from the FIFA World Cup Russia 2018, this model is constructed to forecast the expected fan attendance at the FIFA World Cup Qatar 2022. The overarching aim of this research is to provide a valuable tool that future FWC hosts can utilize to optimize their planning, ultimately enhancing the overall fan experience.

The study uses automated machine learning (AutoML) to experiment with different models and validate the results. AutoML is a method of automating the machine learning model selection and hyperparameter tuning process, making it easier and faster for non-experts to develop predictive models [28]. With AutoML, the system can automatically search for the best combination of algorithms and parameters to use based on the data being analyzed and the goals of the prediction model [28]. This helps in reducing the time and effort required to develop a predictive model, as well as improving its accuracy [29]. However, we are aware that AutoML is not a silver bullet and still requires careful data preparation, feature engineering, and validation to ensure that the results are reliable and accurate.

This study aims to advance sports event management by developing a comprehensive and accurate prediction model for fan attendance that is not limited to the FIFA World Cup, but can be applied to other major sporting events as well. By providing future hosts with a valuable tool, this research enables them to optimize planning, allocate resources efficiently, and ultimately enhance the fan experience. The findings will contribute to the development of best practices for predicting fan attendance at mega sports events, benefiting both researchers and practitioners in the fields of sports event management and fan behavior.

1.2. Paper's Organization

The remainder of the paper is organized as follows. In Section 2, we present the methodology and data used for this study. In Section 3, we present the findings of the study and discuss the implications. In Section 4, we present the limitations of the study and the work that needs to be done. Finally, in Section 5, we conclude the paper and summarize the key findings.

2. Materials and Methods

During the FIFA World Cup qualification process, the 211 member associations of FIFA compete for a spot in the tournament. The FIFA World Cup spots are allocated to the six confederations in the following manner: AFC (Asia: four or five), CAF (Africa: five), CONCACAF (North, Central America, and the Caribbean: three or four), CONMEBOL (South America: four or five), OFC (Oceania: zero or one), and thirteen for UEFA. Additionally, host nations currently qualify automatically for the World Cup. Our objective is to leverage machine learning techniques to accurately forecast the number of visitors from each country prior to the start of the qualifying matches. By utilizing the FIFA rankings of the participating teams and various socio-economic factors of the countries, we aim to provide the host nation with valuable insights that will assist in the efficient planning and execution of the tournament.

To accurately predict visitor counts for World Cup tournaments, access to historical data from previous events is crucial. Unfortunately, this information is not readily available to the public. Despite this challenge, we were able to obtain data for the 2018 Russia World Cup by contacting Russian delegates and for the 2022 Qatar World Cup by contacting the Qatar Supreme Committee. Although we attempted to gather data from other delegates for previous World Cups, we were unfortunately unable to do so. This shortage of data significantly limits our ability to construct a machine learning model that can be generalized to unseen data well. It is important to consider this limitation when evaluating the results of our study.

2.1. Overview

The study involved a thorough data collection approach from numerous sources, followed by data wrangling and feature engineering in order to create a machine learning model to estimate the number of visitors from each country at least one year before the tournament. We carried out experiments with Python Scikit Learn and chose the best-performing model with AutoML in order to build an ideal machine learning model.

To enhance a model's resilience against overfitting, especially in scenarios where certain predictors wield substantial influence, a few measures were implemented. Firstly, employing a technique known as data splitting, the dataset is partitioned into distinct subsets for training, validation, and testing purposes. This segmentation ensures that the model is not assessed on data it has already encountered, thereby providing a more accurate evaluation of its generalizability. Secondly, following the utilization of cross-validation techniques, whereby the dataset is divided into multiple folds, the model is then trained on all but one fold and validated on the excluded fold, iteratively rotating through each partition. This iterative validation process aids in obtaining a more reliable assessment of the model's performance while mitigating variance in performance estimation. Lastly, feature selection strategies play a pivotal role in curbing overfitting by identifying and retaining only the most pertinent predictors. By incorporating these methodologies, the robustness of a model against overfitting, particularly in scenarios with influential predictors, can be substantially fortified.

2.2. System Setup

We used a Dell Precision 7920 Tower Workstation with an Intel Xeon Gold 6244 16-core processor, 64 GB of RAM, and an NVIDIA Quadro RTX 5000 graphics card to carry out the tasks related to this article. To make sure that our work can be replicated on any hardware setup, we used Docker containers to run the AutoML pipeline and Jupyter notebooks for data manipulation.

2.3. Training Dataset

In order to effectively train and validate our machine learning model, we obtained various datasets pertaining to each country. These datasets included historical visitor count data from past World Cups, FIFA rankings of the participating teams, geographical information, and socio-economic data from the World Bank. By incorporating a diverse range of data sources, we aimed to build a robust and comprehensive model that accurately predicts the visitor count for future tournaments.

2.3.1. Historical Dataset

In order to train and validate our model, we collected historical data on past World Cups. However, the availability of these data are limited, and we were able to acquire information specifically only for the 2018 World Cup held in Russia. The dataset we obtained includes the country names and the corresponding visitor count for 75 countries for the 2018 World Cup as shown in Table 1 below:

Table 1. Sample of historical dataset from Russia 2018.

Country	Visitor Count
United States	99,799
Brazil	73,850
Germany	73,050
Colombia	67,563
Mexico	65,595

2.3.2. FIFA Rankings Dataset

Men's national teams are ranked by their performance in games under the FIFA ranking system, which has been in place since 1992. The teams with the best records are given the highest rankings. These rankings are released internationally within predetermined windows. We obtained the team rankings prior to the commencement of the World Cup qualifiers in order to conduct our analysis. The World Cup was held on the following dates: 1994 (31 December 1992), 1998 (21 February 1996), 2002 (16 February 2000), 2006 (27 August 2003), 22 August 2007, 2014 (18 May 2011), 12 March 2015, and 2022 (4 April 2019). To collect the rankings information from the FIFA website, we utilized Python requests and the Pandas packages. The dataset contains data about team names, confederations, current and past points, and rankings. The dataset comprises 8 columns and 1544 rows.

2.3.3. Historical Performance Data

We used specialized sections that include details on the qualification procedure, match schedules, and outcomes to compile data on World Cup qualifiers. We used information from these pages, including the qualification date, the number of times a team has qualified in the past, the most recent qualification, the team's current streak of consecutive appearances, and the team's previous best results. In order to extract this information from the Wikipedia website, we used the Python Pandas and Beautiful Soup 4 tools. A dataset with 336 rows and 9 columns with information on World Cup qualifiers from 1978 to 2022 was created. Earlier World Cup data were utilized for feature engineering and to impute missing values.

2.3.4. Geographical Information Data

In order to incorporate geographical information into our model, we obtained a curated dataset from a CSV file provided as a gist file (Discover gists · github). This dataset includes various geographical attributes, such as the average latitude, average longitude, and ISO country codes of each country. The inclusion of this information allows us to take into account the geographical location of each country and its potential impact on visitor count. We will be using these data to generate meaningful features as shown below in Table 2.

Table 2. Sample of geographical information dataset.

Country	Argentina	Brazil	France	India	United States
Alpha-2 code	AR	BR	FR	IN	US
Alpha-3 code	ARG	BRA	FRA	IND	USA
Numeric code	32	76	250	356	840
Latitude (average)	−34.0	−10.0	46.0	20.0	38.0
Longitude (average)	−64.0	−55.0	2.0	77.0	−97.0

2.3.5. World Bank Data

We leveraged the World Bank's Python package, wbgapi, to gather a range of socio-economic indicators that can potentially impact visitor count [30]. These data were used to gain insight into the economic and social conditions of each country, including population, GDP, remittance, working population, employment percentage, employee percentage, tourism expenses, purchasing power parity, and unemployment percentage. We utilized the Python library wbgapi along with Pandas to access and organize this dataset from the year 2000 to 2022. Our goal was to consider a broad range of socio-economic factors that could affect visitor count and inform our machine learning model.

To achieve this, we initially analyzed 120 features from the World Bank data to determine their potential impact on visitor count. However, after further analysis of the percentage of missing values, some of these features were not deemed useful and were excluded from our study. Some of the features we considered had annual data, while others were only published every 5 years. Some of the features had low data, making them unsuitable for our analysis. Our selection of features was based on the information provided by the World Bank site (indicators). By incorporating these selected socio-economic indicators into our machine learning model, we aimed to provide a more comprehensive and accurate prediction of visitor count from each country.

2.4. Dataset Wrangling

Dataset wrangling, which entails cleaning, preparing, and organizing data so that it is ready for analysis and modeling, is a crucial phase in the data science process.

2.4.1. Dataset Cleaning

We carried out a number of data-cleaning activities to get the data ready for analysis. These procedures were created to make sure the data were reliable, consistent, and prepared for inclusion in our machine learning model. We performed several measures, one of which was to find and fix inconsistencies in the naming of country codes that existed in multiple datasets. Some datasets used ISO codes, while others used country name abbreviations. For instance, the country code for Germany was listed as GER in some datasets, while the ISO country code for Germany is DEU. We standardized the country codes by converting all country codes to the ISO format, which is widely accepted and recognized. This standardization process allowed us to seamlessly integrate the data from different sources and ensure that all data were consistent and accurate.

Removing hyperlink information and other non-numeric data from the Wikipedia dataset was another crucial step we took. In order to make the data consistent, several columns in this dataset that had hyperlinks had to be cleaned. To exclude this information and guarantee that numerical columns contained just numerical data, we used Pandas and regular expressions. In order to improve the quality of the World Bank dataset, we conducted an analysis of all columns to assess the percentage of missing data for each country. We found that many columns had a high number of missing values, which could potentially affect the accuracy of our results. Features with high missing values were removed.

2.4.2. Feature Engineering

The practice of adding new features to a dataset or changing already existing features is known as feature engineering. It is a crucial phase in the data science process because it has the potential to enhance the effectiveness of machine learning algorithms and assist in extracting useful information from the data.

Historical Dataset

We enhanced the historical dataset obtained from Russia in 2018 by adding the necessary information to perform data merging and analysis. To begin with, we added a column for ISO country codes using the python package pycountry to ensure consistent country identification across all datasets. Additionally, we added a year column, with 2018 as the value, to differentiate between the World Cup events. To prepare for predictions for the Qatar 2022 World Cup, we duplicated the country data and added it to the end of the dataset, with the "Visitor Count" column left empty for future predictions. This standardized format enabled us to effectively utilize the historical data and merge them with other relevant data sources for accurate predictions.

FIFA Rankings and Historical Performance Dataset

We developed numerous new features based on the discrepancies between the present rank and previous ranks to comprehend how a team's rating has changed over time and maybe predict their likelihood of qualifying for the World Cup. These elements enabled us to monitor each team's growth (or fall) throughout a variety of time frames, from the most recent rating to the ranking from 20 years prior. These characteristics were developed by comparing the current rank to ranks from various time periods, such as the most recent rank and rank from 4, 8, 12, 16, and 20 years ago. We can find trends and patterns that can be predictive of a team's performance in the future by examining these discrepancies. The raw columns "PreviousRank", "PreviousPoints", "CountryCode", and "TotalPoints" were also eliminated from the dataset so that our research could concentrate on the most significant and valuable attributes.

We developed numerous additional features based on the dataset to enhance the analysis of the historical data provided by Wikipedia. These elements were created to offer insightful data on each team's prior results and assist us in forecasting their chances of making the World Cup.

- Our first feature was a binary column named "IsQualified," which displays whether or not a team has qualified for the World Cup. We set the value of this column to 1 for each team because the Wikipedia data include only teams that made it. The goal variable for our machine learning models' training will be this column.
- The second feature that we developed was the "IsHost" column, which indicates the host nation depending on the "Method of Qualification" column. Understanding the benefits a host team has during the qualification process can be assisted by this information.

- Our third feature was the "Total Times Qualified" column, which shows how many times a national team has qualified for the World Cup. Based on the "Total Times Qualified" column from the Wikipedia dataset, this value was computed. To prevent data leaking, the current qualification was eliminated from the analysis. We can learn more about a team's level of skill and tournament success by knowing how frequently they have qualified.

In order to reflect the team's greatest World Cup performance, we also constructed a set of binary columns. "IsPreviousWinner", "IsPreviousRunnersUp", "IsPreviousFinalist", "IsPreviousThirdPlace", "IsPreviousFourthPlace", "IsPreviousSemiFinalist", "IsPreviousQuarterFinalist", and "IsPreviousRound16Finalist" were among the columns in these lists. In order to concentrate on the most significant and valuable features of our study, we finally deleted the raw columns "Method of Qualification", "Date of Qualification", and "Previous Best Performance" from the dataset.

Geographical Dataset

A major factor that greatly impacts the number of visitors is the geographical distance between their home country and the host country. This affects various factors, such as travel mode, cost, and time of travel, as well as climate conditions. To capture these factors, various features were generated, such as travel costs, climate comparisons, visa restrictions, and the number of expatriates living in the host country. These expatriates could serve as potential sources of accommodation during the tournament, leading to reduced costs. However, obtaining data for these factors for all previous World Cup tournaments is a challenge due to limited availability.

To capture the geographical proximity, we introduced a new feature—the distance between the source country and the host country. This feature considers the impact of various factors like mode of travel, cost and time of travel, and climatic conditions. To calculate the distance, we used the Haversine formula, which measures the angular distance between two points on the surface of a sphere. The latitude and longitude coordinates of the source country (x_1 and y_1) and the host country (x_2 and y_2) were utilized to calculate the distance between them. This was done using the Haversine distance metric from the Scikit Learn Python package. The distance was then converted to kilometers for ease of interpretation. The Haversine formula provides a reliable approximation of the surface distance between two points on Earth, with an average error of less than 1%.

The latitude and longitude coordinates (x_1, y_1) of the source country S and the host country H, with coordinates (x_2, y_2), were utilized to calculate the distance $D(S, H)$ between them. This was achieved using the following Haversine distance metric:

$$D(S, H) = 2 \arcsin \sqrt{\sin^2\left(\frac{x_1 - y_1}{2}\right) + \cos(x_1)\cos(y_1)\sin^2\left(\frac{x_2 - y_2}{2}\right)}$$

The distance was then converted to kilometers for ease of interpretation. The Haversine formula provides a reliable approximation of the surface distance between two points on Earth, with an average error of less than 1%.

2.5. Dataset Merging

Through the use of the country code and the years as the key, we combined all the datasets into one. As a result, we were able to include significant information for each country from all datasets. To make our predictions as accurate as possible, we took into consideration the most recent available socio-economic data from the World Bank. Specifically, we used the data from the last year prior to the tournament year to reflect real-time conditions. For example, when predicting the visitor count for the 2022 World Cup, we used the data from 2021. In cases where data were not available for a specific year, we used the last available data. For instance, since there was no purchasing power parity (PPP) data for Venezuela after 2011, we used the same data for both the 2018 and 2022

World Cup predictions. This approach allowed us to incorporate the latest socio-economic information into our predictions.

We detected missing values that had been added as a result of the merging procedure and eliminated them. These missing values were present in recently established columns of historical performance data that had a value of 0 imputed to them. Missing values for the "Total Times Qualified" column were imputed using the most recent data or, in the absence of data, assigned a value of 0. The backfilling procedure contributed to the merged dataset's accuracy and completeness.

2.6. Data Visualization

We utilized a variety of data visualization techniques to analyze and understand the data. Some of the key visualizations used in this study are as follows Figure 1.

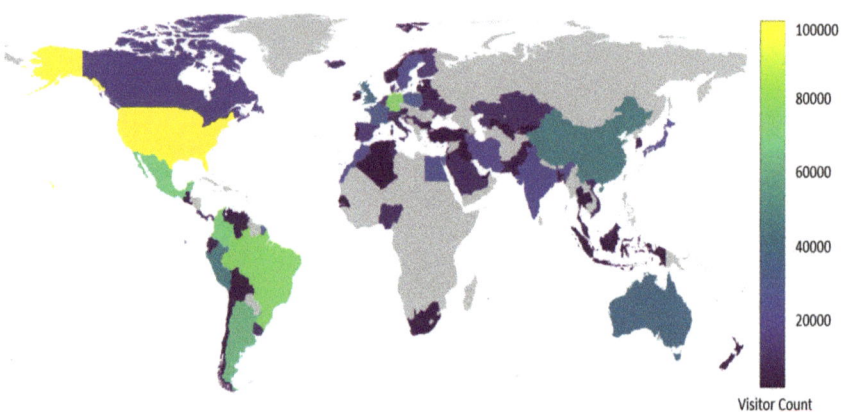

Figure 1. Visitor counts for the fans that attended FWC Russia 2018 illustrated in a world map.

From Figures 2 and 3, it can be observed that the data are highly skewed, with the top country (USA) having more visitors than the number of visitors from the bottom 35 countries combined. The mean number of visitors is 14,289, while the USA has 99,799 visitors.

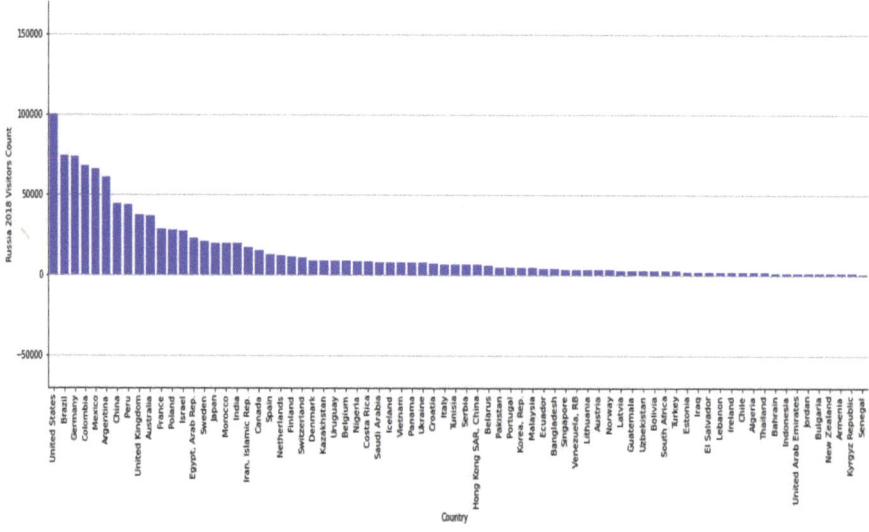

Figure 2. Visitor count distribution for Russia 2018 FIFA World Cup.

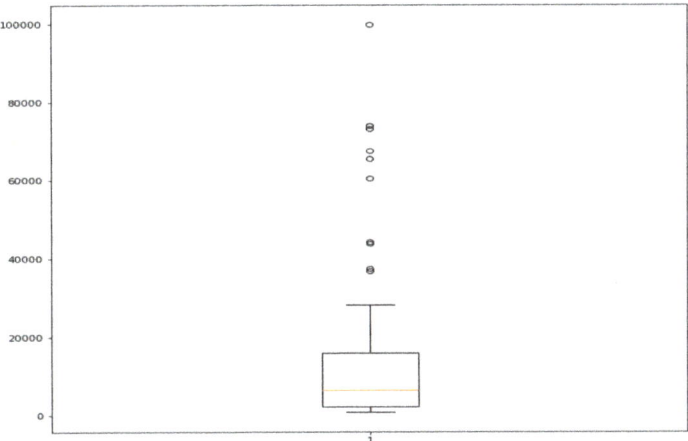

Figure 3. Box plot for visitor count distribution for Russia 2018 FIFA World Cup.

The scatterplot in Figure 4 reveals the relationship between the GDP per capita and the number of visitors per continent. This visualization was critical in gaining insight into how economic prosperity affects the number of visitors from different continents attending the World Cup. A noticeable cluster of four countries—Brazil, Colombia, Mexico, and Argentina—can be seen in the top left of the plot, highlighting that fans participate in the World Cup even from countries with poorer economies.

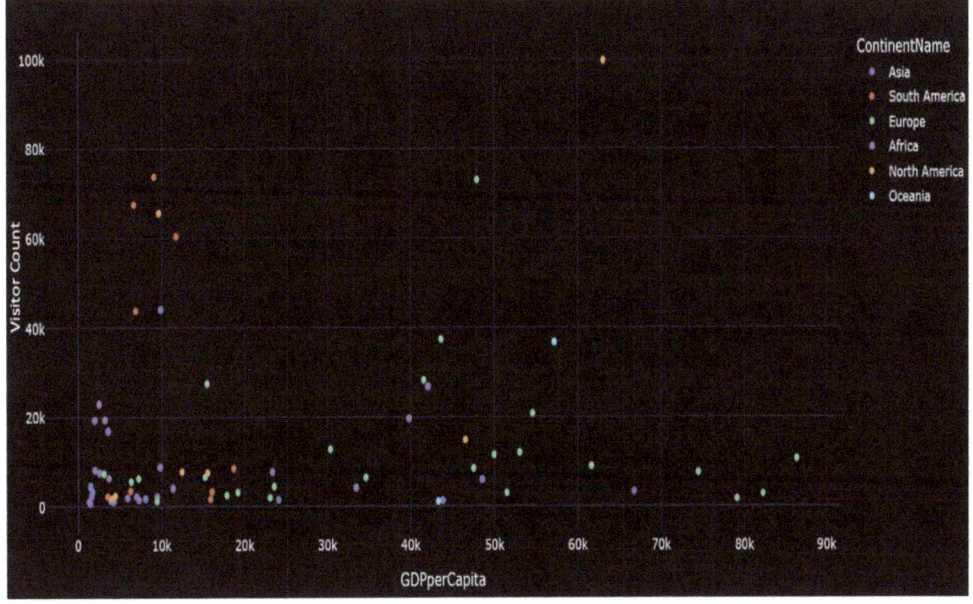

Figure 4. Scatterplot showing the relation of GDP per capita vs. the number of visitors per continent.

2.7. Validation Technique

To assess the performance of our machine learning models, it is ideal to use a holdout validation dataset. This involves training the model on historical data and evaluating its performance on a separate, unseen dataset. In order to evaluate the performance of our machine learning models, we will be using the Qatar 2022 data as a holdout validation dataset and training with the Russia 2018 dataset.

There are several validation techniques that are widely used in the industry. One of the most common techniques is the train–test split, where the dataset is split into two parts—the training set and the testing set. The training set is used to train the model and the testing set is used to evaluate its performance. There are two variations of this technique, one with shuffling of the data and one without shuffling. When the data are shuffled, the model is trained on a random subset of the data, and this helps in avoiding bias due to any patterns in the data. On the other hand, when the data are not shuffled, the model is trained on a contiguous subset of the data, which can help in understanding the model's behavior over time.

Another popular validation technique is k-fold cross-validation, where the dataset is split into k-folds. The model is trained on k-1 folds and tested on the remaining folds. This process is repeated k times with different folds as the testing set, providing a more robust evaluation of the model's performance. There are other validation techniques, such as leave-one-out cross-validation, stratified k-fold cross-validation, and more, each with its own strengths and weaknesses.

Using a 5-fold cross-validation technique, we assess the models while they are being trained. To do this, divide the training data into 5 equal folds, train the model on 4 of those folds, and then evaluate it on the 5th fold. Five repetitions of this process are carried out, with one of each fold serving as the evaluation set. By averaging the assessment scores across each of the five folds, we may obtain a more precise measure of the model's performance (Figure 5).

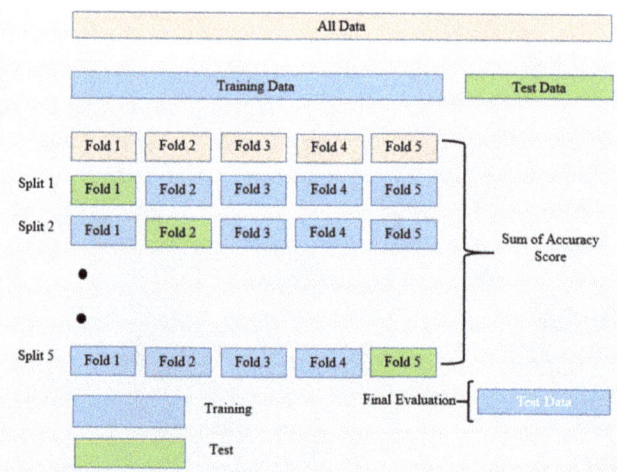

Figure 5. Five-fold cross-validation with holdout test.

2.8. Evaluation Metric

The coefficient of determination, abbreviated R^2, is the optimization metric that we will be using. This is the percentage of the dependent variable's variance that is predicted by the independent variable(s). Based on the percentage of overall variation in outcomes that the model accounts for, it provides a gauge of how well-observed results are duplicated by the model. The maximum score is 1.0, which may be unfavorable. The coefficient of determination, which can be expressed as a percentage while the other measures have arbitrary ranges, can be more intuitively instructive than the MAE (mean absolute error), MSE (mean squared error), MSLE (mean squared log error), MedAE (median absolute error), and RMSE (root mean squared error) in the evaluation of regression analysis. However, we will also be considering other metrics such as MAE, MSE, MSLE, MedAE, and RMSE to get a more comprehensive understanding of the model's performance.

2.9. Modeling

To develop outstanding features, we used an iterative experimentation process with a variety of machine learning models. Using the Python Scikit Learn module, we put this technique to use. We started by building simple models to understand which features the models were emphasizing and to examine their predictions. We used AutoML to fine-tune the parameters and increase model accuracy to create the final high-quality model. In our experimentations, we used the Scikit Learn algorithms with default parameters.

As shown in Figure 3 the target column of the visitor count is highly skewed. This poses a challenge for regression algorithms to fit the data. To overcome this challenge and improve the model performance, we performed a log transformation on the target variable (visitor count) to normalize the data. The log transform of the target variable is a technique used to normalize skewed data. In this technique, the target variable is transformed by taking its logarithmic value. The log transform helps to reduce the impact of outliers and skewness in the data, making the dataset more suitable for regression algorithms. The log transform also helps to convert exponential growth into linear growth, making it easier for the model to understand and predict the target variable. This leads to improved model performance and more accurate predictions. After obtaining the predictions, we will perform an inverse log transformation to obtain the actual visitor count values. This is because the log transformation was applied to normalize the skewed data and improve the model performance, but the actual visitor count values should be in their original format for meaningful interpretation.

We experimented with four sets of features: a selected small set of columns, all columns, highly correlated columns, and important features selected by the models. This enabled us to evaluate how the algorithms are learning from a diverse set of features. We started our experiments with a small subset of features and eventually added more features for experimentation. Figures 6–9 show the correlations for each dataset.

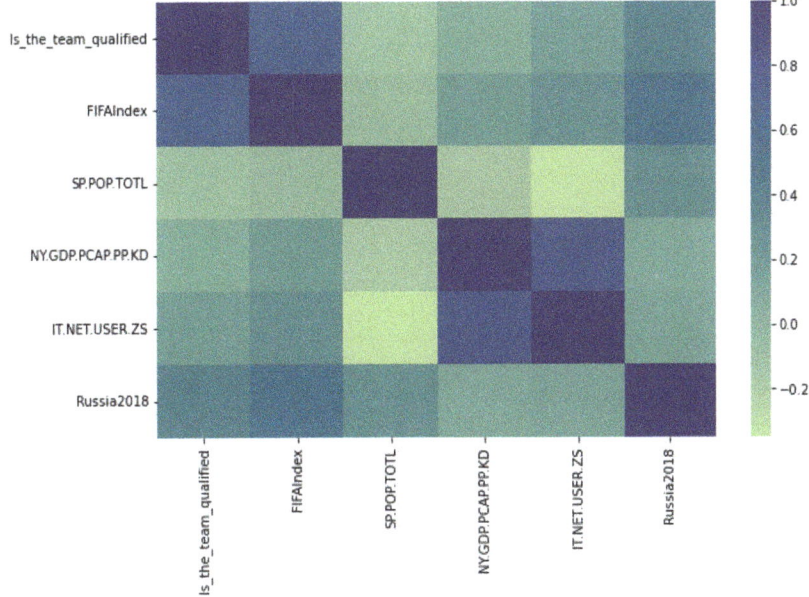

Figure 6. Correlation plot for an initial small subset of data.

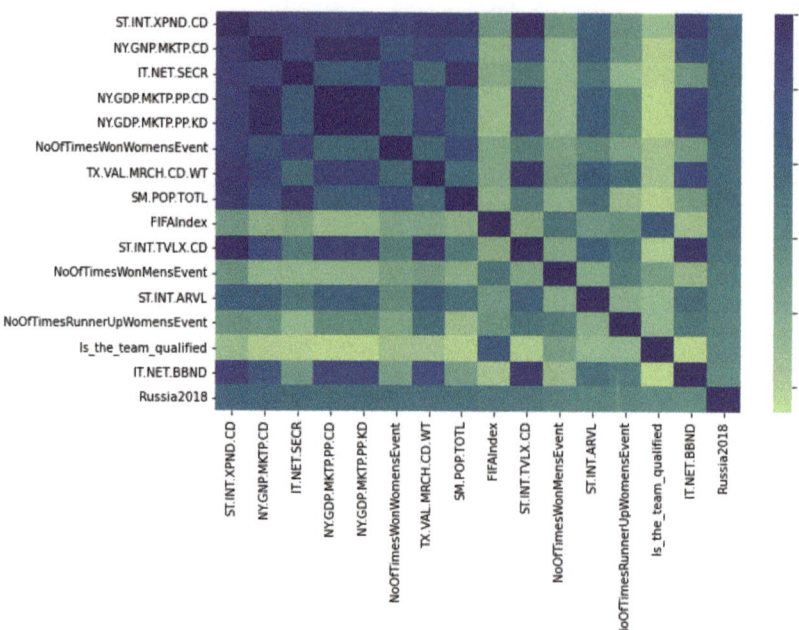

Figure 7. Correlation plot for features highly correlated.

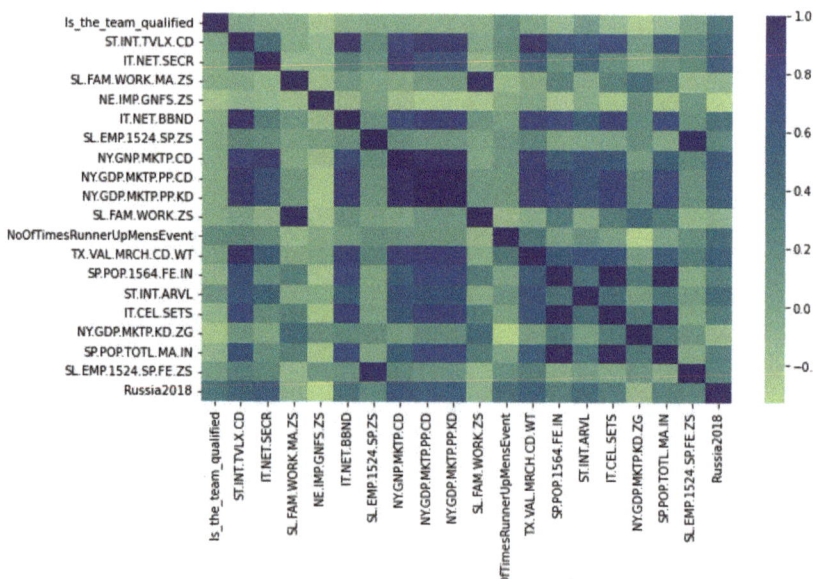

Figure 8. Correlation plot for features with top feature importance.

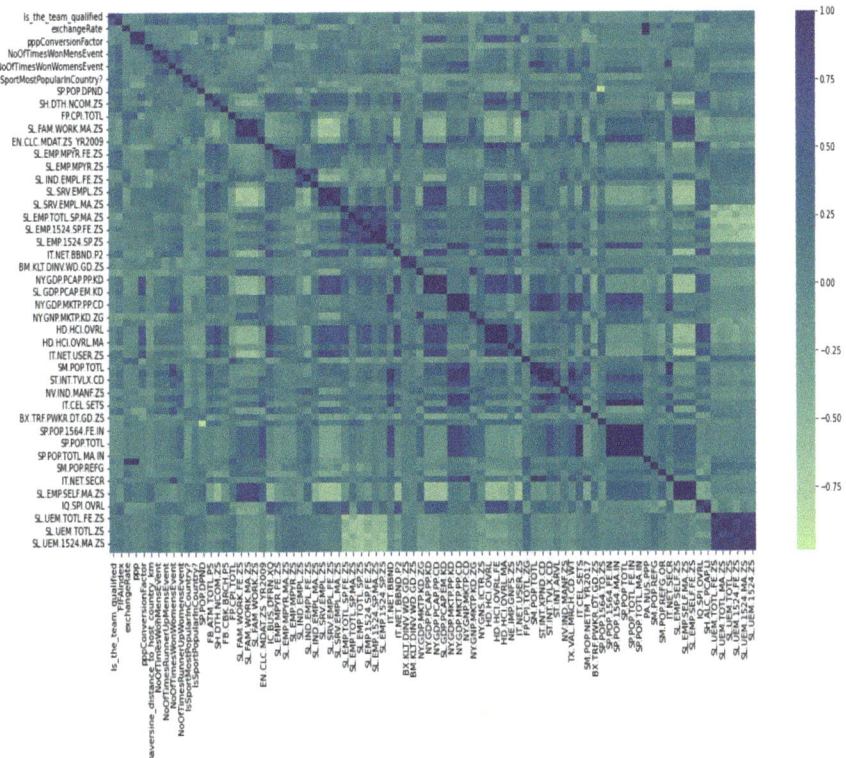

Figure 9. Correlation plot for all features.

2.10. AutoML

The thesis model showcases several innovative aspects of automated machine learning (AutoML), highlighting its ability to simplify and accelerate the entire machine learning pipeline. Key strengths include the following.

End-to-end automation: AutoML automates key steps like data preprocessing, feature engineering, model training, and hyperparameter tuning, enabling faster development of robust models.

Enhanced data quality: Advanced algorithms address data issues like missing values, outliers, and scaling, ensuring data consistency and quality.

Sophisticated feature engineering: AutoML automates feature selection, reduction, and generation, leading to better prediction accuracy by extracting more meaningful insights from the data.

Optimized model selection and training: This evaluates various algorithms, finds the best fit for the data, compares them, and selects the optimal one for deployment, improving model accuracy and reliability.

Diverse optimization techniques: By employing different optimization strategies (like Bayesian optimization, genetic algorithms, and neural architecture search), AutoML demonstrates adaptability and precision in navigating the search space.

Small-dataset proficiency: The model emphasizes AutoML's effectiveness in handling limited data, effectively finding suitable model and hyperparameter combinations while preventing overfitting, ensuring robustness and generalizability.

Accessibility and breadth: By integrating Auto-Sklearn, the model provides accessible APIs and supports a wide range of machine learning models, offering broader applicability.

Comprehensive model assessment: This includes diverse model types like linear models, KNNs, decision trees, ensemble methods, SVMs, and MLPs, facilitating adaptation to different data and tasks.

Innovative training techniques: Techniques like SGD training, ensemble methods, and multilayer perceptrons highlight the model's innovative approach to learning, offering various strategies for improved prediction accuracy and reliability.

By combining these techniques, the thesis model significantly advances AutoML, establishing a robust platform that democratizes access to advanced machine learning capabilities and empowers better decision-making across various domains.

3. Results

We conducted several experiments with various configurations of our machine learning models to optimize performance. We explored different factors, such as the number of columns used, target column transformations, run time, and ensembling. We tested models using all columns, highly correlated columns, and important features selected by the models. We evaluated the impact of target column transformations, including log transformation, quantile transformation, and power transformation from the Scikit Learn preprocessing module. Our results showed that log transformation improved model performance the most. As we increased the run time for Auto-Sklearn, performance continued to improve. This could have been the result of hyperparameters being optimized for individual data points. Ensembling of models also improved the performance of the models. Based on our experiments, we selected the best-performing model for this study: an ensembled model trained on important columns with a log-transformed target column, run for 12 h.

The Auto-Sklearn experiment, which lasted for 12 h, evaluated 2523 models using a diverse range of algorithms and optimizing their hyperparameters. Specifically, we addressed the following key areas.

1. Data preprocessing techniques:
    - The datasets outlined in Appendix A underwent thorough cleansing following the process defined in Section 2.4.1.
    - Preprocessing steps were meticulously executed as specified in Section 2.4.2. These steps ensured that the data were suitably prepared for feeding into the AutoML optimization process.
    - The AutoML process automatically applied additional preprocessing techniques, including feature scaling, during the optimization phase. Given the small size of the dataset, these preprocessing steps remained an integral part of the model pipeline and were not further explored.

2. Algorithms and hyperparameters evaluated:
    - Our AutoML process, as outlined in Section 2.10, systematically evaluated various algorithms and their corresponding hyperparameters.
    - Notably, we did not define a custom range of hyperparameters. Instead, we utilized the default configurations provided by Auto Sklearn regressors.

3. Auto Sklearn configurations:
    - We explored a variety of configurations, including:
    Regression models.
    Data preprocessing steps.
    Feature preprocessing.

4. Algorithms evaluated:
    - Our evaluation encompassed the following algorithms:
    AdaBoostRegressor
    ARDRegression
    DecisionTreeRegressor
    ExtraTreesRegressor

GaussianProcessRegressor
GradientBoostingRegressor
KNNRegressor
Support Vector Regressor

The results of the experiment are analyzed and displayed in Table 3, showcasing the top 10 models for each algorithm.

Table 3. Best fivefold cross-validation scores for top-performing algorithms.

Rank	Model	R^2	MAE	MSE	RMSE	MSLE	MedAE
1	Stochastic Gradient Descent	0.633	0.556	0.480	0.670	0.0050	0.497
302	ARD	0.578	0.546	0.518	0.691	0.0056	0.462
348	Liblinear SVR	0.573	0.574	0.550	0.713	0.0058	0.449
354	LibSVM SVR	0.572	0.578	0.617	0.732	0.0066	0.509
718	Extra trees	0.528	0.618	0.679	0.793	0.0071	0.438
882	Random forest	0.486	0.635	0.692	0.803	0.0073	0.548
936	Gradient boosting	0.464	0.672	0.705	0.828	0.0077	0.529
938	Ada boost	0.463	0.653	0.773	0.842	0.0082	0.472
956	Multilayer perceptron	0.455	0.677	0.721	0.834	0.0076	0.597
984	K-nearest neighbors	0.437	0.718	0.809	0.868	0.0083	0.540

The ranking was based on the R^2 metric, which is a commonly used measure of the goodness of fit in regression problems. The top-performing algorithm was stochastic gradient descent (SGD), which dominated the top 300 ranks with a slight improvement in the R^2 metric. The best SGD model had an R^2 metric of 0.633, while the 300th SGD model had an R^2 metric of 0.578. This highlights the focus of Auto-Sklearn in optimizing the hyperparameters of the best-identified algorithm over a longer period of time.

Table 4 shows how the permutation feature importance calculation approach from Scikit Learn was used to determine the feature importance of the best-performing model. The feature significance score indicates the impact of each feature on the performance of the model. A higher score means that the feature in the study has a bigger impact on the model's prediction result. We can acquire insight into the data, improve the model, and improve its interpretability by comprehending the significance of the feature.

Table 4. Most important features of the best-performing model.

Feature	Description	Importance
Is the team qualified?	Is the team qualified for the tournament?	0.505 +/− 0.044
SL.EMP.1524.SP.ZS	Employment:population ratio, ages 15–24, total (%)	0.043 +/− 0.014
SP.POP.1564.FE.IN	Female population, ages 15–64	0.040 +/− 0.013
SL.FAM.WORK.MA.ZS	Contributing family workers, male (% of male employment)	0.035 +/− 0.019
IT.CEL.SETS	Mobile cellular subscriptions in the country	0.032 +/− 0.011
SP.POP.TOTL.MA.IN	Male population	0.025 +/− 0.010

The permutation feature importance in Scikit Learn provides a feature importance score that is a normalized sum of 1. This means that the relative importance of features derived from permutation is proportional and add up to a total of 1. Given that the relative value of each attribute is measured using the same scale, this can be helpful in situations where you want to compare their respective importance. It can be used to get a rough understanding of the relevance of features independently of the model being used because the feature importance is also calculated without relying on the specific model characteristics.

The contribution of each feature to the prediction generated by the stochastic gradient descent model is shown in Table 4. In almost all studies, a significant amount of weight has consistently been placed on the "Is the team qualified?" element. Table 4 explains the meaning of other features from the World Bank dataset.

We tested the robustness of the best-performing model by evaluating its performance on a holdout validation dataset. The results presented in Table 5 showed that the model was not generalized well with the holdout dataset.

Table 5. Training and holdout test set validation scores for the best-performing model.

Dataset	R^2	MAE	MSE	RMSE	MSLE	MedAE
Training	0.633	0.556	0.480	0.670	0.0050	0.497
Holdout	0.259	1.155	1.889	1.374	0.023	1.063

Additionally, we evaluated how the different validation mechanisms would have performed in evaluating the performance of the models. We experimented with different feature subsets, target column transformations, ensemble configurations, and validation mechanisms. Tables 6 and 7 present some of the results from our experimentation.

Table 6. Training and holdout test set validation scores for models with different validation strategies for top features with target column transformation.

Validation	Dataset	R^2	MAE	MSE	RMSE	MSLE	MedAE
Train–Test Shuffled (0.75/0.25)	Training	0.909	0.248	0.089	0.298	0.001	0.210
	Holdout	0.114	1.189	2.259	1.503	0.029	0.985
Train–Test Not Shuffled (0.75/0.25)	Training	−2.351	0.429	0.253	0.503	0.004	0.338
	Holdout	−0.086	1.339	2.768	1.664	0.033	1.098
Fivefold cross-validation	Training	0.633	0.556	0.480	0.670	0.0050	0.497
	Holdout	0.259	1.155	1.889	1.374	0.023	1.063
Tenfold cross-validation	Training	0.664	0.536	0.469	0.661	0.005	0.438
	Holdout	0.247	1.168	1.918	1.385	0.024	1.010

Table 7. Training and holdout test set validation scores for models with different validation strategies for top features without target column transformation.

Validation	Dataset	R^2	MAE	MSE	RMSE	MSLE	MedAE
Train–Test Shuffled (0.75/0.25)	Training	0.960	2603.70	10,375,390	3221.09	0.990	2607.319
	Holdout	−0.311	13,197.09	749,443,752	27,375.97	2.170	4494.401
Train–Test Not Shuffled (0.75/0.25)	Training	−0.938	432.99	302,851	550.32	0.140	375.000
	Holdout	−0.154	10,789.99	659,404,817	25,678.89	2.646	2588.484
Fivefold cross-validation	Training	0.518	6890.26	152,701,900	11,469.93	1.495	3901.640
	Holdout	−0.132	13,747.16	646,955,961	25,435.39	2.295	6099.449
Tenfold cross-validation	Training	0.629	7252.67	175,867,800	11,188.15	1.381	4199.995
	Holdout	−0.049	12,338.23	599,748,885	24,489.77	2.312	5392.570

4. Discussion

Using Auto-Sklearn, as shown in Table 3, the best fivefold cross-validation score for top-performing algorithms revealed that the algorithm focused heavily on optimizing the hyperparameters of the stochastic gradient descent model with R^2 of 0.633 and MAE of 0.556. The model was tested with different validation techniques like train–test shuffled, train–test not shuffled, and fivefold and tenfold cross-validation in order to observe the best results. According to Yamashita et al. (2022), regardless of the size of the sports, the use of empirical prediction techniques leads to inaccurate results and therefore poor decisions by the organizers. We can confirm this statement when comparing the results against the results of King and Rice (2018), where they examined different prediction techniques and a best result MAE of 1219.

4.1. Reasons for Discrepancies

The deficiency in diverse examples available for learning directly impacts our models' capacity to distinguish meaningful trends and generate reliable predictions. Despite our efforts to enrich the dataset with a diverse array of columns encompassing factors such as geographical distance, FIFA rankings, historical World Cup performances and other socio-geopolitical dynamics, the underlying training data pertain solely to the year 2018. Consequently, our models lack exposure to patterns spanning different years, thereby causing some difficulties in capturing the evolving behavioral trends. As a result, the scarcity of training data serves as a definitive explanation for the disparities observed in our predictions.

The comparison of predicted and actual visitor counts in the Qatar 2022 World Cup can be seen in Figure 10. Figures 11 and 12 reveal that Saudi Arabia and India had higher visitor counts than expected, while there was a significant reduction in visitors from top countries in the Russia 2018 World Cup. This could be attributed to factors such as distance, number of expatriates, visa restrictions, and other socio-geopolitical factors. These findings highlight the need for caution when making predictions based on limited data and suggest the importance of further study to better understand the factors that influence World Cup attendance. The section below discusses the possible causes of the difference between the predicted and actual attendance for Qatar 2022 World Cup.

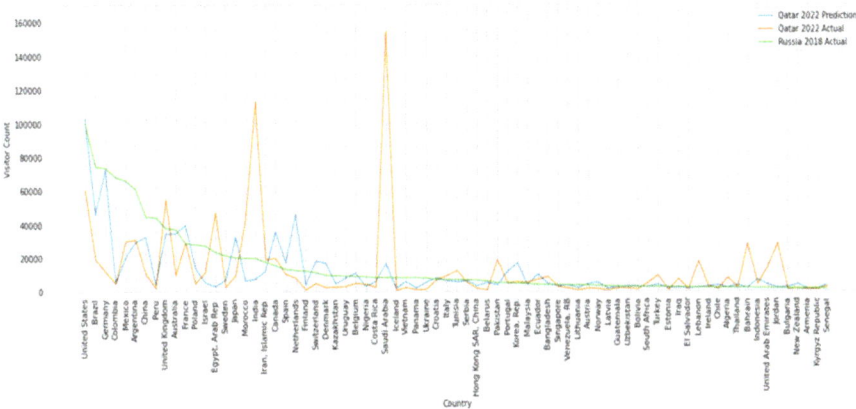

Figure 10. Comparison of predictions: actual visitor counts for Qatar 2022 and Russia 2018.

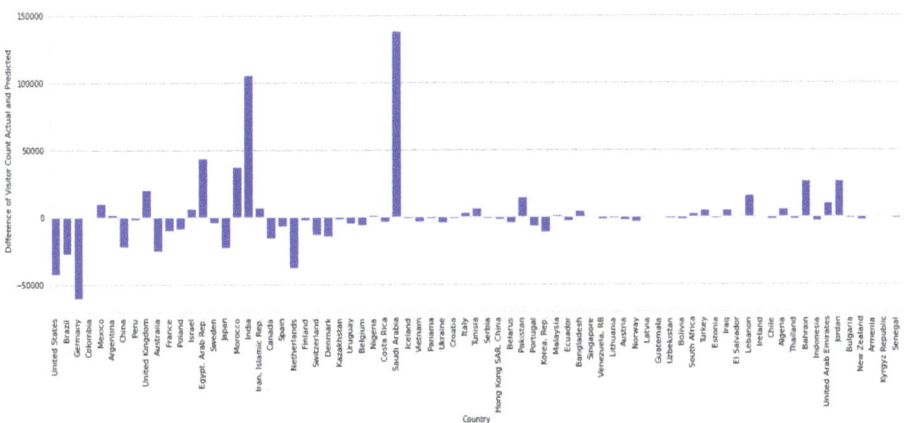

Figure 11. Difference between actual visitor counts and predicted counts for Qatar 2022.

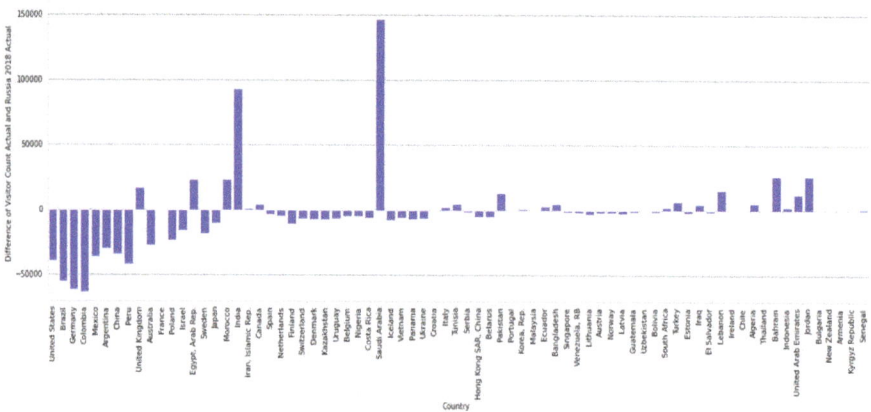

Figure 12. Difference between actual visitor counts for Qatar 2022 and Russia 2018.

4.1.1. COVID-19 Pandemic

It was observed that the actual fan attendance from East Asian countries such as China, Japan, and South Korea was lower than the prediction, and this may be attributed to the COVID-19 pandemic impact on these countries. This is more evident in China, where they had imposed travel restrictions on citizens to travel outside China until January 2023. In addition, COVID-19 caused some financial issues where individuals and employees were dismissed from their work, which affected their ability to travel for tourism and fun. The number of Chinese fans dropped by more than 30,000 when comparing Russia in 2018 and Qatar in 2022.

4.1.2. Unexpected Team Performance during the Tournament

Another factor that seems to have played a role in the difference between actual and predicted fan attendance is the unexpected performance of a team during the tournament. This can be observed in Morocco and Saudi Arabia fans' attendance, whose teams performed very well, which encouraged many fans to travel and attend. Saudi Arabia won the first game against Argentina and later performed strongly against Poland and Mexico. Morocco performed well too, and eliminated Spain and Portugal during the knockout stages and later faced France in the semifinal. The number of chartered flights was organized by the Moroccan government to transport the fans willing to travel and support their team.

4.1.3. Culture and Traditions

As Qatar was the first Middle Eastern and Arab country to host such an event, there will be some factors that could be different from any other tournament. In the case of the Qatar 2022 World Cup, it was observed that some Arab countries contributed more to fan attendance than the model predicted. This is evident in the cases of Morocco, Egypt, Bahrain, UAE, Lebanon, Jordan, and Saudi Arabia. Therefore, factors such as tradition and cultural similarity might play a big role in attracting fans from different countries having similar traditions and cultures.

4.1.4. Number of Residents in the Host Country

The FIFA World Cup in Qatar showed an important factor that could affect the tendency of fans to come to the host country. Qatar has a large number of different communities that make up more than 80 percent of the total population. The impact of this factor can be seen by observing the number of fans who attended the FWC 22 from countries such as India, Pakistan, and Egypt. Indian fans numbered 90,000 more than in Russia in 2018, which might be due to the fact that Indian residents are present in large numbers in Qatar.

4.1.5. Political and Negative Media Coverage

As with any other major sporting event, political controversies and negative media coverage can impact the attendance of fans from certain countries. At the 2022 FIFA World Cup in Qatar, factors unrelated to sports led to lower attendance from countries such as Germany and the Netherlands compared to the 2018 tournament in Russia. These factors are challenging to predict, as the relationships between countries and the media are volatile and can change rapidly. For example, more than 60,000 German fans attended the 2018 FIFA World Cup, but did not attend the Qatar 2022 tournament.

Global uncertainties undeniably affect the accuracy of prediction models. However, those using the approach presented in this paper can take measures to mitigate these uncertainties. For example, political conflict uncertainty can be mitigated by adjusting restrictions and incorporating additional input data, such as the nature of the conflict and travel bans. Training the model requires similar situations from previous tournaments to ensure accurate results. Additionally, postprocessing can involve expert judgment to determine reduction factors for model results.

Regarding pandemic situations, the model can incorporate factors like the number of vaccinated individuals, travel restrictions, and financial impacts. However, requiring similar situations to be included in the training data is crucial for accurate results.

While this paper does not incorporate these mitigation strategies, it is noteworthy that the model is primarily intended for use in the early planning stages, where pandemic regulations and political changes occur rapidly and unexpectedly.

The outcome of our feature importance analysis, which is shown in Table 4, indicates that the model heavily relies on a team's qualification status as a predictor of World Cup attendance. This is a reasonable observation, as fans of qualified teams are more likely to be incentivized to attend the event. However, observations from our holdout data also highlight that other factors such as the distance of the host country, the number of expatriates, and socio-geopolitical factors also play a role in determining visitor counts. To gain a deeper understanding of these factors, more historical data would be necessary. Additionally, the analysis shows that the model places significant importance on socio-economic factors such as employment rate, population size, and mobile phone usage. These factors demonstrate the impact of modern technology and economic stability on travel patterns from different countries.

The validation techniques utilized in our analysis demonstrate that cross-validation, particularly fivefold validation, is an effective method in ensuring stable and reliable results in both training and holdout sets. The transformation of the target column played a crucial role in stabilizing the results, as the holdout set often possesses a different data distribution from the training set. On the other hand, using a traditional train–test split has proven to be unreliable, as the results are heavily dependent on the presence of skewed data in the test or holdout set. The use of k-fold cross-validation mitigates this issue by distributing the data evenly across all iterations. A tenfold cross-validation, however, was found to be slightly less reliable than fivefold, as the validation set size in each iteration was too small.

Incorporating real-time data up to the event starting date could potentially improve the model's results, particularly as team qualification status was the most significant predictor. Access to this real-time information might enhance the model's accuracy and its output.

4.2. Limitations

It is crucial to recognize the limitations of our model in order to fully comprehend its capabilities and limitations. Our approach has several restrictions that must be taken into consideration. Firstly, our dataset consists only of data from a single year, which limits our ability to generalize the model for future World Cup events. As the patterns that influence fans' travel can vary greatly from year to year, it is imperative that a model trained on data from multiple World Cup events is used to truly understand the factors that drive attendance. The feature importance analysis shows that the model heavily relies on socio-economic factors rather than historical performance or distance of travel, which could only be confirmed if the model were trained on data from different World Cups. Additionally, our data are highly skewed, which could mean that the model optimizes for reducing errors in countries with high attendance, rather than generalizing. This issue could be mitigated by incorporating more data from different tournaments. Lastly, it is important to keep in mind that the World Cup is a unique event, and each host country may have its own set of factors that influence the rate of travel. For instance, a European country hosting the event will have different influencing factors from a Middle Eastern country hosting the event. With the expansion of the World Cup to 48 participating countries in 2026, these intricacies must be taken into consideration when making decisions based on the model's output.

While the applicability of this model is currently limited, its methodology can be adapted for future tournaments and further data collection efforts. This adaptation will enhance the accuracy and usability of the model. We hope that this research will inspire additional studies on the use of machine learning in predicting visitor counts for major sports events. Importantly, the model's versatility extends beyond the FIFA World Cup: it can be applied to various sports events such as continental nations cups and the UEFA Champions League, and with minor adjustments, the model can be used for other team sports like basketball, cricket, or volleyball. However, predicting individual sports outcomes remains challenging. Factors such as qualified players and the presence of a fan base in each country significantly impact attendance. Consequently, individual sports events tend to attract primarily citizens and residents of the host country.

5. Conclusions

This paper aimed to enhance the planning of mega sports events by accurately predicting fan attendance from each country. Leveraging attendance data from the 2018 FIFA World Cup in Russia, this research identified several key factors that contributed to the prediction of fan attendance at the 2022 FIFA World Cup in Qatar, utilizing a range of models. Among the models tested, stochastic gradient descent (SGD) emerged as the most suitable, achieving an R^2 value of 0.633. However, it is important to note that the predicted attendance exhibited a discrepancy with the actual attendance, with an R^2 value of 0.259. This discrepancy can be attributed to the limited availability of sufficient data. To achieve higher accuracy in attendance prediction, it is essential to incorporate data from a more diverse range of tournaments. By doing so, the models can capture the nuances and dynamics of different sporting events and fan behaviors, leading to improved predictive performance.

Furthermore, it is crucial to acknowledge that factors beyond the scope of sports can significantly impact attendance at mega events. Political disputes, pandemics, cultural and racial factors, as well as global acceptance or resistance to the event, all play a role in shaping attendance patterns. To enhance prediction accuracy, it is recommended that further research be conducted to explore the influence of these non-sports-related factors on attendance at mega events. By considering a more comprehensive range of variables, future models can provide more nuanced and robust predictions, contributing to better planning and decision-making for host countries. In summary, this study highlights the potential of machine learning in predicting fan attendance at mega sports events. While the stochastic gradient descent model demonstrated promise, the research underscores the need for more extensive data inputs and the inclusion of non-sports-related factors to achieve higher accuracy in attendance prediction. These efforts are encouraged for host countries, as accurate estimation of potential visitors is essential for effective planning, resource allocation, and ensuring a successful and enjoyable experience for fans and players alike.

Author Contributions: Conceptualization, A.A.-B.; Methodology, A.A.-B., M.H. and J.R.J.; Software, J.R.J.; Validation, M.H. and J.R.J.; Formal analysis, A.A.-B.; Investigation, M.H.; Writing—original draft, A.A.-B.; Writing—review & editing, A.A.-B. and M.H.; Visualization, A.A.-B. and J.R.J.; Supervision, M.H.; Project administration, M.H. All authors have read and agreed to the published version of the manuscript.

Funding: This research received no external funding.

Data Availability Statement: All relevant data are included in the paper. Please contact the corresponded author if any data are needed.

Conflicts of Interest: The authors declare no conflicts of interest.

Appendix A

We merged the following datasets to obtain the final dataset used for training and testing the model.

1. Testing Dataset for Qatar 2022

    Summary: This dataset contains the visitor counts for the 2022 Qatar World Cup.
    Source: Supreme Committee for FIFA World Cup 2022.

2. Historical Dataset for Russia 2018

    Summary: This dataset contains the visitor counts for the 2018 Russia World Cup for 75 countries.
    Source: Russian delegation.

3. FIFA Rankings Dataset

    Summary: This dataset contains the FIFA rankings for each country.
    Source: Extracted from the FIFA website using Python requests and Pandas library.

4. Historical Performance Dataset

    Summary: This dataset contains the historical performances in the FIFA World Cup for each country.
    Source: Extracted Python Beautiful Soup 4 and Pandas library.

5. Geographical Information Dataset

    Summary: This dataset contains the geographical information for countries.
    Source: Gist.

6. World Bank Data

    Summary: This dataset contains the socio-economic indicators for countries.
    Source: World Bank's Python package—wbgapi.

References

1. Buarque, D. One country, two cups—The international image of Brazil in 1950 and in 2014: A study of the reputation and the identity of Brazil as projected by the international media during the two FIFA World Cups in the country. *Int. J. Commun.* **2015**, *19*, 9.
2. Lavrentyeva, A.; Kuzmin, S.; Timachev, P. Challenges and perspectives of Volgograd Region place marketing in light of FIFA World Cup Russia 2018. In Proceedings of the International Scientific Conference Competitive, Sustainable and Secure Development of the Regional Economy: Response to Global Challenges (CSSDRE 2018), Volgograd Oblast, Russia, 18–20 April 2018; Atlantis Press: Paris, France, 2018; pp. 395–400. [CrossRef]
3. Florek, M.; Breitbarth, T.; Conejo, F. Mega Event= Mega Impact? Travelling fans' experience and perceptions of the 2006 FIFA World Cup host nation. *J. Sport Tour.* **2008**, *13*, 199–219. [CrossRef]
4. Statista. Average and Total Attendance at FIFA Football World Cup Games from 1930 to 2018. Available online: https://www.statista.com/statistics/264441/number-of-spectators-at-football-world-cups-since-1930/ (accessed on 8 December 2022).
5. Tala, M.; Al Arabiya, E. FIFA World Cup 2022 Qatar Records Highest-Ever Attendance in Tournament's History. Available online: https://english.alarabiya.net/sports/2022/12/04/FIFA-World-Cup-2022-Qatar-records-highest-ever-attendance-in-tournament-s-history#:~:text=The%20FIFA%20World%20Cup%20in,million%20spectators,%20a%20report%20finds (accessed on 28 November 2022).
6. QNA/Doha. Record-Breaking Fan Attendance Registered in World Cup Qatar 2022 Gulf Times. 19 December 2022. Available online: https://www.gulf-times.com/article/651771/qatar/record-breaking-fan-attendance-registered-in-world-cup-qatar-2022 (accessed on 27 February 2023).
7. Müller, M. How mega-events capture their hosts: Event seizure and the World Cup 2018 in Russia. *Urban Geogr.* **2017**, *38*, 1113–1132. [CrossRef]
8. Castro, A.S. The 2018 FIFA World Cup: The gains and constraints of Russia's soft power of attraction through football and sports. *Public Dipl. Rising Reg. Powers* **2018**, *3*, 17–37.

9. Stergiou, D.P.; Karagiorgos, T.; Alexandris, K.; Benetatos, T.; Balaska, P. The contribution of event quality factors on the development of memorable tourism experiences: Evidence from the 2018 FIFA World Cup. *Event Manag.* **2022**, *26*, 1007–1024. [CrossRef]
10. Bishnoi, S.K.; Singh, S. A study on consumer buying behaviour for fashion and luxury brands under emotional influence. *Res. J. Text. Appar.* **2021**, *26*, 405–418. [CrossRef]
11. Kumar, V. Predictive analytics: A review of trends and techniques. *Int. J. Comput. Appl.* **2018**, *182*, 31–37. [CrossRef]
12. Ali, R. Predictive Modeling: Types, Benefits, and Algorithms. 2020. Available online: https://www.netsuite.com/portal/resource/articles/financial-management/predictive-modeling.shtml (accessed on 5 July 2023).
13. Li, J. Assessing the accuracy of predictive models for numerical data: Not r nor r^2, why not? Then what? *PLoS ONE* **2017**, *12*, e0183250. [CrossRef] [PubMed]
14. Ferris, S.P.; Koo, S.; Park, K.; Yi, D.T. The Effects of Hosting Mega Sporting Events on Local Stock Markets and Sustainable Growth. *Sustainability* **2022**, *15*, 363. [CrossRef]
15. Pinakin, A. Deep Dive into Predictive Analytics Models and Algorithms. Available online: https://marutitech.com/predictive-analytics-models-algorithms/ (accessed on 29 December 2023).
16. Gasparrini, A.; Armstrong, B.; Kenward, M.G. Multivariate meta-analysis for non-linear and other multi-parameter associations. *Stat. Med.* **2012**, *31*, 3821–3839. [CrossRef] [PubMed]
17. King, B.E.; Rice, J. Predicting attendance at Major League Soccer Matches: A comparison of four techniques. *J. Comput. Sci. Inf. Technol.* **2018**, *6*, 15–22. [CrossRef]
18. Feurer, M.; Eggensperger, K.; Falkner, S.; Lindauer, M.; Hutter, F. Auto-sklearn 2.0: Hands-Free Automl via Meta-Learning. arXiv.org. 4 October 2022. Available online: https://arxiv.org/abs/2007.04074 (accessed on 28 February 2023).
19. Smith, J.; Nguyen, D. Advanced machine learning in sports analytics: Predicting fan attendance. *Artif. Intell. Rev. Sports* **2023**, *39*, 435–450.
20. Johnson, D.; Lee, W.; Martinez, F. Big data in sports: Transforming fan experience and engagement. *Big Data Res. Sports* **2024**, *11*, 204–220.
21. White, C.; Zhao, L. Real-time data analytics in sports: Applications and implications. *J. Sports Technol. Anal.* **2023**, *10*, 134–145.
22. Martinez, L.; Lee, T. Personalizing fan experiences: New trends in sports analytics. *J. Mark. Sports Manag.* **2024**, *15*, 88–102.
23. Fernandez, J.; Patel, R. Economic and social impacts of mega sports events: A new perspective. *Econ. Anal. Sports* **2023**, *17*, 112–130.
24. Garcia, S.; Robinson, T. Ethical considerations in sports analytics: Towards a sustainable future. *J. Sports Ethics Sustain.* **2024**, *6*, 77–89.
25. Baker, A.; Kumar, S. Interdisciplinary approaches in fan attendance analysis at mega sports events. *J. Sports Anal. Forecast.* **2023**, *29*, 45–59.
26. Yamashita, G.H.; Fogliatto, F.S.; Anzanello, M.J.; Tortorella, G.L. Customized prediction of attendance to soccer matches based on symbolic regression and genetic programming. *Expert Syst. Appl.* **2022**, *187*, 115912. [CrossRef]
27. Neuman, Y.; Israeli, N.; Vilenchik, D.; Cohen, Y. The Adaptive Behavior of a Soccer Team: An Entropy-Based Analysis. *Entropy* **2018**, *20*, 758. [CrossRef]
28. Hutter, F.; Kotthoff, L.; Vanschoren, J. *Automated Machine Learning: Methods, Systems, Challenges*; Springer Nature: Berlin/Heidelberg, Germany, 2019; p. 219.
29. Uribe, R.; Buzeta, C.; Manzur, E.; Alvarez, I. Determinants of football TV audience: The straight and ancillary effects of the presence of the local team on the FIFA world cup. *J. Bus. Res.* **2021**, *127*, 454–463. [CrossRef]
30. Indicators. Data. (n.d.). Available online: https://data.worldbank.org/indicator?tab=all (accessed on 28 February 2023).

Disclaimer/Publisher's Note: The statements, opinions and data contained in all publications are solely those of the individual author(s) and contributor(s) and not of MDPI and/or the editor(s). MDPI and/or the editor(s) disclaim responsibility for any injury to people or property resulting from any ideas, methods, instructions or products referred to in the content.

Article

Improving Adversarial Robustness of Ensemble Classifiers by Diversified Feature Selection and Stochastic Aggregation

Fuyong Zhang *, Kuan Li and Ziliang Ren

School of Computer Science and Technology, Dongguan University of Technology, Dongguan 523808, China; likuan@dgut.edu.cn (K.L.); renzl@dgut.edu.cn (Z.R.)
* Correspondence: zhangfy@dgut.edu.cn

Abstract: Learning-based classifiers are found to be vulnerable to attacks by adversarial samples. Some works suggested that ensemble classifiers tend to be more robust than single classifiers against evasion attacks. However, recent studies have shown that this is not necessarily the case under more realistic settings of black-box attacks. In this paper, we propose a novel ensemble approach to improve the robustness of classifiers against evasion attacks by using diversified feature selection and a stochastic aggregation strategy. Our proposed scheme includes three stages. Firstly, the adversarial feature selection algorithm is used to select a feature each time that can trade-off between classification accuracy and robustness, and add it to the feature vector bank. Secondly, each feature vector in the bank is used to train a base classifier and is added to the base classifier bank. Finally, m classifiers from the classifier bank are randomly selected for decision-making. In this way, it can cause each classifier in the base classifier bank to have good performance in terms of classification accuracy and robustness, and it also makes it difficult to estimate the gradients of the ensemble accurately. Thus, the robustness of classifiers can be improved without reducing the classification accuracy. Experiments performed using both Linear and Kernel SVMs on genuine datasets for spam filtering, malware detection, and handwritten digit recognition demonstrate that our proposed approach significantly improves the classifiers' robustness against evasion attacks.

Keywords: adversarial machine learning; evasion attacks; classifier robustness; ensemble classifiers; gradient correlation

MSC: 68T50

1. Introduction

With the rapid expansion of global data volumes, machine learning has become extensively adopted and serves as a principal tool for data analysis across various sectors such as transportation, computer vision, finance, and security [1,2]. However, a widely acknowledged truth is that machine learning models are susceptible to adversarial examples. Attackers can probe machine learning models and maliciously manipulate their inputs to mislead the recognition outcomes [3,4]. For instance, a machine learning-powered malware detector ingests features extracted from Portable Executable (PE) files and categorizes a test case as either malware or benign software. Here, an adversary could tamper with a malware input by introducing barely perceptible perturbations, thereby tricking the detector into classifying it as benign software [5].

Adversarial samples become serious security threats for many machine learning-based systems, e.g., by extracting sufficient knowledge to exploit Google's phishing pages filter [6] and PDFRATE system-based attack [7].

Various countermeasures against evasion attacks have been proposed. Previous research demonstrates that dimensionality reduction can be an effective defense mechanism against evasion attacks [8]. Another defensive strategy is adversarial training [9], which incorporates adversarial examples into the training process. Some studies indicate that defensive distillation can be leveraged to enhance the robustness of neural networks against adversarial examples [10].

Furthermore, ensemble methods have been put forward as defense mechanisms. Intuitively, it is more challenging for an attacker to undermine a group of models than a single one. Strauss et al. [11] argue that compromising individual classifiers does not necessarily imply that other classifiers within the ensemble will also succumb to the attack. Their experimental findings substantiate that ensemble methods can indeed act as defensive strategies against evasion attacks. Tramèr et al. [12] propose an 'Ensemble Adversarial Training' approach, aimed at training a robust classification model that is resilient to such attacks. Previous research has also demonstrated that ensemble SVMs are generally more robust against evasion attacks compared to a single SVM [13].

However, recent studies have indicated that conventional ensemble learning methods may not necessarily enhance the robustness of learning models. Zhang et al. [14] and Kantchelian et al. [15] have demonstrated that tree ensembles can be more prone to evasion attacks than SVM classifiers, whether they are single or an ensemble. Zhang et al. [16] noted that ensemble SVMs are not necessarily more robust against evasion attacks compared to single SVMs. These studies show that it is still possible for attackers to launch evasion attacks on ensemble models. In 2019, Pang et al. [17] proposed a novel method, Adaptive Diversity Promoting (ADP), which improves the robustness of deep ensembles by promoting diversity in non-maximal predictive scores while keeping the maximal (most likely) prediction consistent with the true label for members in the ensemble. It reveals that promoting the diversity of ensemble models can improve their robustness against adversarial samples.

The main limitations of Linear and Kernel SVM classifiers lie in the fact that their designs do not inherently account for security aspects, rendering them less robust against evasion attacks. Zhang et al. [18] proposed an adversarial feature selection approach that incorporates security considerations into the training process, thereby improving the robustness of single SVM classifiers. Despite this improvement, single SVM classifiers generally exhibit lower classification accuracy when compared to ensemble methods. Smutz et al. [13] advocated for the use of ensemble SVMs to against evasion attacks; however, Zhang et al. [16] pointed out that ensemble SVMs are not necessarily more robust than single SVMs against evasion attacks in practical settings.

Consequently, we propose to improve the robustness of ensemble classifiers by employing diversified feature selection and stochastic aggregation, thus aiming to create a more resilient solution against adversarial threats. The underlying idea of our approach is to build ensemble classifiers not based on the combination of *weaker* classifiers, but the ensemble of classifiers that are robust against adversarial samples. We exploit the adversarial feature selection approach [18] to train the base classifiers because this method makes a trade-off between the generalization capability and its security against evasion attacks. Experimental results on real-world datasets demonstrate that our approach significantly enhances the classifiers' robustness against adversarial examples while maintaining comparable accuracy levels even when there is no attack.

The main contributions are summarized as follows:

- We propose a novel approach to train base classifiers using sequential feature selection, wherein each base classifier encompasses all the features of the preceding trained classifier and subsequently selects an additional new feature.
- We introduce stochastic aggregation, in which m classifiers are randomly selected from the base classifier bank to participate in decision-making, which not only improves the classification accuracy, but also improves the robustness against evasion attacks.
- We re-investigate the security evaluation problem, and update the gradient correlation measure to extend it to be suitable for any real number feature.

- To evaluate the performance of the proposed model, we launched lots of experiments, and the experimental results demonstrate that the proposed ensemble model can improve the robustness against evasion attacks.

2. Related Work

2.1. Evasion Attacks

The susceptibility of machine learning systems to attacks has been extensively researched within the academic community [19]. These studies not only aim to uncover the unknown vulnerabilities present in learning models but also to evaluate and address security concerns when these models face adversarial actions. Among the plethora of such research, evasion attacks during the testing phase have emerged as a prominent area of interest.

Previous studies have shown that the amount and types of knowledge obtained by an adversary can affect the success of the attack [16,19]. Many of the previously proposed attack strategies focus on white-box attacks [15,20–22]. Gradient descent attacks were proposed to employ the discriminant function from the targeted model to probe the decision boundary [20]. Kantchelian et al. [15] proposed two algorithms to attack tree ensemble classifiers. Their experimental results showed that tree ensembles such as random forests and gradient-boosted trees are vulnerable to evasion attacks in terms of white-box attacks.

There exist works that concentrate specifically on black-box attacks. These studies mainly aim to design a robust classifier in terms of the application domains [23]. Liu et al. [24] presented ensemble-based approaches to generate transferable adversarial samples that can be used as a black-box attack against (Available online: clarifai.com). Shokri et al. [25] studied the targeted model where 'machine learning' was used as a service, and presented a *shadow training* approach to launch black-box attacks using realistic datasets. Their work shows that the 'machine learning' service model is vulnerable to membership inference attacks. Alzantot et al. [26] argued that existing black-box attacks usually require many times more queries either in obtaining the training information or in obtaining the gradients based on the output scores. Therefore, they developed a gradient-free optimization approach to create visually imperceptible adversarial samples.

2.2. Defense Against Evasion Attacks

Adversarial training has become a widely adopted approach for training robust machine learning models [27]. The core concept behind adversarial training involves training a classifier by incorporating adversarial examples into the training data set. Goodfellow et al. [28] introduced the idea of considering an augmented objective during the training procedure, which entails adding adversarial examples to the original training dataset. Huang et al. [9], on the other hand, proposed a more efficient method for generating adversarial examples, specifically referring to them as supervised samples. They highlighted that the robustness of neural networks should be learned by utilizing these supervised adversarial samples to train a substantially improved robust model.

Defensive distillation uses the additional information extracted from the distillation to return to the training regimen to improve the robustness of networks [10]. This method is especially robust against gradient-based attacks. However, studies [29,30] showed that distillation is not robust to adversarial samples. Especially, when facing white-box attacks. Thus, Meng and Chen [31] proposed MagNet, which employs several detectors and a reformer network for defending neural networks.

As illustrated by Metzen et al. in [32], they devised subnetworks that are interconnected with the main network, designed to discern whether the input to the network is a non-adversarial sample or an adversarial one. Specifically, their process involves initially training a classification network using non-adversarial samples. Following this, adversarial samples are generated for each individual data point. Subsequently, a subnetwork is further trained using both the generated adversarial samples and the original non-adversarial ones. In another work by Zhang et al. [18], they proposed an adversarial feature selection model which enhances the security of classifiers against evasion attacks. This model improves robustness by incorporating specific assumptions about the attacker's data manipulation strategy.

On the other hand, Smutz et al. [13] demonstrated that ensemble classifiers, such as ensemble trees or SVMs, can serve as a defense strategy against evasion attacks by leveraging the diversity within the ensembles themselves. In contrast, Huang et al. [33] employed deep ensembles as a means of adversarial defense, enhancing their resistance by promoting diversity in the high-level feature representations and gradient dispersion during the simultaneous training of deep ensemble networks. Table 1 presents the defense strategies obtained from a literature review of current defense methods against evasion attacks.

Table 1. Defense strategies against evasion attacks.

Defense Technique	Description	Publication
Adversarial training	Add adversarial samples to the original training data.	[9,28]
Defensive distillation	Employ the extra information extracted from the distillation process to feed back into the training regimen for enhancing the robustness of the network.	[10]
Several detectors	Employ several detectors alongside a reformer network to defend against attacks.	[31]
Statistical tests	Use a statistical test to differentiate adversarial examples from training data.	[34]
Binary detector network	Subnetworks that branch off from the main network are trained to discern the input to the network.	[32]
Pre-trained softmax neural classifier	A framework for identifying out-of-distribution samples and adversarial attacks.	[35]
Random perturbations	Analyze the model's responses to an input subjected to random perturbations.	[36]
Adversarial feature selection	This method enhances the security of the classifier against evasion attacks by incorporating specific assumptions about the adversary's data manipulation tactics.	[18]
Ensemble trees or SVMs	To defend against evasion attacks by examining the diversity within the ensembles themselves.	[13]
Deep ensemble	Encourage diversity in the learning of high-level feature representations and gradient dispersion during the concurrent training of deep ensemble networks.	[33]

However, an adversary can still launch attacks against an ensemble of classifiers because they generalize across classifiers. For example, Zhang et al. [16] conducted research on evasion attacks against ensembles of SVMs and highlighted that, in practical scenarios, ensemble SVMs can be more susceptible to evasion attacks compared to a single SVM. Kantchelian et al. [15] showed that it is possible to employ a Mixed Integer Linear Program solver to generate an evading instance and launch attacks against ensemble of regression trees. In this paper, we focus on improving adversarial robustness of ensemble classifiers by diversified feature selection and stochastic aggregation strategy.

3. Overview of the Proposed Model

In this section, we begin with a review of the evasion attack model, followed by a description of the motivation and structure of the proposed model.

3.1. Evasion Attack Model

In order to efficaciously evaluate the robustness of learning-based classifiers against evasion attacks, we utilize the evasion attack model initially defined in the works [19,20]. In an evasion attack, an adversary's goal is to estimate the decision boundary of the targeted system and manipulate the input sample to mislead the decision of the targeted system. Without the loss of generality, the problem of an evasion attack can be described as: given a machine learning system M, and an input sample $\mathbf{x}$, where $\mathbf{x}$ can be correctly classified by M and the output is $c(\mathbf{x})$. An adversary's goal is to try to find its classification boundary by probing the classifier. Then, an adversary can modify the content of $\mathbf{x}$ after knowing what kinds of instances can be misclassified by the classifier. Therefore, it is possible for $\mathbf{x}$ be modified to $\mathbf{x}'$ by minimally manipulating $\mathbf{x}$, where $\mathbf{x}'$ is classified incorrectly (i.e., $c(\mathbf{x}') \neq c(\mathbf{x})$). Suppose the amount of manipulations is characterized by distance function $d(\mathbf{x}, \mathbf{x}')$, the evasion attack problem can be written as [18]

$$E(\mathbf{x}) = \arg\min_{\mathbf{x}'} d(\mathbf{x}, \mathbf{x}'), \quad s.t. \quad c(\mathbf{x}') \neq c(\mathbf{x}). \tag{1}$$

3.2. Motivation and Architecture of the Proposed Model

Conventional ensemble classifiers, such as Random Forest [37,38], Gradient-Boosting Trees [39], Ensemble SVMs [40,41] and so on, consist of multiple *weak* classifiers, which increase the diversity of classifiers and improve classification performance [42,43], while our primary objective is to enhance the robustness of classifiers. Therefore, the first motivation of our approach is to ensemble with *strong* classifiers. The *strong* classifiers here refer to the robust classifiers without significantly reducing classification accuracy. Intuitively, the ensemble of multiple *strong* classifiers guarantees both robustness and classification accuracy.

Another motivation is that the learning procedure of conventional ensemble classifiers may enable an attacker to train a classifier with a decision boundary that closely mimics the targeted system using a minimal amount of training data, thereby facilitating the attack [16]. Thus, our idea revolves around modifying the learning process to obfuscate the decision boundary, such that even if an attacker possesses knowledge of some or all of the training data, it becomes challenging for them to accurately learn the true decision boundary, thereby enhancing the robustness of the targeted system.

The last point is about the aggregation strategy, which usually adopts voting or averaging [40]. No matter which method, all the classifiers in the ensemble are utilized to make the decision for better performance. However, we intend to use *strong* classifiers as the base classifiers of the ensemble. Any single classifier in the ensemble can achieve good performance. It does not need all classifiers to participate in decision-making. We can randomly selecting m classifiers to make the decision. There are two benefits for doing this. One is that combining the decision of m classifiers can boost the accuracy performance compared with a single classifier. Second, randomly select m classifiers can confuse classification boundaries. Even if an attacker is aware of all the parameters of the targeted system, the real decision boundary remains elusive due to the random selection of classifiers that contribute to the decision-making process.

The architecture of the proposed model is depicted in Figure 1. Within the model, we initially conduct feature selection to identify a set of feature vectors that are advantageous for both robustness and accuracy performance. All selected feature vectors are stored in a feature vector bank. Subsequently, base classifiers are trained using the chosen feature vectors from this bank, and these classifiers are then placed in a classifier bank. Ultimately, the decision made by the proposed model is determined through the consensus of m randomly selected classifiers from the classifier bank.

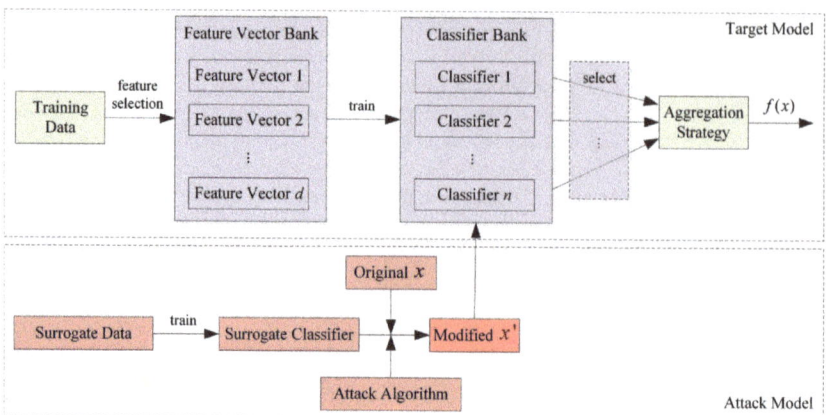

Figure 1. Architecture of the proposed model.

4. Proposed Model

In this section, we present the proposed model for improving adversarial robustness of ensemble classifiers (AREC). In evasion attacks, the more an attacker knows about the decision boundary of the targeted classifier, the easier it becomes to execute a successful evasion. Our fundamental approach is to obfuscate the decision boundary, making it unpredictable, while concurrently maximizing the generalization capacity of the classifier, thus enhancing its resilience against evasion attacks.

4.1. Training Procedure of AREC

As discussed in Section 3, each classifier used in our model should not only optimize accuracy—it is more appropriate to optimize a trade-off between accuracy and robustness. We apply the adversarial feature selection approach to optimize the trade-off [18]. Given a d-dimensional sample **x**, the criterion can be formalized as

$$k^* = \arg\max_{\hat{\mathbf{x}}_k} G(\hat{\mathbf{x}}_k) + \lambda S(\hat{\mathbf{x}}_k) \tag{2}$$

where G symbolizes an estimation of the classifier's generalization ability in the absence of attack. S represents the classifier security against evasion attacks, λ is a trade-off parameter, $\hat{\mathbf{x}}_k, k = 1, 2, \ldots d$, is the mapping of **x** in the subspace of k selected features, and k^* is the kth optimal feature be selected.

Let $g : \mathcal{X} \to \mathcal{Y}$ be a classifier. For a given sample $\mathbf{x} \in \mathcal{X}$ and its label $y \in \mathcal{Y}$, G can be formalized as

$$G = \mathbb{E}_{(\mathbf{x},y) \sim P_{\mathcal{X} \times \mathcal{Y}}} l(g(\hat{\mathbf{x}}_k), y) \tag{3}$$

where $\mathbb{E}$ represents the expectation operator, $P_{\mathcal{X} \times \mathcal{Y}}$ is the data distribution, and $g(\cdot)$ is the discriminant function of classifier g. For binary classifiers $\mathcal{Y} = \{0, 1\}$ and

$$l(g(\hat{\mathbf{x}}_k), y) = \begin{cases} 1, & \text{if } yg(\hat{\mathbf{x}}_k) > 0 \\ 0, & \text{otherwise} \end{cases} \tag{4}$$

As discussed in Section 3, the security term S can be formalized as

$$S = \mathbb{E}_{(\mathbf{x},y) \sim P_{\mathcal{X}|\mathcal{Y}=1}} d(\hat{\mathbf{x}}_k, \hat{\mathbf{x}}'_k) \tag{5}$$

where $\mathcal{Y} = 1$ represents the label of malicious samples, and $\hat{\mathbf{x}}'_k$ is the optimal solution to problem (1).

As the data distribution $P_{\mathcal{X} \times \mathcal{Y}}$ and $P_{\mathcal{X}|\mathcal{Y}=1}$ are typically unknown, we can estimate G and S using a set of n fixed samples, which can be written as

$$G \approx \frac{1}{n} \sum_{i=1}^{n} l(g(\hat{\mathbf{x}}_k^i), y^i) \tag{6}$$

$$S \approx \frac{1}{n^+} \sum_{i=1}^{n^+} d(\hat{\mathbf{x}}_k, \hat{\mathbf{x}}_k') \tag{7}$$

where n^+ denotes the number of malicious samples within the set of n samples. It should be emphasized that the value of S varies depending on the datasets and the distance function $d(\cdot, \cdot)$. Therefore, we can use parameter λ to avoid the dependency, e.g., one may rescale λ by dividing its value by the maximum value of $d(\cdot, \cdot)$. Also, λ can be used to trade-off between G and S.

The criterion (2) can be exploited to select one optimal feature at a time. After each feature selection, the selected features are put in the feature vector bank and also used for the next feature selection step. The base classifiers of AREC are trained using the selected feature vectors in the feature vector bank. The training procedure of the proposed model is shown in Figure 2. The detailed training process is given by Algorithm 1.

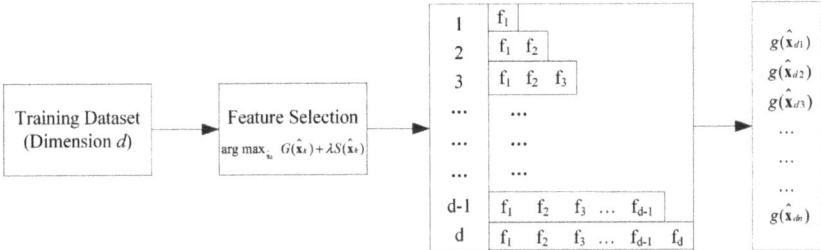

Figure 2. Training procedure of the proposed model.

Algorithm 1 Training AREC

Input: $\mathcal{D} = \{\mathbf{x}^i, y^i\}_{i=1}^{d}$: the training dataset, λ: the trade-off parameter.
Output: $M[d, d]$: the selected feature matrix.
1: $M[a, b] = 0, a = 1, \ldots, d$ and $b = 1, \ldots, d$
2: $\mathcal{S} \leftarrow \emptyset, \mathcal{U} \leftarrow \{1, \ldots, d\}$
3: **for** j from 1 to d **do**
4:    **for** each feature $k \in \mathcal{U}$ **do**
5:       $\mathcal{F} \leftarrow \mathcal{S} \cup \{k\}$
6:       $\theta = 0$, and then $\theta_f = 1$ for $f \in \mathcal{F}$
7:       Estimate $G_k(\theta)$ and $S_k(\theta)$ using cross-validation on $\mathcal{D}_{\subseteq} = \{\mathbf{x}_{\theta}^i, y^i\}_{i=1}^{d}$
8:    **end for**
9:    $\lambda' = \lambda (\max_k S_k)^{-1}$
10:   $k^* = \arg\max_k G_k(\theta) + \lambda' S_k(\theta)$
11:   $\mathcal{S} \leftarrow \mathcal{S} \cup \{k^*\}$
12:   $\mathcal{F} \leftarrow \mathcal{S}$
13:   $\theta = 0$, and then $\theta_f = 1$ for $f \in \mathcal{F}$
14:   $M[j] = \theta$
15: **end for**
16: **return:** M

4.2. Aggregation Strategy of AREC

Following feature selection, each feature vector in the feature vector bank is utilized to train a base classifier and subsequently added to the base classifier bank. Ultimately, m classifiers are randomly selected from the classifier bank for decision-making purposes. This design inherently increases confusion, making it difficult for an attacker to predict which classifiers will be engaged in the decision process. Put simply, this configuration renders evasion attacks more challenging. Moreover, it is important to note that every individual classifier within the ensemble is trained using carefully selected features, striking a balance between accuracy and robustness. Each classifier operates within a unique feature space and assigns different feature weights. Collectively, these characteristics render the proposed approach more robust against evasion attacks. The classification procedure of the proposed model is shown in Figure 3 and Algorithm 2.

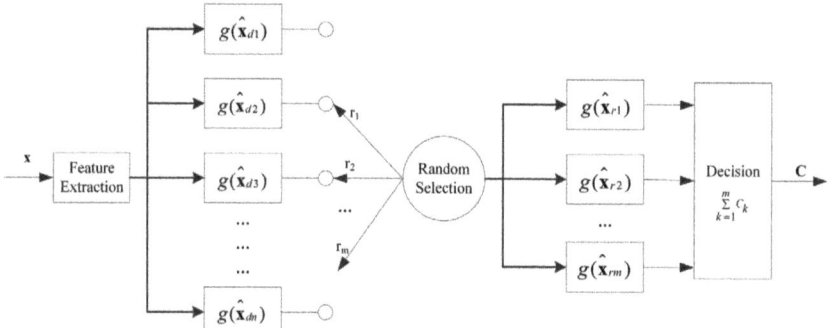

Figure 3. Classification procedure of the proposed model.

Algorithm 2 Classification Procedure of AREC

Input: $\mathbf{x}$: the input sample.
Output: y : the label of $\mathbf{x}$.
1: Randomly select m classifiers from $[G_{d_1}, G_{d_2}, ..., G_{d_n}]$ to form $\mathcal{R} = \{G_{r_1}, ..., G_{r_m}\}$, where m is an odd number and $m < n$
2: $k = 1$
3: **for** $G \in \mathcal{R}$ **do**
4:     If $G(\mathbf{x}) > 0$ then $C_k = 1$, else if $G(\mathbf{x}) < 0$ then $C_k = -1$
5:     $k = k + 1$
6: **end for**
7: If $\sum_{k=1}^{m} C_k > 0$ then $y = 1$, else $y = -1$
8: **return:** y

5. Classifier Security Evaluation

Following the adversary model presented in [19,20,44], an attacker's knowledge can be described in four levels: (1) the training data $\mathcal{D}$; (2) the feature set $\mathcal{X}$; (3) the learning algorithm f, and (4) the targeted model parameters $\mathbf{p}$. Thus, the knowledge can be characterized in terms of $\varphi = (\mathcal{D}, \mathcal{X}, f, \mathbf{p})$. According to this assumption, the knowledge of an attacker can be divided into two categories:

White-box attacks: An attacker is assumed to know all of the targeted model, namely $\varphi = (\mathcal{D}, \mathcal{X}, f, \mathbf{p})$.

Black-box attacks: In this scenario, an attacker is assumed to possess some level of knowledge about the targeted model. In this paper, we suppose that the attacker knows f and $\mathcal{X}$, whereas $\mathcal{D}$ and $\mathbf{p}$ remain unknown to the attacker. However, an attacker can estimate the parameters namely $\hat{\mathbf{p}}$ trained on a subset of $\mathcal{D}$ or a surrogate dataset $\hat{\mathcal{D}} = \{(\hat{\mathbf{x}}_i, \hat{y}_i)\}_{i=1}^{N_s}$ of N_s samples drawn from the resemble distribution of $\mathcal{D}$. The surrogate dataset may be collected from an alternate source. Thus, we can define this scenario as $\hat{\varphi} = (\hat{\mathcal{D}}, \mathcal{X}, f, \hat{\mathbf{p}})$.

In this paper, we examine the robustness of SVM classifiers under black-box attack scenarios (while the evaluation under white-box attacks will be given in discussion). With regard to the attacker's knowledge about the dataset $\mathcal{D}$, we consider two distinct attack situations. One is *subset scenario* which assumes a subset of $\mathcal{D}$ is able to be collected by an attacker, i.e., $\hat{\mathcal{D}} \subset \mathcal{D}$. The other is *surrogate data scenario* which assumes a surrogate dataset $\hat{\mathcal{D}}$ drawn from the resemble distribution of $\mathcal{D}$ can be collected by an attacker.

The gradient descent evasion attack is adopted to solve the optimization problem in Equation (1), which was shown to be effective against SVM-based classifiers [16,20]. The process of the gradient descent evasion attack is detailed in Algorithm 3.

The gradients of single SVMs and ensemble SVMs can be found in [16]. Here, we give the gradients of the proposed ensemble SVMs used in this paper followed by the updated gradient correlation measure.

Algorithm 3 Gradient Descent Evasion Attack

Input: $\mathbf{x}^0$: the initial attack point, α: the gradient step size, d_{max}: the maximum number of iterations.
Output: x: the final attack point.
1: Make $\nabla g(\mathbf{x}^0)$ and $\mathbf{x}^0$ a matrix $[\nabla g(\mathbf{x}^0), \mathbf{x}^0]$
2: $[\mathbf{v}, \mathbf{x}] \leftarrow$ Rearrange the matrix $[\nabla g(\mathbf{x}^0), \mathbf{x}^0]$ according to the descending order of $|\nabla g(\mathbf{x}^0)|$
3: $i \leftarrow 0$
4: **while** $g(\mathbf{x}) > 0$ && $i < d_{max}$ **do**
5: $\quad i \leftarrow i + 1$
6: $\quad$ **if** $v_i > 0$ && $(x_i - \alpha) \in [0, 1]$ **then**
7: $\quad\quad x_i \leftarrow x_i - \alpha$
8: $\quad$ **else if** $v_i < 0$ && $(x_i + \alpha) \in [0, 1]$ **then**
9: $\quad\quad x_i \leftarrow x_i + \alpha$
10: $\quad$ **end if**
11: **end while**
12: **return: x**

5.1. Gradients of the Proposed Ensemble SVMs

Because the classifiers that participate in decision-making are randomly selected from the classifier bank, it is difficult to find the exact gradient. In this section, we give three approaches to find approximate gradients. As discussed above, we assume an attacker knows $\mathcal{X}$ and f. Here, we further assume that the attacker is aware of the number of classifiers selected in the ensemble, which is parameter m.

- Averaging gradient: This means we average each gradient of the classifier from the classifier bank, the gradient function is just like gradients of ensemble SVMs.
- Gradient of the minimal features: Since only one feature is added from one feature vector to the next, the shortest feature vector must be contained within all the other vectors, suggesting that these features could be the most significant in the ensemble. Typically, classifiers do not use very few features, such as just one or two. It is worthwhile to investigate the attack efficiency leveraging this gradient.
- Gradient of the maximal features: Given the difficulty in determining which specific features contribute significantly to the classification process, it is a prudent choice to employ all available features.

5.2. Updated Gradient Correlation

In [16], we proposed a gradient correlation measure to evaluate the similarity of gradient between the surrogate and targeted classifiers, which is given by

$$GC = \frac{\sum_{k=1}^{n} C(k)}{n} \qquad (8)$$

where

$$C(k) = \frac{\sum_{i=1}^{k} v'_i}{\sum_{i=1}^{k} v_i} \qquad (9)$$

Let $\mathbf{v}^+$ denote the original gradient vector of the targeted classifier, $\mathbf{v}$ is the vector which sorted $|\mathbf{v}^+|$ in descending order, i.e., $v_1 \geq v_2 \geq ... \geq v_n$. $\mathbf{v}'$ is the gradient vector of surrogate classifier with the absolute gradient value of target classifier for the same features between the targeted and surrogate classifiers. n is the amount of features adopted in the targeted classifier.

There are two issues with this metric. First, in GC, gradients of all n features are computed, but not all features need to be modified to launch an attack. Therefore, in the updated gradient correlation (UGC), only gradients of the modified features are taken into account. The second issue is that the original GC only considers binary features. In the updated version of GC, we expand it to accommodate any real-valued feature. The updated gradient correlation is given by

$$UGC = \frac{\sum_{i=1}^{l} \alpha v_i'}{\sum_{i=1}^{l} \alpha v_i} = \frac{\sum_{i=1}^{l} v_i'}{\sum_{i=1}^{l} v_i} \qquad (10)$$

where l represents the number of modified features to let $c(\mathbf{x}') \neq c(\mathbf{x})$. α denotes the step size and $\alpha \in (0, 1]$, when each feature value is normalized to $[0,1]$. For binary features, $\alpha = 1$. The detailed procedure of updated gradient correlation measure is given by Algorithm 4. From Algorithm 4, we can see that $UGC \in [0, 1]$, $UGC = 1$ and $UGC = 0$ correspond to the most correlated and the most uncorrelated gradient distribution, respectively.

Algorithm 4 Updated Gradient Correlation

Input: $[\mathbf{v}^+, \mathbf{f}^+]$, $\mathbf{v}^+$: the original gradient vector of the targeted classifier, $\mathbf{f}^+$: the features adopted in the targeted classifier; $[\mathbf{v}^-, \mathbf{f}^-]$, $\mathbf{v}^-$: the original gradient vector of the surrogate classifier, $\mathbf{f}^-$: the features adopted in the surrogate classifier, $\mathbf{f}^- \subseteq \mathbf{f}^+$; n: the amount of features adopted in the targeted classifier; m: the amount of features adopted in the surrogate classifier; l: the amount of modified features.
Output: UGC
1: $[\mathbf{v}, \mathbf{f}] \leftarrow$ sort $|\mathbf{v}^+|$ in descending order;
2: $[\mathbf{v}^*, \mathbf{f}^*] \leftarrow$ sort $|\mathbf{v}^-|$ in descending order;
3: $j \leftarrow 1$;
4: **while** $j \leq m$ **do**
5: $\quad p \leftarrow$ find the position of f_j^* in $\mathbf{f}$ if exist, otherwise $p \leftarrow 0$;
6: $\quad$ **if** $p > 0$ **then**
7: $\quad\quad v_j' \leftarrow v_p$
8: $\quad$ **else**
9: $\quad\quad v_j' \leftarrow 0$
10: $\quad$ **end if**
11: $\quad j \leftarrow j + 1$
12: **end while**
13: **if** $m < n$ **then**
14: $\quad v_j' \leftarrow 0, j = m, m+1, ..., n$
15: **end if**
16: $UGC = \frac{\sum_{i=1}^{l} v_i'}{\sum_{i=1}^{l} v_i}$
17: **return:** UGC

To illustrate how the updated gradient correlation works, consider the following case with five binary features (see Figure 4). The top left of Figure 4 shows the original gradient vector $\mathbf{v}^+$ and the feature vector $\mathbf{f}^+$ from the targeted classifier. $\mathbf{v}$ denotes the vector sorted by $|\mathbf{v}^+|$ in descending order and $\mathbf{f}$ is the feature vector sorted with $\mathbf{v}$. The top right of Figure 4 shows the original gradient vector $\mathbf{v}^-$ and the feature vector $\mathbf{f}^-$ from the surrogate classifier. $\mathbf{v}^*$ denotes the vector sorted by $|\mathbf{v}^-|$ in descending order and $\mathbf{f}^*$ is the feature vector sorted with $\mathbf{v}^*$. $\mathbf{v}'$ is the gradient vector of the surrogate classifier relative to the targeted classifier.

Why use **v**′? From Algorithm 3, one can see that, in a gradient descent attack, an attacker modifies features according to the value of their gradients. In this example, according to the sequence of modifying features obtained by an attacker, the first feature should be modified is f_3, and the gradient change is 3 for the targeted system by modifying f_3. According to the gradient of the targeted system, the feature with the greatest impact is f_5. By modifying f_5, the gradient change is 4. Therefore, in the case of modifying only one feature ($l = 1$), the gradient ratio between the surrogate system and the targeted system is $UGC = 3/4$. If two features need to be modified ($l = 2$), an attacker will modify f_3 and f_2, the sum of the gradients corresponding to these two features is 4, while for the targeted system, modifying two features can make the gradient change 7, so $UGC = 4/7$. In the case, we assume an attacker needs to modify three features to let $c(\mathbf{x}') \neq c(\mathbf{x})$. Thus, $l = 3$ and $UGC = 6/9$. It should be noted that we use GC to represent the updated version of gradient correlation.

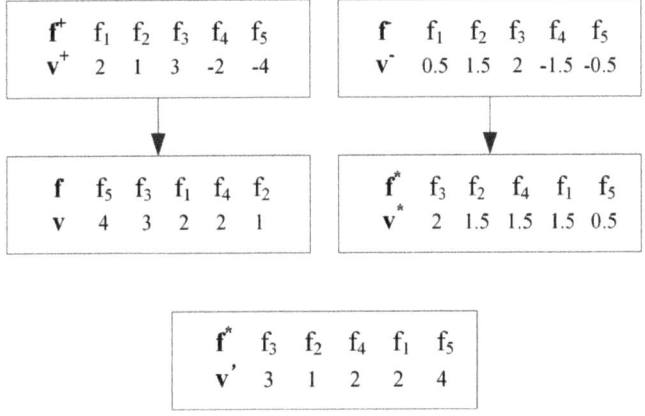

Figure 4. An example of the updated gradient correlation.

6. Experimental Evaluation

In this section, we evaluate the robustness of ARE SVMs, RSE SVMs (Random Subspace Ensemble SVMs [13,37]), a conventional SVM and a SVM trained by adversarial feature selection [18]; we call this approach AFS SVM. However, the authors did not show how to determine the optimal number of selected features. Through the analysis of the results in the paper [18], we discovered that both classification accuracy and robustness perform satisfactorily when approximately half of the total number of features are selected to train the SVM. Consequently, half the number of features were chosen to train the AFS SVM. Three tasks, namely spam email filtering, malware detection and digit recognition, are considered in the evaluation. In both the subset scenario and the surrogate data scenario, we vary an attacker's knowledge by portions of data, 10%, 20%, ..., 100%.

For RSE SVMs, each ensemble classifier contained 100 independent base classifiers and the feature bagging ratio was set to 50%. For ARE SVMs, we applied five-fold cross-validation to train models. For each Linear-SVM-based classifier, the SVM regularization parameter was set to $C = 1$. For all RBF-SVM-based classifiers, we set the regularization parameter $C = 100$ and the kernel parameter $\gamma = 0.01$.

Both the updated gradient correlation and the hardness of evasion [18] measures were adopted for security evaluation. For a single SVM, AFS SVM and RSE SVMs, we ran each experiment 30 times and the results were averaged to produce the figures. For ARE SVMs, 30 independent models were built and we ran 30 times on each model. Thus, the results showed in the figures were averaged by 900. All experiments in the paper were implemented using MATLAB. The following shows the experimental results on three real application datasets.

6.1. Feasibility Analysis on Spam Email Filtering

We consider the PU3 dataset in the spam email filtering task [45,46]. We apply the experimental setup described in [16]. There are three subsets split by 4130 emails—one for training, one is used for the surrogate data, and the last one is used for testing.

Firstly, we give the results based on Linear-SVM and use the spam email filtering case study to show how to select parameters for ARE SVMs. Then we compare the results with single SVM, AFS SVM and RSE SVMs. The left side of Figure 5 shows the classification accuracy achieved by ARE Linear-SVMs trained using single feature vectors. We can see that the more features are selected in the vector, the the higher accuracy, when less than 40 features are selected. The accuracy is not much different when more than 40 features are selected in the vector. In order to obtain high and stable classification accuracy, the feature vectors whose feature number is more than half of the original feature space are selected to train the classifiers in the rest of the experiments. The right side of Figure 5 shows the classification accuracy achieved by ARE Linear-SVMs in which the base classifiers are trained using feature vectors with more than 100 features. It is clear that higher accuracy is achieved with a larger m. We believe $m = 3$ is a good choice for our evaluation tasks.

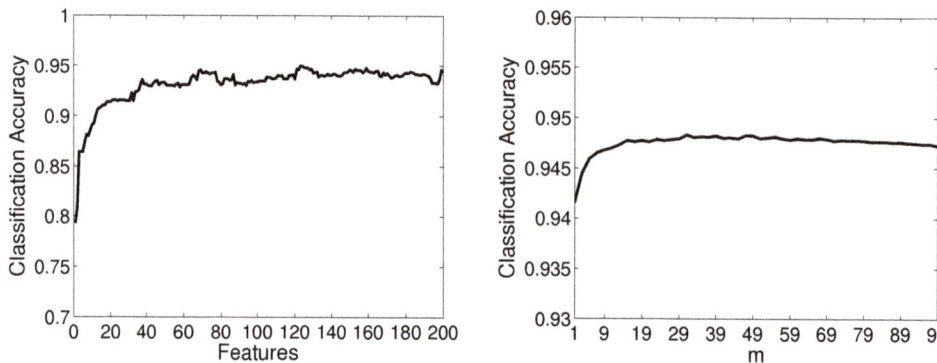

Figure 5. Classification accuracy achieved by ARE Linear-SVMs trained using single feature vector (**left**) and by ARE Linear-SVMs with m (**right**) on the PU3 dataset.

Figure 6 shows the mean ROC curves of the four methods based on Linear-SVM and RBF-SVM, respectively. From the figure, it is evident that ARE SVMs exhibit the second-highest classification performance, with RSE SVMs demonstrating the top performance among them.

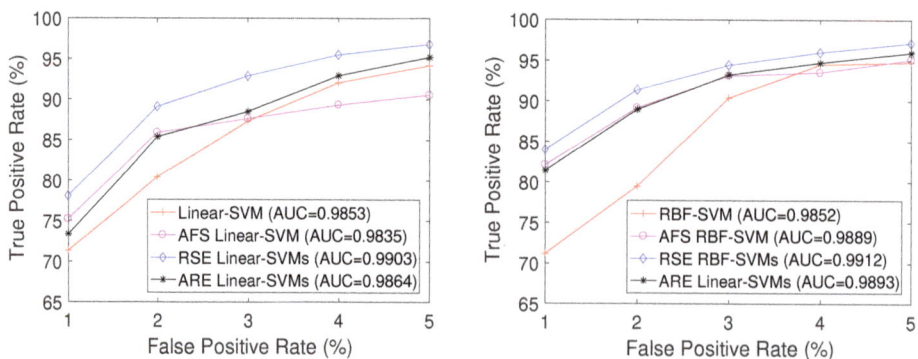

Figure 6. Mean ROC curves based on Linear-SVM (**left**) and RBF-SVM (**right**) on the PU3 dataset.

As illustrated on the left-hand side of Figure 7, ARE SVMs consistently demonstrate higher robustness compared to RSE SVMs and single SVMs, regardless of the amount of data accessible to the attacker. Furthermore, this figure highlights that among the three types of gradients in ARE SVMs, the averaging gradient proves to be more effective than the rest. There is not a significant distinction between the gradient of minimal features and the gradient of maximal features.

On the right side of Figure 7, the gradient correlation measures for the four methodologies are displayed. It can be observed that ARE SVMs consistently exhibit lower *GC* scores than RSE SVMs and single SVMs, corroborating the findings in the left-hand portion of the figure. A higher *GC* score indicates a closer approximation of the gradient estimate between the surrogate and targeted classifiers, rendering the system more susceptible to attacks.

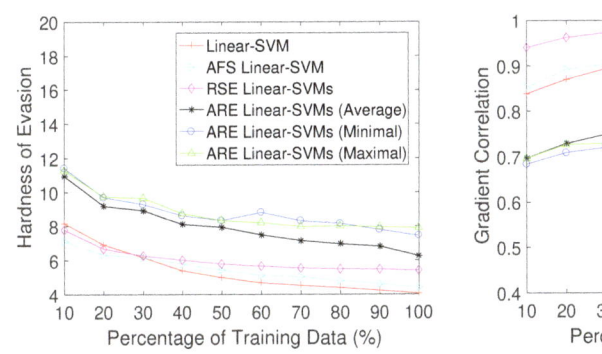
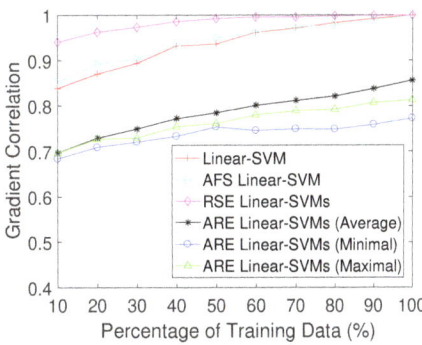

Figure 7. Hardness of evasion (i.e., the average minimum number of modified words required to classify all spam emails as legitimate) (**left**) and gradient correlation *GC* (**right**) based on Linear-SVM in the subset scenario.

Figure 7 also reveals that, for the ARE approach, the averaging gradient attack is more effective than the other two methods. Thus, we only give results of the averaging gradient attack in the rest of the paper.

Figure 8 shows that, under the surrogate data attack scenario, ARE SVMs are still harder to compromise than RSE SVMs and single SVMs. In this scenario, the amount of surrogate data is not as critical as that in the subset scenario and RSE SVMs are always easier to compromise by modifying fewer words on average. The gradient correlation results shown in the right side of Figure 8 also support this observation, which is ARE SVMs always have lower gradient correlation scores than RSE SVMs and single SVMs and the scores of RSE SVMs much higher than the others.

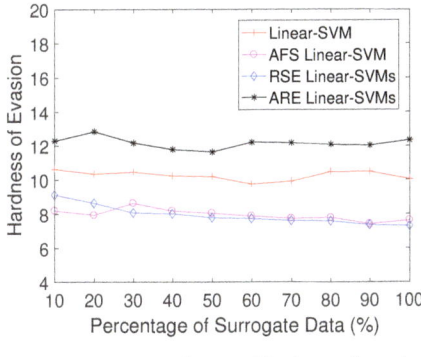
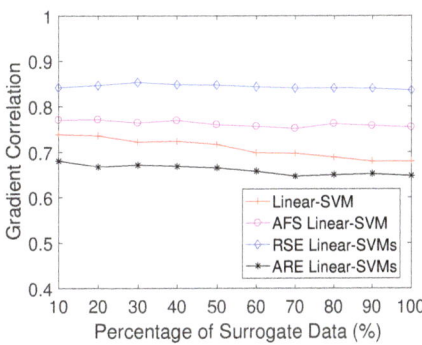

Figure 8. Hardness of evasion (**left**) and gradient correlation *GC* (**right**) based on Linear-SVM in the surrogate data scenario on PU3 dataset.

The results of RBF-SVM-based classifiers are shown in Figure 9. The results show the same trend as Linear-SVM-based classifiers. The ARE classifiers always have the highest hardness of evasion scores and lowest gradient correlation scores, which indicates the ARE approach is more robust than RSE SVMs and single SVMs.

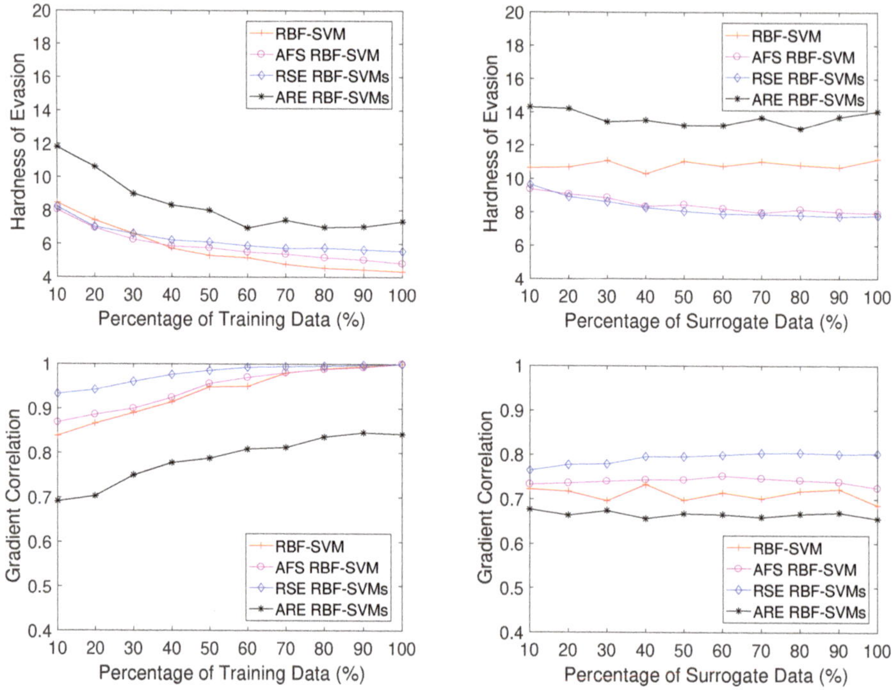

Figure 9. Hardness of evasion (**top**) and gradient correlation GC (**bottom**) based on RBF-SVM on the PU3 dataset.

6.2. Case Study on Malware Detection in PDF

Malware detection is another real-world task we considered in this paper. Also, the PDF dataset and the experimental setup described in [16] are applied in these experiments.

In this task, the gap in evasion difficulty between single SVMs and RSE SVMs is quite narrow for both Linear-based and RBF-based SVMs, and AFS SVMs significantly outperform these two methods according to Figure 10. Notably, ARE SVMs prove to be the most resistant to evasion, requiring almost twice the number of features to be manipulated for successful evasion compared to Linear-SVMs, RBF-SVMs, and RSE SVMs when the attacker possesses identical knowledge about the dataset $\mathcal{D}$. Figure 11 presents the gradient correlation scores, which further substantiate this observation, showing that ARE SVMs consistently display the lowest scores. This suggests that ARE SVMs exhibit enhanced robustness against gradient descent attacks.

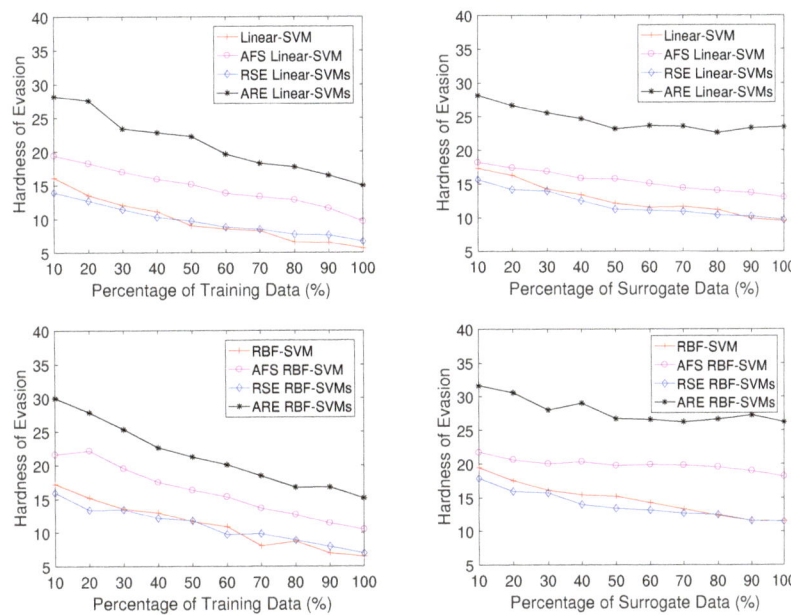

Figure 10. Hardness of evasion (i.e., average minimum number of keywords that need to be added to make each malicious PDF file be misclassified as benign) on the PDF dataset in the subset scenario (**left**) and the surrogate scenario (**right**).

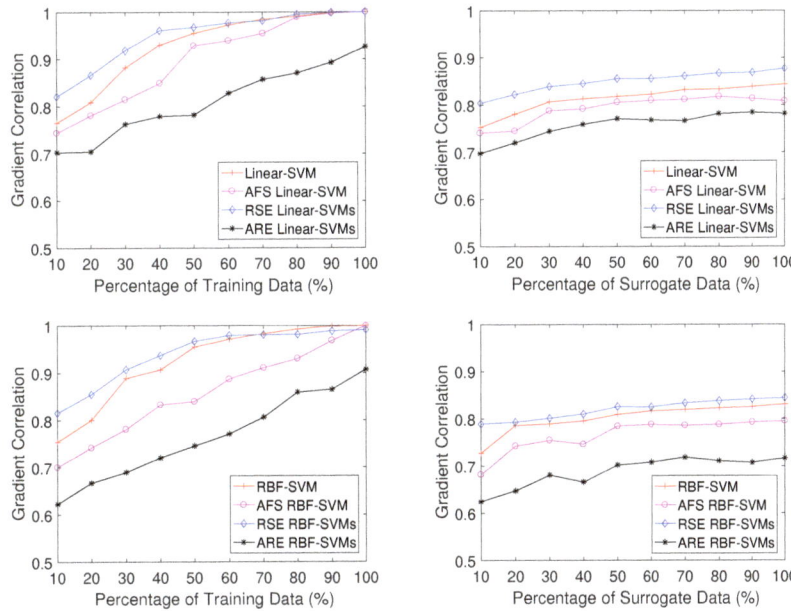

Figure 11. Gradient correlation GC on the PDF dataset in the subset scenario (**left**) and the surrogate data scenario (**right**).

6.3. Case Study on Handwritten Digit Recognition

The third task involves handwritten digit recognition, utilizing the MNIST dataset. In accordance with [14], we specifically discriminate between the digits "2" and "6". Thus, we have 11,876 images for training and 1990 images for testing purposes. From the pool of 11,876 images, we randomly select 1000 samples and partition them into two subsets, each containing 500 images, which serve as the training data and the surrogate data, respectively. To assess robustness, we choose 100 instances of the digit "6" from the test data, ensuring that all the considered models accurately recognize these 100 instances. For evaluating the overall classification performance, all 1990 images are employed.

From Figure 12, it can be discerned that for both Linear-based and RBF-based SVMs, ARE SVMs consistently maintain the second-highest classification performance. However, in the case of Linear-based SVMs, the optimal performance is achieved by RSE Linear-SVMs, while for RBF-based SVMs, the highest degree of performance is attributed to RBF-SVM.

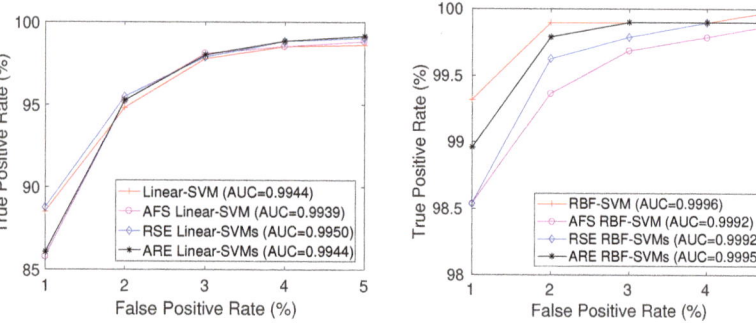

Figure 12. Mean ROC curves on MNIST dataset based on Linear-SVM (**left**) and RBF-SVM (**right**).

In the digit-recognition task, Figure 13 confirms that ARE SVMs remain the most robust classifiers. The performances of the other methods are relatively similar. The gradient correlation scores displayed in Figure 14 further validate this observation, as ARE SVMs consistently exhibit the lowest scores, while the scores of the other three approaches are closely clustered.

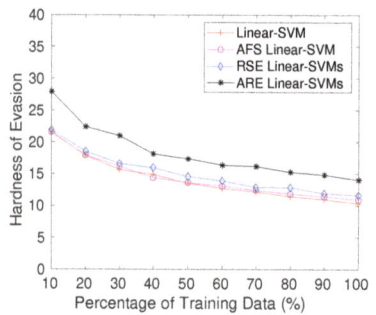 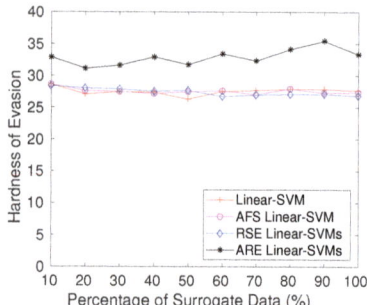

Figure 13. Cont.

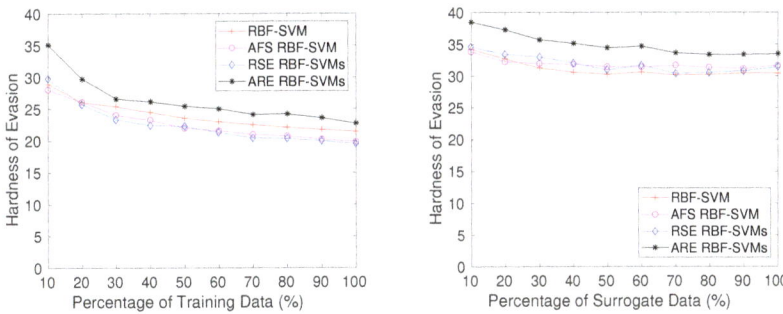

Figure 13. Hardness of evasion (i.e., average minimum number of modified pixels required to misclassify each digit "6" as "2") on MNIST dataset in the subset scenario (**left**) and the surrogate scenario (**right**).

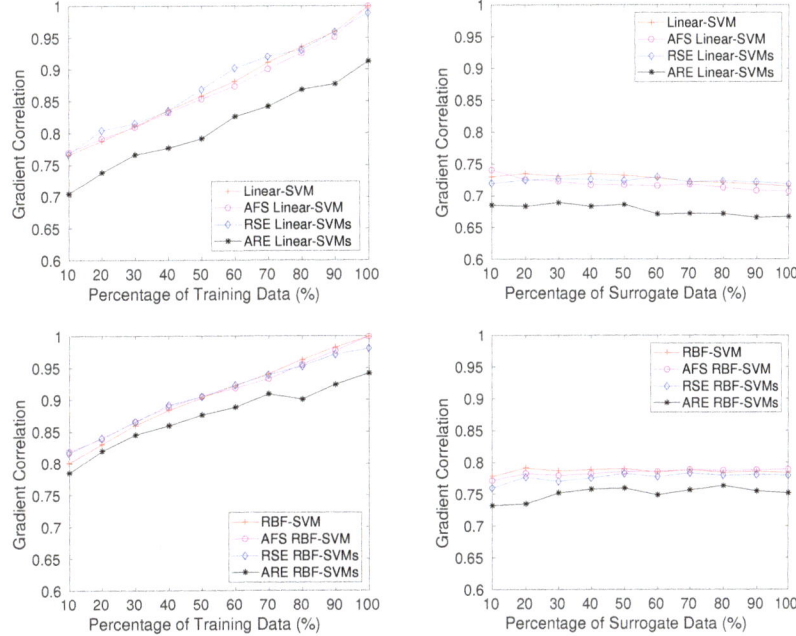

Figure 14. Gradient correlation GC on MNIST dataset in the subset scenario (**left**) and the surrogate data scenario (**right**).

7. Discussion and Limitations

7.1. Robustness under White-Box Attacks

As discussed above, even if an attacker knows all of the training data, they still cannot estimate the targeted model parameters **p** accurately. Usually, an attacker does not have the ability to directly attack the targeted system to obtain the parameters **p**. However, in order to evaluate the robustness of AREC in the worst-case, we show the experimental results under white-box attacks. In this case, an attacker is assumed to know the same knowledge as the targeted system, $\varphi = (\mathcal{D}, \mathcal{X}, F, \mathbf{p})$. Nevertheless, the final classifiers used for making the decision are still selected randomly. The optimal attack for an attacker is applying the average gradient. Experimental results are shown in Table 2. All results are obtained by averaging 30 independent runs. It should be noted that the experimental results of other algorithms in Table 2 are also obtained under the assumption that an attacker knows the same knowledge as the targeted system.

Table 2. Hardness of evasion under white-box attacks.

Model	PU3	PDF	MNIST
Linear-SVM	4.08	5.61	10.44
AFS Linear-SVM	4.41	9.60	8.00
RSE Linear-SVMs	5.21	6.48	11.17
ARE Linear-SVMs	5.43	12.01	11.28
RBF-SVM	4.33	6.44	21.48
AFS RBF-SVM	4.83	10.44	14.87
RSE RBF-SVMs	5.31	6.88	18.76
ARE RBF-SVMs	5.64	13.95	20.96

For the PU3 dataset, the results obtained with ARE SVMs and RSE SVMs are comparable, both outperforming single SVMs. When it comes to the PDF dataset, ARE SVMs notably surpass RSE SVMs and single SVMs in terms of performance. Regarding the MNIST dataset, ARE SVMs continue to deliver strong performance. Based on these observations, we can conclude that even under the most adverse conditions, the proposed method exhibits greater robustness against evasion attacks compared to RSE SVMs and single SVMs.

7.2. Generalization Capability

Each base classifier in AREC is selected by evaluating $G(\theta)$ and $S(\theta)$. According to [18], these classifiers will not reduce the classification accuracy significantly compared with a single classifier. Moreover, decision-making involving m classifiers improves classification accuracy. Our experimental results show that the classification performance of ARE SVMs outperforms single SVMs in most cases. It is noteworthy that almost every malicious PDF is correctly recognized by all eight models in the PDF dataset, hence we do not include these results in Table 3.

Table 3. Classification accuracy.

Model	PU3	MNIST
Linear-SVM	0.9440	0.9729
AFS Linear-SVM	0.9395	0.9698
RSE Linear-SVMs	0.9565	0.9746
ARE Linear-SVMs	0.9447	0.9733
RBF-SVM	0.9448	0.9910
AFS RBF-SVM	0.9410	0.9763
RSE RBF-SVMs	0.9599	0.9874
ARE RBF-SVMs	0.9499	0.9800

7.3. Limitations

While the proposed approach yields encouraging outcomes, there are several limitations to consider. Firstly, the wrapper-based adversarial feature selection technique introduced in [18] is incorporated during the training process. This feature selection method effectively balances accuracy and robustness. However, it entails increased computational complexity relative to single classifiers and RSE classifiers, particularly when dealing with a large initial number of features. Although classifiers with very few features are generally not preferred, employing feature selection via backward elimination can potentially reduce training time. Nonetheless, this does not address the issue at its core. Future work calls for the development of more efficient strategies to overcome this challenge.

Secondly, due to the hierarchical nature of feature selection in the proposed model, each classifier in the ensemble adds only one additional feature based on the previous classifier. In theory, it is possible that an attacker might infer some critical features from the feedback provided by the targeted system. However, practically speaking, this is quite challenging. The reason being that the outcome returned by the targeted system each time is derived from a unique combination of classifiers, and the system only returns the label of a sample, which does not reveal the value of the discriminant function $g(x)$. Hence, it becomes difficult to estimate the features of classifiers from the received results. An extreme scenario that cannot be entirely dismissed is if an attacker gains access to the parameters **p** of the targeted system through social engineering tactics or other means.

8. Conclusions

Machine learning technology was initially designed with the aim of enhancing generalization capabilities. Under this objective, machine learning has thrived and been widely deployed across numerous domains such as image recognition, intrusion detection, among others. However, conventional learning-based algorithms are inherently susceptible to adversarial attacks because their original design did not account for the presence of intelligent adversaries capable of manipulating their behavior to deceive classification algorithms.

In this paper, we propose a method to improve the adversarial robustness of ensemble classifiers through diversified feature selection and stochastic aggregation. Unlike conventional ensemble classifiers that aggregate multiple *weak* classifiers, our ensemble is composed of multiple *strong* classifiers. The *strong* classifiers within AREC are trained by optimizing both their generalization ability and robustness against evasion attacks. For the ensemble integration strategy, the generalization capacity is further bolstered by employing multiple classifier voting. The application of randomly selecting decision classifiers serves to obfuscate the decision boundary of AREC. Additionally, we have updated the gradient correlation measure to ensure it is applicable to any real-number feature. Experimental results across various tasks such as spam email filtering, PDF malware detection, and handwritten digit recognition demonstrate that our proposed approach offers superior robustness compared to conventional single and ensemble classifiers. Furthermore, in contrast to the state-of-the-art algorithm AFS [18], which trades off generalization capability for security, our method significantly boosts robustness while marginally improving generalization capability.

Our future works involve designing an efficient adversarial feature selection algorithm to mitigate the training costs associated with AREC. Additionally, we aim to extend the proposed gradient correlation metric to explore the security performance of diverse learning-based classifiers beyond the current scope.

Author Contributions: Conceptualization, F.Z. and K.L.; methodology, F.Z. and K.L.; software, F.Z. and K.L.; validation, F.Z., K.L. and Z.R.; formal analysis, F.Z., K.L. and Z.R.; investigation, F.Z. and K.L.; resources, F.Z. and K.L.; data curation, F.Z. and K.L.; writing—original draft preparation, F.Z.; writing—review and editing, F.Z., K.L. and Z.R.; visualization, F.Z., K.L. and Z.R.; supervision, F.Z. and K.L.; project administration, F.Z., K.L. and Z.R.; funding acquisition, F.Z. All authors have read and agreed to the published version of the manuscript.

Funding: This research was funded by Dongguan Science and Technology of Social Development Program grant number 20221800905182 and 20231800940522.

Data Availability Statement: No new data were created or analyzed in this study. Data sharing is not applicable to this article.

Conflicts of Interest: The authors declare no conflict of interest. The funders had no role in the design of the study; in the collection, analyses, or interpretation of data; in the writing of the manuscript, or in the decision to publish the results.

References

1. Zhang, W.; Li, X. Federated Transfer Learning for Intelligent Fault Diagnostics Using Deep Adversarial Networks With Data Privacy. *IEEE ASME Trans. Mechatronics* **2022**, *27*, 430–439. [CrossRef]

2. Wang, Z.; Cui, J.; Cai, W.; Li, Y. Partial Transfer Learning of Multidiscriminator Deep Weighted Adversarial Network in Cross-Machine Fault Diagnosis. *IEEE Trans. Instrum. Meas.* **2022**, *71*, 5010010. [CrossRef]
3. Shi, Y.; Han, Y.; Hu, Q.; Yang, Y.; Tian, Q. Query-Efficient Black-Box Adversarial Attack With Customized Iteration and Sampling. *IEEE Trans. Pattern Anal. Mach. Intell.* **2023**, *45*, 2226–2245. [CrossRef] [PubMed]
4. Kravchik, M.; Shabtai, A. Efficient Cyber Attack Detection in Industrial Control Systems Using Lightweight Neural Networks and PCA. *IEEE Trans. Dependable Secur. Comput.* **2022**, *19*, 2179–2197. [CrossRef]
5. Chen, L.; Ye, Y.; Bourlai, T. Adversarial machine learning in malware detection: Arms race between evasion attack and defense. In Proceedings of the 2017 European Intelligence and Security Informatics Conference (EISIC), Athens, Greece, 11–13 September 2017; pp. 99–106.
6. Liang, B.; Su, M.; You, W.; Shi, W.; Yang, G. Cracking classifiers for evasion: A case study on the google's phishing pages filter. In Proceedings of the 25th International Conference on World Wide Web, Montreal, QC, Canada, 11–15 April 2016; pp. 345–356.
7. Laskov, P.; Srndic, N. Practical evasion of a learning-based classifier: A case study. In Proceedings of the Security and Privacy (SP), San Jose, CA, USA, 18–21 May 2014; pp. 197–211.
8. Bhagoji, A.N.; Cullina, D.; Mittal, P. Dimensionality reduction as a defense against evasion attacks on machine learning classifiers. *arXiv* **2017**, arXiv:1704.02654.
9. Huang, R.; Xu, B.; Schuurmans, D.; Szepesvári, C. Learning with a Strong Adversary. *arXiv* **2015**, arXiv:1511.03034.
10. Papernot, N.; McDaniel, P.; Wu, X.; Jha, S.; Swami, A. Distillation as a defense to adversarial perturbations against deep neural networks. In Proceedings of the 2016 IEEE Symposium on Security and Privacy (SP), San Jose, CA, USA, 23–25 May 2016; pp. 582–597.
11. Strauss, T.; Hanselmann, M.; Junginger, A.; Ulmer, H. Ensemble methods as a defense to adversarial perturbations against deep neural networks. *arXiv* **2017**, arXiv:1709.03423.
12. Tramèr, F.; Kurakin, A.; Papernot, N.; Goodfellow, I.; Boneh, D.; McDaniel, P. Ensemble adversarial training: Attacks and defenses. *arXiv* **2017**, arXiv:1705.07204.
13. Smutz, C.; Stavrou, A. When a Tree Falls: Using Diversity in Ensemble Classifiers to Identify Evasion in Malware Detectors. In Proceedings of the Network and Distributed System Security (NDSS), San Jose, CA, USA, 21–24 February 2016.
14. Zhang, F.; Wang, Y.; Liu, S.; Wang, H. Decision-based evasion attacks on tree ensemble classifiers. *World Wide Web Internet Web Inf. Syst.* **2020**, *23*, 2957–2977. [CrossRef]
15. Kantchelian, A.; Tygar, J.; Joseph, A. Evasion and hardening of tree ensemble classifiers. In Proceedings of the International Conference on Machine Learning, New York, NY, USA, 19–24 June 2016; pp. 2387–2396.
16. Zhang, F.; Wang, Y.; Wang, H. Gradient Correlation: Are Ensemble Classifiers More Robust Against Evasion Attacks in Practical Settings? In *WISE 2018, Proceedings of the International Conference on Web Information Systems Engineering, Dubai, United Arab Emirates, 12–15 November 2018*; Springer: Berlin/Heidelberg, Germany, 2018; pp. 96–110.
17. Pang, T.; Xu, K.; Du, C.; Chen, N.; Zhu, J. Improving Adversarial Robustness via Promoting Ensemble Diversity. *arXiv* **2019**, arXiv:1901.08846.
18. Zhang, F.; Chan, P.P.; Biggio, B.; Yeung, D.S.; Roli, F. Adversarial feature selection against evasion attacks. *IEEE Trans. Cybern.* **2016**, *46*, 766–777. [CrossRef] [PubMed]
19. Biggio, B.; Roli, F. Wild patterns: Ten years after the rise of adversarial machine learning. *Pattern Recognit.* **2018**, *84*, 317–331. [CrossRef]
20. Biggio, B.; Corona, I.; Maiorca, D.; Nelson, B.; Šrndić, N.; Laskov, P.; Giacinto, G.; Roli, F. Evasion attacks against machine learning at test time. In *Machine Learning and Knowledge Discovery in Databases, Proceedings of the Joint European Conference on Machine Learning and Knowledge Discovery in Databases, Prague, Czech Republic, 23–27 September 2013*; Springer: Berlin/Heidelberg, Germany, 2013; pp. 387–402.
21. Biggio, B.; Corona, I.; Nelson, B.; Rubinstein, B.I.; Maiorca, D.; Fumera, G.; Giacinto, G.; Roli, F. Security evaluation of support vector machines in adversarial environments. In *Support Vector Machines Applications*; Springer: Berlin/Heidelberg, Germany, 2014; pp. 105–153.
22. Xu, L.; Zhan, Z.; Xu, S.; Ye, K. An evasion and counter-evasion study in malicious websites detection. *arXiv* **2014**, arXiv:1408.1993.
23. Alzaqebah, A.; Aljarah, I.; Al-Kadi, O. A hierarchical intrusion detection system based on extreme learning machine and nature-inspired optimization. *Comput. Secur.* **2023**, *124*, 102957. [CrossRef]
24. Liu, Y.; Chen, X.; Liu, C.; Song, D. Delving into transferable adversarial examples and black-box attacks. *arXiv* **2016**, arXiv:1611.02770.
25. Shokri, R.; Stronati, M.; Song, C.; Shmatikov, V. Membership inference attacks against machine learning models. In Proceedings of the Security and Privacy (SP), San Jose, CA, USA, 22–26 May 2017; pp. 3–18.
26. Alzantot, M.; Sharma, Y.; Chakraborty, S.; Srivastava, M. GenAttack: Practical Black-box Attacks with Gradient-Free Optimization. *arXiv* **2018**, arXiv:1805.11090.
27. Zhang, N.; Zhang, Y.; Song, S.; Chen, C.L.P. A Review of Robust Machine Scheduling. *IEEE Trans. Autom. Sci. Eng.* **2023**. [CrossRef]
28. Goodfellow, I.J.; Shlens, J.; Szegedy, C. Explaining and Harnessing Adversarial Examples. In Proceedings of the 3rd International Conference on Learning Representations, ICLR 2015, San Diego, CA, USA, 7–9 May 2015.
29. Carlini, N.; Wagner, D. Defensive distillation is not robust to adversarial examples. *arXiv* **2016**, arXiv:1607.04311.

30. Carlini, N.; Wagner, D. Towards evaluating the robustness of neural networks. In Proceedings of the 2017 IEEE Symposium on Security and Privacy (SP), San Diego, CA, USA, 22–24 May 2017; pp. 39–57.
31. Meng, D.; Chen, H. Magnet: A two-pronged defense against adversarial examples. In Proceedings of the 2017 ACM SIGSAC Conference on Computer and Communications Security, Dallas, TX, USA, 30 October–3 November 2017; ACM: New York, NY, USA, 2017; pp. 135–147.
32. Metzen, J.H.; Genewein, T.; Fischer, V.; Bischoff, B. On detecting adversarial perturbations. *arXiv* **2017**, arXiv:1702.04267.
33. Huang, B.; Kei, Z.; Wang, Y.; Wang, W.; Shen, L.; Liu, F. Adversarial Defence by Diversified Simultaneous Training of Deep Ensembles. In Proceedings of the Thirty-Fifth AAAI Conference on Artificial Intelligence, Thirty-Third Conference on Innovative Applications of Artificial Intelligence and the Eleventh Symposium on Educational Advances in Artificial Intelligence, Virtual, 2–9 February 2021; Volume 35, pp. 7823–7831.
34. Grosse, K.; Manoharan, P.; Papernot, N.; Backes, M.; McDaniel, P. On the (statistical) detection of adversarial examples. *arXiv* **2017**, arXiv:1702.06280.
35. Lee, K.; Lee, K.; Lee, H.; Shin, J. A simple unified framework for detecting out-of-distribution samples and adversarial attacks. In Proceedings of the Advances in Neural Information Processing Systems, Montreal, QC, Canada, 2–8 December 2018; pp. 7167–7177.
36. Huang, B.; Wang, Y.; Wang, W. Model-Agnostic Adversarial Detection by Random Perturbations. In Proceedings of the 28th International Joint Conference on Artificial Intelligence, Macao, China, 10–16 August 2019; pp. 4689–4696.
37. Ho, T.K. The random subspace method for constructing decision forests. *IEEE Trans. Pattern Anal. Mach. Intell.* **1998**, *20*, 832–844.
38. Breiman, L. Random forests. *Mach. Learn.* **2001**, *45*, 5–32. [CrossRef]
39. Chen, T.; Guestrin, C. Xgboost: A scalable tree boosting system. In Proceedings of the 22nd ACM SIGKDD International Conference on Knowledge Discovery and Data Mining, San Francisco, CA, USA, 13–17 August 2016; ACM: New York, NY, USA, 2016; pp. 785–794.
40. Kim, H.C.; Pang, S.; Je, H.M.; Kim, D.; Bang, S.Y. Constructing support vector machine ensemble. *Pattern Recognit.* **2003**, *36*, 2757–2767. [CrossRef]
41. Dong, Y.S.; Han, K.S. Boosting SVM Classifiers by Ensemble. In Proceedings of the 14th International Conference on World Wide Web (WWW '05), Chiba, Japan, 10–14 May 2005; pp. 1072–1073.
42. Katakis, I.; Tsoumakas, G.; Vlahavas, I. Tracking recurring contexts using ensemble classifiers: An application to email filtering. *Knowl. Inf. Syst.* **2010**, *22*, 371–391. [CrossRef]
43. Vapnik, V. *The Nature of Statistical Learning*, 1st ed.; Springer: New York, NY, USA, 1999.
44. Demontis, A.; Melis, M.; Biggio, B.; Maiorca, D.; Arp, D.; Rieck, K.; Corona, I.; Giacinto, G.; Roli, F. Yes, machine learning can be more secure! a case study on Android malware detection. *IEEE Trans. Dependable Secur. Comput.* **2017**, *16*, 711–724. [CrossRef]
45. Mujtaba, G.; Shuib, L.; Raj, R.G.; Majeed, N.; Al-Garadi, M.A. Email classification research trends: Review and open issues. *IEEE Access* **2017**, *5*, 9044–9064. [CrossRef]
46. Androutsopoulos, I.; Paliouras, G.; Michelakis, E. *Learning to Filter Unsolicited Commercial E-Mail*; Technical Report No. 2004/2; National Center for Scientific Research "Demokritos": Athens, Greek, 2004.

Disclaimer/Publisher's Note: The statements, opinions and data contained in all publications are solely those of the individual author(s) and contributor(s) and not of MDPI and/or the editor(s). MDPI and/or the editor(s) disclaim responsibility for any injury to people or property resulting from any ideas, methods, instructions or products referred to in the content.

Article

Prediction Model of Ammonia Nitrogen Concentration in Aquaculture Based on Improved AdaBoost and LSTM

Yiyang Wang [1], Dehao Xu [2], Xianpeng Li [2] and Wei Wang [2,*]

[1] School of Electrical and Automation Engineering, Liaoning Institute of Science and Technology, Benxi 117004, China; yaopeng17@sohu.com
[2] College of Information Engineering, Dalian Ocean University, Dalian 116023, China; xudehaopro@sina.com (D.X.); 15829169220@163.com (X.L.)
* Correspondence: ww_wangwei@dlou.edu.cn

Abstract: The concentration of ammonia nitrogen is significant for intensive aquaculture, and if the concentration of ammonia nitrogen is too high, it will seriously affect the survival state of aquaculture. Therefore, prediction and control of the ammonia nitrogen concentration in advance is essential. This paper proposed a combined model based on X Adaptive Boosting (XAdaBoost) and the Long Short-Term Memory neural network (LSTM) to predict ammonia nitrogen concentration in mariculture. Firstly, the weight assignment strategy was improved, and the number of correction iterations was introduced to retard the shortcomings of data error accumulation caused by the AdaBoost basic algorithm. Then, the XAdaBoost algorithm generated and combined several LSTM su-models to predict the ammonia nitrogen concentration. Finally, there were two experiments conducted to verify the effectiveness of the proposed prediction model. In the ammonia nitrogen concentration prediction experiment, compared with the LSTM and other comparison models, the RMSE of the XAdaBoost–LSTM model was reduced by about 0.89–2.82%, the MAE was reduced by about 0.72–2.47%, and the MAPE was reduced by about 8.69–18.39%. In the model stability experiment, the RMSE, MAE, and MAPE of the XAdaBoost–LSTM model decreased by about 1–1.5%, 0.7–1.7%, and 7–14%. From these two experiments, the evaluation indexes of the XAdaBoost–LSTM model were superior to the comparison models, which proves that the model has good prediction accuracy and stability and lays a foundation for monitoring and regulating the change of ammonia nitrogen concentration in the future.

Keywords: aquaculture; adaptive boosting algorithm; LSTM; combined prediction

MSC: 37N99

Citation: Wang, Y.; Xu, D.; Li, X.; Wang, W. Prediction Model of Ammonia Nitrogen Concentration in Aquaculture Based on Improved AdaBoost and LSTM. *Mathematics* **2024**, *12*, 627. https://doi.org/10.3390/math12050627

Received: 17 January 2024
Revised: 16 February 2024
Accepted: 19 February 2024
Published: 20 February 2024

Copyright: © 2024 by the authors. Licensee MDPI, Basel, Switzerland. This article is an open access article distributed under the terms and conditions of the Creative Commons Attribution (CC BY) license (https://creativecommons.org/licenses/by/4.0/).

1. Introduction

In the world, China is the first aquaculture country and the first fishery country [1], and the output of aquatic products has ranked first in the world for 29 consecutive years since 1989 [2]. China's fish production from aquaculture has been far more than other countries since 1991. Aquaculture has changed the status quo of traditional capture fisheries, and aquaculture production has exceeded capture production. In the aquaculture process, the complex culture environment, high culture density, biological excretion, and other reasons will lead to the rise of ammonia nitrogen concentration in the water body. The increase in ammonia nitrogen concentration will lead to the rise of toxicity in water, which will lead to the poisoning of large areas of aquatic animals. If water quality control is not carried out in time, it will lead to many deaths [3]. Therefore, in aquaculture, it is crucial to monitor and control the ammonia concentration in advance.

At present, the detection of ammonia nitrogen concentration in China is divided into two categories [4]. One is the sampling laboratory detection method, which is highly accurate, but the time of detection is long, the cost is high, and the experimental results cannot be reproduced. The other is the reagent method, using reagents or test paper on-site inspection; the method is short in time, but the accuracy is low, and both detection methods cannot provide a stable basis for the current water quality control. With the development of deep learning, the emergence of the neural network prediction model provides a new method for monitoring and controlling water quality in aquaculture. In the past, many scholars used mathematical models or statistical models to predict water quality parameters in aquaculture water quality; the standard models mainly included linear regression [5] and multiple regression models [6]. The researchers used these models to establish a linear relationship between water quality parameters and input variables. However, due to the complex environment of aquaculture water quality and the coupling relationship between water quality parameters, although these regression models can realize the prediction of water quality parameters, the prediction accuracy is difficult to guarantee. With deep research, water quality parameter prediction models gradually considered the nonlinear relationship between input and output. Commonly used models include back propagation neural network (BPNN) and support vector machine (SVM) neural network. Chen et al. [7] used backward propagation neural network (BPNN), the adaptive neural fuzzy inference system (ANFIS) method, and multiple linear regression (MLR) models to predict the dissolved oxygen concentration of Feitsui Reservoir in northern Taiwan. The results showed that the BPNN model and MLR model are less accurate than the ANFIS. Nong et al. [8] used an SVM neural network model coupled with data denoising, feature selection technology, and parameter optimization methods to establish a dissolved oxygen model. They used the model to predict dissolved oxygen in different locations of the South-to-North Water Transfer project. The results showed that the SVM neural network coupled with multiple intelligent technologies is more accurate than the comparison model. Liu Ru et al. [9] used the Pearson correlation coefficient (PCC) to analyze the correlation of each index in water and monitor water quality with five indicators with high correlation. The K nearest neighbors (KNN) algorithm was used. The integrated learning AdaBoost algorithm and decision tree three machine learning algorithms predicted the monthly average value of ammonia nitrogen concentration in a water body. This method provided solutions for water body data analysis and adopted a variety of algorithms to verify the prediction. The structure of these models is relatively simple and cannot be predicted with high precision. Recurrent neural networks (RNN) have emerged with the continuous development of theories and techniques. RNN can retain the history information in the data by hiding the state and contributing the included history information to the calculation of the current time step. In addition, RNN can capture historical patterns in the data as it is input, improving the accuracy of the final prediction. Sagar et al. [10] used wireless sensors to collect pollutant concentration data in Indian cities and input the acquired data into the RNN model. Experiments showed that the RNN model performed well on different urban pollutant data sets. However, RNN has the phenomenon of gradient disappearance or explosion, so many scholars have improved the RNN to obtain two models: Long Short-Term Memory Network (LSTM) and Gated Recurrent Unit (GRU). Nitzan et al. [11] combined climate measurement data with water quality data and used LSTM to predict ammonia nitrogen and nitrate concentrations in water after wastewater treatment. The final experiment showed that the accuracy of ammonia nitrogen concentration was 99%, and the accuracy of nitrate concentration was 90%. Huan et al. [12] used a gradient lifting decision tree to select data features and LSTM to predict dissolved oxygen; the results showed that the accuracy was better than that of the comparison model PSO-LSSVM. In data acquisition, the sensor will cause noise in the collected data due to human or environmental factors. Therefore, some scholars have combined the denoising intelligence algorithm with the neural network model and applied it to water quality parameter prediction (see Yan et al. [13]). First, the original ammonia nitrogen concentration data is divided into several sub-sequences using variational modes. Secondly, the GRU model is used to model and predict the subsequence. Finally, the prediction results of the subsequences are added together. The results show that the prediction accuracy is improved compared with the comparison model. In addition, some scholars use intelligent algorithms to enhance the performance of neural network models. Jannatul et al. [14] used the particle swarm optimization (PSO) method to optimize the hyperparameters in the LSTM model to improve the LSTM model's ability to learn time series features. They conducted experiments using the water level observation data of observation stations along the Brahmaputra River, Ganges River, and Megna River in Bangladesh. The final results showed that the PSO–LSTM model was superior to the ANN, PSO–ANN, and LSTM models in predicting water level. Ganiyu et al. [15] adopted adaptive boosting (AdaBoost) to improve the LSTM and GRU models and conducted experiments on the crude oil price data set. By comparing single LSTM and GRU models, it has been proved that AdaBoost improves the prediction performance of the LSTM and GRU models.

This paper proposes a solution to the issue of inaccurate and unstable prediction models for ammonia nitrogen concentration. The proposed solution is a combined XAdaBoost and LSTM prediction model that utilizes turbot culture data collected by the intensive seawater circulation control system. The model takes inputs such as temperature, dissolved oxygen, pH, and conductivity and predicts the ammonia nitrogen concentration for the next moment. To address the error accumulation problem of the AdaBoost base algorithm, the paper proposes a new weight assignment strategy, introduces a corrective iteration number, and combines the improved AdaBoost algorithm with multiple LSTM sub-models for prediction.

2. Introduction of Basic Theory
2.1. Adaptive Enhancement Algorithm

Adaptive boosting [16] (AdaBoost) is a common type of integrated learning algorithm boosting class, first applied to classification problems and gradually used in regression tasks as the algorithm evolves [17]. AdaBoost's key feature is its adaptability. This is achieved by adjusting the weights of data points based on their error rates in the previous sub-prediction model. Data with high error rates are given more weight, while data with low error rates are given less weight. This process is repeated for each sub-prediction model, using the newly weighted data to train the next model. Each sub-prediction model builds on the previous one in the iteration process, aiming to solve the data poorly processed by the earlier sub-model. When the number of iterations or the error rate satisfies the set value, the algorithm will stop the operation and save the final model. The principle of AdaBoost is shown in Figure 1.

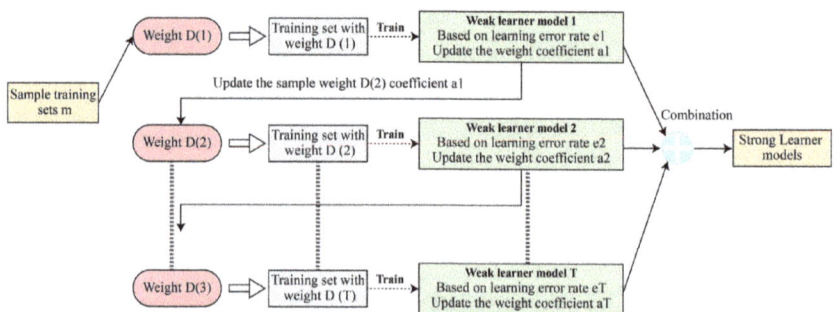

Figure 1. Schematic diagram of adaptive enhancement algorithm.

As can be seen from Figure 1, the algorithm can be divided into three modules: the initial value weight assignment module, the sub-prediction model training module, and the sub-model combination module. The initial value weight assignment module mainly assigns initial values to the data sample weights $D(1)$. m sample training sets are shown in the figure, and then each data initial value is $1/m$. Suppose our training samples are:

$$T = \{(x_1, y_1), (x_2, y_2), (x_3, y_3) \ldots (x_m, y_m)\} \tag{1}$$

where represents the sample set, x_m, y_m represents the input quantity and output quantity, respectively.

Then the output weights of the nth weak learner in the training set are

$$D(n) = (w_{n1}, w_{n2}, w_{n3}, w_{n4}, \ldots, w_{nm}); \quad w_{1i} = \frac{1}{m}; i = 1, 2, 3, \ldots, m \quad (2)$$

The sub-model training module refers to training the weak learner model to the optimal state by selecting part of the data set, comparing the predicted values with the actual values in the training process, obtaining the training data errors, and increasing the data weights with significant error rates; otherwise, reducing them. The updated weights are applied to the next sub-model in the prediction process, and each sub-model puts more operations on the data with more significant error rates based on the previous sub-model. The sub-model combination is the process of combining trained models to form a robust learning model, in which more weights are assigned to the sub-prediction models with small error rates to ensure the accuracy of the vital learning model.

2.2. Long and Short-Term Memory Neural Networks

Recurrent neural networks can handle time series problems, but with the continuous input of time series, the traditional recurrent neural networks are prone to gradient disappearance or gradient explosion due to the abnormal computation of gradients, which leads to the degradation of model accuracy [18]. To solve the impact caused by gradient disappearance or gradient explosion of recurrent neural networks, the LSTM model is generated by introducing three gating units and memory units based on the improvement of traditional recurrent neural networks [19]. The control of the information replaces the information retained in the memory unit through the three gating units; the principle of the LSTM algorithm is shown in Figure 2.

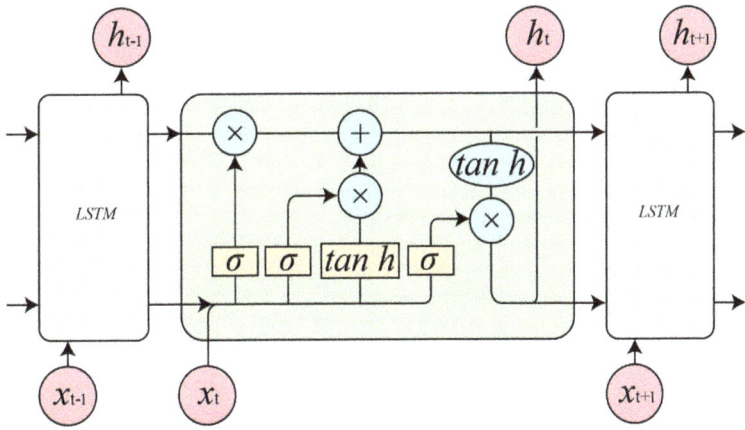

Figure 2. LSTM algorithm schematic.

Figure 2 shows that the input of each LSTM cell contains the current moment input information and the previous moment memory information, and the LSTM cell contains forgetting gates, input gates, and output gates to filter the information in the memory cell by forgetting gates:

$$f_t = \sigma(W_f * [h_{t-1}, x_t] + b_f) \quad (3)$$

where, f_t is the output activation value, σ is the Sigmoid function, after Sigmoid can obtain the number between 0 and 1, it will be multiplied with the memory unit of the previous moment bit by bit for memory retention and forgetting, W_f represents the weight matrix in the forget gate, b_f represents the bias matrix in the forget gate, h_{t-1} represents the output state at the previous time, x_t represents the input at the current time. The final result is a number between 0 and 1. When f_t is zero, the information is forgotten, and when f_t is 1, the information is retained.

The input gate determines how much information about the current moment is retained. The purpose of the input gate is to determine the importance of the current input to the overall situation:

$$i_t = \sigma(W_i * [h_{t-1}, x_t] + b_i) \tag{4}$$

$$\widetilde{C}_t = \tanh(W_c * [h_{t-1}, x_t] + b_c) \tag{5}$$

where i is similar to the formula of the forgetting gate, which filters the input at the current moment. The candidate output state of the current moment of the input gate is a nonlinear transformation of the hidden state of the previous moment and the input of the current moment. tanh is another activation function, no matter how large the input of the activation function is; the final output is the number in the interval $[-1,1]$. W represents the weight matrix in the output gate, and C represents the candidate state weight matrix in the output gate. Both W and C are bias matrices.

The forgetting gate and the input gate work together to update the memory, and the new memory contains the memory retained by the forgetting gate and the memory added by the input gate.

$$C_t = f_t * C_{t-1} + i_t * \widetilde{C}_t \tag{6}$$

C_t represents the state of the cell at the current time; it can be seen from Equation (6) that the current cell state is affected by the forgetting gate as well as the input gate.

Filter which of the current memory cells are used as the hidden state and output for the next moment through the output gate.

$$O_t = \sigma(W_o * [h_{t-1}, x_t] + b_o) \tag{7}$$

O_t is the output value of the output gate at the current time and W_o is the weight matrix of the output gate at the current time. b_o is the bias matrix of the output gate. The output state at the current moment is calculated using the following formula:

$$h_t = O_t * \tanh(C_t) \tag{8}$$

h_t will be fed into the next LSTM cell as the input information at the next moment.

LSTM improves the long-term dependence problem in RNN by introducing the structure of the cell state including the forgetting gate, input gate, and output gate, and its performance is usually better than the temporal recurrent neural network and hidden Markov model. LSTM itself can also be used as a complex nonlinear unit to construct a larger deep network and this sets the stage for our following research.

3. XAdaBoost–LSTM Based Ammonia Concentration Prediction Model

3.1. Fundamentals of Predictive Models

The LSTM ammonia nitrogen concentration prediction model is based on time series prediction, taking into account the effects of temperature, salinity, and pH while also considering the temporal nature of ammonia nitrogen concentration. However, the stability of a single LSTM ammonia nitrogen concentration prediction model is poor, so ensemble learning algorithms are selected to combine multiple sub models to improve model accuracy and robustness. The proposed model mainly combines the advantages of the XAdaBoost algorithm and LSTM model. The basic idea of XAdaboost–LSTM is to use LSTM as the base model and enhance it using the XAdaboost algorithm. Specifically, multiple LSTM models can be trained, each using different data sets and features, and their prediction results can be combined to form a more accurate and robust model. The basic working principle of the XAdaboost LSTM model is as follows: Firstly, the weight W is initialized through the total number of experimental samples, and then the LSTM model is used as a sub model. The LSTM sub model is trained using the sample data with weight W to obtain the prediction results. The weight of the sample data is recalculated based on the prediction results, and the weight of data with high prediction error rates is amplified; the sample weight of data with small prediction error coefficients is reduced. When the number of predicted sample points with an error rate greater than the set error rate is equal to T, the sample weight is set to 0. Linear combination is performed on weak learners based on their performance, and the proportion of each sub model in the strong learning model is determined based on the performance of each sub model. Finally, the final weight is combined with the model to obtain the final prediction model.

3.2. Improved Adaptive Enhancement Algorithm (XAaBoost)

Prediction tasks can have error data during data collection and recording, and since most tasks are used to predict outliers, the sample error data cannot be accurately removed during preprocessing. Therefore, it is essential to identify the error data when AdaBoost is reassigned to the sample data. In this paper, we deal with the prediction task and propose that the XAdaBoost algorithm is used to improve the model prediction accuracy and robustness by combining previous research on classification tasks to address this drawback of AdaBoost's error accumulation.

Suppose the number of iterations of the AdaBoost algorithm is T. Given an error range according to the model, it is divided into four categories according to the number of accurate predictions.

(1) If the prediction error is less than d in each of the T iterations, then the prediction value of each iteration is less than the error range, which means that each sub-model is correct in processing this sample.
(2) The number of errors less than d in T iterations is greater than $T/2$, which means that the number of correct predictions in T sub-models is greater than the number of errors in this data.
(3) Similarly, less than $T/2$ means that the number of correctly predicted sub-models is less than the number of incorrect ones.
(4) The error rate is greater than d in all T iterations, which means that none of the samples are accurate after T iterations.

Based on the above four cases, one more correction iteration is performed, at which point the sample weight update strategy is as follows:

The data in (4) above are considered as wrong data and the weights are assigned to 0; case (3) is assigned a larger value of weights than case (4), and since there are less than the number of correct ones, the weights are low in the previous sub-models and are assigned more in the last time for correction. Then, as per (1), each prediction results in lower correct weights. Therefore, $T + 1$ iterations are used, and the error data are removed in the last iteration, and the weights are assigned more reasonably; the last sub-model is used to correct the previous model containing error data. The previous sub-models are combined on the basis of the last correction.

3.3. Constructing a Prediction Model

In this paper, we used XAdaBoost combined with LSTM, which could effectively take into account the data temporality as the ammonia nitrogen concentration prediction sub-model, and used the AdaBoost integrated learning algorithm to iteratively enhance the LSTM sub-model.

(1) Assume that the number of iterations $t = 1, 2, \ldots, T$ and the initialized data weights are

$$W_t(i) = 1/N \tag{9}$$

where $W_{T-1}(i)$ denotes the sample weight of the algorithm at the Tth iteration of the LSTM sub-model, and N denotes the total number of samples of the experiment.

(2) The LSTM was used to build the sub-model $W_{T-1}(i)$ to train the sample data with the weight of $W_{T-1}(i)$ to obtain the prediction result $\hat{y}$ and save the obtained sub-model.

(3) The sample data weights were recalculated by the prediction results $\hat{y}$, and the weights of the data with large prediction error rate were enlarged and trained by sub-model iterations.

$$e_{max}(x) = max(y - \hat{y}) \tag{10}$$

$$e_{T-1}(x) = \frac{(y - \hat{y})}{e_{max}} \tag{11}$$

where: e_{max} denotes the maximum error, and e_{T-1} denotes the error rate of the sub-model at $T-1$ iterations.

(4) After repeating iterations T times.

At the $T+1$ st iteration, given the error rate d, $e_T(i)$ denotes the error of the ith sample in t iterations. If the number of $e_T(i) > d$ is equal to T let $W_T(i) = 0$.

(5) The weak learners were combined linearly according to their performance, and their weight in the strong learning model was judged by the performance of each sub-model:

$$\partial_T = \frac{1 - e_T}{e_T} \tag{12}$$

where, ∂_T denotes the weight of the Tth sub-model to the strong learning model.

(6) After each training session, the training data weights could be updated by the data error rate and the model share:

$$W_{T+1} = \frac{W_T}{Z_T} \partial_T^{1-e_T} \tag{13}$$

$$Z_T = \sum_{i=1}^{N} W_T \partial_T^{1-e_T} \tag{14}$$

where Z_T denotes the normalization factor, in order to normalize the data weights after the iteration.

(7) The strong learning model was obtained by the combination of the final weights and the model.

$$H(x) = \sum_{t=1}^{T} \partial_t M_t(x) \tag{15}$$

where the output result of the final combined model represented the output of each sub-model, which represented the weight of the T-th sub-model. The above improved AdaBoost combination was used to generate the LSTM sub-model; the model structure is shown in Figure 3.

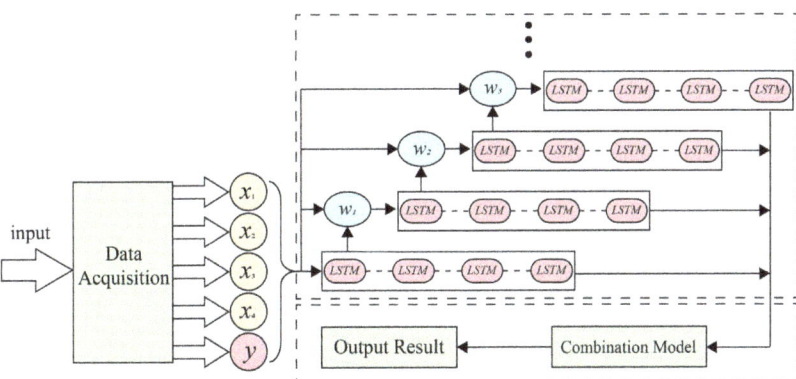

Figure 3. XAdaBoost–LSTM model frame diagram.

In Figure 3, We can divide the diagram into four parts: data input, sub-model training, sub-model combination, and result output. The data input part was mainly used to preprocess the data and specify the input and output variables for the preprocessed data. The sub-model training part was mainly used for data to train the XAdaBoost and LSTM models and update and determine model weights. The sub-model combination part was used to obtain the strong learning model by combining the final weights and the model and then outputting the final result. Such a model architecture inevitably has some defects. The model architecture contained two algorithms, XAdaBoost and LSTM, so the overall combined model also had problems, such as the model accuracy being affected by the balance of data set division and long training time.

3.4. Forecasting Process

The flow chart is divided into four parts: data acquisition, data pre-processing, model training and combination, and output. The data acquisition test object was turbot, which was reared in intensive recirculating seawater culture mode. The temperature, dissolved oxygen, pH, and conductivity data in the culture water were collected by sensors and saved to the corresponding database through PLC (programmable logic controller). A programmable controller was mainly used in the experiment to automatically realize the water level regulation, oxygen pump work, and sensor acquisition of the circulation aquaculture system. The nano reagent method [20] was used to measure ammonia nitrogen concentration, which was simple, rapid, and sensitive to meet the data collection requirements. The data pre-processing part consisted of three primary operations, namely: outlier processing, normalization, and partitioning of the training data set. If the original data contained outliers then the outliers were cleaned up and supplemented by linear interpolation. Since the original data had different units of each feature variable, the actual data was normalized in order to eliminate the effect of dimensionality [21], and was used to divide the data into training set and test set. The model training and combination part mainly used the training data to train the XAdaBoost–LSTM model and saved the final parameters to combine into a robust learner model. The output section outputted the prediction results of the training and test sets; the model prediction process is shown in Figure 4.

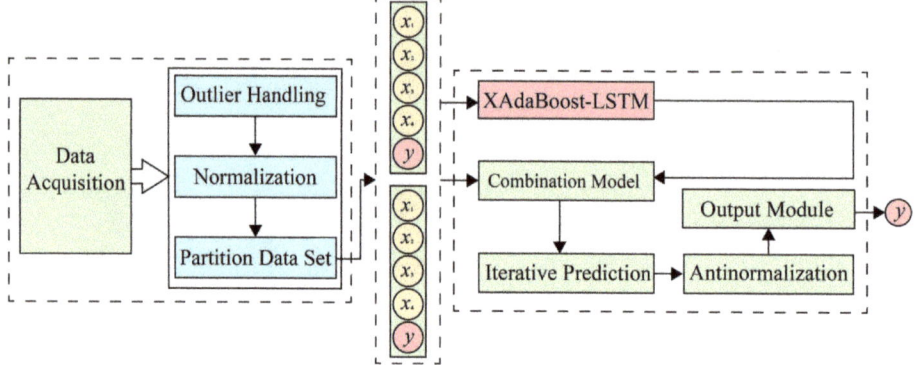

Figure 4. Model prediction flow chart.

4. Analysis of Results

4.1. Raw Data

To verify the feasibility of the XAdaBoost algorithm improvement strategy and the accuracy and stability of the XAdaBoost–LSTM algorithm modeling prediction, the turbot breeding data measured by the intensive seawater circulation control system was used as the modeling data in the experiment. The data collection period was from 08:00 to 18:00 every day from April to June 2017, with a time interval of 2 h; a total of 236 data groups were collected. In the experiment, the corresponding sensor module was used to collect water quality parameters such as temperature, dissolved oxygen, pH value, and electrical conductivity of each group, and the ammonia nitrogen concentration of each group was measured using the chemical reagent method. Among them, the temperature sensor model used was a PT100-type platinum resistance contact sensor; the sensor range was −5–60 °C. The dissolved oxygen concentration sensor used was the FDO 700 IQ sensor of the German WTW company; the measurement range of the dissolved oxygen sensor was 0–20 mg/L. The pH sensor used was a Senso-Lyt 700 IQ SEA sensor from WTW, Germany, which had a measurement range of 2–14. The conductivity sensor used was the TetraCon700 IQ sensor of WTW company in Germany; the measurement range was 0.1–500 ms/cm. Of course, there are some accuracy errors in the actual data acquisition process of the sensor that could be avoided; for example, the temperature sensor had an error of ±0.5%, and the dissolved oxygen concentration also had an error of ±0.01 mg/L. However, these errors are minor compared to the numerical value, and you can make negligible assumptions. Among them, the measured value of ammonia nitrogen concentration was the predicted quantity, which was the model output, and the other water quality factors were used as auxiliary variables as the model input. Some experimental data are shown in Table 1.

Table 1. Partial data of water quality parameters of turbot culture.

Moment	Temperature °C	Dissolved Oxygen (mg·L^{-1})	pH	Electrical Conductivity (ms·cm^{-1})	Ammonia Nitrogen Concentration (mg·L^{-1})
8:00	14.9	8.2	7.85	41.1	0.18
10:00	14.7	8.26	7.85	41.1	0.21
12:00	14.5	8.27	7.91	41.2	0.23
...	...	...	...	...	...
18:00	14.3	8.33	7.91	41.1	0.24

Table 1 shows that the turbot culture data contained four input features, temperature, dissolved oxygen, pH, and conductivity, and one output feature, ammonia nitrogen concentration.

4.2. Data Pre-Processing

The 3σ rule and median filtering method have been used to detect outliers in previous research in the lab [22]. The 3σ criterion, where σ stands for standard deviation, measures how far a number in a data set deviates from its mean. In typically or nearly normally distributed data sets, approximately 68.27% of the data is within the mean $\pm 1\sigma$, 95.45% of the data is within the mean $\pm 2\sigma$, and 99.73% of the data is within the mean $\pm 3\sigma$. Therefore, if the value of a data point is outside the range of the mean $\pm 3\sigma$, we can consider this data point as an outlier.

Since the input variables are not unique and have different values and units, it is necessary to normalize the data to eliminate the influence of the magnitude [23]. There are two standard normalization methods: the first is linear function normalization, which converts all input values into values in the interval [0, 1]. The second method is zero-mean normalization, which transforms the data set into a data set with zero mean and one variance. This experiment uses the first normalization method, i.e., linear function normalization, with the following equation:

$$X_N = \frac{X - X_{MIN}}{X_{MAX} - X_{MIN}} \tag{16}$$

where X_N represents the normalized data, X_{MIN} represents the smallest number in a feature data set, and X_{MAX} represents the largest number in a feature data set. For the missing values among them, linear interpolation is used to fill the missing data. If there is a missing value at time t, a linear interpolation operation is performed using the known data before and after time t, and the result is supplemented as the value at time t with the following formula:

$$x_t = x_{t_q} + \frac{(x_{t_h} - x_{t_q})(t - t_q)}{t_h - t_q} \tag{17}$$

where x_t represents the missing value at the time t, x_{t_q} represents the most recent known data before time t, and x_{t_h} represents the most recent known data after time t.

4.3. Operating Environment and Evaluation Criteria

The ammonia nitrogen concentration prediction is a multivariate prediction model that uses SciPy(1.5.4), NumPy(1.14.3), Matplotlib(2.2.2), Pandas(0.23.0), and Scikit-learn(0.24.2) libraries in machine learning and Theano, TensorFlow(2.0), and Keras(2.3.1) libraries in deep learning. This experiment used the LSTM model as a sub-model, which contained 150 neurons in the input layer, 50 neurons in the hidden layer, and 1 neuron in the output layer. In order to prevent the occurrence of overfitting, the value of Dropout was set to 0.3, the Optimizer selected the ADAM algorithm to optimize, and the loss function selected the mean square error (MAE) to calculate. After experimental verification in the XAdaBoost model, the number of iterations was finally selected as three, and the model used for iteration was the LSTM model, in which the loss function was linear. The experiment used the temperature, conductivity, pH value, and dissolved oxygen concentration as the feature data input, and the ammonia nitrogen concentration was used as the output to train the model. Before training the model, the data was divided into 76% of the training set and 24% of the test set. In the laboratory culture process, temperature, electrical conductivity, water pH and dissolved oxygen concentration changes all affect the change of ammonia nitrogen concentration in the water. Therefore, in aquaculture, temperature, electrical conductivity, water pH, dissolved oxygen concentration, and ammonia nitrogen concentration interact with each other, and the relationship is coupled. Therefore, in this experiment, temperature, electrical conductivity, water pH, and dissolved oxygen concentration closely related to ammonia nitrogen concentration were used as inputs.

In evaluating the model, the evaluation criteria used in this paper were as follows: the root mean square error (RMSE), the mean absolute error (MAE), and the mean absolute percentage error (MAPE) [24].

The formulas of the three evaluation criteria are shown below:

$$RMSE = \sqrt{\frac{\sum_{i=1}^{n}(y^*_i - y_i)^2}{n}} \quad (18)$$

$$MAE = \frac{\sum_{i=1}^{n}\left|\frac{y^*_i - y_i}{y_i}\right|}{n} \quad (19)$$

$$MAPE = \frac{\sum_{i=1}^{n}\left|\frac{y^*_i}{y_i}\right|}{n} \quad (20)$$

where y^*_i represents the predicted value of the model, y_i represents the true value, and n represents the number of samples. $RMSE$, MAE, $MAPE$ represent three evaluation criteria containing information on the error between the predicted and true values as well as the sample proportion.

4.4. Experimental Analysis and Evaluation

Since the last iteration of the XAdaBoost algorithm was to be based on the comparison of multiple error rate results, the number of iterations T = 3 was finally selected in this paper after several experiments; the last one was used as the corrected iteration after improvement. The error rate range d in the experiment was selected based on the distribution of the first 2 error rates in the model. A comparison of the LSTM prediction model with the AdaBoost–LSTM prediction model and the prediction results are shown in Figure 5.

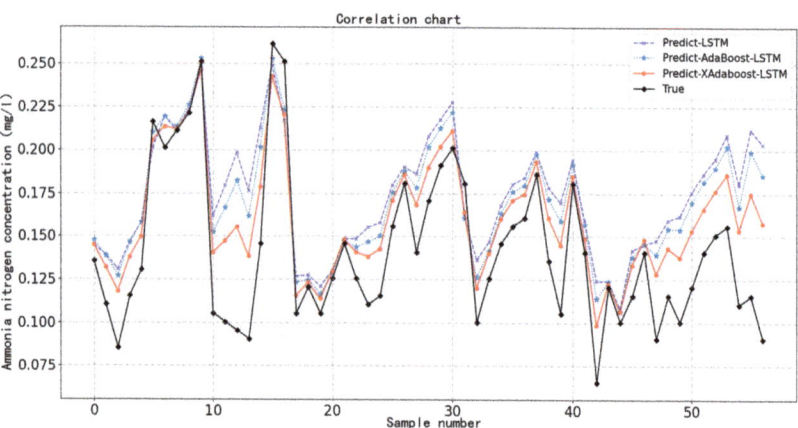

Figure 5. Comparison chart of experimental results.

In the figure, the XAdaBoost–LSTM is the prediction model of the improved AdaBoost algorithm for LSTM enhancement and compares the two models of LSTM and AdaBoost–LSTM. Firstly, it can be seen that the AdaBoost algorithm could improve the accuracy of the LSTM prediction model through iteration, which was better in some details compared to the LSTM; secondly, it can be seen that the XAdaBoost–LSTM prediction graph is more obvious in the fitting effect, which verifies the feasibility of the improved AdaBoost algorithm. It can be seen that the change trends before and after the improvement are very similar, but its results in some details are better and more stable compared to the improved one. In Figure 5, when the XAdaBoost–LSTM model predicts the low value of ammonia nitrogen concentration, the prediction accuracy is insufficient, but compared with the other two models, the accuracy is the highest when the low value of ammonia nitrogen concentration is predicted.

Meanwhile, a comparison experiment was set up to compare the effectiveness of the proposed method with MLP and another LSTM method using CNN improvement; the prediction results are shown in Figure 6.

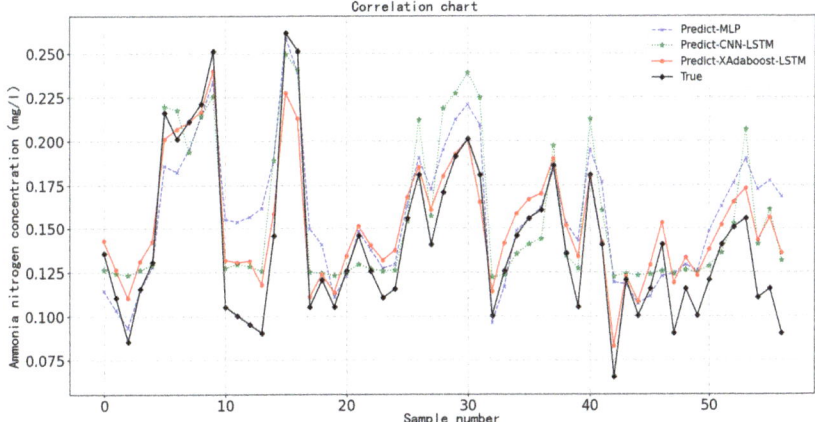

Figure 6. Comparison chart of multi-model experimental results.

As can be seen from the figure, adding the CNN network before the recurrent neural network to extract the features of the data, the CNN–LSTM model was better in some details, but the overall fitting effect was not as good as the XAdaboost–LSTM model; the MLP model had abrupt variability in the prediction points in the figure several times, which was because the network did not consider the temporality of the sequence. On the contrary, the LSTM model with XAdaBoost boost had high error tolerance, so it had better results in dealing with the task of temporality and the presence of errors.

In this paper, three sub-models were generated after iteration, and each sub-model handled data with different weights. To facilitate the observation of features, some data points were intercepted to show the prediction effects of the three sub-models, as shown in Figures 7–9.

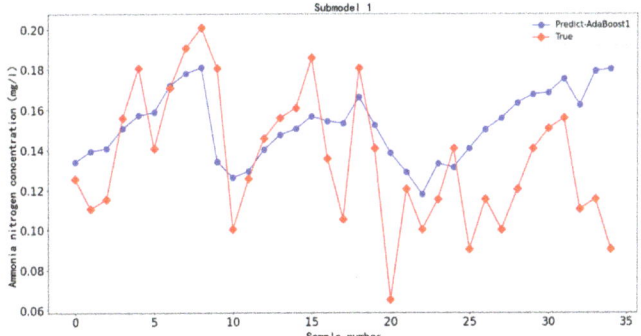

Figure 7. Sub-model 1 result plot.

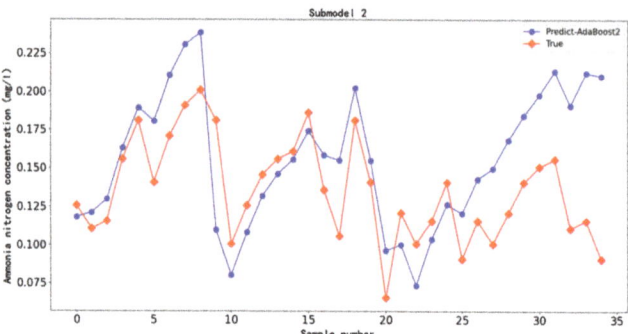

Figure 8. Sub-model 2 result plot.

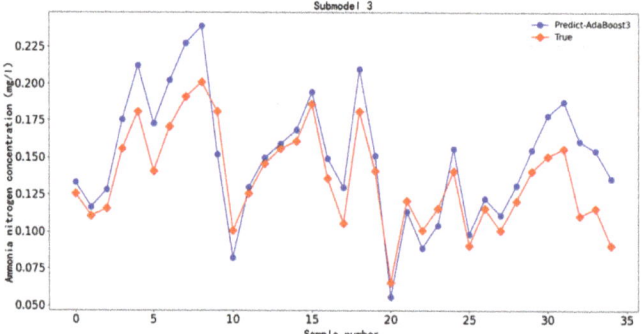

Figure 9. Sub-model 3 result plot.

Figure 7 shows the first generated sub-model 1; it can be seen that the trend of most points in the figure is not apparent and has a significant error. After the first weak model was obtained, the data weights were reassigned according to the prediction results.

Figure 8 shows sub-model 2 generated after iteration. The weights of the poorly predicted data were enlarged based on the results predicted by sub-model 1, so the model was more accurate in dealing with the points that did not work well in sub-model 1. At the same time, the image was better fitted because the weights of other points are reduced.

Figure 9 shows the sub-model 3 generated after the iteration, which was also the corrective iteration. The model was built based on the first two iterations, and by comparing the magnitude of the error rate, the weights of the cases where both error rates were not satisfied were set to 0. After zooming in again for the data with poor prediction results, it can be seen that the distribution of some points in the weak model 3 differs from sub-models 1 and 2, but the overall effect was better than the first two prediction results.

In the last iteration, the error rate d was selected as 0.058 by the results of the first two model processing results of the data. If the first two sub-model prediction results' error rate was greater than d, the weight was set to 0 in the third correction iteration process. The model error rate distribution is shown in Figure 10.

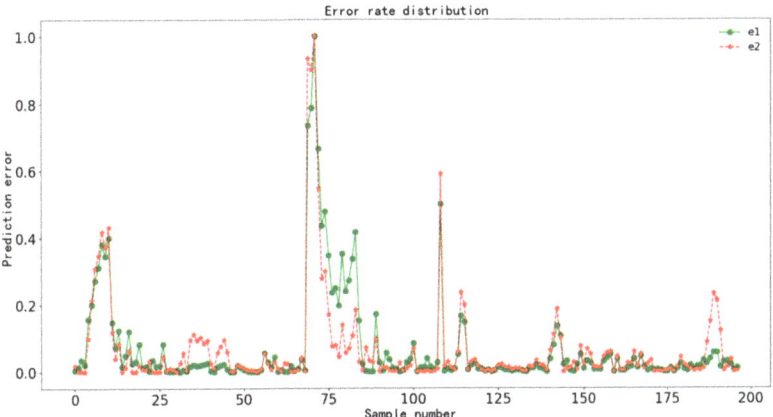

Figure 10. Two model prediction error rate distributions.

e1, e2 were the first and second iteration error rate distributions; we can see that through the change of data weights most of the data in the two prediction results error rate difference was not large, but there were also noticeable differences in the second rather than the first good point, which provides a the basis that AdaBoost can improve the accuracy rate. There are also some points where the error rate became larger with the amplification of the data, and the combination of different data changes could effectively improve the stability. Some of the data in the figure have large error rates on both occasions, and treating such data as error data and disregarding their effects in the last iteration can effectively improve model stability and accuracy. The same three metrics, RMSE, MAE, and MAPE, were used in this experiment to assess the accuracy and stability of the model. The results are shown in Table 2.

Table 2. Model evaluation index.

Models	RMSE	MAE	MAPE
MLP	0.0634	0.0523	41.4199
LSTM	0.0601	0.0456	38.1255
CNN–LSTM	0.0489	0.0412	31.9996
ADABOOST-LSTM	0.0441	0.0348	31.7202
XADABOOST-LSTM	0.0352	0.0276	23.0314

Table 2 shows the average of the results of 20 experiments. After AdaBoost's iterative enhancement to LSTM, the three indicators were significantly reduced so that AdaBoost could improve the accuracy of the model prediction. The three indicators of the XAdaBoost–LSTM model were lower than those of AdaBoost, which could prove the effect of the improved algorithm and the effect of the model. These three indicators could intuitively reflect that the indicators of the XAdaBoost–LSTM prediction model are significantly lower than those of other machine learning models and artificial intelligence models such as MLP.

In addition, the GRU series models have fewer parameters, which makes the model widely used in the field of aquaculture. Therefore, we also used the evaluation criteria to verify that the prediction accuracy of XAdaBoost–LSTM was higher than that of the GRU series models. Since its introduction, the CNN model has been widely used and achieved good performance in different fields. Therefore, we also added the CNN model to make the supplementary experiment more perfect. The comparison of evaluation criteria of the supplementary model is shown in Table 3.

Table 3. Supplementary model evaluation indicators.

Models	RMSE	MAE	MAPE
CNN	0.0685	0.0610	52.8130
GRU	0.0546	0.0424	37.307
CONV-GRU	0.0416	0.0313	26.4624
XADABOOST–LSTM	0.0352	0.0276	23.0314

It can be seen from Table 3 that the XAdaBoost–LSTM model had more accurate prediction performance than the GRU series models with fewer parameters and computational complexity and the CNN model with a wide range of applications.

4.5. Model Stability Analysis

To verify that the XAdaBoost algorithm and AdaBoost algorithm could improve the stability of the models, the stability and robustness of the models were reacted by observing the changes of RMSE, MAE, and MAPE for 20 predictions of the LSTM, AdaBoost–LSTM, and XAdaBoost–LSTM models, as shown in Figures 11–13.

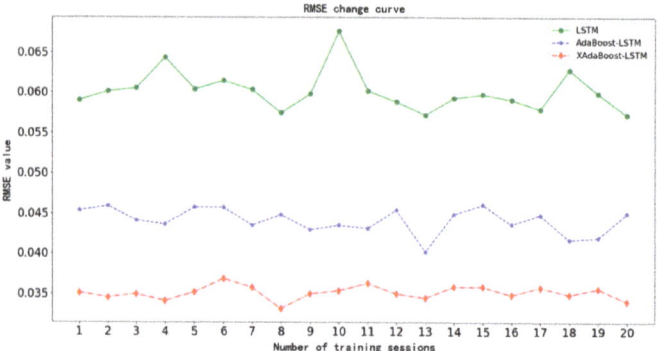

Figure 11. RMSE change chart.

It can be seen from the figure that the changes in the three indicators of the prediction model were smoother than those of the LSTM model after the iterative enhancement of XAdaBoost and AdaBoost during multiple experiments. The changes of XAdaBoost indicators were the smoothest and the changes were the smallest, indicating that the XAdaBoost–LSTM prediction model was more stable. It proves that the XAdaBoost algorithm can effectively solve the problems of poor single prediction robustness and low stability of traditional prediction models.

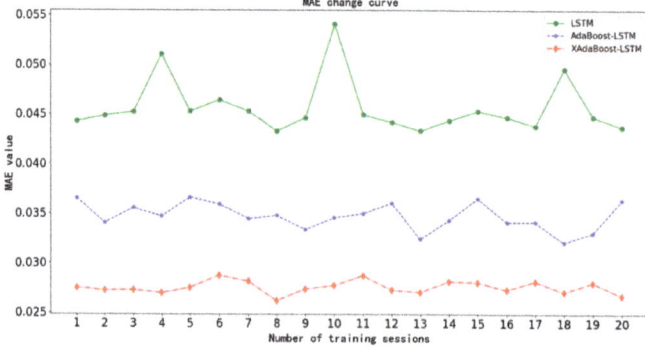

Figure 12. MAE change chart.

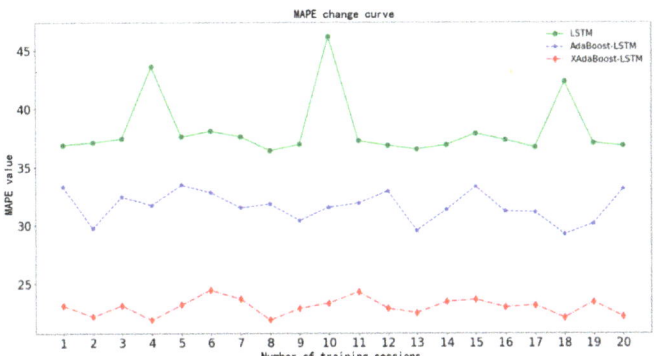

Figure 13. MAPE change chart.

AdaBoost improves model stability and accuracy from the perspective of data weights, but the different number of iterations will affect the model performance. The XAdaBoost–LSTM ammonia nitrogen concentration prediction model is the traditional Adaboost–LSTM algorithm when the number of iterations is less than 3, and corrective iterations can be introduced when T > 3. The RMSE, MAE, and MAPE for different iterations are shown in Table 4.

Table 4. The results of XAdaBoost–LSTM in different iterations.

Number of Iterations	RMSE	MAE	MAPE
1	0.0591	0.0443	38.1255
2	0.0441	0.0348	31.7202
3	0.0352	0.0276	23.0314
4	0.0426	0.0344	28.1742

The table shows the average results of 20 experiments. The model works best at the third iteration, and the model prediction effect starts to decrease when the number of iterations continues to increase, because the AdaBoost integrated learning model keeps amplifying the error data when assigning weights to the training data each time, so after the model reaches the optimum, increasing the number of iterations will only increase the error rate of the model, and the number of iterations will change depending on the data type. XAdaBoost introduces corrective iterations, but the error accumulation is not eliminated, so the effect of the model will still decrease with more iterations.

5. Conclusions

To solve the problem that a single LSTM ammonia nitrogen prediction model is susceptible to sudden changes and error information in the prediction process, which leads to low prediction accuracy and robustness, an XAdaBoost integrated algorithm with an improved combination approach was proposed to consider the feature that the combined learning algorithm can build multiple sub-models; the XAdaBoost–LSTM ammonia nitrogen concentration prediction model was proposed. The ammonia nitrogen concentration prediction sub-model was established using LSTM, and the data weights were updated by the XAdaBoost integrated learning algorithm so that the model could fully consider the sample characteristics. The distribution of the sub-model on different data was analyzed, and the model changes were compared for multiple experiments. It was verified that XAdaBoost could improve the accuracy and stability of the prediction model, and the effect was better than AdaBoost. The algorithm had universal applicability to different models, and the proposed method was verified to be more effective than MLP and CNN–LSTM in the task of ammonia nitrogen concentration prediction through comparison experiments, and more suitable for the design of an ammonia nitrogen concentration prediction system in aquaculture water quality.

Applying the prediction model in this paper to the aquaculture system is of great significance for formulating the regulation strategy in advance. By setting the prediction time step, the change curve of ammonia nitrogen concentration can be predicted in the future. By analyzing the change curve of ammonia nitrogen concentration, the safe range of ammonia nitrogen concentration corresponded to determine the exceedance time of ammonia nitrogen concentration, and the reasons for the exceedance of ammonia nitrogen concentration were analyzed. Suppose the ammonia nitrogen concentration in the water body increases due to the accumulation of food residues and excreta in the aquaculture pond without water change operation for a long time. In that case, management strategies such as water change and silt removal should be adopted at that point. If the water change interval is short, the concentration of ammonia nitrogen is also in the excessive range, which is the method of oxygen increase that can be used to reduce the concentration of ammonia nitrogen. High oxygen content means that ammonia nitrogen has little toxic effect on aquaculture. In addition, in this case, it is necessary to check whether the pH value of the water and the temperature are within the reasonable range for the survival of the aquaculture. When the pH value is higher, the ammonia nitrogen concentration increases more rapidly; otherwise, it is slower. When the temperature is too high, it will also increase the concentration of ammonia nitrogen in the water. When the above methods have not solved the problem of unreasonable concentration of ammonia nitrogen, the method of drug delivery can be used to reduce the concentration of ammonia nitrogen. If the previous methods have failed to address the issue of excessive concentration of ammonia nitrogen, drug delivery can be used to reduce its concentration. However, applying this model in aquaculture systems poses certain challenges. The model's prediction accuracy can be impacted by large-scale data, and it is yet to be determined whether the model can maintain stability and prediction accuracy across different aquaculture species. The application of the prediction model in aquaculture management systems involves designing the function and relationship of each module and encapsulating all modules into a platform system, which includes data acquisition and processing, prediction, output, and storage modules. Water quality data is collected by sensors and transmitted to the database, and a prediction model module is established in the system. The data is then inputted into the prediction module to obtain the predicted value.

In the future, we will further use the data sets collected by different aquaculture systems to verify the model, proving that the model also has good prediction accuracy and stability in different systems. In addition, we will use feature construction, merging data, and other methods to increase the number of features of aquaculture water quality in the data and combine the model with the actual Internet of Things devices to further improve the model's generalization. Finally, we will apply the model to the water quality management system to assess the practice.

Author Contributions: Conceptualization, Y.W.; methodology, Y.W., X.L. and W.W.; software, Y.W., D.X., X.L. and W.W.; data curation, D.X.; writing—original draft, D.X.; writing—review & editing, X.L.; visualization, W.W.; supervision, Y.W. and W.W.; project administration, W.W.; funding acquisition, W.W. All authors have read and agreed to the published version of the manuscript.

Funding: This work is supported by the Open Project of Key Laboratory of Environment Controlled Aquaculture, Ministry of Education, China (Project Number: 202314), the General Scientific Research Projects of Liaoning Provincial Department of Education, China (Project Number: JYTMS20230489), and the data came from the intensive mariculture system of the modeling laboratory of Dalian Ocean University.

Data Availability Statement: The data will be made available by the authors on request.

Acknowledgments: Special thanks to the editors and the four reviewers for their constructive comments.

Conflicts of Interest: The authors declare no conflict of interest.

References

1. Wang, J.X.; Li, J.Y.; Li, S.J.; Shi, Y.Q.; Gao, Y.; Ji, G.J. Exploration of aquaculture standardization in China. *China Aquac.* **2019**, *4*, 31–34.
2. Zhang, C.L.; Xu, H.; Wang, S.M.; Liu, H.; Chen, X.J. Current situation and considerations on the development of deep-sea fisheries based on large-scale fisheries platforms. *China Agron. Bull.* **2020**, *36*, 152–157.
3. Nagaraju, T.V.; Sunil, B.M.; Chaudhary, B.; Prasad, C.D.; Gobinath, R. Prediction of ammonia contaminants in the aquaculture ponds using soft computing coupled with wavelet analysis. *Environ. Pollut.* **2023**, *331 Pt 2*, 121924. [CrossRef] [PubMed]
4. Le, P.T.T.; Boyd, C.E. Comparison of Phenate and Salicylate Methods for Determination of Total Ammonia Nitrogen in Freshwater and Saline Water. *J. World Aquac. Soc.* **2012**, *43*, 885–889. [CrossRef]
5. Xu, G.; Xu, G.; Wei, H.; Wei, H.; Wang, J.; Wang, J.; Chen, X.; Chen, X.; Zhu, B.; Zhu, B. A Local Weighted Linear Regression (LWLR) Ensemble of Surrogate Models Based on Stacking Strategy: Application to Hydrodynamic Response Prediction for Submerged Floating Tunnel (SFT). *Appl. Ocean. Res.* **2022**, *125*, 103228. [CrossRef]
6. Ottaviani, F.M.; De Marco, A. Multiple Linear Regression Model for Improved Project Cost Forecasting. *Procedia Comput. Sci.* **2022**, *196*, 808–815. [CrossRef]
7. Chen, W.B.; Liu, W.C. Artificial neural network modeling of dissolved oxygen in the reservoir. *Environ. Monit. Assess.* **2014**, *186*, 1203–1217. [CrossRef] [PubMed]
8. Nong, X.; Lai, C.; Chen, L.; Shao, D.; Zhang, C.; Liang, J. Prediction modeling framework comparative analysis of dissolved oxygen concentration variations using support vector regression coupled with multiple feature engineering and optimization methods: A case study in China. *Ecol. Indic.* **2023**, *146*, 109845. [CrossRef]
9. Zhao, S.; Gui, F.L.; Liu, H.Q. Prediction of nitrogen concentration in Taihu Lake based on AdaBoost machine learning model. *China Rural. Water Hydropower* **2022**, *6*, 24–28.
10. Belavadi, S.V.; Rajagopal, S.; Ranjani, R.; Mohan, R. Air Quality Forecasting using LSTM RNN and Wireless Sensor Networks. *Procedia Comput. Sci.* **2020**, *170*, 241–248. [CrossRef]
11. Farhi, N.; Kohen, E.; Mamane, H.; Shavitt, Y. Prediction of wastewater treatment quality using LSTM neural network. *Environ. Technol. Innov.* **2021**, *23*, 101632. [CrossRef]
12. Huan, J.; Li, H.; Li, M.; Chen, B. Prediction of dissolved oxygen in aquaculture based on gradient boosting decision tree and long short-term memory network: A study of Chang Zhou fishery demonstration base. *Comput. Electron. Agric.* **2020**, *175*, 105530. [CrossRef]
13. Yan, K.; Li, C.; Zhao, R.; Zhang, Y.; Duan, H.; Wang, W. Predicting the ammonia nitrogen of wastewater treatment plant influent via integrated model based on rolling decomposition method and deep learning algorithm. *Sustain. Cities Soc.* **2023**, *94*, 104541. [CrossRef]
14. Ruma, J.F.; Adnan, M.S.G.; Dewan, A.; Rahman, R.M. Particle swarm optimization based LSTM networks for water level forecasting: A case study on Bangladesh river network. *Results Eng.* **2023**, *17*, 100951. [CrossRef]
15. Busari, G.A.; Lim, D.H. Crude oil price prediction: A comparison between AdaBoost-LSTM and AdaBoost-GRU for improving forecasting performance. *Comput. Chem. Eng.* **2021**, *155*, 107513. [CrossRef]
16. Xiao, C.; Chen, N.; Hu, C.; Wang, K.; Gong, J.; Chen, Z. Short and mid-term sea surface temperature prediction using time-series satellite data and LSTM-AdaBoost combination approach. *Remote Sens. Environ.* **2019**, *233*, 111358. [CrossRef]
17. Wadud, M.A.H.; Kabir, M.M.; Mridha, M.F.; Ali, M.A.; Hamid, M.A.; Monowar, M.M. How can we manage Offensive Text in Social Media—A Text Classification Approach using LSTM-BOOST. *Int. J. Inf. Manag. Data Insights* **2022**, *2*, 100095. [CrossRef]
18. Shi, W.; Hu, L.; Lin, Z.; Zhang, L.; Wu, J.; Chai, W. Short-term motion prediction of floating offshore wind turbine based on muti-input LSTM neural network. *Ocean Eng.* **2023**, *280*, 114558. [CrossRef]
19. Qiu, K.; Li, J.; Chen, D. Optimized long short-term memory (LSTM) network for performance prediction in unconventional reservoirs. *Energy Rep.* **2022**, *8*, 15436–15445. [CrossRef]
20. Zhou, L.; Boyd, C.E. Comparison of Nessler, phenate, salicylate, and ion selective electrode procedures for determination of total ammonia nitrogen in aquaculture. *Aquaculture* **2016**, *450*, 187–193. [CrossRef]
21. Li, Y.; Li, R. Predicting ammonia nitrogen in surface water by a new attention-based deep learning hybrid model. *Environ. Res.* **2023**, *216 Pt 3*, 114723. [CrossRef] [PubMed]
22. Wang, W.; Guo, G. Soft-sensing model of ammonia nitrogen concentration in perception based on random configuration network. *Trans. Chin. Soc. Agric. Mach.* **2020**, *51*, 214–220.
23. Nasiri, A.; Yoder, J.; Zhao, Y.; Hawkins, S.; Prado, M.; Gan, H. Pose estimation-based lameness recognition in broiler using CNN-LSTM network. *Comput. Electron. Agric.* **2022**, *197*, 106931. [CrossRef]
24. Yu, H.; Yang, L.; Li, D.; Chen, Y. A hybrid intelligent soft computing method for ammonia nitrogen prediction in aquaculture. *Inf. Process. Agric.* **2021**, *8*, 64–74. [CrossRef]

Disclaimer/Publisher's Note: The statements, opinions and data contained in all publications are solely those of the individual author(s) and contributor(s) and not of MDPI and/or the editor(s). MDPI and/or the editor(s) disclaim responsibility for any injury to people or property resulting from any ideas, methods, instructions or products referred to in the content.

Article

Developer Assignment Method for Software Defects Based on Related Issue Prediction

Baochuan Liu, Li Zhang, Zhenwei Liu and Jing Jiang *

State Key Laboratory of Software Development Environment, Beihang University, Beijing 100191, China; liubc@buaa.edu.cn (B.L.); lily@buaa.edu.cn (L.Z.); meetliuzhenwei@gmail.com (Z.L.)
* Correspondence: jiangjing@buaa.edu.cn

Abstract: The open-source software platform hosts a large number of software defects, and the task of relying on administrators to manually assign developers is often time consuming. Thus, it is crucial to determine how to assign software defects to appropriate developers. This paper presents DARIP, a method for assigning developers to address software defects. First, the correlation between software defects and issues is considered, predicting related issues for each defect and comprehensively calculating the textual characteristics of the defect using the BERT model. Second, a heterogeneous collaborative network is constructed based on the three development behaviors of developers: reporting, commenting, and fixing. The meta-paths are defined based on the four collaborative relationships between developers: report–comment, report–fix, comment–comment, and comment–fix. The graph-embedding algorithm metapath2vec extracts developer characteristics from the heterogeneous collaborative network. Then, a classifier based on a deep learning model calculates the probability assigned to each developer category. Finally, the assignment list is obtained according to the probability ranking. Experiments on a dataset of 20,280 defects from 9 popular projects show that the DARIP method improves the average of the Recall@5, the Recall@10, and the MRR by 31.13%, 21.40%, and 25.45%, respectively, compared to the state-of-the-art method.

Keywords: defect fixing; developer assignment; prediction of related issues; heterogeneous collaborative network

MSC: 68M20

1. Introduction

GitHub is a web-based project-hosting platform [1–3] that provides an Issue-Tracking System to help users manage issues that occur in their projects. In the Issue-Tracking System [4,5], users can report software defects found during development [6–8], project managers can assign software defects to appropriate developers, and other developers can participate in discussions around defects of interest. However, with over 200 million open-source projects and 1.2 billion issues hosted on the GitHub platform worldwide, there are a large number of software defects that need to be fixed every day. Manually assigning developers to software defects by managers alone can be a tedious and time-consuming task [9–12]. To streamline this process, researchers have conducted studies on the task of assigning or recommending developers [13–22]. For example, Yang et al. [13] filtered developers from historical defects by calculating textual similarities between different software defects, and then assigned developers to software defects based on their development experience. Aung et al. [14] processed code snippets and text information in defect reports separately and improved the performance of developer assignments through joint learning of developer assignment tasks and label classification tasks.

Empirical studies have shown that some software defects may be related [23,24], and two related software defects could involve the same source code file. Almhana and Kessentini [25] define dependencies based on two software defects involving the same source code

file. They leverage the dependencies to help resolve the task of developer assignment on the Mozilla platform. Jahanshahi et al. [26] discovered that some software defects may be blocked by others during the repair process. They studied how to assign developers for software defects based on their blocking relationships. Since there are correlations between software defects for reasons such as involving the same source code files or blocking relationships, referring to related software defects may help assign appropriate developers to software defects. However, most existing studies only consider the characteristics of the current software defect itself and overlook the correlation between software defects when automatically assigning developers to software defects.

Meanwhile, existing studies do not consider developers' different development behaviors when collecting candidates and extracting their characteristics [27,28]. For example, Xuan et al. [28] considered the commenting behavior among developers to build social networks and designed a model for assigning developer priorities. Considering the different behaviors of developers can help to understand their characteristics, which can help to assign the appropriate developer to a software defect.

This paper proposes an automated Developer Assignment method for open-source software defects based on Related Issue Prediction, named DARIP. First, this paper extracts the text vectors of software defects and all their historical software defects using the BERT model, predicts the Top-N potential related software defects for each software defect from all the historical software defects based on cosine similarity, takes the text information of related software defects as an extension of the text information of software defects, and takes the text information of software defects together with the text information of related software defects as text input. The text characteristics of software defects are obtained by comprehensively calculating the text vectors of software defects and related software defects. Second, a heterogeneous collaborative network is constructed based on the three development behaviors of developers: reporting, commenting, and fixing. The meta-paths are defined based on the four collaborative relationships between developers: report–comment, report–fix, comment–comment, and comment–fix. The graph-embedding algorithm metapath2vec extracts developer characteristics from the heterogeneous collaborative network. Then, a classifier based on a deep learning model calculates the probability assigned to each developer category. Finally, the assignment list is obtained according to the probability ranking.

In order to evaluate the effectiveness of the DARIP method, this paper collects 20,280 software defects from 9 popular open-source projects. The experimental results show that the average values of the Recall@5, the Recall@10, and the MRR of the method DARIP in 9 projects are 0.5902, 0.7160, and 0.4136, respectively. Compared with the existing method Multi-triage, the average values of the Recall@5, the Recall@10, and the MRR of the DARIP method in 9 projects are increased by 31.13%, 21.40%, and 25.45%, respectively.

2. Background

In the GitHub open-source community, the Issue Tracker System supports developers to contribute freely to open-source projects. In the Issue Tracker System, users can report software defects or functional requirements found during the development process. For example, managers may identify an issue as a software defect [29] by adding the label "bug", "defect" or other synonyms. After the issue is reported, other interested developers participate in the issue comments to discuss the solution. In response to the reported software defects, managers have the option of assigning appropriate developers. Moreover, developers can create a pull request to submit fixable code for code review based on the solution to a software defect. After passing the code review, the code is merged into the repository, and the software defect is fixed. Therefore, this paper refers to the literature [14], which defines the fixer of a software defect as the assignee or the creator who creates the corresponding pull request and is successfully merged into the repository.

In this paper, we study the software defects in the Issue-Tracking System. Take the software defect of No. 29391 (https://github.com/tensorflow/tensorflow/issues/29391, (accessed on 14 December 2023)) in the project *tensorflow/tensorflow* as an example, and its basic structure is shown in Figure 1.

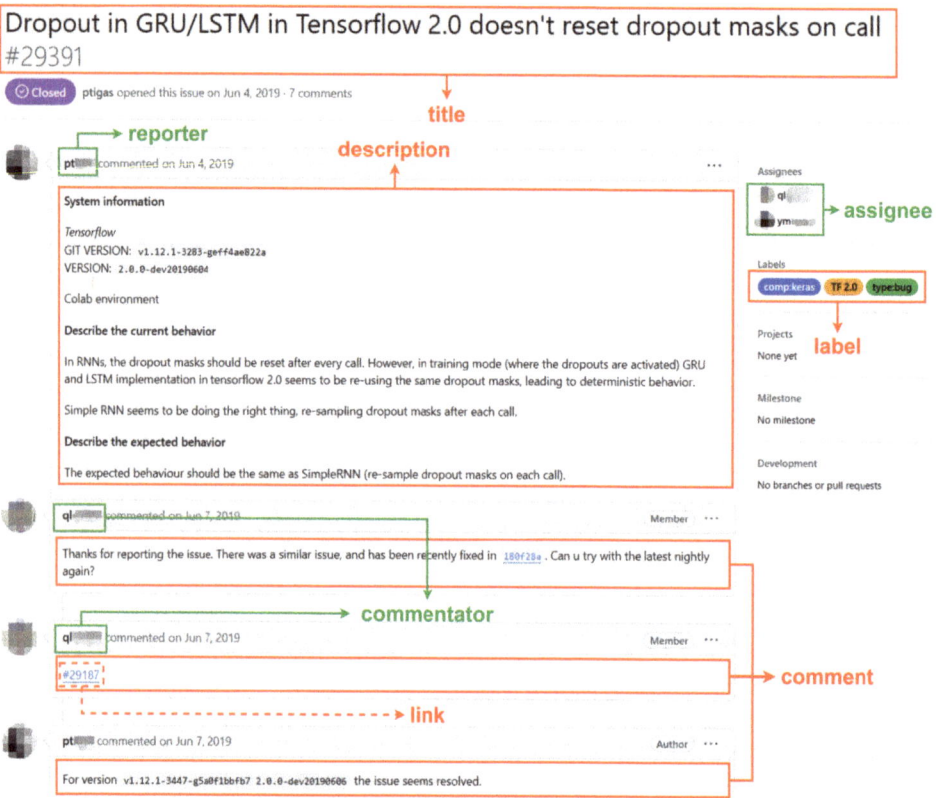

Figure 1. A sample of a software defect.

(1) Title: A brief overview of the software defect.

(2) Description: The body of the defect report, including a specific description of the software defect.

(3) Comment: Information about developers participating in discussions about a software defect.

(4) Label: Managers add labels to identify the category of a issue. For example, add the label *type:bug* to indicate that the current issue is a software defect.

(5) Reporter: The developer who reported the current software defect.

(6) Commentator: Developers involved in the discussion of a software defect.

(7) Assignee: A developer assigned by the manager to fix the software defect.

(8) Link: A hyperlink left by a developer during the discussion of an issue, often used to refer to other relevant information.

As shown in Figure 1, the developer *pt***** reported a software defect number 29391, which was assigned to developers *ql****** and *ym***** on the project *tensorflow/tensorflow*. Subsequently, the developer *ql****** indicated that the current software defect was related to the historical software defect number 29187 (https://github.com/tensorflow/tensorflow/issues/29187, (accessed on 14 December 2023)) in the same project, and the submitted code had fixed the related software defect. By validation from the developer *pt*****, the current software defect can also be fixed using the same version of the fixed code. The historically related software defect number 29187 was reported earlier than the software defect number

29391 and has been fixed by the developer $ql*****$. In particular, the assignee $ql*****$ of the software defect number 29391 was also the assignee of the related software defect number 29187. Already familiar with the resolution of the historically related software defect number 29187, the developer $ql*****$ immediately fixed the software defect number 29391 with the same fixable code.

As a related issue, the resolution of software defect number 29391 helped to fix the software defect number 29187. At the same time, the experience of developer $ql*****$ in fixing related issues helped reduce the resolution time for software defect number 29187. Therefore, referring to the issues associated with the software defect may help to assign the appropriate developer to the software defect.

3. Related Work

3.1. Related Issue

Due to the fact that open-source software can share or reuse code, many open-source projects rely on the same libraries and components [12]. Dependencies between open-source projects further affect software defects in the project, and issues in one project may be linked to related issues from the same or other projects [30–33]. Ma et al. [30] conducted an empirical study of software defects in seven open-source projects in the Python ecosystem on the GitHub platform. They found that developers point to related issues by leaving links in the text messages of software defects. Zhang et al. [31] performed both qualitative and quantitative analysis of links in the Rails ecosystem and found that the percentage of issues with links reached 24.8%. Of these, 82.8% were links within projects, and 17.2% were links between different projects. Li et al. [32] analyzed 16,584 Python projects on the GitHub platform. They classified the relationship between software defects and related issues into six different types through qualitative analysis, and each type of related issue could help to fix software defects. Previous studies have shown that referencing related issues may help fix corresponding software defects.

Zhang et al. [34] stated that issue reports on GitHub are essential knowledge in software development and proposed iLinker, a method to automatically obtain related issues to help fix issues by sharing knowledge of related issues. The Linker method calculated three similarity scores between query issues and candidate issues using TF-IDF, word embedding, and document embedding, respectively. Then, the final scores of the query issues and the candidate issues are combined, and the related issues of query issues are recommended based on the final scores. In our previous work [35], we focused on software defects and related issues and proposed an algorithm, CPIRecom, to predict cross-project related issues automatically. Firstly, the pre-selecting set construction method is proposed to filter the massive issues. Secondly, the BERT pre-training model is used to extract text features and analyze project features. Then, the random forest algorithm is used to calculate the probability of the pre-selecting issues and the software defects. Finally, the recommendation list is obtained according to the ranking.

In this paper, we draw on the idea of the CPIRecom method of related issue recommendation to predict potentially related issues for each software defect in order to help solve the task of developer assignment. Our existing work and our current work are different because they are designed to solve different research questions. Our prior work [35] aimed at predicting relevant issues from other projects for software defects. However, the purpose of the current work is to assign appropriate developers for software defects.

3.2. Developer Assignment

In this section, we present existing research on developer assignment and divide existing work into four categories: information retrieval-based approaches, machine learning-based approaches, social network-based approaches, and defect relationship-based approaches.

3.2.1. Information Retrieval-Based Approach

Information retrieval refers to the process of finding information from a collection of data that meets information needs. The developer assignment method based on information retrieval assumes that developers can fix specific types of software defects because they have some specialized knowledge. Some researchers introduced the concept of topic model for assigning developers [13,15–17]. Among them, Yang et al. [13] proposed a developer assignment method with a multi-feature combination, extracted topics from historical defect reports, extracted features such as components, products, priorities, and severity of software defects, calculated textual similarities among software defects, and collected developers who contributed as candidates. Finally, they obtained a ranking list of candidate developers based on development experience. Xia et al. [16] proposed a multi-featured topic model that extends the Latent Dirichlet Allocation(LDA) to the developer recommendation task. They considered product information and component information of software defects and assigned appropriate developers to software defects based on the affinity of the developer to the topics.

Most of the above information retrieval-based methods are divided into two steps: filtering out a small number of eligible historical software defects and collecting all the developers from them to obtain a candidate set, then extracting the characteristics of all the candidates in the candidate set and finally assigning appropriate developers to the software defects. If the real developers do not appear in the candidate set, it will directly affect the effectiveness of the method.

3.2.2. Machine Learning-Based Approach

With the continuous development of machine learning technology, some researchers utilized traditional machine-learning and deep-learning algorithms to solve the developer assignment task [14,18–22,36–39]. Jonsson et al. [19] proposed a defect assignment method based on ensemble learner, using TF-IDF technology to extract features from the title information and description information of defect reports and combining Naive Bayes, Support Vector Machines, KNN, and Decision Tree classifiers to create a stacked generalization classifier for improving the prediction accuracy of automatic developer assignment. Lee et al. [21] propose a developer assignment method based on a CNN and word embedding, using the word2vec model to convert each word in the summary and description in defect reports into a word vector and then using a CNN to learn the text features of software defects to solve the defect classification task. Mani et al. [22] proposed a developer assignment method based on deep bidirectional recurrent neural networks, which learns paragraph-level representations of software defects based on deep learning algorithms, learned word order and semantic relationships from the context of defect reports, and finally, realized defect classification using a softmax classifier. Aung et al. [14] proposed a multi-task learning classification model using a text encoder to extract text features from defect reports and an AST encoder to extract code features from code snippets to improve the performance of the model by jointly learning defect assignment and label classification tasks.

Most of the existing methods based on machine learning use various models to learn feature representations from the text information of software defects and apply the text classification to solve the developer assignment task. However, many of these methods only focus on the software defects themselves and overlook the correlation between them. Therefore, it is crucial to consider the related issues of software defects when extracting textual characteristics, as this can aid in solving the task of developer assignment by extending the text information of software defects.

3.2.3. Social Network-Based Approach

Some researchers utilized methods based on social network analysis to solve the task of developer assignment [14,40–45]. For example, Banitaan and Alenezi [40] proposed DECOBA, a developer assignment method based on developer communities. They used developers' commenting behavior on software defects to construct a developer social network. Then, they detected developer communities and ranked developers by their experience in each community to obtain a developer assignment list. Zhang et al. [41] took commentators on software defects as potential developers. They constructed heterogeneous social networks based on developers, software defects, comments, components, and products. They then calculated three types of collaborative proximity among developers in these networks based on defects, components, and products. The researchers ranked developers according to their comprehensive score and generated a recommended list of potential developers. Zaidi and Lee [42] proposed a graphical representation of defect reports, extracted the title and description information from the defect reports, took the defect report as a document, the document and the word in a document as two types of nodes, and built a heterogeneous network with the document-to-word and the word-to-word as two types of edges. The Graph Convolutional Network was used to learn the graph representation of software defects, and the task of defect classification was solved by using node classification.

The social network-based approaches mentioned above did not consider the reporting, commenting, and fixing behavior of developers in software defects. Therefore, it is essential to analyze the personal characteristics of developers when extracting developer characteristics for software defects. This analysis can help in assigning appropriate developers to software defects.

3.2.4. Defect Relationship-Based Approach

A few researchers consider the relationship between software defects in the developer assignment task of studying software defects [12,25,26]. Almhana and Kessentini [25] proposed a defect classification method based on the dependency between defect reports, which defined the dependency between two defect reports as the number of shared files to be inspected to localize the defects. Then, they adopted a multi-objective search to rank the bug reports for developers based on both of their priorities and the dependency between them. Jahanshahi et al. [26] introduced a defect-triaging method called DABT, which considered the text information, the cost associated with each defect, and the dependency among them. They leveraged natural language processing and integer programming to assign software defects to appropriate developers.

Although the defect relationship-based methods mentioned above have proven to be effective, they rely on platforms like Mozilla and Bugzilla that contain information such as dependency relationships and source code files. Unfortunately, the GitHub platform lacks this information, making it impossible to apply these methods directly to it. Therefore, it is necessary to draw on the related issue recommendation method to predict the potential related issues for each software defect to assist in the task of assigning developers.

4. Method

Given the difficulty of manually assigning developers to software defects in GitHub, this paper proposes a method for automatically assigning developers to software defects. Then, we present the design idea and the individual modules of the DARIP method.

4.1. Design Idea

After a software defect is reported, it may be assigned to different developers. This allows us to label the type of software defect as the assignee and convert the developer assignment task into a multi-classification task in the field of machine learning. In this paper, we propose the automated developer assignment method, DARIP, which is divided into two phases: the training phase and the testing phase. The overall architecture is shown in Figure 2. The DARIP methodology consists of the following components:

(1) Collect historical software defects and developers.
(2) Predict potentially related issues for software defects based on their textual information.

(3) The feature vectors of text information in software defects and the feature vectors of text information in related issues are used to calculate the textual features of software defects comprehensively.

(4) Consider the three development behaviors of developers in software defects: reporting, commenting, and fixing. Construct a heterogeneous collaborative network with developers and software defects as two types of nodes and three development behaviors as three types of edges.

(5) A graph-embedding algorithm is used to extract the developer features of software defects from heterogeneous collaborative networks.

(6) The textual features and textual features of software defects are input into the classifier for training and learning, and the developer assignment model is obtained.

(7) Extract the text feature and developer feature for a newly reported software defect.

(8) Input the extracted text feature and developer feature into the trained developer assignment model and output the developer assignment list.

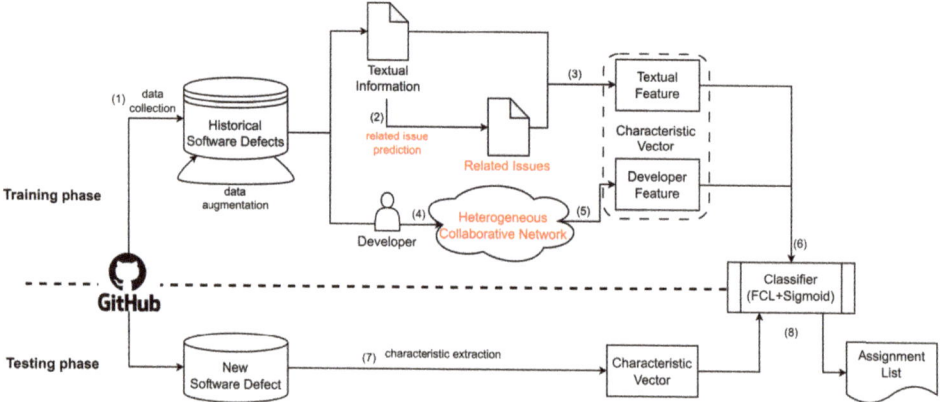

Figure 2. Overall procedure of DARIP method.

In the training phase, this paper first collects software defects from the GitHub platform and the developers. Then, potentially related issues are predicted for software defects, and text features are calculated comprehensively. At the same time, a heterogeneous collaborative network is constructed based on three development behaviors of developers: reporting, commenting, and fixing. The graph-embedding algorithm is used to learn the feature representation of developers. Finally, the feature vectors of software defects are input to the classifier for training and learning, and the developer assignment model is obtained.

During the testing phase, when new software defects are reported on the GitHub platform, the DARIP method extracts the textual and developer characteristics of the software defects. It then calculates the probability of each candidate developer being able to fix the software defects using the assignment model generated during the training phase. Finally, the candidate developers are ranked based on their probability, from highest to lowest, to create an assignment list of potential developers.

4.2. Textual Characteristic

When developers report software defects, they provide detailed information about the problem using both the title and description. Therefore, text information is an essential reference to help assign developers. At the same time, a software defect in open-source software may be related to other issues, and referring to the related issues may help fix the software defect. Therefore, the following section describes how to extract the textual characteristic.

To prepare the text information of software defect for analysis, we first preprocess the text information. The pre-processing includes removing non-text information, converting all letters to lowercase, removing stop words, segmenting the text, and lemmatization. In our study, we remove non-text information such as phone numbers, email addresses, and emoticons from the title and description. We then use blank spaces to separate the remaining text into individual words, creating an array of words for analysis.

Secondly, for a software defect, the potentially related issue is predicted, and the text information of the related issue is taken as an extension of the text information of the software defect. The text information of the software defect and the text information of the related issue are taken as the text input. Specifically, the DARIP method collects all historical software defects corresponding to each software defect from the dataset. Then, natural language processing techniques are used to extract the textual vectors of software defects and all their historical software defects. Currently, the BERT pre-training model [46] is an important technique in the field of natural language processing. We use the BERT pre-training model to transform the preprocessed word arrays into text vectors that can characterize the semantic information. Then, we use cosine similarity to calculate the textual similarity of feature vectors between the software defect and each historical software defect, rank all its historical software defects from highest to lowest according to the textual similarity, and select the Top-N historical software defects with the highest textual similarity as the potential N related issues of the software defect. Extend the text information of related issues as the text information of software defect, and take the text information of software defect and related issues together as text input.

Finally, the textual vectors of software defects and the textual vectors of Top-N related issues are weighted to get the final textual characteristic of the software defect. Specifically, the cosine similarity between the textual vector of the related issues and the textual vector of the software defect is calculated as the correlation coefficient of the related issues. For each related issue, the weighted value is then obtained by multiplying its textual vector with the correlation coefficient. Next, we calculate the cumulative weighted value of N related issues. Then, we calculate the sum of the cumulative weighted values of N related issues and the textual vector of software defect. Finally, divide the sum by N+1 to obtain the final textual feature of the software defect. The formula for calculating the textual characteristic of software defect is as follows:

$$tFeat(i) = \frac{1}{N+1}\left(bf(i) + \sum_{k=1}^{N}(Cosine(i)_k * bf(i)_k)\right) \quad (1)$$

where N represents the number of potentially related issues predicted by the i-th software defect, $bf(i)$ represents the text vector of the i-th software defect, $bf(i)_k$ represents the text vector of the i-th software defect corresponding to the k-th related issue, $Cosine(i)_k$ represents the cosine similarity between the i-th software defect and the corresponding k-th related issue, and $tFeat(i)$ represents the final textual characteristic of the i-th software defect. According to Section 6.3, the value of N is set to 1. This means that the text information of a software defect is used as textual input together with the text information of the TOP-1 related issue.

4.3. Developer Characteristic

The development behaviors of developers in software defects mainly include reporting, commenting, and fixing, and developers can participate in the development of different software defects based on different development behaviors according to their personal wishes. For the newly reported software defects, the DARIP method considers the three development behaviors of developers: reporting, commenting, and fixing. Based on the three development behaviors of developers in a software defect and its historical software defects, a heterogeneous collaborative network is constructed. The graph-embedding algorithm is then used to mine the personal features of developers from the heterogeneous collaborative network and learn the vector representations of developers. Finally, the feature vector of the reporter of the new software defect is used as the developer characteristic of the current software defect.

4.3.1. Heterogeneous Collaborative Network

First, for a software defect and all corresponding historical software defects, collect the participating developers, including reporters, commentators, and fixers. Then, based on the three development behaviors of reporting, commenting, and fixing software defects, a heterogeneous collaborative network is built corresponding to current software defect, all historical software defects, and all developers involved in the above defects. In this paper, we consider assigning appropriate developers to the software defect as soon as they are reported, so that the only participant in newly reported software defects is the reporter.

The definition of a heterogeneous collaborative network is shown in Table 1. The flowchart for constructing a heterogeneous collaborative network for a software defect is shown in Figure 3. First, we collect all historical software defects. Second, we select a software defect to be addressed from the historical software defects. Third, we collect the developers from the software defect, including reporter, commentator, and fixer. Fourth, we construct the reporting relationship, the commenting relationship, and the fixing relationship between developers and software defects, respectively. Fifth, we determine whether there are any software defects to be addressed. If so, go back to the second step. If not, it indicates that all software defects have been handled and the final heterogeneous collaborative network is output.

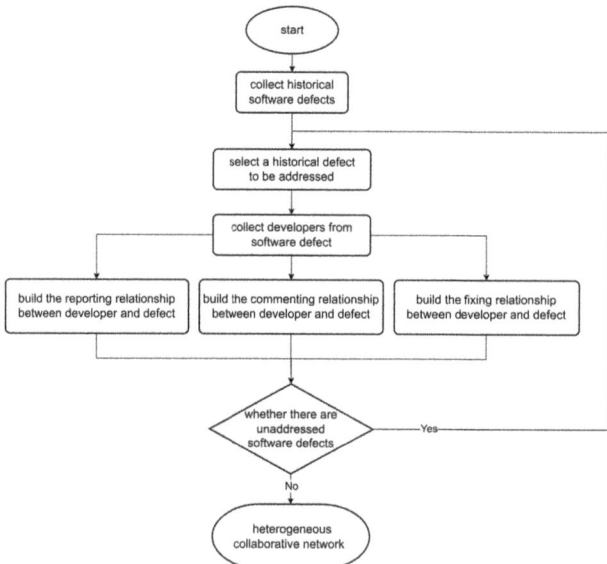

Figure 3. The flowchart for construct heterogeneous collaborative network.

In heterogeneous collaborative networks, the node types include software defects and developers, and the edge types include developers' reporting behavior, commenting behavior, and fixing behavior. We represent a software defect as B (also known as _Bug_), a _Developer as D, a _reporting behavior as r, a _commenting behavior as c, and a _fixing behavior as f. An example of a heterogeneous collaborative network is shown in Figure 4, where B_{new} is the newly reported software defect, developer D_3 is the reporter of the software defect, B_1 and B_2 belong to the historical software defects, and D_1 and D_2 are the developers involved. At the same time, developer D_3 also participated in commenting on historical software defect B_1 and historical software defect B_2. So far, the DARIP method has obtained a heterogeneous collaborative network built for software defect B_{new}.

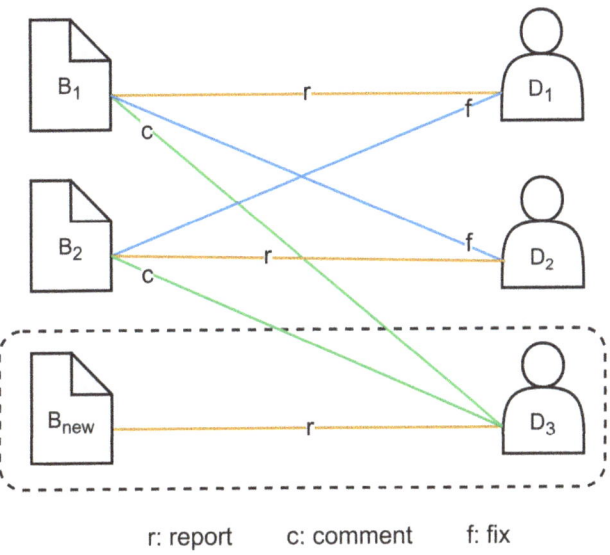

r: report   c: comment   f: fix

Figure 4. A sample of a heterogeneous collaborative network.

It should be noted that the heterogeneous collaborative network constructed by the DARIP method is undirected, because D-c-B and B-c-D illustrate the same scenario in the real software development process: the developer D comments on the software defect B. Since each software defect is reported at a different time, the historical software defects collected for each software defect are not the same. This makes the heterogeneous collaborative network built by each software defect unique. Therefore, this paper needs to build a separate heterogeneous collaborative network for each software defect.

Table 1. Definition of the heterogeneous collaborative network.

Structure	Type	Description
Node	Software Defect/Bug (B)	Software defects in a heterogeneous collaborative network include: current software defect and its historical software defects.
	Developer (D)	Developers in a heterogeneous collaborative network include: reporters, commentators, and fixers. Among them, the only developer involved in the current software defect is the reporter.
Edge	Report (r)	Developer report a software defect.
	Comment (c)	Developer comment on a software defect.
	Fix (f)	Developer fix a software defect.

4.3.2. Developer Characteristic Extraction

The heterogeneous collaborative network constructed for software defects is typical non-Euclidean spatial data. Therefore, it is necessary to select a suitable graph-embedding algorithm to extract the feature vectors of the reporter in current software defect from the heterogeneous collaborative network. Since the heterogeneous collaborative network constructed in this paper contains two types of nodes and three types of edges, it is crucial to select an algorithm that can handle heterogeneous networks. Dong et al. [47] proposed a graph-embedding algorithm, metapath2vec, which can deal with heterogeneous information networks, support custom meta-paths to guide the random wandering of nodes, and is able to obtain semantic and structural information between different nodes. Therefore, the metapath2vec algorithm is used in this paper to extract the reporter's feature vector in the current software defect from heterogeneous collaborative networks.

Extracting feature vectors of nodes from the network based on graph-embedding algorithm metapath2vec usually involves three steps: (1) Customising meta-paths. Meta-paths are paths formed by connecting different types of nodes in a heterogeneous network in a specific way. The metapath2vec algorithm supports researchers in fixing personalized problems by customizing meta-paths. (2) For a heterogeneous network, the metapath2vec algorithm guides random walks of nodes and obtains all node walk sequences based on metapath2vec. Considering the nodes in the network as words and the walk sequences of nodes as sentences, all possible node sequences form a corpus. (3) Feature vectors of nodes in the network are obtained by using the skip-gram model to extract word vectors in the corpus. According to the above steps, this paper needs to propose the custom meta-paths and then guide nodes in the heterogeneous collaborative network to walk around based on the custom meta-paths and obtain all possible walk sequences. Finally, all walk sequences are input into the skit-gram model, and the feature vector of the reporter in new software defect from the heterogeneous collaborative network are output.

(1) Custom meta-paths.

This paper defines the meta-paths based on the different collaborative relationships between developers. When constructing a heterogeneous collaborative network, we consider the three behaviors of developers: reporting, commenting, and fixing. According to the three development behaviors of developers, we can get six kinds of collaborative relationships among developers: report–report, report–comment, report–fix, comment–comment, comment–fix, and fix–fix. In this case, the report–report collaboration does not really exist because there is only one reporter for a software defect. Furthermore, the analysis of the dataset in Section 5 reveals that most software defects have only one fixer, and the percentage of defects with multiple fixers (two or more) is less than eight percent on average. Therefore, we ignore the collaborative relationship of fix–fix and finally obtain four types of collaborative relationships between developers and define the meta-paths. The meta-paths and the corresponding collaborative relationships are shown in Table 2.

Table 2. The meta-paths and collaborative relationships.

Meta-Paths	Collaborative Relationships
$D - f - B - r - D \ / \ D - r - B - f - D$	A developer fixed a software defect reported by another developer.
$D - c - B - r - D \ / \ D - r - B - c - D$	A developer commented on a software defect reported by another developer.
$D - c - B - f - D \ / \ D - f - B - c - D$	A developer commented on a software defect fixed by another developer.
$D - c - B - c - D$	Both developers commented on the same software defect.

It is important to note that collaboration between developers does not take direction into account. For example, $D_1 - f - B - r - D_2$ and $D_2 - r - B - f - D_1$ illustrate the same scenario in the real software development process, where developer D_2 reported software defect B and developer D_1 fixed it.

(2) Guide random walks.

The defined meta-paths guide the nodes to walk randomly on the heterogeneous collaborative network, so that the node sequence containing the semantic information of the collaborative relationship can be obtained. Then, all the node sequences containing semantic information of collaborative relationships are inputted into the skip-gram model.

(3) Extract feature vectors.

The skip-gram model is a kind of Word2Vec model that predicts the context based on the central word. Specifically, it predicts other words before and after the word in the sliding window. Among them, the number of prediction words is determined by the size of the sliding window w. Thus, this paper essentially uses the skip-gram model to predict the other developers in a sequence of nodes that collaborate with a developer. For example, given a sequence of nodes as follows:

$$D_1 - c - B_1 - f - D_2 - f - B_2 - c - D_3 - c - B_3 - r - D_4 - f - B_4 - r - D_5 \quad (2)$$

Assuming that the central word is D_2, when the sliding window $w = 2$, the model can learn the set of developers $S_1 = \{D_1, D_3\}$ that has collaborative relationships with D_2. The collaborative distance between developer D_2 and developers D_1 and D_3 is 0. When the sliding window $w = 4$, the model can learn the set of developers $S_2 = \{D_1, D_3, D_4\}$ that has collaborative relationships with D_2. Among them, the collaborative distance between developer D_2 and developers D_1 and D_3 is 0, the collaborative distance between developer D_2 and developers D_4 is 1. When the sliding window $w = 6$, the model can learn the set of developers $S_3 = \{D_1, D_3, D_4, D_5\}$ that has collaborative relationships with D_2. Among them, the collaborative distance between developer D_2 and developers D_1 and D_3 is 0, the collaborative distance between developer D_2 and developers D_4 is 1, the collaborative distance between developer D_2 and developers D_5 is 2.

Finally, the skip-gram model outputs the feature vector of each node in the heterogeneous collaborative network. We take the feature vector of the reporter in the current software defect as the developer characteristic of the current software defect. According to the experimental results in Section 6.3, this paper sets the value of sliding window $w = 4$.

4.4. Classifier

In this paper, the DARIP method takes the fixers as the labels of software defects. Therefore, the task of assigning a developer to a software defect can be transformed into a classification task, and the developer assignment task can be solved by using the method of classification task.

In this paper, a fully connected neural network is used to build a classifier, which trains and learns the textual characteristics, developer characteristics, and labels input of software defects in the classifier and uses the ReLU function as the activation function. Since there are cases where there are multiple fixers for a software defect, i.e., multiple labels for a single sample, our classification task belongs to multi-label classification. For this purpose, for the last layer of full connectivity, we use the Sigmoid activation function to calculate the probability of assigning a software defect to each developer category. The mathematical formula of the Sigmoid function is shown in Formula (3),

$$\sigma(x) = \frac{1}{1 + e^{-x}} \quad (3)$$

In the field of mathematics, the Sigmoid function is monotonically increasing, derivable, and continuous. Its value domain $R(s) \in (0, 1)$. When the input value tends to negative infinity, the output value is close to 0. When the input value tends to positive infinity, the output value is close to 1. The mathematical properties of the Sigmoid function allow it to be used in neural networks as an activation function to normalize the output of each neuron. In addition, since the probability also takes values in the range of 0 to 1, the Sigmoid function is often applied to prediction probability models to solve classification problems. This paper uses the Sigmoid function to predict the probability of each label in the software defect separately [48], and the probability of different categories do not affect each other. In the classifier, the formula for calculating the probability of assigning the i-th software defect to the j-th fixer is defined by Formulas (4)–(6),

$$\sigma(z_j) = \frac{1}{1 + e^{-z_j}} \quad (4)$$

$$\sigma(z_j) = p(dev_j|bug_i) \quad (5)$$

$$p(dev_j|bug_i) = \frac{1}{1 + e^{-z_j}} \quad (6)$$

where z_j is the ouput of the fully connected layer and the input of the Sigmoid function. Formula (4) is obtained by inserting $x = z_j$ into Formula (3). In Formula (5), bug_i is the i-th software defect, and dev_j is the j-th fixer. $\sigma(z_j)$ is expressed as the probability of assigning the i-th software defect to the j-th fixer. The final probability calculation Formula (6) can be obtained by substituting Formula (5) with Formula (4).

In addition, the number of software defects fixed by each developer varies, making the sample size different for different developer types, which may lead to a category imbalance in the dataset. This paper addresses the problem of category imbalance by using data augmentation technique [49], which extends the dataset by generating new training data from existing data, effectively reducing model overfitting. Specifically, we first delete the categories with a sample size of 1 in the dataset because too few samples will affect the training effect of the model. Secondly, the sample size of the largest category in the dataset is denoted as $maxNum$. Then, the formula $Threshold = p * maxNum$ for the small number of samples is proposed by setting the parameter $p = 0.8$. For each category, when the sample size of the category is less than $Threshold$, a sample is randomly selected from the original dataset of the category, and the original textual content in the sample is randomly exchanged to generate new textual content. For the newly generated text, the same processing method is used to obtain the textual characteristic of the sample. At the same time, we keep the developer characteristic unchanged and finally get the characteristic vector of the new sample. When the sample size of the category is not less than $Threshold$, the data augmentation process for the current category is stopped. Finally, the problem of category imbalance in the dataset is solved by traversing and processing each category.

We evaluate the performance of the model by splitting the training set and the test set and dividing them by a ratio of 8:2. During the training phase, we obtain the augmented training set based on the above data-augmentation method. We construct the cross-entropy loss function, train the classifiers based on the gradient descent optimization algorithm, use the dropout strategy to prevent the overfitting phenomenon, and finally generate the assignment model. During the test phase, the assignment model generated in the training phase is used to recommend appropriate developers for each software defect based on the data in the test set.

5. Dataset

In order to study the assignment of software defects, this paper needs to collect data on software defects and construct a dataset.

In order to collect software defects, this paper needs to select suitable open-source projects from the GitHub platform. First, we sorted projects in GitHub from highest to lowest based on the number of stars in order to select some popular projects. For the Top-50 open-source projects with the highest number of stars, we further filtered out projects that shared documentation or books and only considered projects that involved software development work. Then, for such projects, we counted the number of software defects in each project from inception until 2023. Since GitHub supports developers to identify features for reported issues by adding labels, we manually checked the label described as a bug in each software project and selected the issue with that label as a software defect. In order to ensure that software defects do not change in the future, this paper only considers software defects whose status is closed. At the same time, in order to ensure that the collected software defects can be used for the training and learning of the assignment model, we selected the software defects with fixers. For the software defects that meet the above conditions, we filtered out the projects with a number of software defects that were less than 500 to ensure that there were enough software defects in each software project. Finally, we selected the Top-9 open-source software projects with a high number of stars and more than 500 software defects. The details of the 9 open-source projects are shown in Table 3. In Table 3, the number of software defects in the 9 open-source projects reached 20,280, using programming languages such as C++, C#, JavaScript, Go, and other mainstream programming languages.

For the software defects in nine open-source projects, we used GitHub Rest API to extract the title, body, reporter, commentator, and fixer information of each defect. At the same time, we collected the reporting time and closing time of the software defects. We define other software defects whose closing time is earlier than the reporting time of the current defect as their historical software defects. Some software defects may be assigned to virtual bots (users registered on the platform with a "bot" string in their name) instead of real developers. Since no real developers were used, these software defects were not useful for the training and learning the automated developer assignment task. Therefore, we removed these software defects assigned to virtual bots based on the "bot" string contained in the registered name. At the same time, we also removed the virtual bots when collecting developers. In addition, there are a small number of cases where the reporters of software defects are also their fixers. In order to better study the developer assignment method, we treated these software defects as follows: (1) If there was only one fixer and the fixer was also the reporter, the software defect was deleted directly. (2) If the software defect had more than one fixer, the defect was retained, and the fixer, who was also the reporter, was deleted from the fixer list.

Table 3. Information of nine open-source projects.

Open-Source Project	Period	Number of Stars	Label of Defects	Number of Defects	Number of Fixers	Main Programming Language
tensorflow/tensorflow	2015/11–2022/12	170k	type:bug	7208	341	C++
flutter/flutter	2015/11–2022/12	148 k	P4	741	143	Dart
electron/electron	2014/05–2022/12	105 k	bug	755	35	C++
vercel/next.js	2016/10–2022/12	97.9 k	kind: bug	592	33	JavaScript
kubernetes/kubernetes	2014/06–2022/12	94.5 k	kind/bug	3768	778	Go
microsoft/TypeScript	2014/07–2022/12	87 k	Bug	4601	51	TypeScript
microsoft/terminal	2017/10–2022/12	86.7 k	Issue-Bug	577	30	C++
microsoft/PowerToys	2019/09–2022/12	83.7 k	Issue-Bug	973	56	C#
ant-design/ant-design	2015/07–2022/12	83.5 k	Bug	1065	44	TypeScript

In addition, software defects may have one or multiple fixers. We measured the percentage of software bugs with multiple fixers across 9 projects and found that only 7.57%

of software defects had two or more fixers, and 92.43% of software defects had only one fixer. Therefore, when we customized the meta-paths, we did not consider the collaboration of two developers fixing a software defect at the same time.

6. Experimental Evaluation

6.1. Evaluation Metrics

For the developer assignment method DARIP, this paper evaluates the DARIP method by using two metrics: Mean Reciprocal Rank(MRR) [50] and Recall@k [51].

(1) Mean Reciprocal Rank (MRR)

The Mean Reciprocal Rank is a widely used evaluation metric in recommendation algorithms. It represents the average reciprocal ranking of the real fixers in the assignment list. The higher the ranking of a real fixer in the assignment list, the higher the average reciprocal ranking. If there are multiple real fixers, the one with the highest ranking is selected for the calculation. In this paper, we denote N as the number of software defects, and $rank(i)$ as the rank of the real fixer in the assignment list for the i-th software defect. The formula for calculating the Mean Reciprocal Rank is as follows:

$$MRR = \frac{1}{N}\sum_{i=1}^{N}\frac{1}{rank(i)} \quad (7)$$

(2) Recall@k

The k indicates a configurable option. The $Recall@k$ is the number of real fixers in the top-k ranking divided by the number of real fixers. The research goal of this paper is to assign appropriate fixers to software defects, so we hope to find out the real fixers of software defects as much as possible, so we use the $Recall@k$ to evaluate the ability of the model to predict the fixers. In this paper, we denote N as the number of software defects, $real(i)_k$ as the number of real fixers in the top-k ranking of the assignment list for the i-th software defect, and $real(i)_{all}$ as the number of all real fixers for the i-th software defect. Finally, the average of the $Recall@k$ of N software defects is calculated. The calculation formula is as follows:

$$Recall@k = \frac{1}{N}\sum_{i=1}^{N}\frac{real(i)_k}{real(i)_{all}} \quad (8)$$

In addition, in order to compare the difference in the assignment effect of different methods, this paper defines the gain value to calculate the difference in the assignment effect of method M_1 and method M_2, including the gain value of MRR and the gain value of $Recall@k$. The definitions are as follows:

$$Gain(MRR) = \frac{MRR(M_1) - MRR(M_2)}{MRR(M_2)} \quad (9)$$

$$Gain(Recall@k) = \frac{Recall@k(M_1) - Recall@k(M_2)}{Recall@k(M_2)} \quad (10)$$

6.2. Research Questions

This paper studies the following three questions:

RQ1: How is the performance of the DARIP method in assigning developers for software defects?

In this paper, we compare the DARIP method with the Multi-triage method proposed by Aung et al. [14] and validate the effect of the DARIP method of developer assignment for software defects in the datasets of nine open-source projects, respectively.

RQ2: Does the combination of different characteristics improve the assignment effect of the DARIP method?

The automatic developer assignment method proposed in this paper considers the textual and developer characteristics of software defects, respectively. In order to evaluate the necessity of selecting the above characteristics, this paper compares the assignment effect of different characteristic combinations and selects the appropriate characteristic combinations to apply to the DARIP method.

RQ3: How do different parameter settings affect the assignment effect of the DARIP method?

Different parameters are involved in the developer assignment method DARIP designed in this paper. We predict Top-N potentially related issues for software defects when extracting textual characteristics. We use the skip-gram model with a specified value of sliding window w to learn the feature representations of developers in heterogeneous collaborative networks. In order to evaluate the effect of different parameter settings on the developer assignment effect, this paper compares the assignment effect under different parameter values and selects the appropriate parameter size for the DARIP method.

6.3. Evaluation Results

6.3.1. RQ1: How Is the Performance of the DARIP Method in Assigning Developers for Software Defects?

Aung et al. [11] proposed multi-triage, a multi-task learning multi-classification method, which extracted the feature representation of bug descriptions and code snippets using a text encoder and an AST encoder, and improved the performance of the model by jointly learning the developer assignment and label classification tasks. In this paper, the Multi-triage method is used as a comparison method.

The experimental results are shown in Table 4. The average values of the Recall@5, the Recall@10, and the MRR of the method DARIP in 9 projects are 0.5902, 0.7160, and 0.4136, respectively. It can be seen that the assignment method DARIP in this paper outperforms the Multi-triage method in the Recall@5, the Recall@10, and the MRR.

Table 4. Definition of the heterogeneous collaborative network.

Project	Method	Recall@5	Recall@10	MRR
ant-design	DARIP	**0.9156**	**0.9778**	**0.6708**
	Multi-traige	0.7426	0.7919	0.5741
electron	DARIP	**0.7319**	**0.8795**	**0.5784**
	Multi-traige	0.7219	0.8278	0.5699
flutter	DARIP	0.2000	**0.3125**	**0.1412**
	Multi-traige	**0.2569**	0.2926	0.1306
kubernetes	DARIP	0.1271	0.1766	**0.1073**
	Multi-traige	**0.1286**	**0.2084**	0.0998
next.js	DARIP	**0.8202**	**0.9071**	**0.5997**
	Multi-traige	0.3517	0.6695	0.2397
PowerToys	DARIP	**0.6501**	**0.8347**	**0.4284**
	Multi-traige	0.5155	0.6443	0.4020
tensorflow	DARIP	**0.2980**	**0.4344**	**0.1770**
	Multi-traige	0.1446	0.3174	0.1333
terminal	DARIP	**0.8281**	**0.9676**	**0.5439**
	Multi-traige	0.5725	0.7812	0.4174
TypeScript	DARIP	**0.7410**	**0.9542**	**0.4757**
	Multi-traige	0.6163	0.7750	0.4004
Average	DARIP	**0.5902**	**0.7160**	**0.4136**
	Multi-traige	0.4501	0.5898	0.3297

Then, the gains of the DARIP method over the Multi-triage method are calculated on 9 projects for the two evaluation metrics, as shown in Table 5. Compared with the existing method Multi-triage, the average values of the Recall@5, the Recall@10, and the MRR of the DARIP method in 9 projects are increased by 31.13%, 21.40%, and 25.45%, respectively.

Table 5. The gain values of the DARIP method relative to the Multi-triage method.

Project	Gain(%)		
	Recall@5	Recall@10	MRR
ant-design	23.30%	23.48%	16.84%
electron	1.39%	6.25%	1.49%
flutter	−22.15%	6.80%	8.12%
kubernetes	−1.17%	−15.26%	7.52%
next.js	133.21%	35.49%	150.19%
PowerToys	26.11%	29.55%	6.57%
tensorflow	106.09%	36.86%	32.78%
terminal	44.65%	23.86%	30.31%
TypeScript	20.23%	23.12%	18.81%
Average	31.13%	21.40%	25.45%

6.3.2. RQ2: Does the Combination of Different Features Improve the Assignment Effect of the DARIP Method?

The assignment method proposed in this paper considers the textual and developer characteristics of software defects, respectively. In order to evaluate the necessity of selecting the above characteristics, this paper compares the assignment effect of different characteristic combinations and selects the appropriate characteristic combinations to apply to the DARIP method.

We remove textual characteristics and developer characteristics, respectively, and compare the differences in the assignment effect between the method of removing textual characteristic, the method of removing developer characteristic, and the DARIP method, as shown in Table 6. The results show that the DARIP method has higher Recall@5, Recall@10, and MRR on nine projects than the methods with textual characteristic removed and developer characteristic removed. This shows that considering both textual and developer characteristics can help improve the effect of developer assignment.

In conclusion, compared with the method of removing textual characteristic and the method of removing developer characteristic, the DARIP method shows a better assignment effect on nine projects. This fully demonstrates the importance of selecting the above characteristics in this paper.

Table 6. Comparison of different characteristics.

Project	Experimental Group	Recall@5	Recall@10	MRR
ant-design	DARIP	**0.9156**	**0.9778**	**0.6708**
	Remove Text	0.8828	0.9294	0.5418
	Remove Developer	0.8891	0.9682	0.6462
electron	DARIP	**0.7319**	**0.8795**	**0.5784**
	Remove Text	0.6632	0.8160	0.5477
	Remove Developer	0.6899	0.8501	0.5636
flutter	DARIP	**0.2**	**0.3125**	**0.1412**
	Remove Text	0.1761	0.2689	0.1298
	Remove Developer	0.1714	0.2642	0.1294

Table 6. *Cont.*

Project	Experimental Group	Recall@5	Recall@10	MRR
kubernetes	DARIP	**0.1271**	**0.1766**	**0.1073**
	Remove Text	0.1136	0.1655	0.1005
	Remove Developer	0.1253	0.1725	0.0980
next.js	DARIP	**0.8202**	**0.9071**	**0.5997**
	Remove Text	0.7598	0.8993	0.5928
	Remove Developer	0.8046	0.9013	0.5961
PowerToys	DARIP	**0.6501**	**0.8347**	**0.4284**
	Remove Text	0.6275	0.7264	0.3344
	Remove Developer	0.6359	0.8002	0.4220
tensorflow	DARIP	**0.2980**	**0.4344**	**0.1770**
	Remove Text	0.2275	0.3893	0.1402
	Remove Developer	0.2764	0.4250	0.1734
terminal	DARIP	**0.8281**	**0.9676**	**0.5439**
	Remove Text	0.7016	0.9656	0.4303
	Remove Developer	0.8221	0.9656	0.5414
TypeScript	DARIP	**0.7410**	**0.9542**	**0.4757**
	Remove Text	0.5089	0.8407	0.3271
	Remove Developer	0.7304	0.9404	0.4724

6.3.3. RQ3: How Do Different Parameter Settings Affect the Assignment Effect of the DARIP Method?

Different parameters are involved in the developer assignment method DARIP designed in this paper. This section analyzes the parameter settings of the number of predicted related issues N and the sliding window w in the skip-gram model.

When extracting the textual characteristics of software defects, we predict Top-N potential related issues for each software defect, weight them based on the cosine similarity between software defects and related issues, and finally get the textual characteristics of each software defect. If the parameter N takes different values, the resulting textual characteristics also have certain differences. We set the parameter N to 0, 1, 3, and 5, respectively, and compare the difference in the assignment effect when N takes different values, as shown in Table 7. Among them, $N = 0$ means that we do not consider the related issues and only extract textual characteristics based on the text information of software defects.

Table 7. Comparison of different characteristics.

Project	Top-N	Recall@5	Recall@10	MRR
ant-design	Without Issues	0.8989	0.9689	0.6451
	Top-1	**0.9156**	**0.9778**	**0.6708**
	Top-3	0.8891	0.9597	0.6507
	Top-5	0.8859	0.9640	0.6415
electron	Without Issues	0.7064	0.8716	0.5738
	Top-1	**0.7319**	**0.8795**	**0.5784**
	Top-3	0.6914	0.8501	0.5606
	Top-5	0.6751	0.8472	0.5552
flutter	Without Issues	0.1897	0.2773	0.1360
	Top-1	**0.2**	**0.3125**	**0.1412**
	Top-3	0.1811	0.3062	0.1323
	Top-5	0.1748	0.3046	0.1279

Table 7. Cont.

Project	Top-N	Recall@5	Recall@10	MRR
kubernetes	Without Issues	0.1261	0.1638	0.0911
	Top-1	**0.1271**	**0.1766**	**0.1073**
	Top-3	0.1015	0.1575	0.0976
	Top-5	0.1184	0.1572	0.0875
next.js	Without Issues	0.7549	0.8961	0.5677
	Top-1	**0.8202**	**0.9071**	**0.5997**
	Top-3	0.7851	0.8974	0.5698
	Top-5	0.7618	0.8916	0.5844
PowerToys	Without Issues	0.6376	0.8259	0.4202
	Top-1	**0.6501**	**0.8347**	**0.4284**
	Top-3	0.6085	0.7787	0.3865
	Top-5	0.6049	0.7859	0.3702
tensorflow	Without Issues	0.2937	0.4025	0.1698
	Top-1	**0.2980**	**0.4344**	**0.1770**
	Top-3	0.2773	0.3899	0.1598
	Top-5	0.2836	0.4105	0.1680
terminal	Without Issues	0.7916	0.9652	0.5345
	Top-1	**0.8281**	**0.9676**	**0.5439**
	Top-3	0.8221	0.9834	0.5371
	Top-5	0.8004	0.9755	0.5394
TypeScript	Without Issues	0.7119	0.9535	0.4519
	Top-1	**0.7410**	**0.9542**	**0.4757**
	Top-3	0.7286	0.9487	0.4666
	Top-5	0.7195	0.9509	0.4560

When considering related issues, it can be found that the Recall@5, the Recall@10, and the MRR when N is 1 are better than the Recall@5, the Recall@10, and the MRR when N is 3 and 5. This indicates that the method considering Top-1 related issues has better assignment effect than the methods considering Top-3 and Top-5 related issues. Moreover, with the increase of N, the assignment effect of the DARIP method decreases.

In the case of not considering related issues, it can be found that the Recall@5, the Recall@10, and the MRR when N takes the value of 1 are better than the Recall@5, the Recall@10, and the MRR without related issues on 9 projects. This suggests that considering the text information of related issues can help to improve the developers' assignment effect.

In conclusion, the DARIP method is the most effective when predicting the Top-1 potentially related issues for software defects. Therefore, in this paper, we set the value of N to 1.

At the same time, this paper uses the skip-gram model to extract developer characteristics from the walk sequences. The size of the sliding window w in the skip-gram model limits the collaborative distance between developers that can be learned. When w takes different values, the developer characteristics extracted from software defects are also different.

We set the sliding window w to 2, 4, and 6, respectively, and compare the differences in the assignment effect when w is set to different values, as shown in Table 8. The results show that the Recall@5, the Recall@10, and the MRR of the DARIP method when w is set to 4 are better than that of the methods when w is set to 2 and 6. Therefore, we set the value of w to 4 in this paper.

Table 8. Comparison of different characteristics.

Project	w	Recall@5	Recall@10	MRR
ant-design	2	0.8649	0.9564	0.5979
	4	**0.9156**	**0.9778**	**0.6708**
	6	0.8992	0.9682	0.6544
electron	2	0.7018	0.8532	0.5656
	4	**0.7319**	**0.8795**	**0.5784**
	6	0.6815	0.8408	0.5476
flutter	2	0.1968	0.3043	0.1353
	4	**0.2**	**0.3125**	**0.1412**
	6	0.1841	0.2991	0.1326
kubernetes	2	0.1254	0.1188	0.0888
	4	**0.1271**	**0.1766**	**0.1073**
	6	0.1229	0.1745	0.0978
next.js	2	0.7949	0.8976	0.5645
	4	**0.8202**	**0.9071**	**0.5997**
	6	0.8194	0.8863	0.5435
PowerToys	2	0.6199	0.7878	0.3946
	4	**0.6501**	**0.8347**	**0.4284**
	6	0.6206	0.7892	0.4050
tensorflow	2	0.2860	**0.4554**	0.1685
	4	**0.2980**	0.4344	**0.1770**
	6	0.2892	0.4298	0.1625
terminal	2	0.8180	0.9660	0.5274
	4	**0.8281**	**0.9676**	**0.5439**
	6	0.8101	0.9556	0.5395
TypeScript	2	0.6930	0.8995	0.4393
	4	**0.7410**	**0.9542**	**0.4757**
	6	0.6951	0.8953	0.4348

7. Discussion

In this paper, we propose the developer assignment method DARIP, which assigns appropriate developers to software defects by considering the prediction of related issues and the collaborative relationship between developers. Experimental results validate the effectiveness of the DARIP method in several ways.

The DARIP method takes into account the possible correlation between software defects and other issues, and mines additional valuable text information for software defects by predicting related issues. As shown in Table 7, the Recall@5, the Recall@10, and the MRR when N is 1 are better than the Recall@5, the Recall@10, and the MRR when N is 0. This indicates that the method considering Top-1 related issues has better assignment effect than the method without considering related issues. However, we find that the assignment effect of the DARIP method decreases with the increase of N. In the ant-design project, the Recall@5, the Recall@10, and the MRR when N is 5 are lower than the Recall@5, the Recall@10, and the MRR when N is 0. We analyze the difference of the assignment effect when N takes different values, and find that it is optimal when predicting Top-1 related issues for software defects.

Meanwhile, the DARIP method considers four types of collaborative relationships between developers: report–comment, report–fix, comment–comment, and comment–fix, and uses graph-embedding algorithm to learn collaboration between developers from the constructed heterogeneous collaborative network. We analyze the difference in assignment effect with different values of sliding window w, as shown in Table 8. The Recall@5, the Recall@10, and the MRR of the DARIP method when w is set to 4 are better than that of the method when w is set to 2. This indicates that it is not sufficient to consider collaborative relationships where the collaborative distance between developers is 0 (direct collaboration, where two developers collaborate on the same software defect) but also collaborative relationships where the collaborative distance between developers is 1 (indirect collaboration, where both developers have a direct collaborative relationship with the same developer). However, the Recall@5, the Recall@10, and the MRR of the DARIP method when w is set to 4 are better than that of the method when w is set to 6. This indicates that the assignment effect decreases when considering collaborative relationships with greater distances. Therefore, when assigning developers for software defects, direct and indirect collaborative relationships between developers need to be considered, and collaborative relationships with greater distances are not recommended.

8. Threats to Validity

Threats to construct validity is concerned with the suitability of experimental results to the concepts or theories behind the experiments. Firstly, we selected 9 popular projects from the GitHub platform to verify our method. The 9 open-source projects involve a variety of common programming languages and contain 20,280 software defects, which is representative. Future work can collect more open-source projects to validate our method. Then, we predict related issues for a software defect from its historical software defects. These historical software defects belong to the same project as the software defect. However, when Li et al. [29] studied the correlation between issues, they found that the related issues of an issue in a project may originate from other projects on the GitHub platform. In future work, we will expand the data sources of related issues to evaluate the DARIP method.

Threats to internal validity is the degree to which research establishes a credible causal relationship between disposition and outcome. First, we investigate the assignment effect of the method based on the standard answer of the assignee to the software defect as the fixer. However, the real fixer may not be the best developer to fix the software defect, and other developers may also be capable of fixing it. Future work can manually label the developers who are capable of fixing software defects to construct the dataset. Then, this paper uses cosine similarity to calculate the correlation between software defects and related issues. In future work, we try to use different text similarity calculation methods and analyze the impact of using different similarity calculation methods on developer assignment methods.

Threats to external validity have to do with the universality of our research. This paper selects the GitHub platform to study the developer assignment of software defects but is uncertain about the effect of this method on other open-source platforms. Future work can collect data from more platforms to validate the DARIP method. Meanwhile, this paper investigates the developer assignment method for software defects in the Issue-Tracking System. However, the issues recorded in the Issue-Tracking System include not only software defects but also functional requirements proposed by developers. Such issues may also be assigned to developers to complete software development tasks. In future work, we consider extending the DARIP method to assign developers to all issues in the Issue-Tracking System.

9. Conclusions

In this paper, we propose a developer assignment method, DARIP, for open-source software defects. First, the DARIP method uses the BERT model to extract the textual vectors from software defects and all its historical software defects. Based on the cosine similarity, Top-N potential related issues are predicted for each software defect from all the historical software defects, and takes the text information of related issues together with the text information of software defects as textual input. The textual characteristics of software defects are obtained by comprehensively calculating the text vector of software defects and related issues. Secondly, a heterogeneous collaborative network is constructed based on the three development behaviors of developers: reporting, commenting, and fixing. The meta-paths are defined based on the four collaboration relationships between developers:

report–comment, report–fix, comment–comment, and comment–fix. The graph-embedding algorithm metapath2vec is used to extract developer characteristics from the heterogeneous collaborative network. Then, a classifier based on a deep learning model calculates the probability assigned to each developer category. Finally, the assignment list is obtained according to the probability ranking.

This paper verifies the performance of the DARIP method on 20,280 software defects in 9 popular projects. The experimental results show that the average values of the Recall@5, the Recall@10, and the MRR of the DARIP method in 9 projects are 0.5902, 0.7160, and 0.4136, respectively. Compared with the existing method Multi-triage, the average values of the Recall@5, the Recall@10, and the MRR of the DARIP method in 9 projects are increased by 31.13%, 21.40%, and 25.45%, respectively.

Author Contributions: Conceptualization, B.L. and J.J.; methodology, B.L. and J.J.; validation, B.L. and Z.L.; formal analysis, B.L.; investigation, B.L.; resources, L.Z. and J.J.; data curation, B.L.; writing—original draft preparation, B.L.; writing—review and editing, J.J.; supervision, L.Z.; project administration, J.J.; funding acquisition, L.Z. and J.J. All authors have read and agreed to the published version of the manuscript.

Funding: This research was funded by the National Natural Science Foundation of China under grant No. 62177003.

Data Availability Statement: Data are contained within the article.

Acknowledgments: This research was supported by the National Natural Science Foundation of China.

Conflicts of Interest: The authors declare no conflicts of interest.

References

1. Dabbish, L.; Stuart, C.; Tsay, J.; Herbsleb, J. Social coding in GitHub: Transparency and collaboration in an open software repository. In Proceedings of the ACM 2012 Conference on Computer Supported Cooperative Work, Seattle, WA, USA, 11–15 February 2012; pp. 1277–1286.
2. Lima, A.; Rossi, L.; Musolesi, M. Coding together at scale: GitHub as a collaborative social network. In Proceedings of the International AAAI Conference on Web and Social Media, Oxford, UK, 27–29 May 2014; Volume 8, pp. 295–304.
3. Yang, B.; Yu, Q.; Zhang, W.; Wu, J.; Liu, C. Influence Factors Correlation Analysis in GitHub Open Source Software Development Process. *J. Softw.* **2017**, *28*, 1330–1342.
4. Bissyandé, T.F.; Lo, D.; Jiang, L.; Réveillere, L.; Klein, J.; Le Traon, Y. Got issues? who cares about it? a large scale investigation of issue trackers from github. In Proceedings of the 2013 IEEE 24th International Symposium on Software Reliability Engineering (ISSRE), Pasadena, CA, USA, 4–7 November 2013; pp. 188–197.
5. Bertram, D.; Voida, A.; Greenberg, S.; Walker, R. Communication, collaboration, and bugs: The social nature of issue tracking in small, collocated teams. In Proceedings of the 2010 ACM Conference on Computer Supported Cooperative Work, Savannah, GA, USA, 6–10 February 2010; pp. 291–300.
6. Xu, C.; Cheung, S.C.; Ma, X.; Cao, C.; Lu, J. Adam: Identifying defects in context-aware adaptation. *J. Syst. Softw.* **2012**, *85*, 2812–2828. [CrossRef]
7. Yan, A.; Zhong, H.; Song, D.; Jia, L. How do programmers fix bugs as workarounds? An empirical study on Apache projects. *Empir. Softw. Eng.* **2023**, *28*, 96–120. [CrossRef]
8. Wang, Y.; Chen, X.; Huang, Y.; Zhu, H.N.; Bian, J.; Zheng, Z. An empirical study on real bug fixes from solidity smart contract projects. *J. Syst. Softw.* **2023**, *204*, 96–120. [CrossRef]
9. Guo, S.; Zhang, X.; Yang, X.; Chen, R.; Guo, C.; Li, H.; Li, T. Developer activity motivated bug triaging: Via convolutional neural network. *Neural Process. Lett.* **2020**, *51*, 2589–2606. [CrossRef]
10. Shokripour, R.; Anvik, J.; Kasirun, Z.M.; Zamani, S. Why so complicated? simple term filtering and weighting for location-based bug report assignment recommendation. In Proceedings of the 2013 10th Working Conference on Mining Software Repositories (MSR), San Francisco, CA, USA, 18–19 May 2013; pp. 2–11.
11. Jeong, G.; Kim, S.; Zimmermann, T. Improving bug triage with bug tossing graphs. In Proceedings of the 7th Joint Meeting of the European Software Engineering Conference and the ACM SIGSOFT Symposium on the Foundations of Software Engineering, Amsterdam, The Netherlands, 24–28 August 2009; pp. 111–120.
12. Jahanshahi, H.; Cevik, M. S-DABT: Schedule and Dependency-aware Bug Triage in open-source bug tracking systems. *Inf. Softw. Technol.* **2022**, *151*, 107025. [CrossRef]

13. Yang, G.; Zhang, T.; Lee, B. Towards semi-automatic bug triage and severity prediction based on topic model and multi-feature of bug reports. In Proceedings of the 2014 IEEE 38th Annual Computer Software and Applications Conference, Vasteras, Sweden, 21–25 July 2014; pp. 97–106.
14. Aung, T.W.W.; Wan, Y.; Huo, H.; Sui, Y. Multi-triage: A multi-task learning framework for bug triage. *J. Syst. Softw.* **2022**, *184*, 111133. [CrossRef]
15. Naguib, H.; Narayan, N.; Brügge, B.; Helal, D. Bug report assignee recommendation using activity profiles. In Proceedings of the 2013 10th Working Conference on Mining Software Repositories (MSR), San Francisco, CA, USA, 18–19 May 2013; pp. 22–30.
16. Xia, X.; Lo, D.; Ding, Y.; Al-Kofahi, J.M.; Nguyen, T.N.; Wang, X. Improving automated bug triaging with specialized topic model. *IEEE Trans. Softw. Eng.* **2016**, *43*, 272–297. [CrossRef]
17. Zhang, W.; Cui, Y.; Yoshida, T. En-lda: An novel approach to automatic bug report assignment with entropy optimized latent dirichlet allocation. *Entropy* **2017**, *19*, 173. [CrossRef]
18. Bhattacharya, P.; Neamtiu, I. Fine-grained incremental learning and multi-feature tossing graphs to improve bug triaging. In Proceedings of the 2010 IEEE International Conference on Software Maintenance, Timisoara, Romani, 12–18 September 2010.
19. Jonsson, L.; Borg, M.; Broman, D.; Sandahl, K.; Eldh, S.; Runeson, P. Automated bug assignment: Ensemble-based machine learning in large scale industrial contexts. *Empir. Softw. Eng.* **2016**, *21*, 1533–1578. [CrossRef]
20. Sarkar, A.; Rigby, P.C.; Bartalos, B. Improving bug triaging with high confidence predictions at ericsson. In Proceedings of the 2019 IEEE International Conference on Software Maintenance and Evolution (ICSME), Cleveland, OH, USA, 29 September–4 October 2019; pp. 81–91.
21. Lee, S.R.; Heo, M.J.; Lee, C.G.; Kim, M.; Jeong, G. Applying deep learning based automatic bug triager to industrial projects. In Proceedings of the 2017 11th Joint Meeting on Foundations of Software Engineering, Paderborn, Germany, 4–8 September 2017; pp. 926–931.
22. Mani, S.; Sankaran, A.; Aralikatte, R. Deeptriage: Exploring the effectiveness of deep learning for bug triaging. In Proceedings of the ACM India Joint International Conference on Data Science and Management of Data, Mumbai, India, 4–7 January 2019; pp. 171–179.
23. Canfora, G.; Ceccarelli, M.; Cerulo, L.; Di Penta, M. How long does a bug survive? An empirical study. In Proceedings of the 2011 18th Working Conference on Reverse Engineering, Limerick, Ireland, 17–20 October 2011; pp. 191–200.
24. Li, Z.; Tan, L.; Wang, X.; Lu, S.; Zhou, Y.; Zhai, C. Have things changed now? An empirical study of bug characteristics in modern open-source software. In Proceedings of the 1st Workshop on Architectural and System Support for Improving Software Dependability, San Jose, CA, USA, 21 October 2006; pp. 25–33.
25. Almhana, R.; Kessentini, M. Considering dependencies between bug reports to improve bugs triage. *Autom. Softw. Eng.* **2021**, *28*, 1–26. [CrossRef]
26. Jahanshahi, H.; Chhabra, K.; Cevik, M.; Başar, A. DABT: A dependency-aware bug triaging method. In Proceedings of the Evaluation and Assessment in Software Engineering, Trondheim, Norway, 21–23 June 2021; pp. 221–230.
27. Hong, Q.; Kim, S.; Cheung, S.C.; Bird, C. Understanding a developer social network and its evolution. In Proceedings of the 2011 27th IEEE International Conference on Software Maintenance (ICSM), Williamsburg, VA, USA, 25–30 September 2011; pp. 323–332.
28. Xuan, J.; Jiang, H.; Ren, Z.; Zou, W. Developer prioritization in bug repositories. In Proceedings of the 2012 34th International Conference on Software Engineering (ICSE), Zurich, Switzerland, 2–9 June 2012; pp. 25–35.
29. Wang, Q.; Xu, B.; Xia, X.; Wang, T.; Li, S. Duplicate pull request detection: When time matters. In Proceedings of the 11th Asia-Pacific Symposium on Internetware, Fukuoka, Japan, 28–29 October 2019; pp. 1–10.
30. Ma, W.; Chen, L.; Zhang, X.; Zhou, Y.; Xu, B. How do developers fix cross-project correlated bugs? a case study on the github scientific python ecosystem. In Proceedings of the 2017 IEEE/ACM 39th International Conference on Software Engineering (ICSE), Buenos Aires, Argentina, 20–28 May 2017; pp. 381–392.
31. Zhang, Y.; Yu, Y.; Wang, H.; Vasilescu, B.; Filkov, V. Within-ecosystem issue linking: A large-scale study of rails. In Proceedings of the 7th International Workshop on Software Mining, Montpellier, France, 3 September 2018; pp. 12–19.
32. Li, L.; Ren, Z.; Li, X.; Zou, W.; Jiang, H. How are issue units linked? empirical study on the linking behavior in github. In Proceedings of the 2018 25th Asia-Pacific Software Engineering Conference (APSEC), Nara, Japan, 4–7 December 2018; pp. 386–395.
33. Liu, B.; Zhang, L.; Jiang, J.; Wang, L. A method for identifying references between projects in GitHub. *Sci. Comput. Program.* **2022**, *222*, 102858. [CrossRef]
34. Zhang, Y.; Wu, Y.; Wang, T.; Wang, H. iLinker: A novel approach for issue knowledge acquisition in GitHub projects. *World Wide Web* **2020**, *23*, 1589–1619. [CrossRef]
35. Liu, B.; Zhang, L.; Liu, Z.; Jiang, J. Cross-project Issue Recommendation Method for Open-source Software Defects. *J. Softw.* **2023**, 1–19. [CrossRef]
36. Zaidi, S.F.A.; Woo, H.; Lee, C.G. Toward an effective bug triage system using transformers to add new developers. *J. Sens.* **2022**, *2022*, 4347004. [CrossRef]
37. Kim, M.H.; Wang, D.S.; Wang, S.T.; Park, S.H.; Lee, C.G. Improving the Robustness of the Bug Triage Model through Adversarial Training. In Proceedings of the International Conference on Information Networking, Jeju, Republic of Korean, 12–15 January 2022; pp. 478–481.

38. Zhang, W.; Zhao, J.; Wang, S. SusTriage: Sustainable Bug Triage with Multi-modal Ensemble Learning. In Proceedings of the International Conference on Web Intelligence and Intelligent Agent Technology, Melbourne, VIC, Australia, 14–17 December 2021; pp. 441–448.
39. Jahanshahi, H.; Cevik, M.; Mousavi, K.; Basar, A. ADPTriage: Approximate Dynamic Programming for Bug Triage. *Trans. Softw. Eng.* **2023**, *49*, 4594–4609. [CrossRef]
40. Banitaan, S.; Alenezi, M. Decoba: Utilizing developers communities in bug assignment. In Proceedings of the 2013 12th International Conference on Machine Learning and Applications, Miami, FL, USA, 4–7 December 2013; Volume 2, pp. 66–71.
41. Zhang, W.; Wang, S.; Wang, Q. KSAP: An approach to bug report assignment using KNN search and heterogeneous proximity. *Inf. Softw. Technol.* **2016**, *70*, 68–84. [CrossRef]
42. Zaidi, S.F.A.; Lee, C.G. Learning graph representation of bug reports to triage bugs using graph convolution network. In Proceedings of the 2021 International Conference on Information Networking (ICOIN), Jeju, Republic of Korean, 13–16 January 2021; pp. 504–507.
43. Hu, H.; Zhang, H.; Xuan, J.; Sun, W. Effective bug triage based on historical bug-fix information. In Proceedings of the 2014 IEEE 25th International Symposium on Software Reliability Engineering, Naples, Italy, 3–6 November 2014; pp. 122–132.
44. Yadav, A.; Singh, S.K.; Suri, J.S. Ranking of software developers based on expertise score for bug triaging. *Inf. Softw. Technol.* **2019**, *112*, 1–17. [CrossRef]
45. Su, Y.; Xing, Z.; Peng, X.; Xia, X.; Wang, C.; Xu, X.; Zhu, L. Reducing bug triaging confusion by learning from mistakes with a bug tossing knowledge graph. In Proceedings of the 2021 36th IEEE/ACM International Conference on Automated Software Engineering (ASE), Melbourne, Australia, 15–19 November 2021; pp. 191–202.
46. Devlin, J.; Chang, M.W.; Lee, K.; Toutanova, K. Bert: Pre-training of deep bidirectional transformers for language understanding. *arXiv* **2018**, arXiv:1810.04805.
47. Dong, Y.; Chawla, N.V.; Swami, A. metapath2vec: Scalable representation learning for heterogeneous networks. In Proceedings of the 23rd ACM SIGKDD International Conference on Knowledge Discovery and Data Mining, Halifax, NS, Canada, 13–17 August 2017; pp. 135–144.
48. Goel, P.; Kumar, S.S. Certain class of starlike functions associated with modified sigmoid function. *Bull. Malays. Math. Sci. Soc.* **2020**, *43*, 957–991. [CrossRef]
49. Wei, J.; Zou, K. Eda: Easy data augmentation techniques for boosting performance on text classification tasks. *arXiv* **2019**, arXiv:1901.11196.
50. Zhao, J.; Zhou, Z.; Guan, Z.; Zhao, W.; Ning, W.; Qiu, G.; He, X. Intentgc: A scalable graph convolution framework fusing heterogeneous information for recommendation. In Proceedings of the 25th ACM SIGKDD International Conference on Knowledge Discovery & Data Mining, Anchorage, AK, USA, 4–8 August 2019; pp. 2347–2357.
51. Altosaar, J.; Ranganath, R.; Tansey, W. RankFromSets: Scalable set recommendation with optimal recall. *Stat* **2021**, *10*, e363. [CrossRef]

Disclaimer/Publisher's Note: The statements, opinions and data contained in all publications are solely those of the individual author(s) and contributor(s) and not of MDPI and/or the editor(s). MDPI and/or the editor(s) disclaim responsibility for any injury to people or property resulting from any ideas, methods, instructions or products referred to in the content.

Article

Research on a Non-Intrusive Load Recognition Algorithm Based on High-Frequency Signal Decomposition with Improved VI Trajectory and Background Color Coding †

Jiachuan Shi [1,‡], Dingrui Zhi [2,‡] and Rao Fu [2,*]

1. Shandong Key Laboratory of Intelligent Buildings Technology, Shandong Jianzhu University, Jinan 250101, China; jc_shi@sdjzu.edu.cn
2. School of Information and Electrical Engineering, Shandong Jianzhu University, Jinan 250101, China; 2021080123@stu.sdjzu.edu.cn
* Correspondence: furao20@sdjzu.edu.cn
† This paper is an extended version of our paper published in the 4th International Conference on Neural Computing for Advanced Applications, Hefei, China, 7–9 July 2023.
‡ These authors contributed equally to this work.

Abstract: Against the backdrop of the current Chinese national carbon peak and carbon neutrality policies, higher requirements have been put forward for the construction and upgrading of smart grids. Non-intrusive Load Monitoring (NILM) technology is a key technology for advanced measurement systems at the end of the power grid. This technology obtains detailed power information about the load without the need for traditional hardware deployment. The key step to solve this problem is load decomposition and identification. This study first utilized the Long Short-Term Memory Denoising Autoencoder (LSTM-DAE) to decompose the mixed current signal of a household busbar and obtain the current signals of the multiple independent loads that constituted the mixed current. Then, the obtained independent current signals were combined with the voltage signals to generate multicycle colored Voltage–Current (VI) trajectories, which were color-coded according to the background. These color-coded VI trajectories formed a feature library. When the Convolutional Neural Network (CNN) was used for load recognition, in light of the influence of the hyperparameters on the recognition results, the Bayesian Optimization Algorithm (BOA) was used for optimization, and the optimized CNN network was employed for VI trajectory recognition. Finally, the proposed method was validated using the PLAID dataset. The experimental results show that the proposed method exhibited better performance in load decomposition and identification than current methods.

Keywords: denoising autoencoder; Bayesian optimization; non-intrusive load recognition; convolutional neural network

MSC: 86T20

Citation: Shi, J.; Zhi, D.; Fu, R. Research on a Non-Intrusive Load Recognition Algorithm Based on High-Frequency Signal Decomposition with Improved VI Trajectory and Background Color Coding. *Mathematics* 2024, 12, 30. https://doi.org/10.3390/math12010030

Academic Editor: Ke-Lin Du

Received: 15 November 2023
Revised: 18 December 2023
Accepted: 19 December 2023
Published: 22 December 2023

Copyright: © 2023 by the authors. Licensee MDPI, Basel, Switzerland. This article is an open access article distributed under the terms and conditions of the Creative Commons Attribution (CC BY) license (https://creativecommons.org/licenses/by/4.0/).

1. Introduction

Given the ongoing increase in domestic electricity consumption, incorporating effective daily electricity usage planning is important to minimize energy waste. In this regard, NILM can help identify domestic electrical appliances and their states, enabling domestic consumers to have a better understanding of their electricity consumption behavior and improve their usage patterns [1]. Moreover, NILM can also enhance the management and optimization of the demand side of the power grid to achieve energy saving goals. Therefore, NILM holds great significance for energy conservation and emission reduction [2]. Unlike traditional methods requiring the installation of multiple sensors, NILM integrates electricity information into a single collection signal, making it more cost-effective and practical [3]. NILM can be primarily divided into two categories based on its objectives.

The first is load identification, which involves recognizing the electrical appliances that users are currently using or identifying changes in the switch status of the appliances. The second is load decomposition, where the total power is broken down into the power consumption of individual electrical devices. By analyzing information from these two categories, NILM can provide users and power suppliers with accurate device-level electricity consumption details, including startup and shutdown times, operating duration, power consumption, and the associated costs. In terms of event changes, NILM can be classified into event-based load identification and non-event-based load decomposition [4]. Event-based load identification methods typically include three steps: event detection, feature extraction, and load classification [5]. Non-event-based load decomposition usually does not require event detection; instead, it directly uses the total power sequence as the model input. This is because its purpose is not to identify the electrical appliances running during a specific time period but to decompose the total power based on the differences in the power and operating modes of different appliances, directly obtaining the power sequences of individual electrical devices.

Regarding load identification technology, a 2019 study [6] utilized the Dynamic Time Warping (DTW) algorithm to calculate the similarity between test templates and reference templates, using transient waveforms and the power change values of household load switching events as feature quantities for load recognition. A more recent study [7] clustered load data based on steady-state values and proposed a non-intrusive load recognition method using Feature Weighted K-Nearest Neighbor (FWKNN), which improved the feature distance calculations with feature weights and achieved high accuracy. A further study [8] presented an attention model that combined global and sliding window approaches, employing bidirectional Long Short-Term Memory (LSTM) networks as encoders to extract information, utilizing an attention mechanism to capture the current load information and decode the output decomposition results. A 2020 study [9] encoded different power states of target appliances using a deep recurrent convolutional model, extracting spatiotemporal features of input total load power, and implemented state modeling of different target appliances through transfer learning, achieving significant improvements compared to Markov models. In another recent study [10], a lightweight recognition task was accomplished by combining CNN and K-Nearest Neighbor (KNN) networks. Simultaneously, for unknown loads, user feedback may not be required, allowing the system to operate in unfamiliar home environments. Even more recently [11], a novel method was proposed to extract distorted images of current harmonics from aggregated signals over 60 cycles, enabling appliance classification within 1 s with low computational complexity. Earlier, a study [12] described in detail eight shape features such as the asymmetry observed in VI trajectories and conducted recognition using hierarchical clustering. Subsequently, researchers [13] used the elliptical Fourier descriptor of VI trajectory contours as input for a classification algorithm. A further study [14], based on [12], introduced a new feature called "span" and compared it with the harmonic content, active power, and reactive power of the current, utilizing four classification algorithms. The results showed that the VI trajectories had good recognition capability. The authors of [15] introduced a transfer learning methodology grounded in the VI trajectory to address the challenge of limited data label acquisition. Additionally, the VI trajectory underwent a transformation into a visual representation through color encoding. This process not only heightened the uniqueness of the appliance signature but also facilitated the integration of transfer learning into NILM. The authors of [16] proposed adaptive weighted recurrence graph blocks for the representation of appliance signatures in event-based NILM. By converting the activation current of a single cycle into a weighted recursive graph, the proposed method ensured the distinctiveness of appliance signatures. Consequently, this approach demonstrated superior recognition performance on the LILACD and PLAID public datasets compared to traditional VI-trajectory-based methods. A reconstructed VI trajectory was introduced, incorporating the Particle Swarm Optimization (PSO) algorithm to ascertain the optimal threshold parameters. This enhancement aims to maximize the model's classification capability, addressing the challenge faced by conventional VI-trajectory-based methods in effectively distinguishing similar appliances [17]. A 2021 study [18] introduced the Asymmetric Deep Supervised Hashing (ADSH) method, utilizing VI trajectory signatures for NILM. This approach employed the VI trajectory as the model input, effectively addressing challenges related to the inefficient computation of massive data and the limited discrimination of manually extracted signatures. Simultaneously, an asymmetric learning architecture was applied for hash code learning. Specifically, a convolutional neural network model was used for high-dimensional feature extraction and hash function learning in some training trajectories to establish coding rules. For all training trajectories, the direct learning of coding rules ensured consistency in the codes, thereby achieving accurate appliance recognition. This approach significantly enhanced recognition accuracy while maintaining a small code length and reducing the space complexity. To tackle the difficulties associated with acquiring label data and correctly identifying the VI trajectory of multistate appliances, a semi-supervised learning method based on the semi-supervised teacher graph network [19] was proposed. This method compacted the feature distribution of multistate appliances by constructing a teacher graph, leading to improved recognition results. However, while significant progress has been made in the accuracy of load identification using VI trajectories as features, several challenges persist. Firstly, the current approach normalizes the voltage and current data to derive the VI trajectories, leading to a loss of energy information. Secondly, appliances with continuous power variations, such as computers, are difficult to represent using steady-state VI trajectories. Lastly, VI trajectories fail to capture the stability characteristics of a load's operational state during runtime, specifically the amplitude of the current oscillations.

In the realm of load decomposition techniques, traditional methods rely on low-frequency data to decompose aggregated data into device-level information. This process does not necessitate event detection and typically focuses on power data as the primary research object. The Hidden Markov Model (HMM) has been a commonly used regression model. Kim et al. validated four HMM extension models and introduced non-electrical characteristics such as the load switching duration, load usage frequency, and interdependence among loads, which improved the decomposition accuracy to a certain extent [20]. Kolter et al. applied the Factorial Hidden Markov Model (FHMM) algorithm to establish a load decomposition model, using the total current signals as the research object. When a signal change was detected, the signal differences between the load currents were encoded, resulting in the optimal solution for the model and achieving a high decomposition accuracy [21]. With the continuous development of deep learning technology, non-intrusive load decomposition models based on deep learning have emerged [22]. In 2015, Kelly introduced deep learning methods into the NILM field and coined the term "Neural NILM". Kelly proposed three neural network structures: LSTM, Recurrent Neural Network (RNN), and Distributed Agent Environment (DAE), which were effective in handling long time-series data [23]. Roberto improved Kelly's DAE model by combining it with a median filter, which partially eliminated the noise interference and improved the model's robustness [24]. Odysseas modified Kelly's LSTM network to tackle the issue of the high number of network neurons, which led to long training times and thus, its unsuitability for embedded devices. Instead, the Gated Recurrent Unit (GRU) algorithm was used, reducing the network's depth while maintaining the accuracy and reducing the computational complexity [25]. Zhang proposed a load decomposition framework that mapped sequences to individual load points, with aggregated power data of windows as the network's input and the corresponding single-point load data as the network's output. This mapping pattern accelerated the training speed and improved the load decomposition's real-time performance [26]. Barsim proposed a general deep decomposition model that automatically adjusted the model parameters based on the characteristics of different loads, thus obtaining more accurate load-switching state sequences [27]. Piccialli adopted a neural network model with an attention mechanism, which strengthened the correlation between the input and output and improved the decomposition accuracy [28].

The tasks of load decomposition and load identification have conventionally been regarded as independent processes. However, during load identification tasks, it is imperative to conduct load decomposition. Distinctive load characteristics can only be further extracted by obtaining the independent electrical signals of individual loads through load decomposition. In the load identification process, the commonly employed method for decomposition is the differencing technique. This involves taking the difference between the total voltage and current data before and after the occurrence of an "event". However, practical challenges arise in obtaining accurate current–voltage data through differencing during actual operations, particularly when loads with substantial fluctuations exist on the user bus. Obtaining precise current signals is especially challenging. Consequently, this study introduces the notion of traditional load decomposition into the load identification task to replace the differencing method. Given that voltage signals are minimally affected by load switch actions, only current signals require decomposition. Hence, a deep learning approach is employed for current decomposition, obtaining independent current signals. The current decomposition in load identification differs from traditional load decomposition, which employs low-frequency signals with a sampling frequency typically ranging from 1/6 Hz to 1 Hz. Traditional methods require neural networks to learn the features of the entire load operating cycle over an extended period. In contrast, load identification necessitates high-frequency features, often employing data exceeding 1 kHz. As high-frequency signals exhibit strong periodicity, this study transforms the decomposition issue in load identification into a denoising problem. By denoising mixed current signals, independent current signals for individual loads are obtained.

Thanks to the higher discriminability of electrical quantities in VI trajectories compared to other features and its effective integration with image recognition, the complexity of feature extraction and load identification was reduced. Consequently, the current study opted for VI trajectories as the distinctive feature for load recognition. Despite the significant progress achieved in load recognition accuracy by using VI trajectories as features, the existing issues still exerted a considerable impact on the precision of load identification.

To address these issues, this paper proposed an approach based on LSTM-DAE. This method was employed to decompose complex mixed current signals and obtain independent current signals of unknown loads. The decomposed current signals were combined with voltage signals, and the resulting VI trajectories were plotted as features for load identification. Recognizing the limitations inherent in VI trajectories, traditional single-cycle VI trajectories were enhanced by transforming them into multicycle VI trajectories to capture fluctuations during load operation. Additionally, color coding was applied to VI trajectories to enhance the distinctiveness between different loads. Different background colors were assigned to VI trajectories based on varying current amplitudes, addressing the issue of energy information loss caused by the normalization of current–voltage data.

Following the completion of VI trajectory feature extraction, the improved VI trajectories were subjected to image recognition using the AlexNet architecture within a CNN to accomplish the load identification task. Given the numerous parameters of the AlexNet network and their significant influence on recognition accuracy, the BOA was employed to optimize the hyperparameters of the AlexNet network, aiming to achieve the optimal solution. The specific methodology was as follows:

(1) The high-frequency mixed current signals were decomposed using the LSTM-DAE. This work accurately acquired the current signals of each load by exploiting the high sensitivity of LSTM to temporal signal features and the ability of the DAE to transform the load decomposition problems into denoising problems, which were then utilized as the fundamental data for load recognition;

(2) Colored VI trajectories were generated by plotting the VI trajectories obtained from the multicycle voltage and current data. The R channel represented the normal multicycle VI trajectory, the G channel represented the current variation slope between adjacent sampling points, and the B channel represented the rate of power changes.

(3) Additionally, the VI trajectory background was color processed based on the difference in the current amplitude to obtain a multicycle color-encoded VI trajectory feature library with filled background colors;
(3) The VI trajectory feature library was transformed into an n×n image format and input into the AlexNet network for training. Since the traditional AlexNet network was not suitable for load recognition tasks, the BOA algorithm was employed to optimize the network parameters, thereby achieving better recognition performance;
(4) The PLAID dataset was utilized in the experiments, and the results demonstrated that the six selected load decomposition accuracies all exceeded 94.

2. LSTM-DAE-Based Load Decomposition

2.1. Load Decomposition

Load decomposition is the process of decomposing one mixed telecommunications signal into the independent telecommunications signals for each load. This research transformed this process into a denoising problem to obtain accurate information about the current of each load. Assuming there were N loads, the total current [29] at time t was:

$$I(t) = \sum_{k=1}^{N} I_k(t) + I_\delta(t), \tag{1}$$

where $I(t)$ was the total current at the current moment, $I_k(t)$ was the current generated by the kth load, and $I_\delta(t)$ was the noise disturbance.

Assuming the target load current represented the actual signal and considering the total current signal as the composite of the actual signal and noise interference, the equation was modified as follows:

$$I(t) = I_\eta(t) + I_\beta(t), \tag{2}$$

where $I_\eta(t)$ is the current of the target load and also the real current in the denoising process, and $I_\beta(t)$ is the noise in the denoising process, which is the superposition of the currents of the loads other than the current of the target load and the real noise, expressed as:

$$I_\beta(t) = \sum_{k=1}^{N-1} I_k(t) + I_\delta(t). \tag{3}$$

2.2. Denoising Autoencoder

As shown in Figure 1, the Autoencoder (AE) had an equal number of nodes for the input and output, with the aim of minimizing the reconstruction error between the input and output. The AE consisted of an encoder ϕ and a decoder ψ, where the encoder mapped the input to a low-dimensional feature space, and the decoder mapped the data from the low-dimensional feature space back to the original input. In Figure 1, x represented the input data to the encoder, h represents the data mapped from x to the hidden feature space, and x' represents the data reconstructed by the decoder using the hidden feature space data h. Assuming the input space was $I = R^n$ (where n was the number of variables), the working principle of the autoencoder was defined as follows:

$$\begin{aligned} \phi &: I \to F \\ \psi &: F \to I \\ \phi, \psi &= \underset{\phi,\psi}{\arg\min} \|x - x'\|^2 \end{aligned}, \tag{4}$$

where $\|\cdot\|$ denoted the Frobenius norm. Taking an AE with one hidden layer as an example, the encoder mapped the input $x \in I$ to the hidden feature space $h \in F = R^p$ (p was the dimension of the hidden layer), and the mapping process was

$$h = \sigma(Wx + b), \tag{5}$$

where σ was the activation function in the encoder, W was the weight matrix, and b was the bias vector. After the encoder mapped the input variable to the hidden layer, the decoder reconstructed the variable x' into a variable of the same size as the input variable x based on the information in the hidden layer h. The mapping process was as follows:

$$x' = \sigma'(W'x + b'), \tag{6}$$

where σ' represented the activation function in the decoder, and W' and b' corresponded to the weight matrix and deviation vector in the decoder, respectively. The goal of the self-encoder was to find the process that minimized the residuals between the input and the reconstructed quantity x':

$$\begin{aligned} L(x, x') &= \frac{1}{m} \|x - x'\|^2 \\ &= \frac{1}{m} \|x - \sigma'(W'\sigma(Wx + b)) + b'\|^2, \end{aligned} \tag{7}$$

where m represented the number of sample points in the AE network. The optimization problem of the self-encoder was solved by backpropagation.

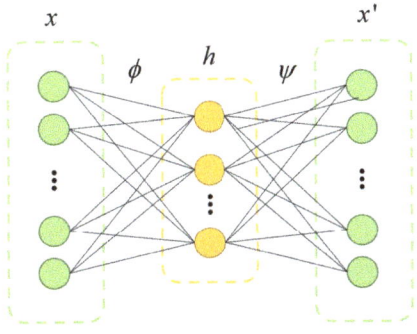

Figure 1. Basic structure of an Autoencoder.

The Denoising Autoencoder (DAE) is a variant of an AE first proposed by Vincent et al. [30]; its network structure is shown in Figure 2. The difference between the DAE and an AE is that it uses partially corrupted data to train the DAE network in order to recover the real inputs, and its function is to separate and remove the noise in the data to obtain the real data. The workflow of a DAE is as follows:

(1) We obtain the corrupted data by adding noise to the normal data or randomly discarding parts of the normal data;

$$\tilde{x} = q(\tilde{x} \mid x) \tag{8}$$

(2) In this study, the corrupted data $\tilde{x}$ is mapped to the low-dimensional hidden feature space by the self-encoder coding process $h = \sigma(Wx + b)$;
(3) The decoder decodes the corrupted data's mapping in the hidden feature space using Equation (6) and obtains the reconstructed data;
(4) The minimization problem of Equation (7) is solved using the backpropagation algorithm.

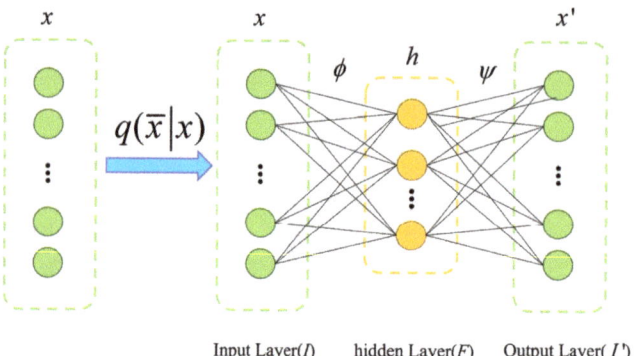

Figure 2. Structure of the Denoising Autoencoder.

In this way, in this paper, signal decomposition was converted into a denoising problem. Specifically, the mixed current signals were treated as noisy signals, and the independent load signals were seen as real data after undergoing denoising processing.

2.3. Decomposition Model Based on LSTM-DAE

The LSTM network has exhibited good performance in extracting features from time-series signals [31,32]. Therefore, LSTM was combined with DAE. The encoder and decoder parts of the DAE were composed of a dual-layer LSTM and Dropout layers, respectively. The input data were the mixed current data, and a sliding window approach was employed in which multiple cycles of a mixed current were used as inputs. This work selected a window size of 10 cycles to achieve the functionality of seq2seq and obtain the output of the independent current. The structure is shown in Figure 3.

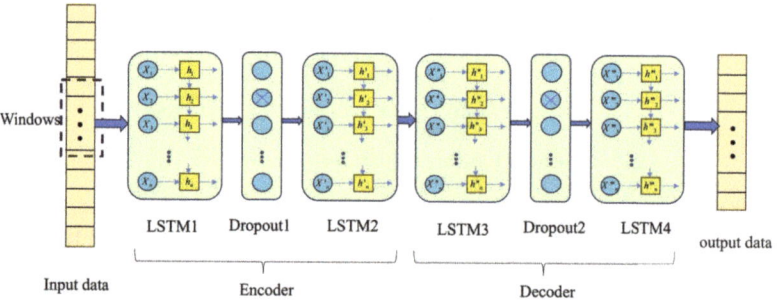

Figure 3. The LSTM-DAE neural network model.

3. Load Recognition of VI Traces Based on Background Color Coding

3.1. Construction of the VI Trajectory Pixelization

The VI trajectory refers to the voltage–current relationship curve used to describe the performance characteristics of electrical equipment. Traditional VI trajectory analysis methods mapped the curve onto a unit grid, where each grid cell represented the presence or absence of VI trajectory information (0 or 1). The grid was then transformed into an image, thereby converting the load recognition problem into an image recognition problem for automated identification. However, previous methods only utilized binary values to represent each grid cell, resulting in relatively limited information content. Therefore, the current study proposes an improved approach aimed at enhancing the expressive power of the VI trajectory data.

(1) Conventional VI traces typically analyzed changes in a single cycle, which failed to capture the characteristic changes of the load across different operating cycles.

Therefore, this work utilized 20 consecutive cycles of current–voltage signals to generate VI traces, aiming to provide a more comprehensive reflection of the changes across different cycles;

(2) Color coding the VI trajectory: The multicycle VI trajectory was represented in red (R channel), the slope of the straight line segment between adjacent sampling points of the VI trajectory was represented in green (G channel), and the instantaneous power value was represented in blue (B channel), thereby generating a VI trajectory image with colored tracks;

(3) Due to the significant differences in current amplitude between certain loads with similar VI trajectories, and considering that current amplitude is an important load characteristic, this research assigned different colors to the background of the VI trajectories based on the varying current amplitudes in order to highlight the differences in current amplitude.

The specific steps were as follows:

(1) In this study, the voltage and current values were standardized, and the resulting standardized data were used to plot the standardized VI trajectory. The standardization formula employed in this research is as follows:

$$\Delta V_m = \frac{V_m}{\max|V|} \tag{9}$$

$$\Delta I_m = \frac{I_m}{\max|I|}, \tag{10}$$

where $\max|V|$ was the maximum value of the voltage in the steady-state sequence and $\max|I|$ was the maximum value of current in the steady state sequence. V_m and I_m were the voltage and current values of the mth sampling point in the sequence, respectively, and ΔV_m and ΔI_m were the voltage and current values of the mth sampling point after normalization, respectively;

(2) In this study, the VI trajectory was created using normalized data, and the resultant VI trajectory served as the R channel of the colored VI trajectory. Subsequently, the green (G) and blue (B) channels were established in sequence, facilitating the amalgamation of the RGB channels to form a colorful VI trajectory;

(3) In this study, the G channel was created by mapping the slope of the straight line segments to the (0, 1) range using the arctan function.

$$K_j = \frac{i_f(j+1) - i_f(j)}{V(j+1) - V(j)} \times \frac{\max(|V|)}{\max(|I_f|)} \tag{11}$$

$$G_j = \frac{1}{2} + \frac{\arctan(K_j)}{\pi}, \tag{12}$$

where K_j was the slope of the jth straight line segment, and G_j was the G-channel depth value of the jth straight line segment. $i_f(j)$ signified the current value at the present data point, and $i_f(j+1)$ represented the subsequent data point's current value. $V_f(j)$ corresponded to the voltage value at the current data point, while $V_f(j+1)$ represented the voltage value at the next data point. $max|V|$ was utilized to extract the absolute value of the maximum voltage obtained from the data used to plot the VI trajectory, and $max|I_f|$ was employed to extract the absolute value of the maximum current obtained from the data depicting the VI trajectory.

The G_j was mapped to the VI trajectory to obtain the corresponding G-channel depth value $G_{m,n}$ for each grid, which was then normalized to obtain the G-channel value for each grid point;

$$G_{m,n}' = \frac{G_{m,n}}{\max G} \tag{13}$$

$$maxG = \max\{G_{1,1}, G_{1,2}, G_{1,3}, \cdots, G_{n,n}\} \tag{14}$$

(4) The B channel was created with the following instantaneous power values:

$$P_j = I_j V_j \tag{15}$$

Mapping P_j onto the VI trajectory results in depth values $P_{m,n}$ for each grid. Following this, the multiperiod power was normalized.

$$P_{m,n}' = \frac{P_{m,n}}{\max P} \tag{16}$$

$$\max P = \max\{P_{1,1}, P_{1,2}, P_{1,3}, \cdots, P_{n,n}\}, \tag{17}$$

where P_j was the instantaneous power value, $P_{m,n}$ was the power superimposed on each grid in the grid, max P was the maximum value of power in all the grids, and the resulting $P'_{m,n}$ was the value of the B channel;

(5) For the addition of the background color, the average of the RMS values of the current energy of 25 adjacent cycles was obtained and matched with the set background color to determine the background color.

Figure 4 shows the multicycle monochromatic VI trajectory, the multicycle color-coded VI trajectory, and the color-coded VI trajectory with background fill.

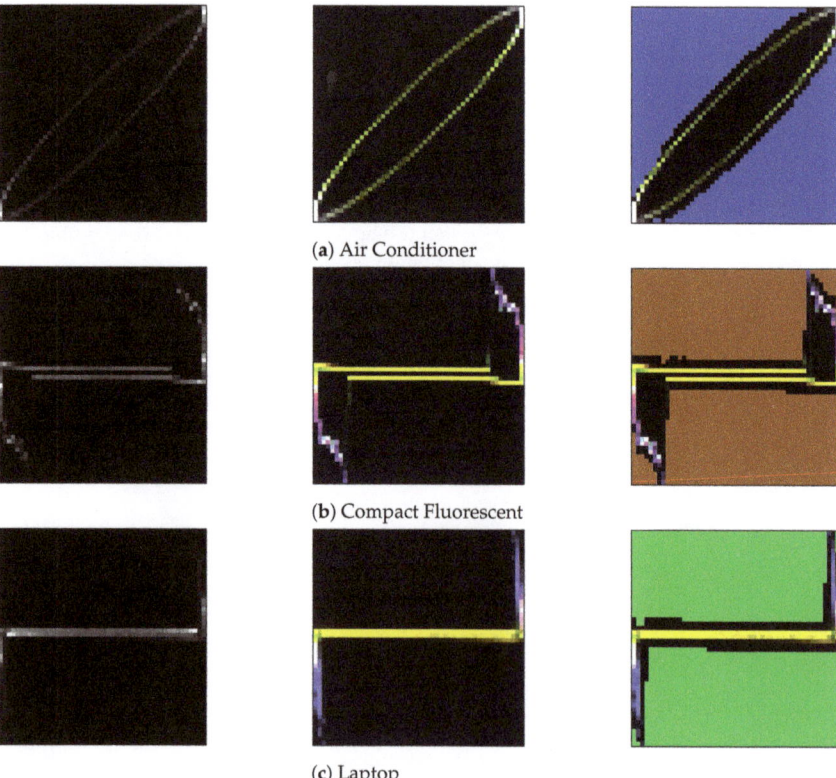

(a) Air Conditioner

(b) Compact Fluorescent

(c) Laptop

Figure 4. *Cont.*

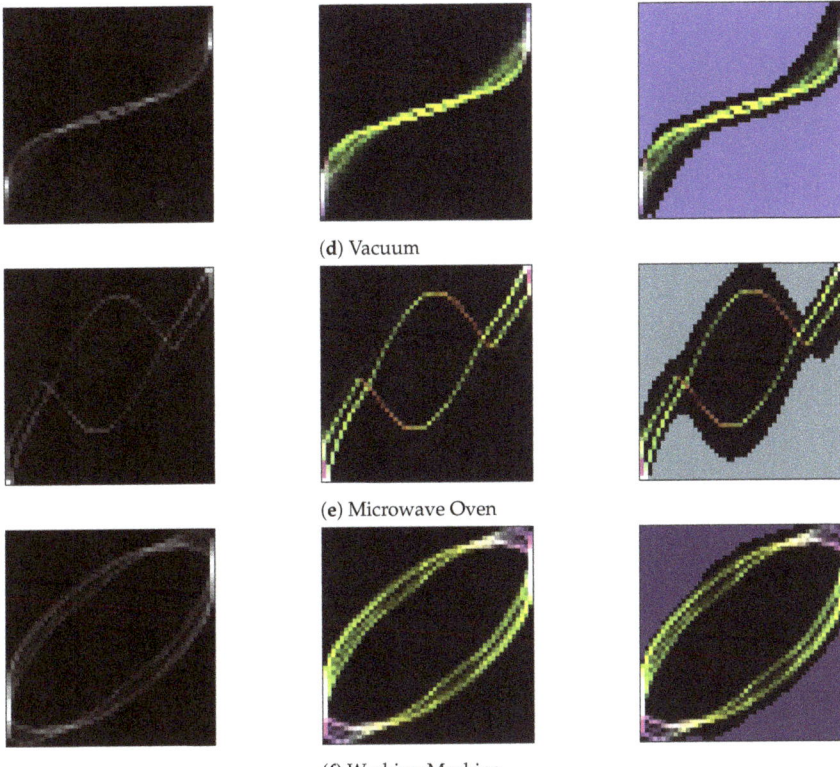

(d) Vacuum

(e) Microwave Oven

(f) Washing Machine

Figure 4. Monochromatic VI trajectory, VI trajectory with color coding, and color-coded VI trajectory with background colors.

3.2. Construction of a Convolutional Neural Network

CNN possess outstanding advantages in handling two-dimensional input data [33,34]. Therefore, the AlexNet network, proposed in 2012, was chosen for load recognition, as it represented a significant breakthrough in deep learning in the field of image recognition. The structure of this model consisted of five convolutional layers, three pooling layers, two Dropout layers, and three fully connected layers, with the activation function being Rectified Linear Units (ReLU). To accomplish the recognition task, the encoded VI trajectory image with filled background color was used as the model input (an $n \times n$ matrix, where $n = 50$). The schematic diagram of the AlexNet network is shown in Figure 5.

The classic AlexNet network could not be directly applied to load recognition tasks and required some modifications to make it work properly. Additionally, due to the numerous hyperparameters, there was a need to optimize the hyperparameters of the convolutional layers, pooling layers, and fully connected layers in order to obtain a highly accurate recognition model.

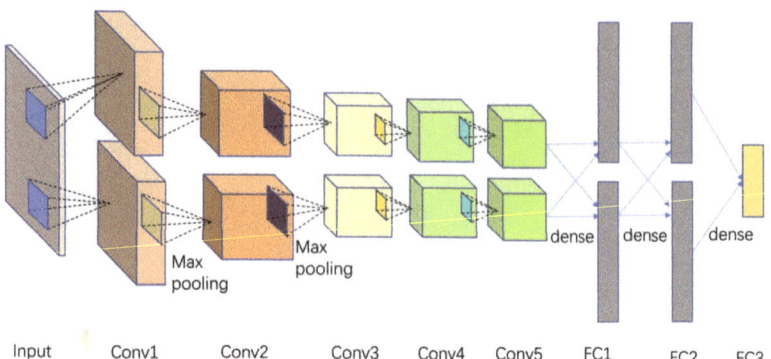

Figure 5. AlexNet network model diagram.

3.3. Bayesian Optimization Algorithm

Bayesian Optimization (BO) is used to estimate the maximum value of a function based on existing sampled points when the functional equation is unknown [35]. It effectively addresses the classical problem of finding the next evaluation point based on the information acquired about the unknown objective function, to quickly search for the optimal solution [36]. Bayesian Optimization has been highly applicable in evaluating costly and complex optimization problems and has been widely used in the optimization of machine learning hyperparameters, deep learning model hyperparameters, and other related areas. In this study, the hyperparameters selected for optimization were the number of convolutional kernels, the size of the convolutional kernels, the stride of the convolutional kernels, the size of pooling kernels, the stride, and the Dropout probability. The optimization ranges are presented in Table 1. The parameter definitions for Bayesian Optimization are provided in Table 2.

Table 1. Hyperparameters to be optimized and their ranges.

Layers	Hyperparameters	Dynamic Range
Conv	Number of convolution kernels	30~135
	Convolution kernel size	2~6
	Convolution kernel step	1~3
Pool	Pool core size	2~6
	Pool nucleation step size	1~3
Dropout	Dropout rate	0~1

Table 2. Parameter definitions in the Bayesian Optimization algorithms.

Layers	Hyperparameters
a1, a2, a3, a4, a5	The number of convolution kernels in five convolutional layers
b1, b2, b3, b4, b5	Convolutional kernel size for five convolutional layers
c1, c2, c3, c4, c5	Convolutional kernel step size for five convolution layers
d1, d2, d3	The number of pooling kernels in three pooling layers
e1, e2, e3	Step size of pooling kernels in three pooling layers
f1, f2	Dropout rate of the two layers

4. Dataset and Evaluation Criteria

This research validated the effectiveness of the algorithm using the PLAID dataset from Carnegie Mellon University in the United States. The dataset included instantaneous values of current and voltage for 11 different types of appliances, sampled at 30 kHz, recorded in multiple households in Pittsburgh, Pennsylvania. In this dataset, mixed currents with multiple loads are missing, and only individual current data when each load operated separately are available. Therefore, before analysis, it was necessary to align and superimpose the current values based on the voltage values to obtain mixed currents. This article selected six loads for load decomposition verification, namely, an air conditioner, an energy-saving lamp, a laptop, a vacuum cleaner, a microwave oven, and a washing machine.

5. Experimental Analysis

5.1. Assessment of Indicators

5.1.1. Evaluation Indexes of Decomposition Process

The root mean square error (RMSE), mean absolute error (MAE), phase error, and correlation coefficient were selected as the evaluation metrics. The RMSE is a commonly used metric that measures the mean square difference between the predicted and actual values, representing the average magnitude of the prediction errors. A lower RMSE value indicates that the predicted results are closer to the actual values. The MAE is another common evaluation metric that measures the average absolute difference between the predicted and actual values, reflecting the absolute error of the predictions. The phase error is an important metric for high-frequency current decomposition, measuring the error between the predicted and actual phase of the signals. The correlation coefficient is used to measure the linear correlation between the predicted and actual values. A correlation coefficient closer to 1 indicates a better linear relationship between the predictions and the actual values. The definitions of these four evaluation metrics are as follows:

$$RMSE = \sqrt{\frac{1}{n}\sum_{i=1}^{n}\left(I_i - \widehat{I_i}\right)^2}; \tag{18}$$

$$MAE = \frac{1}{n}\sum_{i=1}^{n}\left|I_i - \widehat{I_i}\right|; \tag{19}$$

$$Phase\ Error = \arccos\left(\frac{\sum_{i=1}^{n} I_i \widehat{I_i}}{\sqrt{\sum_{i=1}^{n} I_i^2 \sum_{i=1}^{n} \widehat{I_i}^2}}\right); \tag{20}$$

$$Correlation = \frac{\sum_{i=1}^{n}(I_i - \bar{I})\left(\widehat{I_i} - \bar{\widehat{I}}\right)}{\sqrt{\sum_{i=1}^{n}(I_i - \bar{I})^2 \sum_{i=1}^{n}\left(\widehat{I_i} - \bar{\widehat{I}}\right)^2}}. \tag{21}$$

5.1.2. Evaluation Metrics for the Load Recognition Process

For the evaluation of non-intrusive load identification performance, common evaluation metrics such as recognition accuracy (Acc), F1 score, and F-measure [37] were primarily utilized. The calculation formulas are depicted in Equations (22)–(25).

$$Acc = \frac{m}{n}, \tag{22}$$

where m denotes the number of correct classifications of the model, and n is the total number of samples;

$$F_{1_i} = 2 \cdot \frac{precision \cdot recall}{precision + recall}; \tag{23}$$

$$precision = \frac{TP}{TP+FP};\qquad(24)$$

$$recall = \frac{TP}{TP+FN}.\qquad(25)$$

In the above equation, TP represents the number of true positives, where both the true value and the predicted value are positive; FP represents the number of false positives, where the true value is negative, but the predicted value is positive; and FN represents the number of false negatives, where the true value is positive, but the predicted value is negative. The following equation was used to obtain the average value for each device:

$$F_{i,mean} = \frac{1}{L}\sum_{g=1}^{L} F_{1_{g,i}}.\qquad(26)$$

In this equation, L represents the total number of occurrences of device i in the test set; $F_{1_{g,i}}$ represents the F_1 value of device i in the g-th occurrence; and $F_{i,mean}$ represents the average F_1 score for the i-th device over L trials, explicitly portraying the F-measures for device i. Finally, by calculating the average of all the F-measures using Equation (26), the macro-average value F_{macro} is obtained.

$$F_{macro} = \frac{1}{A}\sum_{i=1}^{A} F_{i,mean},\qquad(27)$$

where A represents the total number of different equipment types.

5.2. Example Analysis

5.2.1. Load Decomposition

The input of the LSTM-DAE model was a mixed current obtained by superimposing multiple load currents. The window size of the data input was set to 10 cycles of current data. In the PLAID dataset, one cycle contains 500 data points. Therefore, the size of each window was set to 5000. The sliding step was one cycle of data, which was 500 data points. The training times (epochs) were set to 1000. The decomposition results are shown in Figure 6. Each figure contains three curves representing, from top to bottom, the mixed current, the true target load current, and the predicted target load current.

From Figure 6, it can be observed that the latent information of strongly correlated current sequences was effectively extracted, and the temporal features within the time-series signals were mined using the LSTM-DAE network model. Even in cases where irregular variations were present in the mixed signals and actual signals, the target signal was accurately decomposed by the model. Overall, the decomposed current signals output by this model were well able to track the variations in the actual current signals and essentially fit the rising and falling trends of the actual current curves. These results suggest that the decomposition and fitting of current signals were performed effectively by the model.

From Table 3, it can be seen that out of the six types of loads, five had correlation coefficients exceeding 98%. Even the load with the lowest correlation coefficient, which belonged to the laptop (notebook) category, had a coefficient close to 95%. This indicated a strong linear relationship between the predicted results of the algorithm and the actual values, effectively capturing the changing trends in the load current. Additionally, the maximum values for the RMSE, MAE, and phase error were 0.866, 0.551, and 0.332, respectively. In comparison to the four network models listed in Reference [38], the algorithm in this study achieved a minimum MAE score of 5.97 and a minimum RMSE of 10.52, demonstrating a significant improvement in algorithm performance. Overall, the algorithm exhibited high precision, a low phase error, and a strong correlation in current signal decomposition tasks, making it particularly suitable for handling high-frequency currents. These advantages give the algorithm potentially high practical value in applications such as power load analysis and energy management, providing a reliable tool.

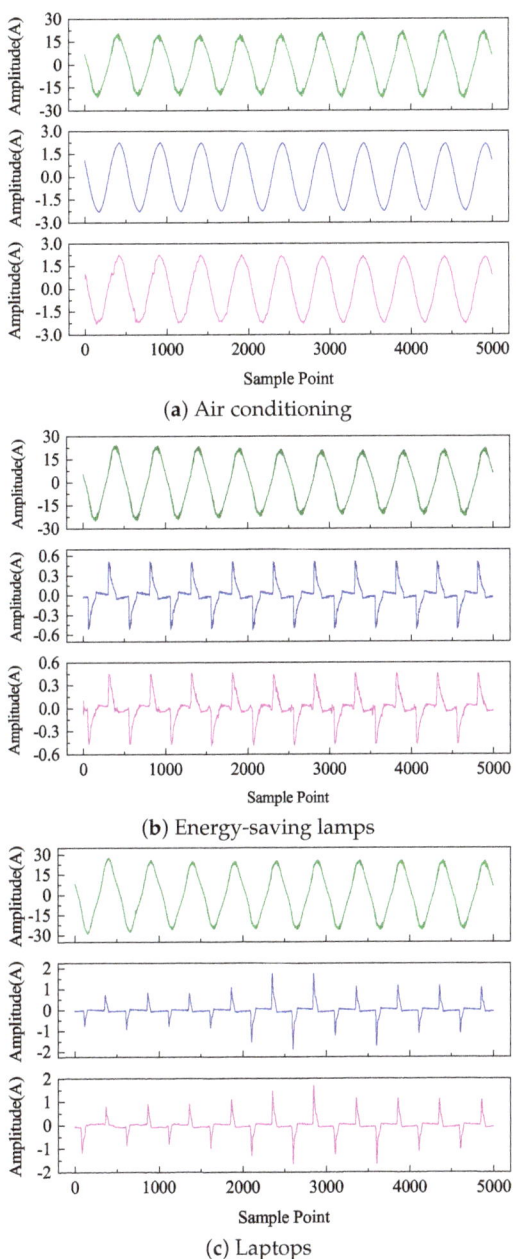

(**a**) Air conditioning

(**b**) Energy-saving lamps

(**c**) Laptops

Figure 6. *Cont.*

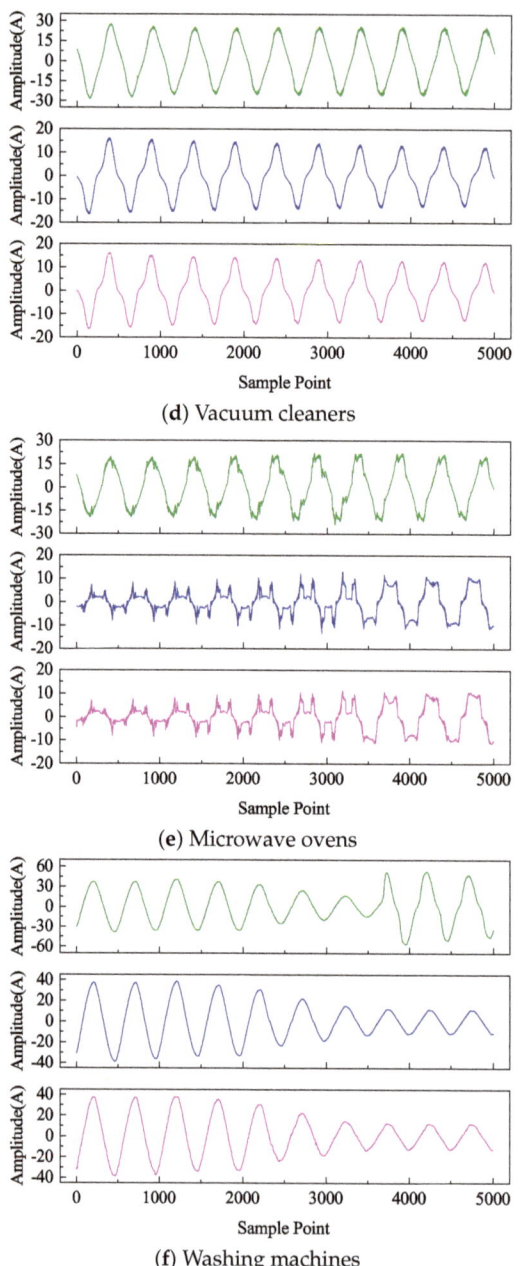

(d) Vacuum cleaners

(e) Microwave ovens

(f) Washing machines

Figure 6. Monochromatic VI trajectory, VI trajectory with color coding, and color−coded VI trajectory with background colors.

Table 3. Evaluation metrics scores of the LATM-DAE algorithm.

Load Type	RMSE	MAE	Phase Error	Correlation Coefficient (%)
Air conditioner	0.109	0.081	0.068	99.8
Energy-saving lamps	0.033	0.020	0.196	98.1
Notebook	0.097	0.040	0.332	94.5
Vacuum cleaner	0.295	0.220	0.035	99.9
Microwave oven	0.668	0.456	0.129	99.2
Washing machines	0.866	0.551	0.046	99.9

5.2.2. Load Recognition

After converting the dataset into VI trajectory images with background color coding, it was input into the CNN network, and the Bayesian Optimization algorithm was used to optimize the hyperparameters of the convolutional layers, pooling layers, and Dropout layers. There were a total of five convolutional layers, three pooling layers, and two Dropout layers. The comparison of the hyperparameters before and after optimization is shown in Table 4. The data in the table indicate, for example, that the parameters of Conv1 layer were $3 \times 3/48/1$, which meant the convolutional kernel size was 3×3, the number of convolutional kernels was 48, and the stride was 1. The parameter of Dropout1 layer was 0.5, indicating a Dropout probability of 0.5.

Table 4. Comparison of the hyperparameter information between CNN and BOA-CNN.

Catagory	CNN	BOA-CNN
Conv1	$3 \times 3/48/1$	$4 \times 4/60/1$
Pool1	$3 \times 3/2$	$2 \times 2/1$
Conv2	$5 \times 5/128/2$	$4 \times 4/121/1$
Pool2	$3 \times 3/2$	$2 \times 2/1$
Conv3	$3 \times 3/192/1$	$4 \times 4/126/1$
Conv4	$3 \times 3/192/1$	$3 \times 3/55/1$
Conv5	$3 \times 3/192/1$	$3 \times 3/125/1$
Droout1	0.5	0.4
Droout1	0.5	0.1

The accuracy of the optimized model was compared with the recognition accuracy of other models in the literature, as shown in Table 5. The accuracy of the CNN network optimized by Bayesian Optimization was approximately 96.5%, while the accuracy of the regular CNN network was approximately 93.1%, indicating a 3.4% improvement. The recognition accuracy was also higher than that of other models in the literature.

Table 5. Comparison of the recognition accuracy of various algorithms.

Model	Accuracy (%)
BOA-CNN	96.5%
CNN	93.1%
Model in [39]	90.0%
Model in [19]	92.8%
Model in [40]	91.7%
Model in [41]	93.20%

In order to test the stability of the BOA-CNN algorithm, 12 experiments were conducted on the PLAID dataset. As shown in Figure 7, the recognition accuracy of the BOA-CNN algorithm was superior to that of the ordinary CNN model in all experiments, with good robustness. However, in terms of stability, the BOA-CNN algorithm performed poorly and fluctuated significantly. Specifically, in the 12 experiments, the difference between the maximum and minimum accuracy of the BOA-CNN algorithm was about 4.7%, while the difference between those of the ordinary CNN model was about 3.5%. This indicates that the BOA-CNN algorithm is unstable across different experiments. Further analysis showed that this instability may be caused by the randomness and local optimal solution of Bayesian Optimization algorithms. However, its automatic search for the optimal hyperparameters of the convolution layer, pooling layer, and Dropout layer reduces the time and labor costs of manual parameter adjustment.

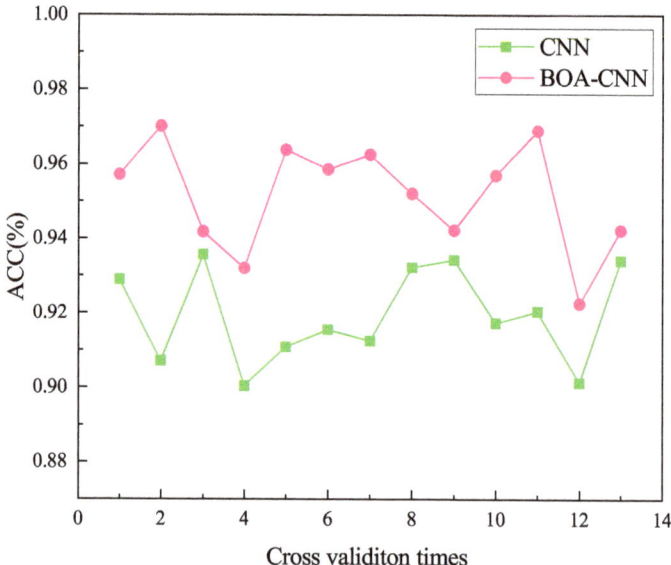

Figure 7. Comparison of the recognition accuracy between the BOA-CNN and CNN.

The model confusion matrix is shown in Figure 8, in which the number in each cell represents the number of corresponding devices, the abscissa represents the predicted value for an appliance, and the ordinate represents the actual value for that appliance. It can be seen that in the PLAID dataset, compared to the ordinary CNN model, the BOA-CNN model reduced the number of false negatives (FN) and false positives (FP) for each electrical appliance and also reduced the number of device types that were incorrectly classified for each electrical appliance. This indicates that the BOA-CNN model showed excellent results in the accuracy of electrical identification and has practical value.

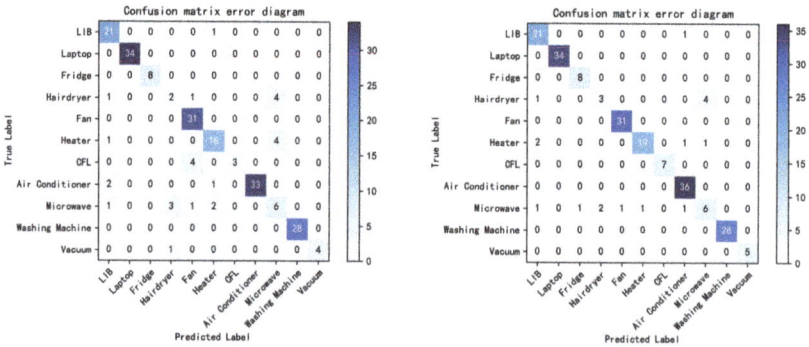

Figure 8. Comparison of the BOA-CNN and CNN confusion matrices.

In the case of the *F*-measure indicators and F_{macro} indicators, as shown in Figure 9, the F_{macro} indicator for the BOA-CNN was 87%, while the F_{macro} indicator for the CNN was 81%. In addition, the *F*-measure values for the hair dryers were lower than the macro average. This may be due to the small amount of measurement data for some devices in the dataset, which limits the learning ability of the model, resulting in lower *F*-measure values for some devices. However, in general, the convolutional neural network model based on Bayesian Optimization proposed in this paper showed improved performance compared to the original convolutional neural network model for 11 types of electrical appliances in the PLAID dataset, with a maximum improvement of 21%. Therefore, the model has good performance.

The incremental addition of numerous features during the CNN construction process led to a significant increase in computational workload. The experiment was conducted on a laptop equipped with 16 GB of RAM and 16 cores (12th Gen Intel(R) Core(TM) i5-1240P @1.70 GHz). On this platform, the time required for VI trajectory construction was 2016.47 milliseconds, while the recognition of input images took 868.01 milliseconds, resulting in a total of 2884.48 milliseconds, which is less than 3 s. In comparison, the total time spent in Reference [11] was 388.24 milliseconds, and in Reference [42], it was 923 milliseconds. Despite the relatively substantial computational workload, the CNN exhibits the capability to perform load recognition within seconds in the context of NILM tasks, aligning with the intended goals and requirements of recognition.

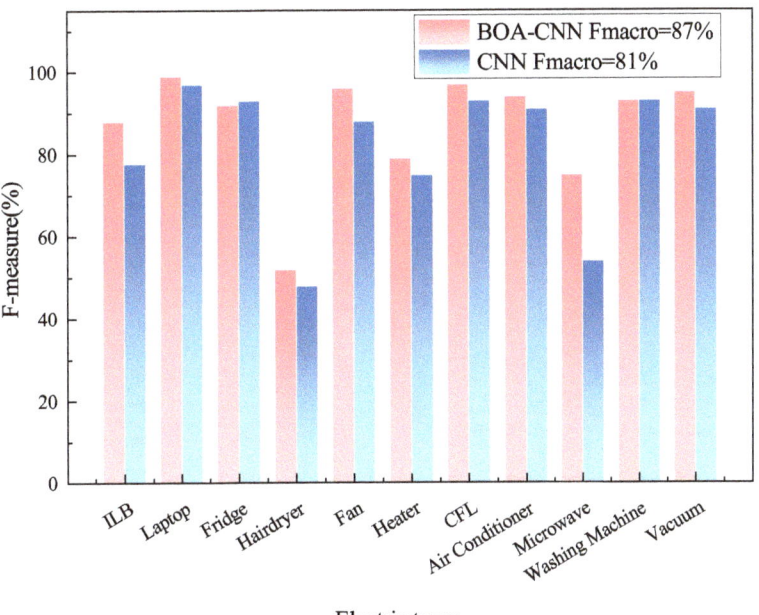

Figure 9. Comparison between the BOA-CNN and CNN *F*-measure indicators and F_{macro} indicators.

6. Conclusions

This paper introduced a load decomposition method based on the LSTM-DAE and presented a load recognition approach that employed color-coded VI trajectories with background color filling. The experimental results revealed that the proposed load decomposition method achieved an accuracy exceeding 98%, accompanied by a notable current reproduction effect, thereby providing precise data support for high-frequency load recognition. The amalgamation of multicycle signals, the color coding of VI trajectories, and the background color filling enhanced the distinguishability among different load VI trajectories. Moreover, the utilization of a BOA-optimized AlexNet network for

VI trajectory recognition illustrated that the BOA-CNN model effectively mitigated the issue of confusing devices compared to existing algorithms, showcasing elevated accuracy and robustness. Relative to conventional CNN models, this method excelled in various aspects of electrical appliance recognition. Although the algorithm presented in this paper imposed a higher computational load than other lightweight algorithms, the processing time aligned seamlessly with the requirements of load recognition. Nevertheless, despite the high accuracy of the proposed decomposition method, it required preliminary data training, unlike the differencing method, which does not require data pretraining. Consequently, the proposed decomposition method exhibited certain limitations compared to the differencing approach. Additionally, errors might have arisen in the CNN's recognition of VI trajectories due to significant differences among similar loads resulting from variations in brand and power. Therefore, future research should further explore the scalability of the load recognition capabilities of the proposed algorithm.

Author Contributions: methodology, D.Z. and J.S.; software, D.Z.; validation, J.S., R.F. and D.Z.; investigation, R.F.; resources, J.S.; data curation, D.Z. and R.F.; writing—original draft preparation, D.Z. and J.S.; writing—review and editing, J.S. and R.F.; visualization, D.Z.; supervision, R.F.; project administration, J.S. All authors have read and agreed to the published version of the manuscript.

Funding: Shandong Jianzhu University Doctoral Fund (Project No.: X21103Z).

Data Availability Statement: Publicly available datasets were analyzed in this study. The data can be found here: https://figshare.com/articles/dataset/PLAID_2014/11605074.

Conflicts of Interest: The authors declare no conflict of interest.

References

1. Qi, B.; Liu, L.; Han, L.; Wang, L.; Ruan, W. Home appliance load identification algorithm based on system model. *Electr. Meas. Instrum.* **2018**, *55*, 23–30.
2. Deng, X.; Zhang, G.; Wei, Q.; Peng, W.; Li, C. A survey on the non-intrusive load monitoring. *Acta Autom. Sin.* **2022**, *43*, 644–663.
3. Li, P. Non-Intrusive Method for Power Load Disaggregation and Monitoring. Master's Thesis, Tianjin University, Tianjin, China, 2009.
4. Basu, K.; Debusschere, V.; Douzal-Chouakria, A.; Bacha, S. Time series distance-based methods for non-intrusive load monitoring in residential buildings. *Energy Build.* **2015**, *96*, 109–117. [CrossRef]
5. Ruano, A.; Hernandez, A.; Ureña, J.; Ruano, M.; Garcia, J. NILM Techniques for Intelligent Home Energy Management and Ambient Assisted Living: A Review. *Energies* **2019**, *12*, 2203. [CrossRef]
6. Piccialli, V.; Sudoso, A. A nonintrusive recognition method of household load behavior based on DTW algorithm. *Electr. Meas. Instrum.* **2019**, *56*, 17–22.
7. Zhu, H.; Cao, N.; Lu, H. Non-intrusive load identification method based on feature weighted KNN. *Electron. Meas. Technol.* **2022**, *56*, 70–75.
8. Dong, Z.; Chen, Y.; Xue, T.; Shao, R. Non-intrusive load monitoring algorithm based on attention mechanism combined with global and sliding window. *Electr. Meas. Instrum.* **2023**, *60*, 74–80.
9. Yu, D.; Liu, M. A non-invasive load decomposiontion method base on deep circular convolutional model. *Electr. Meas. Instrum.* **2020**, *57*, 47–53.
10. Athanasiadis, C.L.; Papadopoulos, T.A.; Doukas, D.I. Real-time non-intrusive load monitoring: A light-weight and scalable approach. *Energy Build.* **2021**, *253*, 111523. [CrossRef]
11. Papageorgiou, P.; Mylona, D.; Stergiou, K.; Bouhouras, A.S. A Time-Driven Deep Learning NILM Framework Based on Novel Current Harmonic Distortion Images. *Sustainability* **2023**, *15*, 12957. [CrossRef]
12. Lam, H.Y.; Fung, G.S.K.; Lee, W.K. A novel method to construct taxonomy electrical appliances based on load signatures. *IEEE Trans. Consum. Electron.* **2007**, *53*, 653–660. [CrossRef]
13. De Baets, L.; Develder, C.; Dhaene, T.; Deschrijver, D. Automated classification of appliances using elliptical fourier descriptors. In Proceedings of the 2017 IEEE International Conference on Smart Grid Communications, Dresden, Germany, 23 October 2017.
14. Hassan, T.; Javed, F.; Arshad, N. An Empirical Investigation of V-I Trajectory Based Load Signatures for Non-Intrusive Load Monitoring. *IEEE Trans. Smart Grid* **2014**, *5*, 870–878. [CrossRef]
15. Liu, Y.; Wang, X.; You, W. Non-intrusive load monitoring by voltage–current trajectory enabled transfer learning. *IEEE Trans. Smart Grid* **2018**, *10*, 5609–5619. [CrossRef]
16. Faustine, A.; Pereira, L.; Klemenjak, C. Adaptive weighted recurrence graphs for appliance recognition in non-intrusive load monitoring. *IEEE Trans. Smart Grid* **2020**, *12*, 398–406. [CrossRef]

17. Jia, D.; Li, Y.; Du, Z.; Xu, J.; Yin, B. Non-intrusive load identification using reconstructed voltage–current images. *IEEE Access* **2021**, *9*, 77349–77358. [CrossRef]
18. Han, Y.; Xu, Y.; Huo, Y.; Zhao, Q. Non-intrusive load monitoring by voltage–current trajectory enabled asymmetric deep supervised hashing. *Iet Gener. Transm. Distrib.* **2021**, *15*, 3066–3080. [CrossRef]
19. Han, Y.; Li, K.; Feng, H.; Zhao, Q. Non-intrusive load monitoring based on semi-supervised smooth teacher graph learning with voltage–current trajectory. *Neural Comput. Appl.* **2022**, *34*, 19147–19160. [CrossRef]
20. Kim, H.; Marwah, M.; Arlitt, M.; Lyon, G.; Han, J. Unsupervised Disaggregation of Low Frequency Power Measurements. In Proceedings of the 2011 SIAM International Conference on Data Mining, Mesa, AZ, USA, 28–30 April 2011.
21. Kolter, Z.; Jaakkola, T.; Kolter, J.Z. Approximate Inference in Additive Factorial HMMs with Application to Energy Disaggregation. *J. Mach. Learn. Res.* **2012**, *22*, 1472–1482.
22. Li, D.; Li, J.; Zeng, X.; Stankovic, V.; Stankovic, L.; Xiao, C.; Shi, Q. Transfer learning for multi-objective non-intrusive load monitoring in smart building. *Appl. Energy* **2023**, *329*, 1472–1482. [CrossRef]
23. Kelly, J.; Knottenbelt, W. Neural NILM: Deep Neural Networks Applied to Energy Disaggregation. In Proceedings of the 2nd ACM International Conference on Embedded Systems for Energy-Efficient Built, BuildSys 2015, Seoul, Republic of Korea, 4 November 2015.
24. Roberto, B.; Felicetti, A.; Principi, E. Denoising Autoencoders for Non-Intrusive Load Monitoring: Improvements and Comparative Evaluation. *Energy Build.* **2018**, *158*, 1461–1474.
25. Odysseas, K.; Christoforos, N.; Dimitris, V. Sliding Window Approach for Online Energy Disaggregation Using Artificial Neural Networks. In Proceedings of the 10th Hellenic Conference on Artificial Intelligence, Patras, Greece, 9 July 2018.
26. Zhang, C.; Zhong, M.; Wang, Z.; Goddard, N.; Sutton, C. Sequence-to-Point Learning with Neural Networks for non-intrusive Load Monitoring. In Proceedings of the 32nd AAAI Conference on Artificial Intelligence, New Orleans, LA, USA, 2–7 February 2018.
27. Xu, X.; Zhao, S.; Cui, K. Non-intrusive load decomposition algorithm based on convolution block attention model. *Power Syst. Technol.* **2021**, *45*, 3700–3705.
28. Piccialli, V.; Sudoso, A. Improving Non-Intrusive Load Disaggregation through an Attention-Based Deep Neural Network. *Energies* **2021**, *14*, 847. [CrossRef]
29. Hart, G. Nonintrusive appliance load monitoring. *Proc. IEEE* **1992**, *80*, 1870–1891. [CrossRef]
30. Vincent, P.; Larochelle, H.; Bengio, Y.; Manzagol, P.A. Extracting and composing robust features with denoising autoencoders. In Proceedings of the 25th International Conference on Machine Learning, Helsinki, Finland, 5 July 2008.
31. Liu, H.; Liu, Y.; Deng, S.C.; Shi, S.B.; Min, R.L.; Zhou, D.G. A power load identification method based on LSTM model. *Electr. Meas. Instrum.* **2019**, *56*, 62–69.
32. Han, T.; Chen, X.; Liu, Q. Short-Term Load Forecasting for Distribution Network in the Presence of TOU Price Based on Long-Short-Term Memory Network. *J. Northeast Electr. Power Univ.* **2020**, *40*, 19–28.
33. Song, X.; Jin, L.; Zhao, Y.; Yue, S.; Tong, L. Plant Image Recognition with Complex Background Based on Effective Region Screening. *Laser Optoelectron. Prog.* **2020**, *57*, 181–191.
34. Liu, F.; Li, M.; Hu, J.; Xiao, Y.; Qi, Z. Expression Recognition Based on Low Pixel Face Images. *Laser Optoelectron. Prog.* **2020**, *57*, 97–104.
35. Zhu, H.; Liu, X.; Liu, Y. Bayesian-based novel deep learning hyperparameter optimization. *Data Commun.* **2019**, *2*, 35–38.
36. Jones, D.; Schonlau, M.; Welch, W. Efficient global optimization of expensive black-box functions. *J. Glob. Optim.* **1998**, *13*, 455–492. [CrossRef]
37. Yu, X.; Xu, L.; Li, J.; Ji, X. MagConv: Mask-Guided Convolution for Image Inpainting. *IEEE Trans. Image Process.* **2023**, *32*, 4716–4727. [CrossRef]
38. Cui, H. Non-Intrusive Load Monitoring and Decomposition Technology Based on Deep Learning and Application of Typical Scenarios. Master's Thesis, Northeast Electric Power University, Dalian, China, 2023.
39. Wu, X.; Jiao, D.; Liang, K.; Han, X. A fast online load identification algorithm based on VI characteristics of high-frequency data under user operational constraints. *Energy* **2019**, *188*, 63–70. [CrossRef]
40. Zhao, A.; Zhao, X.; Jing, J.; Xi, J.; Cui, P. Non-intrusive Electric Load Identification Algorithm for Optimizing CNN Hyperparameters. *Laser Optoelectron. Prog.* **2023**, *60*, 63–70.
41. Zhi, D.; Shi, J.; Fu, R. Non-intrusive Load Identification Based on Steady-state V-I Trajectory. In Proceedings of the 4th International Conference on Neural Computing for Advanced Applications, Hefei, China, 7 July 2023.
42. Wu, B.; Gu, W.; He, X. Low-power consumption high-precision non-invasive electrical appliance identification algorithm. *J. Xidian Univ.* **2023**, *50*, 149–157.

Disclaimer/Publisher's Note: The statements, opinions and data contained in all publications are solely those of the individual author(s) and contributor(s) and not of MDPI and/or the editor(s). MDPI and/or the editor(s) disclaim responsibility for any injury to people or property resulting from any ideas, methods, instructions or products referred to in the content.

Article

A Visually Inspired Computational Model for Recognition of Optic Flow

Xiumin Li [1,*], Wanyan Lin [1], Hao Yi [2], Lei Wang [1] and Jiawei Chen [1]

[1] College of Automation, Chongqing University, Chongqing 400030, China
[2] Huawei Technologies Co., Ltd., Shenzhen 518129, China
* Correspondence: xmli@cqu.edu.cn

Abstract: Foundation models trained on vast quantities of data have demonstrated impressive performance in capturing complex nonlinear relationships and accurately predicting neuronal responses. Due to the fact that deep learning neural networks depend on massive amounts of data samples and high energy consumption, foundation models based on spiking neural networks (SNNs) have the potential to significantly reduce calculation costs by training on neuromorphic hardware. In this paper, a visually inspired computational model composed of an SNN and echo state network (ESN) is proposed for the recognition of optic flow. The visually inspired SNN model serves as a foundation model that is trained using spike-timing-dependent plasticity (STDP) for extracting core features. The ESN model makes readout decisions for recognition tasks using the linear regression method. The results show that STDP can perform similar functions as non-negative matrix decomposition (NMF), i.e., generating sparse and linear superimposed readouts based on basis flow fields. Once the foundation model is fully trained from enough input samples, it can considerably reduce the training samples required for ESN readout learning. Our proposed SNN-based foundation model facilitates efficient and cost-effective task learning and could also be adapted to new stimuli that are not included in the training of the foundation model. Moreover, compared with the NMF algorithm, the foundation model trained using STDP does not need to be retrained during the testing procedure, contributing to a more efficient computational performance.

Keywords: foundation model; MT-MSTd; STDP; SNN; optic flow

MSC: 62M45

Citation: Li, X.; Lin, W.; Yi, H.; Wang, L.; Chen, J. A Visually Inspired Computational Model for Recognition of Optic Flow. *Mathematics* **2023**, *11*, 4777. https://doi.org/10.3390/math11234777

Academic Editor: Georgios Tsekouras

Received: 30 October 2023
Revised: 22 November 2023
Accepted: 23 November 2023
Published: 27 November 2023

Copyright: © 2023 by the authors. Licensee MDPI, Basel, Switzerland. This article is an open access article distributed under the terms and conditions of the Creative Commons Attribution (CC BY) license (https://creativecommons.org/licenses/by/4.0/).

1. Introduction

Recently, foundation models based on deep artificial neural networks have shown robust representations of their modeling domain and achieved breakthroughs for accurately predicting neuronal responses to arbitrary natural images in a visual cortex [1–6]. However, despite the appearance of deep learning artificial neural networks, which have recently shown remarkable capability on a broad range of computational tasks, these models require high energy consumption and need to run on graphics processors that consume many kilowatts of power [7]. Therefore, brain-inspired algorithmic models and neuromorphic hardware processors are increasingly emerging and can potentially lead to low-power intelligent systems for large-scale real-world applications.

Spiking neural networks (SNNs) have attracted significant attention from researchers across various domains due to their brain-like information processing mechanism. However, training SNNs directly on neuromorphic hardware remains a significant challenge due to the non-differentiable nature of the spike-generation function. Amirhossein T. proposed a method called BP-STDP, which uses the difference between the desired output sequence and the actual firing sequence for backpropagation [8]. Converting the well-trained rate-based ANNs to SNNs by directly mapping the connection weights has also been broadly studied [9,10]. Zhang et al. demonstrate that both the learning speed and the robustness of computation accuracy can be significantly improved by applying the biologically inspired intrinsic plasticity learning scheme into spiking feed-forward neural networks [11,12]. Kim S. from Seoul National University proposed Spiking-YOLO, which was the first application of SNNs in object detection, achieving a performance comparable to CNNs with extremely low power consumption [13]. However, these efforts to improve learning algorithms based on gradient descent iterations are far from the mechanism of real visual processing in the brain cortex, with the limitations of single network structure, high computational cost, and lack of biological plausibility.

It has been known that sparse coding, also known as sparse representation, uses a small number of elements to represent most or all of the original signals and explains how the visual cortex achieves efficient encoding and processing of information using a small number of neurons in an iterative manner. Therefore, modeling SNNs based on visually inspired information processing is of great significance for improving computational performance. In 1999, Professor Daniel D. proposed non-negative matrix factorization (NMF), which enables neural networks to achieve modular recognition of images and has significant implications for visual cognitive computational models [14]. Some evidence suggests that its dimensionality reduction and sparsity constraints are an effective form of population coding [15]. Beyeler M. proposed a hypothesis that the medial superior temporal region (MSTd) effectively encodes various visual flow patterns from neurons in the middle temporal region (MT) [16], and the sparse coding process is similar to NMF [17]. Further, an SNN model based on evolved and homomorphic synaptic scaling (STDP-H) learning rules was proposed and confirmed this hypothesis [18]. This model learns a compressed and efficient representation of input patterns similar to NMF, thus generating a receptive field similar to what is observed in the MSTd of monkeys. This suggests that the observed STDP-H in the neural system may have similar functionality to NMF with sparse constraints, providing an experimental platform for theoretical mechanisms on how MSTd efficiently encodes complex visual motion patterns to support robust self-motion perception.

Neurons in the visual cortex receive optic flow-like input and inherit their speed and direction preferences to process video sequences of realistic visual scenes. Optic flow can be used to avoid obstacles and approach goals in novel cluttered environments for animals by perceiving the heading direction of self-motion and guiding locomotion. Therefore, accurate recognition of optic flow is crucial for the development of visually based navigation models, such as the ViSTARS neural model, which was developed to describe neuronal information processing of the V1, MT, and MSTd areas in the primate visual dorsal pathway [19,20]. In [21], a biologically inspired neural network that learns patterns in optic flow is proposed based on fuzzy adaptive resonance theory. The paper [22] presented an artificial neural network that accurately estimates the parameters describing the observer's self-motion from MSTd-like optic flow templates. However, how to efficiently recognize the patterns of optic flow based on spiking neural networks and spike-based learning rules has not been fully studied yet.

Based on the above-mentioned literature, a visually inspired computational model inspired by the image processing mechanisms of the primary visual cortex for the recognition of optic flow is proposed in this paper. The visually inspired SNN model serves as a foundation model that is trained using spike-timing-dependent plasticity (STDP) on large amounts of optic flows for extracting core features. The ESN model trained using the linear regression method makes readout decisions for recognition tasks of optic flow. The results show that STDP can perform similar functions as non-negative matrix decomposition (NMF), i.e., generating sparse and linear superimposed readout based on local features, which is an ideal core/foundation model to accurately reconstruct input stimuli for image reconstruction. Based on the well-trained core network, ESN can accurately recognize not only optical flows but also new stimuli such as the grating stimulus. Moreover, ESN requires significantly less training data than the one without a fully trained core SNN model. Compared with the NMF algorithm, the foundation model trained with STDP does not need to be retrained during the testing procedure for new stimuli, contributing to more efficient computational performance.

In summary, our main contributions are: (1) a foundation model for the recognition of optic flow is established based on biologically realistic spiking neural networks and trained with a neurophysiologically observed learning rule (STDP); (2) the efficiency and necessity of feature extraction from the foundation model is confirmed from our simulation results. That is, the computational performance mainly depends on feature extraction instead of readout training, indicating that learning is a multi-stage feature-extraction process instead of end-to-end training, as commonly used in neural networks.

2. Materials and Methods

The overall architecture of the model is depicted in Figure 1. There are two sub-networks: the foundational model of SNN and the decision model of ESN, which are trained separately. Since it is known that neurons in the MSTd region of the visual cortex can efficiently recognize firing patterns from neurons in the MT region, here the SNN model consists of two visual cortical layers, i.e., the MT layer and the MSTd layer. The input optic flow stimuli are initially processed by a group of MT neurons, which encode the information into Poisson spike trains. These spike trains are then transmitted to a group of excitatory spiking neurons representing MSTd. The connection weights from MT to MSTd are updated using spike-timing-dependent plasticity (STDP) based on large amounts of optic flow with different patterns to extract the core features of the training dataset. After training, all core features are saved in the form of MT-MSTd synaptic weights. Then, the firing rate of the MSTd layer encoding the relative importance of the core's features to the current visual input is transformed into an ESN model trained using the linear regression method, which makes readout decisions to recognize which patterns the input stimuli belong to. Detailed models are described in the below subsections.

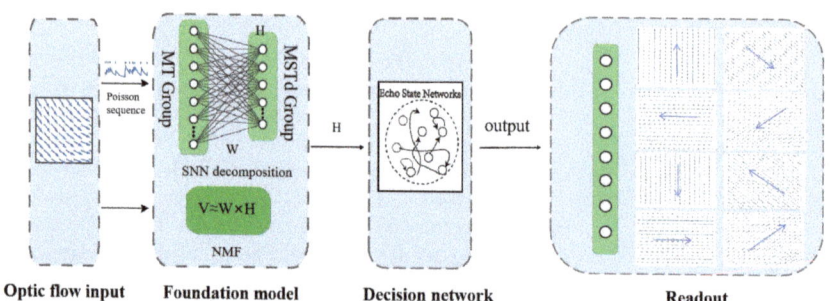

Figure 1. Model architecture. This model consists of three aspects: visual input, foundation model of the visual cortex, and decision network. The input stimuli to the network are computer-generated 15 × 15 pixel arrays representing optic flow. Inputs encode information into Poisson spike trains, which are then transmitted to the MT layer. The architecture of the MT group is 15 × 15 × 8, that of the MSTd group is 8 × 8 × 1, and the Inh group is 8 × 8 × 8. Both MSTd-to-Inh and Inh-to-MSTd connections follow uniform random connectivity with a 0.1 probability. STDP learning rule is employed to adjust the network weights from MT to MSTd. ESN consisting of a random reservoir network and readout layer is trained for making decisions for recognition tasks.

2.1. Visual Input

The input stimuli to the network are computer-generated 15 × 15 pixel arrays representing optic flow. To simulate the visual motion on the retina caused by an observer moving in a 3D environment, a motion field model is utilized to generate the optic flow stimuli. Please refer to the papers [17,23] for details. Using computer-generated data, we created 6000 samples of optic flow data. Each sample contains input information for different directions and velocities, where the values represent the length of the optic flow vectors. Therefore, when plotting, the information of the 8 directions and velocity is superimposed within a 15 × 15 grid. This means that the vectors are converted into values on the x and y coordinates and added together to obtain the coordinates of the vector endpoints. The MATLAB function "quiver" can be used to plot the optic flow vector map. Figure 2 depicts optic flow maps with different patterns that simulate the projection of three-dimensional coordinates onto the retina as the observer moves in a three-dimensional world. From the figures, it can be observed how the projection of the three-dimensional points on the retina changes when the observer moves backward, rotates, and translates in the three-dimensional world. Input stimuli encode information into Poisson spike trains, which are then transmitted to a group of excitatory spiking neurons in the MT layer.

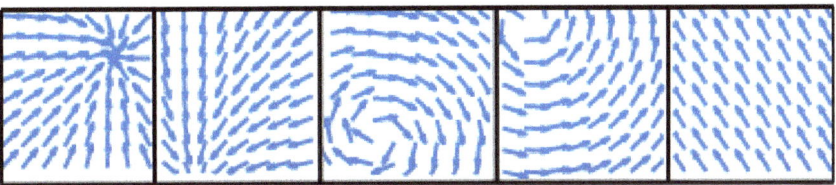

Figure 2. Sample plots of visual optic flow to simulate the projection of three-dimensional coordinates on the retina as the observer moves in the three-dimensional world [17].

2.2. Foundation Model of Spiking Neural Networks

This SNN model focuses on extracting core features of optic flow patterns resulting from self-movement. Each optic flow field is processed by MT units that resemble the orientation selectivity of MT neurons, which selectively respond to optic flows with specific positions, directions, and velocities. Here, the MT layer is composed of $15 \times 15 \times 8 = 1800$ units, representing the responses to the specified eight directions ($45°$, $90°$, $135°, 180°, 225°, 270°, 315°, 360°$) and one velocity. The population code of local direction and speed of motion acts as the activity pattern of these 8 units/pixel. All neurons within the MT layer are isolated and the neural activity is modeled using Izhikevich neurons [24] exhibiting excitatory regular spiking behavior. The input optic flow stimuli are initially processed by a group of MT neurons, which encode the information into Poisson spike trains. The average pixel value of input determines the mean firing rate of spike trains. These spike trains are then transmitted to the MSTd layer. The MSTd group contains 64 isolated Izhikevich neurons corresponding to 64 core features. The weight connections from MT to MSTd follow a Gaussian distribution, in which close neurons have a higher probability of connectivity and higher initial connection weights. Additionally, the MSTd group projects to a set of inhibitory neurons (Inh), providing feedback inhibition to regulate network activity. The inhibitory group has 512 neurons. The population size of MT is $15 \times 15 \times 8$, that of MST is $8 \times 8 \times 1$, and that of the inhibitory group is $8 \times 8 \times 8$. Both MSTd-to-Inh and Inh-to-MSTd connections follow uniform random connectivity with a 0.1 probability [25]. The detailed models for the Izhikevich neuron and synapses are as follows:

$$\frac{dV(t)}{dt} = 0.04V(t)^2 + 5V(t) + 140 - U(t) + I^{syn}(t) \quad (1)$$

$$\frac{dU(t)}{dt} = a(bV(t) - U(t)) \quad (2)$$

$$\text{if } V > V_{cutoff} \text{, then} \begin{cases} V = c \\ U = U + d \end{cases} \quad (3)$$

where V and U represent membrane potential and membrane recovery variables, respectively. I^{syn} is the external synaptic current, the membrane potential V has an mv scale, and time has a ms scale. The parameters a, b, c, d in (2) and (3) are set as $a = 0.02, b = 0.2$,

$c = -65, d = 8$ or $a = 0.1, b = 0.2, c = -65, d = 2$, representing regular-spiking (RS) neurons (excitatory neurons) or fast-spiking (FS) neurons (inhibitory neurons). Here, we use the conductance-based description for synaptic models, which calculates the synaptic current using complex conductance equations for each synaptic receptor type. AMPA and NMDA are excitatory synaptic connection types. $GABA_A$ and $GABA_B$ are inhibitory synaptic connection types.

$$\begin{aligned} i_e &= i_{NMDA} + i_{AMPA} \\ i_i &= i_{GABA_A} + i_{GABA_B} \end{aligned} \quad (4)$$

The total current I_{syn} can be expanded to:

$$\begin{aligned} i_{syn} = &-g_{AMPA}(v - v^{rev}_{AMPA}) - g_{NMDA}\frac{[\frac{v+80}{60}]^2}{1 + [\frac{v+80}{60}]^2}(v - v^{rev}_{NMDA}) \\ &- g_{GABA_a}(v - v^{rev}_{GABA_A}) - g_{GABA_B}(v - v^{rev}_{GABA_B}) \end{aligned} \quad (5)$$

where g and v_{rev} are specific to a particular ion channel or receptor. The synaptic conductance g obeys the exponential decay and changes when presynaptic spikes arrive.

$$\frac{dg_r(t)}{dt} = -\frac{1}{\tau_r}g_r(t) + w\sum_i \delta(t - t_i) \quad (6)$$

where δ is the Dirac delta function, and r is the receptor type ($AMPA, NMDA, GABA_a, GABA_b$). t_i is the presynaptic spikes arrival time [24].

Since topological structure enhances temporal-spatial processing ability and biological plausibility, the training of the synaptic matrix W from MT to MSTd directly affects the effectiveness of feature extraction of the foundation model. In this paper, all connections in SNN are plastic, whose weight values are modulated by the heterosynaptic STDP (STDP-H) to optimize the learning rule parameters based on an evolutionary algorithm, as proposed in [18]. Simulations were conducted using the CARLSim SNN simulator platform https://github.com/UCI-CARL/CARLsim6 (accessed on 1 March 2022) [26,27].

The model of STDP-H can be described as follows [18]:

$$\frac{dw_{i,j}}{dt} = [\overbrace{\alpha \cdot w_{i,j}(1 - \overline{R}/R_{t\,arg\,et})}^{\text{hom}eostasis} + \overbrace{\beta(LTP_{i,j} + LTD_{i,j})}^{STDP}] \cdot K \quad (7)$$

Equation (7) describes the cumulative impact of STDP-H on a specific synapse $w_{i,j}$ that connects the presynaptic neuron i and the postsynaptic neuron j. Equation (7) consists of two key components. The first component pertains to homeostatic scaling, which is determined by the ratio of the average firing rate R to the target firing rate $R_{t\,arg\,et}$ of neuron j. Homeostatic scaling modulates the rate of synaptic weight changes, reducing it when the neuron is excessively active and increasing it when the neuron is too inactive. The second component in Equation (7) deals with spike-timing-dependent plasticity (STDP [28], encompassing both long-term potentiation (LTP) and long-term depression (LTD). STDP adjusts the strength of synaptic connections based on the timing of spikes between presynaptic and postsynaptic neurons. Specific details can be found in reference [18].

For STDP learning, parameter optimization was performed with the Parameter Tuning Interface in CARLsim 6, which used the Evolutionary Computations in JAVA library (ECJ) [29]. By leveraging the parallel execution capabilities provided by CARLsim, the computations were distributed among GPU and CPU cores, resulting in a significant acceleration of the simulation process. ECJ was used to evolve suitable parameters for STDP learning. It automatically constructs multiple independent individuals based on the network structure and selects the best-adapted parameters according to evaluation rules. During learning, the input data were shuffled. A portion of the samples was used for training to adjust the MT-to-MST connection weights. The remaining samples were used for testing and parameter evaluation. Each sample ran for 0.5 s before stopping the Poisson process for spike generation. An additional 0.5 s of idle time was added between samples to allow neuronal voltages to decay without affecting subsequent inputs. The evaluation metric was the correlation coefficient between the input and reconstructed samples.

$$fitness = \frac{\sum_m \sum_n (A_{mn} - \bar{A})(B_{mn} - \bar{B})}{\sqrt{\sum_m \sum_n (A_{mn} - \bar{A}) \sum_m \sum_n (B_{mn} - \bar{B})}} \qquad (8)$$

The correlation coefficient is calculated as: $\bar{A}$ and $\bar{B}$ are the column-wise mean values of matrices A and B, respectively. A is the test samples from the input data, and B is the product of the MT-to-MST connection weight matrix W and the MST neuronal firing rate matrix H. The ECJ parameters were configured with adjustment ranges as mentioned in [25]. Each iteration evaluated 15 network individuals, and after 100 iterations the best fitness of 72.66% was achieved. The 18 parameters corresponding to the highest fitness network were selected as the adapted parameters.

2.3. Decision Model of Echo State Network

Based on the above well-trained foundation SNN model, all core features are saved in the form of MT-MSTd synaptic weights. Then, the firing rates of MSTd neurons encoding the relative importance of the core features to the current visual input are transferred to the readout decision model. In this paper, an echo state network (ESN) proposed by Jaeger [30–32] is utilized as the decision model. It consists of a random sparse network (reservoir) and one readout layer. The reservoir acts as an information processing medium, which maps the low-dimensional input signal to the high-dimensional state space.

Specifically, we have the following weight matrices: W_{in}, W_{res}, W_{back}, and W_{out}. W_{in} signifies the weight matrix governing connections from the input layer to the reservoir, W_{res} represents the internal weight matrix regulating connections within the reservoir, and W_{back} is responsible for feedback connections from the output layer to the reservoir. Lastly, W_{out} corresponds to the weight matrix that manages connections from the reservoir to the output layer. In terms of variables, we use $u(n)$ to denote the network input at time n, $x(n)$ signifies the state vector representing the network's reservoir, and $y(n)$ represents the network's output.

The updated reservoir status is calculated according to Formula (9) and the network output is calculated according to the following Formula (10):

$$x(n+1) = f(W_{in}u(n+1) + W_{res}x(n) + W_{back}y(n)) \qquad (9)$$

$$y(n+1) = f_{out}(W_{out}[x(n+1)|u(n+1)]) \qquad (10)$$

where $f(\bullet)$ is the activation function of the neuron of the network reservoir. $f(\bullet)$ can be typically defined as a sigmoid or tanh function [33], and $f_{out}(\bullet)$ represents the output function of the output layer neurons. In ESN, W_{in}, W_{res}, and W_{back} are randomly generated before training and no longer adjusted. W_{out} is the only matrix that needs to be learned. Algorithms such as the ridge regression algorithm are used to learn W_{out}.

There are 500 units in the reservoir network. Only synaptic weights from the readout layer to the reservoir are updated using the linear regression method and connections within the reservoir are randomly generated. Furthermore, the connection weights in the foundation model of SNN are also frozen and unchanged during the readout training process. This ESN model for recognition tasks makes readout decisions to recognize which patterns of the input stimuli belong. The ESN network structure parameters for this experiment are shown in Table 1.

Table 1. Key parameters of ESN model.

ESN Parameters	Values
Reservoir Sparsity (SP)	0.5
Displacement Scale (IS)	1
Input Unit Scale (IC)	1
Spectral Radius (SR)	0.85
Reservoir Activation Function (f)	Tanh
Output Unit Activation Function (f_{out})	1
Regularization Coefficient (λ)	1×10^{-3}

3. Results

The proposed model framework, as shown in Figure 1, consists of three aspects: input layer, feature extraction in the foundation model of the visual cortex, and decision layer. First, optic flow data V are encoded as spike sequences using Poisson frequency encoding, serving as the input to the MT-group neurons in the SNN model. Synaptic weights from MT to MSTd are saved in the W matrix, and the firing frequency of the MSTd group is represented as the H matrix. The STDP learning rule is employed to adjust the network parameters, aiming to reconstruct the original optic flow data V with the $W \times H$ matrix and automatically optimize the network by evaluating the reconstruction performance at each iteration. Finally, the effectiveness of the foundation SNN model is validated through image recognition of the optic flow and grating stimulus by training the ESN model. The pseudo-code is as follows (Algorithm 1):

Algorithm 1: A visually inspired computational model for recognition of optic flow

1 **Step 1: Foundation model of SNN**
2 **for** *each optic flow data* **do**
3   Encode input optic flow into Poisson spike trains
4   Adjust MT-MSTd weight connections W with STDP-H learning
5   Compute MSTd firing rates H
6   Reconstruct input data V to verify the efficiency of feature extraction using $V \approx W \times H$
7 **Step 2: Decision model of ESN**
8 **for** *each H_i* **do**
9   Initialize synaptic weights randomly
10   Use ridge regression algorithm to obtain W_{out} while keeping the other weights fixed
11   Achieve recognition for optic flow

3.1. Feature Extraction of SNN Model

Non-negative matrix factorization (NMF) is known for its key feature of feature extraction by decomposing data into linear combinations of different local features [14,34]. This algorithm is a sparse decomposition processing with dimensional reduction, which has been previously shown to be capable of mimicking a wide range of monkey MSTd visual response properties [15,17]. The input stimuli can be accurately reconstructed from a linear superposition of the sparse, parts-based features regarded as basis flow fields (see Figure 3a). Considering the columns of an input matrix V with a set of samples, these data can be linearly decomposed as $V \approx W \times H$, where the columns of the matrix W contain the basis feature vectors of the decomposition and the rows of H contain the corresponding coefficients that give the contribution of each basis vector. In NMF, the basis functions W and the corresponding coefficient vector H are obtained simultaneously in one calculation.

Although the basis matrix W obtained in NMF can be considered the synaptic weights of a population of simulated neurons in a neural network, both the W and H matrices need to be retrained every time a new sample is added to the input matrix V, that is, all of the data must be re-decomposed.

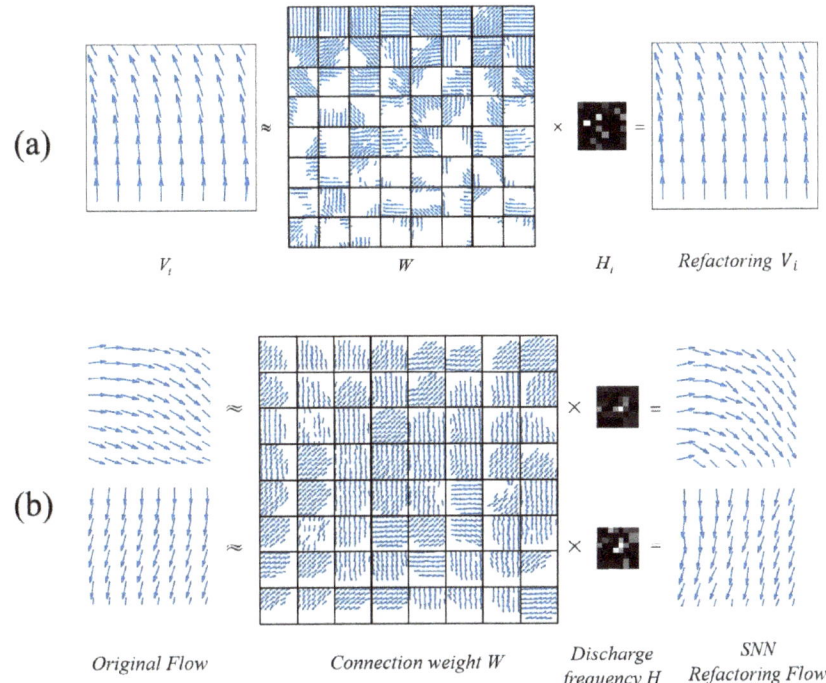

Figure 3. Decomposition and reconstruction of optic flow from NMF (**a**) and STDP learning (**b**). V_i is a single sample. Basis flow fields are shown in an 8×8 MT-MSTd weight matrix W, which is visualized using the population vector decoding method. H is a grayscale image containing weight information of core features. Input optic flow V can be reconstructed from a sparse activation of model MSTd neurons, i.e., $V \approx W \times H$. The optic flow of each square in the basis matrix W is different, indicating that the features are separated and contain the local features of the original data. By multiplying the coefficient matrix H, the features in W are combined to reconstruct the original data. Therefore, the coefficient matrix H contains the weight of each local feature and can represent the original data for classification verification.

Recent studies have shown that the SNN model can learn efficient representations and reconstructions of the input patterns similar to that emerging from NMF [18]. Therefore, we adopt SNN with STDP learning to achieve feature extraction of optic flow. Figure 3b demonstrates that a set of basis flow fields (shown in an 8×8 MT-MSTd weight matrix W, which is visualized as basis flow fields using the population vector decoding method) can emerge from both NMF and STDP learning, indicating that the core features are successfully extracted from the original input data. Meanwhile, optic flow fields can be reconstructed from a sparse firing activation of model MSTd neurons that prefer various orientations of the basis flow fields. That is, the optic flow input samples V can then be approximated by a linear superposition of basis flow fields, i.e., $V \approx W \times H$, which means that the original 1800-dimensional input data V are compressed into a 64-dimension coefficient matrix H. In this way, sparse coding reduces the overall neural activity necessary to represent the information. This not only reduces the number of nodes in the MSTd layer but also improves the learning efficiency of the decision layer.

Unlike the NMF method, once the connection MT-MSTd weight matrix W is well-trained, it can be frozen and the parts-based features saved in W can be re-used or shared for new input stimuli. The coefficient vector H that gives the contribution of each basis feature for the current input stimuli can be directly obtained through the firing responses of the MSTd layer. Inputs belonging to the same patterns share similar value distributions of the H vector, while H coefficients are different for different input patterns. To validate the effectiveness of this feature-extraction method, an ESN model is used to train the readout decision layer for the recognition task of optic flow.

3.2. Recognition Performance

Image reconstruction based on feature extraction is shown in Figure 3b, which indicates that good image reconstruction means accurate feature representation of the MSTd neurons. In order to test the effectiveness of the SNN model, eight categories with different directions ranging from 0° to 360° in 45° increments are selected from a sample of 6000 MT optic streams that had previously been generated. As shown in Figure 1, the readout neurons are divided into eight classes corresponding to the superimposed directions. Each class included 120 samples, resulting in a total of 960 samples. A fully trained foundation model has the capability to achieve more diverse parts-based features than the partially trained foundation model (see Figure 4a). The weight visualization of a fully trained model demonstrates more distinct and concrete feature extraction compared to the incompletely trained model. Therefore, we can see from Figure 4b that the fully trained base model significantly outperforms the incompletely trained counterpart, contributing to the reduction in training samples for readout learning.

Furthermore, we conducted a comparative analysis of the classification performance between the fully trained SNN model and a basic CNN model, as depicted in Figure 4c. The CNN architecture employed in this paper consists of six layers. The initial layer is the input layer, which receives data of size $15 \times 15 \times 8$. Following this is the second layer, a convolutional layer comprising 16 convolutional kernels of size 3×3 utilized to extract features from the input. Subsequently, the third layer is the activation function, employing the rectified linear unit (ReLU) activation function to introduce non-linear characteristics and enhance the network's expressive capability. The fourth layer is a pooling layer, utilizing a 2×2 max-pooling operation to reduce the dimensions of the feature maps. Next is the fully connected output layer containing ten nodes. Finally, through the combination of a Softmax layer and a classification layer, the network completes its output and transforms it into a probability distribution for executing the ultimate classification task. Since CNN is trained end-to-end for all layers, pattern recognition is examined with different numbers of training data.

Remarkably, we observed that our two-layer SNN model with ESN readout outperforms the six-layer CNN throughout the whole experimental process. Note that even when inputting different pattern samples, retraining for SNN is unnecessary, i.e., the weights in the SNN model are frozen and only the ESN readout is trained to learn new patterns. In contrast, the CNN model shows lower classification accuracy, and all layers need to be end-to-end retrained when new input patterns are added. This result demonstrates the advantages of our model in terms of low power consumption and high precision of computation.

Our model not only excels in recognizing visual optic flow (in-domain) but also accurately recognizes out-of-domain stimuli, such as the sinusoidal grating stimulus [35]. We use the model of the V1 visual cortex proposed in [36] to transfer the stimuli into the optic flow, as shown in Figure 5a. The left image represents the input grating stimulus, where v represents the direction of the grating motion. The right image represents the integrated optic flow. The results demonstrate that the V1 response accurately identifies the motion direction of the grating stimulus, indicating that the grating stimulus is transformed into optic flow stimuli and can be used for recognition validation of this model.

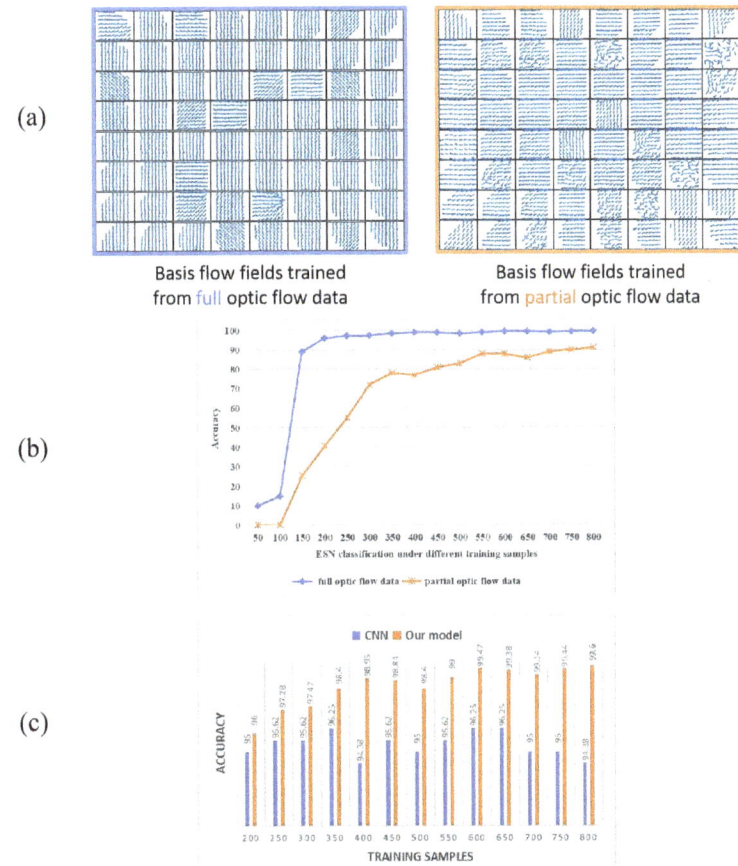

Figure 4. Fully trained foundation model can considerably reduce the training samples required for recognition tasks during the readout learning. (**a**) Basis flow fields trained from full or partial input data. (**b**) Performance comparison of fully trained or not fully trained foundation models under different training samples for readout learning. (**c**) Comparison of classification performance between a six-layer CNN model and our proposed model on optic flow data.

Based on the above-obtained foundation model trained from the optic flow stimulus, here the MT-MSTd connection weights in SNN are fixed. Training data from the new stimulus are only used to fit the readout weights of the ESN model. The recognition performance for the grating input is shown in Figure 5b. It can be seen that the training accuracy for the grating stimulus can reach up to 99.85% and the testing accuracy is 99.25%. This indicates that the foundation SNN model performs exceptionally well in classifying new stimulus data with no need to retrain the basis features, even when compared to its performance in recognizing optic flow data. This result reveals that a foundation model trained from vast quantities of data has remarkable capabilities and generalization in performing computational tasks.

However, if the grating stimulus is directed and projected to the SNN model without the processing of the V1 layer, recognition will not succeed. Because the MT layer can only process orientation-based input, images must be processed with V1 before input to the MT layer. Preliminary feature extraction for stripe shapes with V1 is also crucial for image recognition. Therefore, further study considering the V1 and V2 visual cortex as the foundation model is necessary for expanding its applicability to the recognition of broader image datasets.

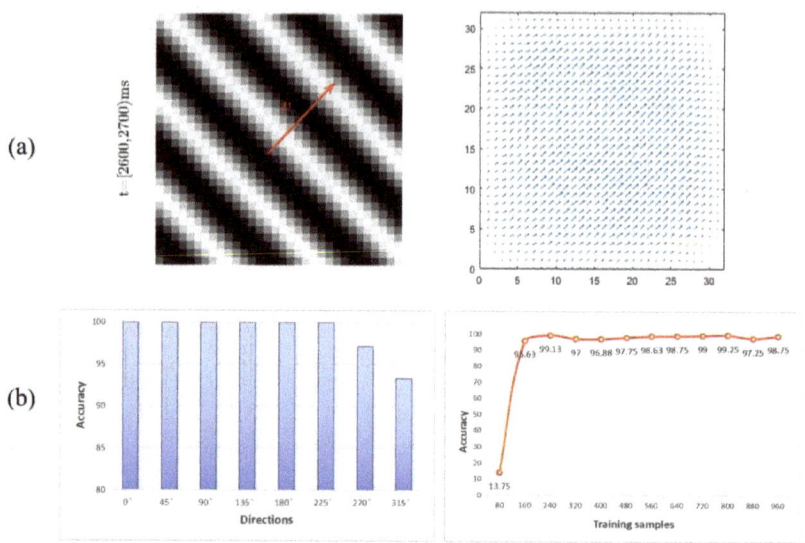

Figure 5. Recognition performance for grating stimulus. (**a**) **Left**: grating motion stimulus sample. **Right**: optic flow transformed from the original grating stimuli using V1 visual cortex model proposed in [36]. (**b**) **Left**: Average classification accuracy in each direction. **Right**: Classification accuracy with different numbers of grating training samples.

4. Conclusions

We introduce a visually inspired computational model that achieves efficient performance in the recognition of optic flow. Here, a foundation model based on SNNs with STDP learning is shown to be an efficient sparse coding for parts-based representation, where any flow field could be represented by only a small set of simulated MSTd neurons (H coefficient) as compared with vast quantities of input samples. The results show that STDP can perform similar functions as NMF, i.e., generating sparse and linear superimposed readouts based on basis flow fields. The visually inspired SNN is an ideal core/foundation model to accurately reconstruct input stimuli for image reconstruction. Based on the well-trained SNN, the readouts can accurately recognize not only optic flow but also new stimuli such as the grating stimulus. Moreover, the ESN requires significantly less training data than the one without a fully trained core SNN model.

Our model based on biologically realistic SNNs offers a powerful new approach for the efficient recognition of visual optic flow, which has the potential to be used in neuromorphic applications to reduce computations. This study may give insight into the development of visually based navigation models, brain-inspired robots, and new-generation artificial intelligence machines.

Author Contributions: Methodology, W.L.; Formal analysis, J.C.; Resources, L.W.; Data curation, H.Y.; Supervision and Writing editing, X.L. All authors have read and agreed to the published version of the manuscript.

Funding: This paper is supported by STI 2030-Major Project 2021ZD0201300.

Data Availability Statement: The Evolutionary Computations in JAVA library (ECJ) used to evolve suitable parameters for STDP learning is available on https://cs.gmu.edu/eclab/projects/ecj/. The sinusoidal grating stimulus was generated from the Visual Stimulus Toolbox (https://zenodo.org/records/154061 for details).

Acknowledgments: The authors would like to give sincere appreciation to Jeffrey Krichmar and Kexin Chen for their insightful suggestions and discussions for this work.

Conflicts of Interest: Hao Yi was employed by the Huawei Technologies Co., Ltd. The remaining authors declare that the research was conducted in the absence of any commercial or financial relationships that could be construed as a potential conflict of interest

References

1. Bommasani, R.; Hudson, D.A.; Adeli, E.; Altman, R.; Arora, S.; von Arx, S.; Bernstein, M.S.; Bohg, J.; Bosselut, A.; Brunskill, E.; et al. On the Opportunities and Risks of Foundation Models. *arXiv* **2022**, arXiv:cs.LG/2108.07258.
2. Bashivan, P.; Kar, K.; Dicarlo, J.J. Neural Population Control via Deep Image Synthesis. *Science* **2018**, *364*, eaav9436. [CrossRef]
3. Walker, E.Y.; Sinz, F.H.; Cobos, E.; Muhammad, T.; Froudarakis, E.; Fahey, P.G.; Ecker, A.S.; Reimer, J.; Pitkow, X.; Tolias, A.S. Inception loops discover what excites neurons most using deep predictive models. *Nat. Neurosci.* **2019**, *22*, 2060–2065. [CrossRef]
4. Ponce, C.R.; Xiao, W.; Schade, P.F.; Hartmann, T.S.; Kreiman, G.; Livingstone, M.S. Evolving Images for Visual Neurons Using a Deep Generative Network Reveals Coding Principles and Neuronal Preferences. *Cell* **2019**, *177*, 999–1009.e10. [CrossRef]
5. Franke, K.; Willeke, K.F.; Ponder, K.; Galdamez, M.; Zhou, N.; Muhammad, T.; Patel, S.; Froudarakis, E.; Reimer, J.; Sinz, F.H.; et al. State-dependent pupil dilation rapidly shifts visual feature selectivity. *Nature* **2022**, *610*, 128–134. [CrossRef] [PubMed]
6. Höfling, L.; Szatko, K.P.; Behrens, C.; Qiu, Y.; Klindt, D.A.; Jessen, Z.; Schwartz, G.W.; Bethge, M.; Berens, P.; Franke, K.; et al. A chromatic feature detector in the retina signals visual context changes. *bioRxiv* **2022**. [CrossRef]
7. Chen, K.; Kashyap, H.J.; Krichmar, J.L.; Li, X. What can computer vision learn from visual neuroscience? Introduction to the special issue. *Biol. Cybern.* **2023**, *117*, 297–298. [CrossRef] [PubMed]
8. Tavanaei, A.; Maida, A. BP-STDP: Approximating backpropagation using spike timing dependent plasticity. *Neurocomputing* **2019**, *330*, 39–47. [CrossRef]
9. Rueckauer, B.; Liu, S.C. Conversion of analog to spiking neural networks using sparse temporal coding. In Proceedings of the 2018 IEEE International Symposium on Circuits and Systems (ISCAS), Florence, Italy, 27–30 May 2018; pp. 1–5. [CrossRef]
10. Diehl, P.U.; Neil, D.; Binas, J.; Cook, M.; Liu, S.C.; Pfeiffer, M. Fast-classifying, high-accuracy spiking deep networks through weight and threshold balancing. In Proceedings of the 2015 International Joint Conference on Neural Networks (IJCNN), Killarney, Ireland, 12–17 July 2015; pp. 1–8. [CrossRef]
11. Zhang, A.; Li, X.; Gao, Y.; Niu, Y. Event-Driven Intrinsic Plasticity for Spiking Convolutional Neural Networks. *IEEE Trans. Neural Netw. Learn. Syst.* **2022**, *33*, 1986–1995. [CrossRef]
12. Zhang, A.; Zhou, H.; Li, X.; Zhu, W. Fast and robust learning in Spiking Feed-forward Neural Networks based on Intrinsic Plasticity mechanism. *Neurocomputing* **2019**, *365*, 102–112. [CrossRef]
13. Kim, S.; Park, S.; Na, B.; Yoon, S. Spiking-YOLO: Spiking Neural Network for Energy-Efficient Object Detection. *Proc. AAAI Conf. Artif. Intell.* **2020**, *34*, 11270–11277. [CrossRef]
14. Lee, D.D.; Seung, H.S. Learning the parts of objects by non-negative matrix factorization. *Nature* **1999**, *401*, 788–791. [CrossRef] [PubMed]
15. Beyeler, M.; Rounds, E.L.; Carlson, K.D.; Dutt, N.; Krichmar, J.L. Neural correlates of sparse coding and dimensionality reduction. *PLoS Comput. Biol.* **2019**, *15*, e1006908. [CrossRef] [PubMed]
16. Nishimoto, S.; Gallant, J.L. A Three-Dimensional Spatiotemporal Receptive Field Model Explains Responses of Area MT Neurons to Naturalistic Movies. *J. Neurosci.* **2011**, *31*, 14551–14564. [CrossRef]
17. Beyeler, M.; Dutt, N.; Krichmar, J.L. 3D Visual Response Properties of MSTd Emerge from an Efficient, Sparse Population Code. *J. Neurosci.* **2016**, *36*, 8399–8415. [CrossRef]
18. Chen, K.; Beyeler, M.; Krichmar, J.L. Cortical Motion Perception Emerges from Dimensionality Reduction with Evolved Spike-Timing-Dependent Plasticity Rules. *J. Neurosci.* **2022**, *42*, 5882–5898. [CrossRef]
19. Browning, N.A.; Grossberg, S.; Mingolla, E. A neural model of how the brain computes heading from optic flow in realistic scenes. *Cogn. Psychol.* **2009**, *59*, 320–356. [CrossRef] [PubMed]
20. Logan, D.J.; Duffy, C.J. Cortical Area MSTd Combines Visual Cues to Represent 3-D Self-Movement. *Cereb. Cortex* **2005**, *16*, 1494–1507. [CrossRef]
21. Layton, O.W. ARTFLOW: A Fast, Biologically Inspired Neural Network that Learns Optic Flow Templates for Self-Motion Estimation. *Sensors* **2021**, *21*, 8217. [CrossRef]
22. Layton, O.W.; Powell, N.; Steinmetz, S.T.; Fajen, B.R. Estimating curvilinear self-motion from optic flow with a biologically inspired neural system*. *Bioinspir. Biomimetics* **2022**, *17*, 046013. [CrossRef]
23. The interpretation of a moving retinal image. *Proc. R. Soc. Lond. Ser. B. Biol. Sci.* **1980**, *208*, 385–397. [CrossRef]
24. Izhikevich, E. Which Model to Use for Cortical Spiking Neurons? *IEEE Trans. Neural Netw.* **2004**, *15*, 1063–1070. [CrossRef] [PubMed]
25. Lin, W.; Yi, H.; Li, X. Image Reconstruction and Recognition of Optical Flow Based on Local Feature Extraction Mechanism of Visual Cortex. In *Proceedings of the International Conference on Neural Computing for Advanced Applications, Hefei, China, 7–9 July 2023*; Zhang, H., Ke, Y., Wu, Z., Hao, T., Zhang, Z., Meng, W., Mu, Y., Eds.; Springer: Singapore, 2023; pp. 18–32.
26. Niedermeier, L.; Krichmar, J.L. Experience-Dependent Axonal Plasticity in Large-Scale Spiking Neural Network Simulations. In Proceedings of the 2023 International Joint Conference on Neural Networks (IJCNN), IEEE, Gold Coast, Australia, 18–23 June 2023. [CrossRef]

27. Niedermeier, L.; Chen, K.; Xing, J.; Das, A.; Kopsick, J.; Scott, E.; Sutton, N.; Weber, K.; Dutt, N.; Krichmar, J.L. CARLsim 6: An Open Source Library for Large-Scale, Biologically Detailed Spiking Neural Network Simulation. In Proceedings of the 2022 International Joint Conference on Neural Networks (IJCNN), IEEE, Padua, Italy, 18–23 July 2022. [CrossRef]
28. Kheradpisheh, S.R.; Ganjtabesh, M.; Thorpe, S.J.; Masquelier, T. STDP-based spiking deep convolutional neural networks for object recognition. *Neural Netw.* **2018**, *99*, 56–67. [CrossRef]
29. Luke, S. ECJ then and now. In Proceedings of the Genetic and Evolutionary Computation Conference Companion, ACM, Berlin Germany, 15–19 July 2017. [CrossRef]
30. Liu, B. A Prediction Method Based on Improved Echo State Network for COVID-19 Nonlinear Time Series. *J. Comput. Commun.* **2020**, *8*, 113. [CrossRef]
31. Jaeger, H. *Tutorial on Training Recurrent Neural Networks, Covering BPPT, RTRL, EKF and the "Echo State Network" Approach*; German National Research Center for Information Technology: Bonn, Germany, 2002.
32. Jaeger, H. *The "Echo State" Approach to Analysing and Training Recurrent Neural Networks-with an Erratum Note*; GMD Technical Report; German National Research Center for Information Technology: Bonn, Germany, 2001; Volume 148, p. 13.
33. Rodan, A.; Tino, P. Minimum Complexity Echo State Network. *IEEE Trans. Neural Netw.* **2011**, *22*, 131–144. [CrossRef] [PubMed]
34. Wang, G.; Kossenkov, A.V.; Ochs, M.F. LS-NMF: A modified non-negative matrix factorization algorithm utilizing uncertainty estimates. *BMC Bioinform.* **2006**, *7*, 1–10. [CrossRef] [PubMed]
35. Beyeler, M. *Visual Stimulus Toolbox: v1.0.0.*; Zenodo: Genève, Switzerland, 2016. [CrossRef]
36. Beyeler, M.; Richert, M.; Dutt, N.D.; Krichmar, J.L. Efficient Spiking Neural Network Model of Pattern Motion Selectivity in Visual Cortex. *Neuroinformatics* **2014**, *12*, 435. [CrossRef]

Disclaimer/Publisher's Note: The statements, opinions and data contained in all publications are solely those of the individual author(s) and contributor(s) and not of MDPI and/or the editor(s). MDPI and/or the editor(s) disclaim responsibility for any injury to people or property resulting from any ideas, methods, instructions or products referred to in the content.

Article

Minimization of Active Power Loss Using Enhanced Particle Swarm Optimization

Samson Ademola Adegoke [1,*], Yanxia Sun [1,*] and Zenghui Wang [2]

1 Department of Electrical and Electronic Engineering Science, University of Johannesburg, Johannesburg 2006, South Africa
2 Department of Electrical Engineering, University of South Africa, Florida 1709, South Africa; wangz@unisa.ac.za
* Correspondence: adsam4u@gmail.com (S.A.A.); ysun@uj.ac.za (Y.S.)

Abstract: Identifying the weak buses in power system networks is crucial for planning and operation since most generators operate close to their operating limits, resulting in generator failures. This work aims to identify the critical/weak node and reduce the system's power loss. The line stability index (L_{mn}) and fast voltage stability index (FVSI) were used to identify the critical node and lines close to instability in the power system networks. Enhanced particle swarm optimization (EPSO) was chosen because of its ability to communicate with better individuals, making it more efficient to obtain a prominent solution. EPSO and other PSO variants minimized the system's actual/real losses. Nodes 8 and 14 were identified as the critical nodes of the IEEE 9 and 14 bus systems, respectively. The power loss of the IEEE 9 bus system was reduced from 9.842 MW to 7.543 MW, and for the IEEE 14 bus system, the loss was reduced from 13.775 MW of the base case to 12.253 MW for EPSO. EPSO gives a better active power loss reduction and improves the node's voltage profile than other PSO variants and algorithms in the literature. This suggests the feasibility and suitability of EPSO to improve the grid voltage quality.

Keywords: voltage stability; identification of weak bus; FVSI and L_{mn}; diminish power loss; PSO variants; EPSO

MSC: 90C11; 90C30

Citation: Adegoke, S.A.; Sun, Y.; Wang, Z. Minimization of Active Power Loss Using Enhanced Particle Swarm Optimization. *Mathematics* 2023, 11, 3660. https://doi.org/10.3390/math11173660

Academic Editor: Nicu Bizon

Received: 10 July 2023
Revised: 15 August 2023
Accepted: 17 August 2023
Published: 24 August 2023

Copyright: © 2023 by the authors. Licensee MDPI, Basel, Switzerland. This article is an open access article distributed under the terms and conditions of the Creative Commons Attribution (CC BY) license (https://creativecommons.org/licenses/by/4.0/).

1. Introduction

Voltage stability (VS) is a major focus of modern power system (PS) utility companies. Therefore, VS is the ability of systems to keep the voltage profile stable when undergoing large or small disturbances. Different means have been used to improve the voltage profile in modern PS, such as battery storage systems and distributed energy resources (DER) [1–4]. The increase in the infrastructure and load demand rate leads to the high utilization of PS energy equipment. This has made systems experience voltage instability that has led to blackouts in some parts of the world, destruction of some businesses and daily activities, and increased power loss. Based on this problem, this study is motivated by identifying the weak bus that could cause a blackout in a system and reducing system transmission loss, which is caused by a shortage of reactive power (RP), which significantly affects the quality of energy delivery to the consumer end. Environmental and economic factors are two leading causes for establishing a new transmission line (TL). As the load increases, the system is heavily loaded, and maintaining stability becomes difficult; thus, the system operates close to the instability point [5–8]. Evaluation of system stability is based on the node/bus voltage profile. Presently, there are numerous techniques for finding system stability. The line voltage stability index (LVSI) [9], a simplified voltage stability index (SVSI) [10], L-index [11], a global voltage stability index (GVSI) [12], etc. Some classical voltage stability assessments and various techniques have been proposed for weak bus identification in power system networks. Some of them are genetic algorithms based on support vector machine (GA-VSM) [13], ant colony (AC) [14], electric cactus structure (ECS) [15], and network response structural characteristic (NRSC) [16].

A shortage of RP in a PS network causes a tremendous waste of electricity in the distribution system, resulting in extra emission of carbon and power generation cost. Therefore, reducing losses in transmission line networks (TLN) is essential for system safety. However, the best way to reduce losses in TLs of PS networks is RP optimization (RPO). Two methods used in solving the RPO problem are traditional and evolutionary algorithms. Traditional methods include the Newton–Raphson (NR) method, interior point methods, quadratic programming, and linear programming [17]. Recently, evolution algorithms have been used to solve RPO problems, such as the hybrid pathfinder algorithm (HPFA) [18], hybrid PSO (HPSO-PFA) [17], modified PFA (mPFA) [19], chaotic krill herd [20], ant lion optimizer (ALO) [21], the tree seed algorithm (TSA) [22], and the improved pathfinder algorithm (IPFA) [23]. However, PSO is good in search capacity and has less programming than others [17].

Harish et al. used the fast voltage stability index (FVSI) and line stability index (L_{mn}) to identify the location of flexible alternating current transmission system (FACTS) devices along with PSO, artificial bee colony (ABC), and the hybrid genetic algorithm (H-GA) to find the sizing of the FACTS devices [24]. Also, a novel method for strengthening PS stability was proposed by Jaramillo et al. [25]. FVSI was used to identify the node on which the SVC should be installed under an N-1 scenario. It was reported that the result obtained could reestablish the FVSI in each contingency before the outage [25]. The voltage collapse critical bus index (VCCBI) [26], L-Index, voltage collapse proximity index (VCPI), and modal analysis [27], which are part of voltage stability indices (VSI), were used to identify weak/vulnerable buses in electrical power systems. Power loss reduction was made using a hybrid loop-genetic-based algorithm (HLGBA) [28], the Jaya algorithm (JAYA), diversity-enhanced (DEPSO), etc. [29].

This research considers the identification of critical nodes and loss reduction, which serve as merit over the previous work mentioned above. FVSI and L_{mn} were used to find the critical node in the system based on load flow (LF) results from MATLAB 2018b software (MathWorks, Inc., Natick, MA, USA). FVSI and L_{mn} were chosen because of their efficiency in identifying the weak/vulnerable bus (i.e., the fastness of FVSI and the accuracy of L_{mn}) [30]. The critical node was determined by the value of the indices (i.e., FVSI and L_{mn}). When the indices value reaches unity or is close to unity, that node is the critical node of the system. The reactive powers of all the load buses were increased one after the other to determine the maximum RP on each of the load buses/nodes. Also, each line's value of FVSI and L_{mn} was computed to determine the load-ability limit on each load bus. The ranking was carried out based on the indices value of each node; hence, the node with the highest indices values is the system's critical bus. This bus contained the smallest RP when the load bus was varied. The identified node needs reactive power support to avoid voltage collapse. Also, enhanced PSO (EPSO) was used to minimize the PS network loss along with PSO variants that have been developed by previous research, such as PSO-based time-varying acceleration coefficients (PSO-TVAC) [31], random inertia weight PSO (RPSO), and PSO based on success rate (PSO-SR) [32]. To overcome the premature convergence of PSO, the chosen EPSO was applied, and it uses neighborhood exchange to share more information with the other best individual (neighborhood) to improve itself, which makes it more efficient in getting a prominent solution (i.e., exploitation stage) to optimizing the objective function. The novelty of this research and this paper's contribution is that each particle learns from its own personal and global positions in the PSO algorithm in the social cognitive system. Apart from personal experience and better information received from the search areas, it is advisable to share with better individuals to enhance or improve itself. Therefore, a new acceleration constant (c_3) is added to the original PSO equation, making obtaining the best solution more efficient. Also, additional c_3 gives the swarm the capability to reach the exploitation stage, which helps to overcome the premature convergence of PSO.

However, this paper has contributed by (1) comparing different PSO variants and EPSO for power loss reduction; (2) identifying the power system critical node for the perfect operation of generators to avoid breakdown.

The rest of the paper is structured as follows: Section 2 presents the problem formulation of voltage stability indices and RPO, and Section 3 discusses the PSO, its variants, and EPSO. The results and discussion are presented in Section 4, and the conclusion and future work is the last section.

2. Problem Formulation

2.1. Formulation of Voltage Stability Indices

FVSI and L_{mn} are part of the VSI methods for identifying weak buses. They were formed based on two bus systems. For a system to be stable, the value of FVSI and L_{mn} must be smaller than unity and unstable when it equals unity and above.

2.1.1. FVSI

FVSI was developed [33] based on the concept of a single line of power flow (PF). The FVSI is evaluated by:

$$\text{FVSI} = \frac{4Zj^2 Q_1}{V_1^2 Xr} \leq 1 \quad (1)$$

where Zj is the impedance, Q_1 is the RP at sending ends, Xr is the reactance of the line, and V_1 is the voltage at the sending end.

2.1.2. L_{mn}

L_{mn} was proposed by the authors of [34]. Using the concept of PF from a single-line diagram, the discriminant of the quadratic voltage equation is set to be higher than or equal to zero. The equation is given below.

$$L_{mn} = \frac{4XQ_2}{[V_1 \sin(\theta - \delta)]^2} \leq 1 \quad (2)$$

where θ is the angle of the TL, δ is the power angle, and Q_2 is the RP at receiving end.

2.2. Steps Involve in Identifying Critical Node in EPS

Identifying critical nodes in EPS is essential for delivering stable electricity to the consumer end. The following steps are involved:

1. Input the line and bus data of the IEEE test case;
2. Run the PF solution in MATLAB using the NR method at the base case;
3. Calculate the stability values of FVSI and L_{mn} of the IEEE test system;
4. Gradually increased the RP of the load bus until the values of FVSI and L_{mn} are closer to one (1);
5. The load bus with the highest FVSI and L_{mn} value is selected at the critical node;
6. Steps 1 to 5 are repeated for all the load buses;
7. The highest RP loading is selected and called maximum load-ability;
8. The voltage magnitude at the critical loading of a particular load bus is obtained and is called the critical voltage of a specific load bus.

2.3. Formulation of RPO

The main objective of RPO is to reduce the network's actual power loss.

2.3.1. Objective Function

The main goal of RPO is to reduce the network's actual power losses, which are described as follows.

$$\text{Minimize } f = P_{loss}(x, u) \quad (3)$$

which satisfying

$$\begin{cases} g(x,u) = 0 \\ h(x,u) \leq 0 \end{cases} \quad (4)$$

where $f(x,u)$ is the objective function, $g(x,u)$ is the equality constraints, $h(x,u)$ is the inequality constraints, x is the vector of the state variables, and u is the vector of the control variables.

The real power loss minimization in the TL is given below, and its purpose is to reduce the overall loss in the TLN.

$$Min f = P_{loss} \sum_{K=1}^{N_L} G_k \left(v_i^2 + v_j^2 - 2V_i V_j \cos \theta_{ij} \right) \quad (5)$$

where P_{loss} is the real total losses, k is the branch, G_k is the conductance of the branch k, Vj and V_i is the voltage at the ith and jth bus, N_L is the total number of TL, and θ_{ij} is the voltage angle between bus i and j.

2.3.2. Equality Constraints

The PS network's active and reactive PF equation are called the equality constraints.

$$P_{gi} - P_{di} - V_i \sum_{j=1}^{N} V_j (g_{ij} \cos \theta_{ij} + b_{ij} \sin \theta_{ij}) = 0 \quad (6)$$

$$Q_{gi} - Q_{di} - V_i \sum_{j=1}^{N} V_j (g_{ij} \sin \theta_{ij} - b_{ij} \cos \theta_{ij}) = 0 \quad (7)$$

Here, g_{ij} and b_{ij} are conductance and susceptance, and θ_{ij} is the phase difference of voltages.

2.3.3. Inequality Constraints

Inequality constraints are operational variables that must be kept within acceptable limits.

(1). Generator constraints

$$V_{gi}^{min} \leq V_{gi} \leq V_{gi}^{max} \quad i = 1 \ldots, N_g \quad (8)$$

$$Q_{gi}^{min} \leq Q_{gi} \leq Q_{gi}^{max} \quad i = 1 \ldots, N_g \quad (9)$$

(2). Reactive compensation constraints

$$Q_{ci}^{min} \leq Q_{ci} \leq Q_{ci}^{max} \quad i = 1 \ldots, N_C \quad (10)$$

(3). Transformer tap ratio constraints

$$T_k^{min} \leq T_k \leq T_k^{max} \quad i = 1 \ldots, N_T \quad (11)$$

where V_{gi}^{min} and V_{gi}^{max} are voltage amplitude limits, Q_{gi}^{min} and Q_{gi}^{max} are the generation limits of reactive power, P_{gi}^{min} and P_{gi}^{max} are the limits of active power, Q_{ci}^{min} and Q_{ci}^{max} are the reactive compensation limits, and T_k^{min} and T_k^{max} are the transformer tap limits.

The penalty function is used to make optimization problems more straightforward and rigorous. In other to solve the optimization problem, the penalty function has to be selected. The primary function of the penalty function is to keep system security within the acceptable limits.

$$f_T = f + \lambda_V \sum_{K=1}^{N_B} \left(V_i - V_i^{lim}\right)^2 + \lambda_g \sum_{K=1}^{N_B} \left(Q_{gi} - Q_{gi}^{lim}\right)^2 + \lambda_s \sum_{K=1}^{N_B} \left(S_i - S_i^{lim}\right)^2 \quad (12)$$

where λ_V, λ_g, and λ_s

$$V_i^{lim} = \begin{cases} V_i^{lim}, if\ V_i < V_i^{min} \\ V_i^{lim}, if\ V_i > V_i^{max} \end{cases} \quad (13)$$

$$Q_{gi}^{lim} = \begin{cases} Q_{gi}^{lim}, if\ Q_{gi} < Q_{gi}^{min} \\ Q_{gi}^{lim}, if\ Q_{gi} > Q_{gi}^{max} \end{cases} \quad (14)$$

$$S_i^{lim} = \begin{cases} S_i^{lim}, if\ S_i < S_i^{min} \\ S_i^{lim}, if\ S_i > S_i^{max} \end{cases} \quad (15)$$

3. Particle Swarm Optimization (PSO)

3.1. PSO and Its Variants

3.1.1. Overview of PSO

PSO was created in 1995 by Kennedy and Eberhart [35]. The social behavior of birds and schooling fish was the basis for the population-based stochastic optimization method known as PSO. In the search space, PSO makes use of the promising area. Each particle moves and adjusts its position following its past behavior and the best particle within a decision time. Each particle is identified by a d-dimensional vector that depicts its location in the search space. The position of the vector is represented as a possible solution to the optimization issue. Whenever an iterative process is performed, the velocity is added to update each particle's position [36]. The best particle in the swarm (population) and the distance from the best cognitive both impact the particle's velocity. The formulae for velocity and position are shown below.

$$V_i^{k+1} = wv_i^k + c_1 \times r_1 \left(p_{best} - s_i^k\right) + c_2 \times r_2 \left(g_{best} - s_i^k\right) \quad (16)$$

$$s_i^{k+1} = s_i^k + V_i^{k+1} \quad (17)$$

where V_i^k is the velocity of the particle, s_i^k is the position of the particle, r_1 and r_2 are two randomly generated numbers between (0, 1), c_1 and c_2 are the coefficients of accelerated particles, w is the inertia weight, p_{best} is the personal best, and g_{best} is the global best.

3.1.2. RPSO

In RPSO, the weight factor was usually between 0.5 and 1 [37]. Roy Ghatak et al. claim that the random inertia weight component enhanced the initial objective function. Stocking to the local optimal at the end of the iteration may affect the accuracy of the solution [32]. The value of w is found in Equation (19).

$$w = 0.5 + rand()/2 \quad (18)$$

3.1.3. PSO-SR

To find the best method for the effective management of inertia weight (w), a novel adaptive w was developed based on success rate (SR) [37]. At each iteration, the swarm position is determined using the SR. Indicate that a big value of w is necessary to advance toward the optimal point when the SR is large. Additionally, for a low value, the particle oscillates around the ideal location and requires a small increase in the w value to reach the perfect result [32].

$$w(t) = \left(w^{max} - w^{min}\right) * \text{SR} + w^{min} \tag{19}$$

where SR is the success rate and is chosen to be 1 (otherwise, it is zero), w^{min} and w^{max} are the minimum and maximum limits of the w [32].

3.1.4. PSO-TVAC

Due to the lack of diversity towards the end of the search area, PSO with PSOTV-w was utilized, which locates the optimal solution more quickly but is less effective at tuning the optimal solution. The accuracy and effectiveness of the PSO to obtain optimal solutions are significantly influenced by the tuning parameter [31,38]. Based on this concept, a TVAC was proposed to enhance the global search at the start of optimization, allowing the particle to move to the global optimum at the end of the search space. As the search progresses, c_1 and c_2 alter over time, decreasing the cognitive components and increasing the social components. This indicates that the particle converges to the global optimum towards the end of the search process due to minor cognitive and greater social components. Additionally, the particle can roam throughout the search area rather than initially gravitating toward the best population due to enhanced cognitive and minor social components [31].

$$C_1 = (C_{1t} - C_{1k})\frac{z}{iter_{max}} + C_{1k} \tag{20}$$

$$C_2 = (C_{2t} - C_{2k})\frac{z}{iter_{max}} + C_{2k} \tag{21}$$

where z is the current iteration, $iter_{max}$ is the maximum iteration, and C_{1k}, C_{1t}, C_{2t}, and C_{2k} are the initial and final values of the cognitive and social acceleration factors. The value for C_{1t} and C_{2k} is 0.5, and 2.5 for C_{1k} and C_{2t} is the most accurate value [39].

3.2. EPSO

To overcome the issue of falling into a local optimal from the standard PSO, the chosen EPSO added some expansion to the basic PSO, such as a constriction factor and a neighborhood model.

3.2.1. Exchange of Neighborhood

Since each particle learns from its own personal and global positions in the PSO algorithm in the social cognitive system, apart from personal experience and better information received from the search areas, it is advisable to share with better individuals to enhance or improve itself [40]. Therefore, using that concept, a new acceleration constant (c_3) is added to the original PSO equation, making it more efficient to obtain the best solution. The additional c_3 gives the swarm the capability to reach the exploitation stage.

$$V_i^{k+1} = \varphi\left(w_1 v_i^k + c_1 r_1 \left(p_{best} - s_i^k\right) + c_2 r_2 \left(g_{best} - s_i^k\right) + c_3 \times r_3 \left(p_{best,\ t} - s_i^k\right)\right) \tag{22}$$

where $p_{best,t}$ is the vector position for an excellent individual domain (i.e., the overall best position), φ is the constriction factor, and r_3 is random numbers in the interval of (0,1).

3.2.2. Implementation of EPSO to RPO

The steps involved in solving the RPO problem are given below, and the flow chart is shown in Figure 1:

1. Initialize: Set the number of particles, initial velocity, the total number of iterations, generator voltages, the transformer tap settings, and accelerated constants;
2. Run load flows to determine the objective function (real power loss) and evaluate the penalty function concerning inequality constraint violation;

3. Counter updating: Update the iter = iter + 1;
4. Evaluate each particle and save the global and personal best positions;
5. Update the velocity as given in Equation (22);
6. Update the position as given in Equation (17);
7. Check whether solutions in Steps 3 and 4 are within the limit; if it is above the limit, apply Equation (12) to keep the violation;
8. The position of the local best should be updated if the current fitness value is smaller than the best one;
9. Update global best;
10. Search for minimum value: The minimum value in all the individual iterations is considered the best solution;
11. Stopping criteria: If the stopping criteria have been satisfied, stop; if not, go back to Step 5.

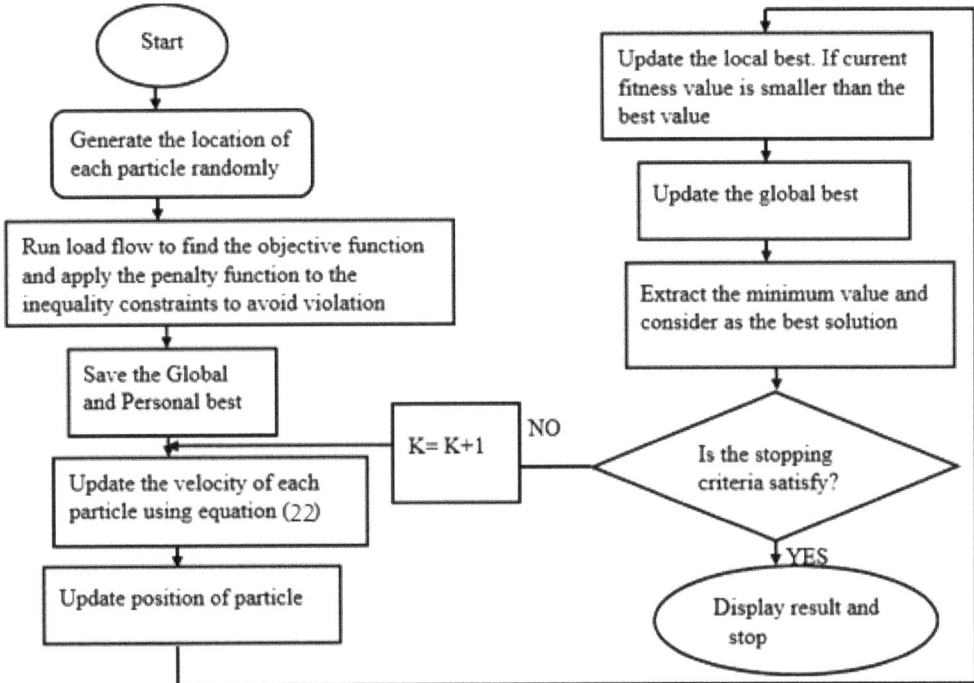

Figure 1. Flow chart of EPSO.

4. Result and Discussion

This section is divided into two. The first section discusses the results of voltage stability indices. The second section discusses the results of the RPO algorithm. The algorithm settings used in the second section is shown in Table 1. The simulation was executed using MATLAB 2018b. The IEEE 9 and 14 bus systems were employed to evaluate the effectiveness of the techniques for actual power reduction. The best outcomes are documented after each test system has been run 30 times.

Table 1. Optimum setting of the algorithm.

Parameters	Value
Number of iterations	200
Particle number	50
Acceleration constant	C1 = C2 = C3 = 2.05
Maximum and minimum w	0.9 and 0.4
Constriction factor	0.729

4.1. Voltage Stability Indices

4.1.1. IEEE 9 Bus System

The system consists of three generators located at buses 1, 2, and 3; three load buses located at buses 5, 6, and 8; and three transformers located at buses 1, 2, and 3. Also, the system has six transmission lines and 100 MVA at the base. The line and bus data are taken [41,42]. The single-line diagram/scheme of the IEEE 9 bus system was given in Figure 2. The MATLAB 2018b software was used to validate the FVSI and L_{mn} and the results obtained after varying reactive power of load buses are presented in Table 2. The critical node of the system was selected by varying/increasing the RP of the load bus until one of the indices values approaches unity, and the bus contains the lowest permissible RP. The load buses' RP was increased one after the other to find the maximum reactive power of each load bus. In Table 2, the value of the indices, the voltage magnitude, and each load bus ranking are presented. The bus with the highest values of the index and a smaller load-ability value of RP is ranked first and is the system's critical node. Node 8 is the critical node and ranks first in the system because it contains a small RP load variation of 240 MVar and a value of 1.028 for FVSI. The lines connected to it are 7–8 and 8–9. This bus needs urgent attention to avoid the breakdown of the generator.

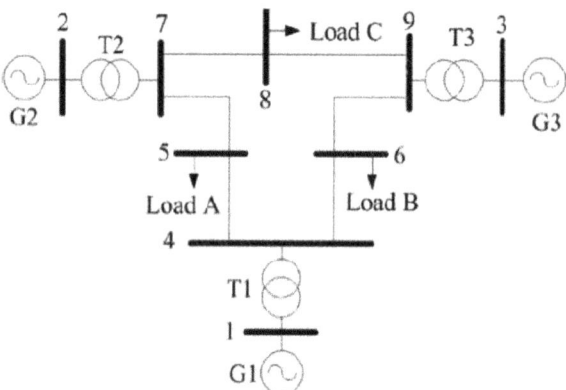

Figure 2. Single-line diagram of the IEEE 9 bus system [43].

Table 2. The indices value and ranking of the bus in the IEEE 9 bus system.

Bus Numbers	Q (MVar)	L_{mn}	FVSI	Voltage Magnitude (p.u)	Ranking
5	260	0.902	0.933	0.800	2
6	290	0.865	0.889	0.824	3
8	240	0.998	1.028	0.802	1

4.1.2. IEEE 14 Bus System

The IEEE 14 bus system contains four generators, a slack bus, twenty transmission lines, and nine load buses located at buses 4, 5, 7, 9, 10, 11, 12, 13, and 14. The line and bus data were taken [29,30]. The single-line diagram/scheme of the IEEE 14 bus system is given in Figure 3. Table 3 shows each load bus's indices value, ranking, and voltage magnitude. The validation was carried out on MATLAB 2018b software, the FVSI and L_{mn} results were obtained after varying the reactive power of load buses. The RP of the load bus was varied one bus at a time until the value of indices reached unity, or the LF solution failed to converge. When varying the RP of each load bus, one of the indices values makes the bus vulnerable to voltage collapse; at this stage, the indices values were noted, and the bus was selected as the critical bus. The result obtained was compared with the previous study reported by Samuel et al. [30], and it was observed that the result of this study shows its validity and effectiveness as it aligned with that of the literature [30]. It also presents the ranking of each bus, which was carried out based on the highest values of the indices and the least RP injected into the load bus. The load node/bus with the highest indices value and the small permissible reactive load was selected as the critical node of the system and ranked first. It clearly shows that node 14 is the critical bus/node of the system because it had the highest values of the index of 1.023 for FVSI and a small permissible reactive load of 76.5 MVar. This node/bus had two connected lines, 9–14 and 13–14. The load connected to the line experienced voltage instability. This was identified as the weakest bus that needs proper attention to avoid voltage collapse. The most stable bus are nodes/buses 4 and 5. They had the height value of RP injected into the bus, 360 MVar, and 352.5 MVar, respectively.

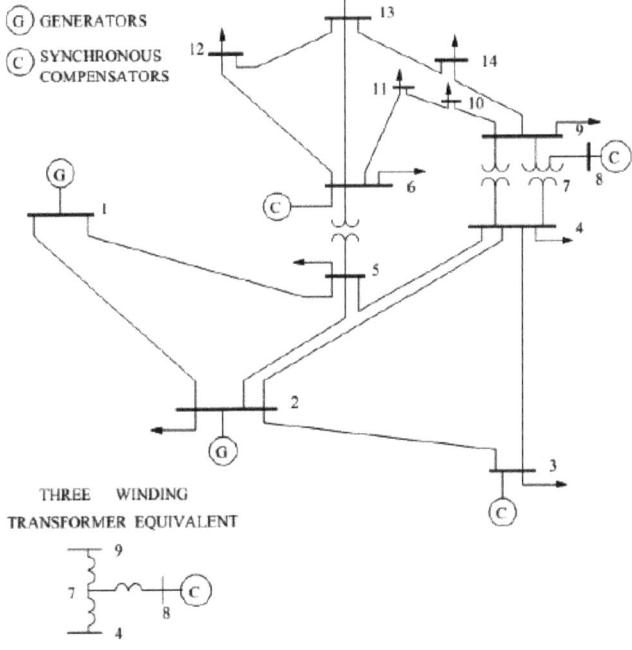

Figure 3. Single-line diagram of the IEEE 14 bus system [30].

Table 3. The indices value and ranking of the bus in the IEEE 14 bus system.

Bus Number	Q (Var)	Voltage Magnitude (p.u)	Ranking	L_{mn}	FVSI
4	360	0.833	9	0.944	0.892
5	352.5	0.997	8	0.998	0.999
7	160	0.771	7	0.929	0.928
9	150	0.712	5	0.981	0.970
10	120	0.663	4	0.942	0.904
11	103	0.748	3	0.912	0.974
12	78	0.790	2	0.865	0.868
13	151.8	0.747	6	0.923	0.993
14	76.5	0.693	1	0.966	1.023

4.2. Reactive Power Optimization

To test the chosen EPSO for RPO, EPSO and other PSO variants are coded in MATLAB 2018b software. Table 4 shows the control variable limits of the two test systems. The maximum and minimum limits for voltage magnitude are 1.1 p.u and 0.95 p.u, respectively. Also, the maximum and minimum limits for the transformer tab limits are 1.025 and 0.975, respectively. However, the limits for the shunt compensator are set in the ranges of 0 MVar and 20 MVar [44].

Table 4. Control variable limits for the IEEE 9 and 14 bus system.

Voltage	Test Systems
V_{max}	1.10
V_{min}	0.95
T_{max}	1.025
T_{min}	0.975
Q_{max}	20
Q_{min}	0.0

4.2.1. IEEE 9 Bus System

Table 4 illustrates the variable control limits of the algorithms used in this research. The N-R was used to obtain the base case power loss. EPSO and other PSO variants are compared to obtain the smallest power loss. Figure 4 illustrates the convergence curve of the system. The loss of PSO, EPSO, PSO-TVAC, PSO-SR, and RPSO are 7.608 MW, 7.543 MW, 7.589 MW, 7.600 MW, and 7.602 MW, respectively, from the base case of 9.842 MW. The optimized power loss is expected to be smaller than the base case result. Therefore, EPSO gives the smallest power loss of 7.543 MW; this shows the significance of the chosen method in power loss reduction. Figure 5 illustrates the voltage profile at each bus before and after the optimization. It can be seen that EPSO offered the highest voltage profile. This shows that EPSO is more suitable for improving the node voltage than the rest of the PSO variants. Table 5 gives the comparison of power loss for EPSO with other PSO variants and algorithms. It can be seen that EPSO gave the smallest power loss of 7.543 MW. This shows the effectiveness of EPSO in offering accurate results and outperforms all of them.

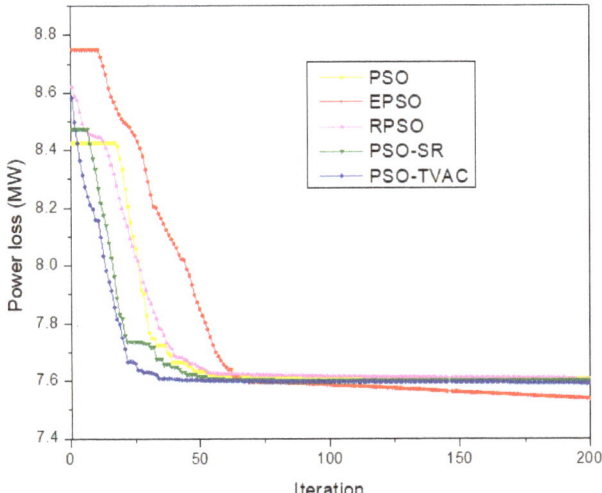

Figure 4. The convergence curve minimizes real power loss for the IEEE 9 bus system.

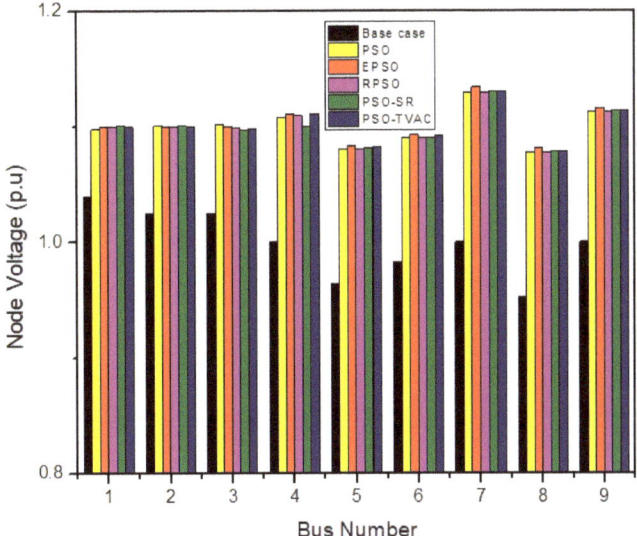

Figure 5. Voltage magnitude before optimization (base case) and after optimization of the IEEE 9 bus system.

Table 5. Comparison of the IEEE 9 bus system with other algorithms.

Algorithms	PSO	EPSO	PSO-TVAC	PSO-SR	RPSO	DA [45]	CA [45]
Best MW	7.6077	**7.543**	7.5894	7.600	7.6023	14.74	14.82
Worst MW	8.957	8.257	8.685	8.878	8.989	-	-
Mean MW	8.282	7.900	8.137	8.239	8.296	-	-
STD	0.954	0.505	0.775	0.902	0.957	-	-

The bold value indicates the lowest power loss and the superiority of this study to others presented in the table.

4.2.2. IEEE 14 Bus System

The control variable is given in Table 4. The N-R was used as the base case, while EPSO was chosen and compared with other PSO variants. The initial/base case system loads, total generation, and power losses of the test system from the LF solution by NR method are given below.

$$P_{load} = 259 \text{ MW}, P_{loss} = 13.775 \text{ MW}, \text{and } P_G = 272.757 \text{ MW}$$

The curve of the real power loss of EPSO is demonstrated in Figure 6. The power loss reduction of PSO, EPSO, PSO-TVAC, PSO-SR, and RPSO are 12.263 MW, 12.253 MW, 12.260 MW, 12.261 MW, and 12.264 MW, respectively, from the base case of 13.775 MW. After optimization, the power loss is expected to be less than the base case result. It can be seen that EPSO outperforms all other PSO variants, giving a lower reduction of 12.253 MW. However, EPSO has more computation times. Furthermore, Figure 7 shows the voltage magnitude of each bus/node before and after optimization. EPSO effectively increases each node's voltage and gives the smallest loss reduction. The superiority of EPSO was validated by comparing the real power loss, mean, and standard deviation (STD) of the result obtained with other algorithms, like PSO, PSO-TVAC, RPSO, LCA, JAYA, and PBIL, as presented in Table 6. Notably, it shows that EPSO reduced the power loss to 12.253 MW, while PSO offers 12.263 MW, PSO-TVAC offers 12.260 MW, RPSO offers 12.259 MW, etc. Thus, EPSO methods give excellent results by lowering power loss and outperforming other techniques.

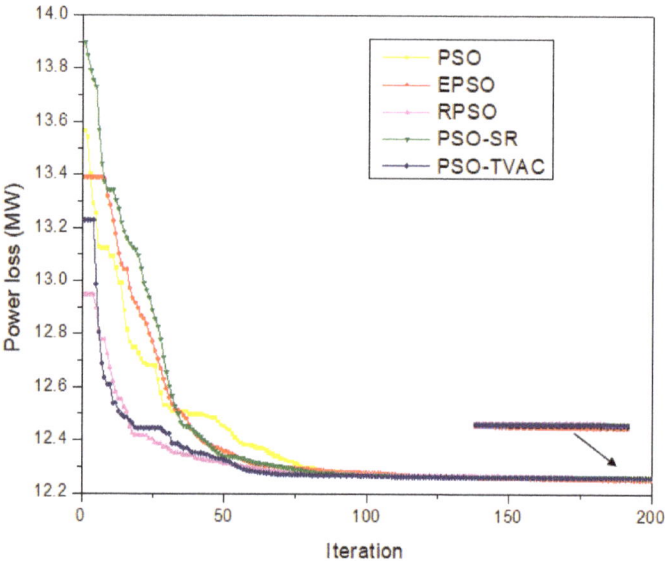

Figure 6. Convergence minimization of real power loss for the IEEE 14 bus system.

Table 6. Comparison of the IEEE 14 bus system with other algorithms.

Algorithms	Best	Worst	Mean	STD
PSO	12.263	12.879	12.571	0.436
EPSO	**12.253**	12.311	12.282	0.041

Table 6. Cont.

Algorithms	Best	Worst	Mean	STD
PSO-TVAC	12.260	12.587	12.424	0.232
PSO-SR	12.261	12.762	12.512	0.354
RPSO	12.259	12.324	12.292	0.046
HLGBA [28]	13.1229	-	-	-
LCA [46]	12.9891	13.1638	-	5.5283×10^{-3}
PBIL [46]	13.0008	13.1947	-	9.7075×10^{-4}
JAYA [47]	12.281	-	-	-
PSO [44]	12.36	-	-	-

The bold value indicates the lowest power loss and the superiority of this study to others presented in the table.

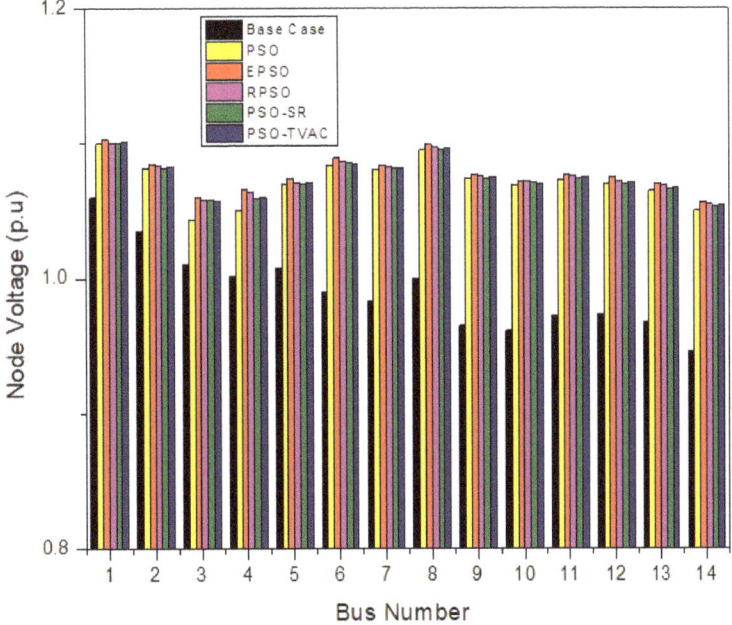

Figure 7. Voltage magnitude before optimization (base case) and after optimization for the IEEE 14 bus system.

5. Conclusions and Future Work

The role of PS operations is to ensure a stable voltage at the consumer end. Unfortunately, the PS failed to meet the desired goal due to generator failures and losses in the TL. This work applied EPSO to reduce the real power loss and other PSO variants. FVSI and L_{mn} were used to identify the critical bus and to learn the stressfulness of the lines in a PS. For the IEEE 9 bus system, bus 8 is the critical node, and the lines connected to it are the most stressful lines of the system. It has the lowest value of RP of 240 MVar, and one of the indices reaches unity (1). Node 14 was the critical node in the IEEE 14 bus system, and the lines connected to it experienced voltage instability. EPSO was used to reduce/diminish the actual/real power loss on the IEEE 9 and 14 bus systems. The loss was reduced from 9.842 MW to 7.543 MW for EPSO and 7.608 MW, 7.602 MW, 7.589 MW, and 7.600 MW for PSO, RPSO, PSO-TVAC, and PSO-SR, respectively, for the IEEE 9 bus system. Also, the losses on the IEEE 14 bus system were reduced from 13.775 MW (the base case) to 12.253 MW for

EPSO and 12.263 MW, 12.259 MW, 12.260 MW, and 12.261 MW for PSO, RPSO, PSO-TVAC, and PSO-SR, respectively. The result shows that the EPSO algorithm gives a better loss reduction than other techniques and PSO variants in the literature. This indicates that EPSO is suitable for improving grid voltage quality, thereby suggesting that the technique will be a valuable tool for PS engineers in the planning and operation of electrical PS networks. This work recommends applying EPSO to other metaheuristic algorithms to form a hybrid method to solve engineering problems and some standard IEEE benchmark functions. Also, the computation time should be improved in future work.

Author Contributions: S.A.A.: Conceptualization, data curation, formal analysis and investigation, methodology, validation, visualization, writing—original draft preparation, writing—review, and editing; Y.S. and Z.W.: Conceptualization, validation, visualization, review, editing, and supervision. All authors have read and agreed to the published version of the manuscript.

Funding: This research work was supported by Global Excellence and Stature, Fourth Industrial Revolution (GES 4.0), University of Johannesburg, South Africa.

Data Availability Statement: All data used in this study are available within this manuscript.

Conflicts of Interest: The authors declare no conflict of interest.

Nomenclature

FVSI	fast voltage stability index
L_{mn}	line stability index
TL	transmission line
RP	reactive power
Zj	is the impedance
Q_1	is the RP at sending end
Xr	is the reactance of the line
θ	is the angle of the TL
V_1	is the voltage at the sending end
δ	is the power angle
Q_2	is the RP at receiving end
P_{loss}	is the real total losses
k	is the branch
G_k	is the conductance of the branch k
Vj and V_i	are the voltage at the ith and jth bus
N_L	is the total number of TL
θ_{ij}	is the voltage angle between bus i and j
g_{ij} and b_{ij}	are conductance and susceptance
V_{gi}^{min} and V_{gi}^{max}	are voltage magnitude limits
Q_{gi}^{min} and Q_{gi}^{max}	are the generation limits of reactive power
P_{gi}^{min} and P_{gi}^{max}	are the limits of active power
Q_{ci}^{min} and Q_{ci}^{max}	are the reactive compensation limits
T_k^{min} and T_k^{max}	are the transformer tap limits
V_i^k	is the velocity of the particle
s_i^k	is the position of the particle
p_{best}	is the personal best
g_{best}	is the global best
r_1 and r_2	are two randomly generated numbers between (0, 1)
c_1 and c_2	are the coefficients of accelerated particles
w	is the inertia weight
SR	is the success rate

w^{min} and w^{max}	is the minimum and maximum limits of the w
z	is the current iteration
$iter_{max}$	is the maximum iteration
C_{1k}, C_{1t}, C_{2t}, and C_{2k}	are the initial and final values of the cognitive and social acceleration factors
$p_{best,t}$	is the vector position for an excellent individual domain (i.e., the overall best position)
φ	is the constriction factor
PSO	particle swarm optimization
PF	power flow
P.U	per unit
RPSO	random inertia weight PSO
TVAC	time-varying acceleration coefficients
VS	is the voltage stability
DER	is the distributed energy resources
PS	is the power system
RPO	is the reactive power optimization

References

1. Hosseinzadeh, N.; Aziz, A.; Mahmud, A.; Gargoom, A.; Rabbani, M. Voltage Stability of Power Systems with Renewable-Energy Inverter-Based Generators: A Review. *Electronics* **2021**, *10*, 115. [CrossRef]
2. Ibrahim, I.A.; Hossain, M.J. Low Voltage Distribution Networks Modeling and Unbalanced (Optimal) Power Flow: A Comprehensive Review. *IEEE Access* **2021**, *9*, 143026–143084. [CrossRef]
3. Shayeghi, H.; Rahnama, A.; Mohajery, R.; Bizon, N.; Mazare, A.G.; Ionescu, L.M. Multi-Area Microgrid Load-Frequency Control Using Combined Fractional and Integer Order Master–Slave Controller Considering Electric Vehicle Aggregator Effects. *Electronics* **2022**, *11*, 3440. [CrossRef]
4. González, I.; Calderón, A.J.; Folgado, F.J. IoT Real Time System for Monitoring Lithium-Ion Battery Long-Term Operation in Microgrids. *J. Energy Storage* **2022**, *51*, 104596. [CrossRef]
5. Subramani, C.; Dash, S.S.; Jagdeeshkumar, M.; Bhaskar, M.A. Stability Index Based Voltage Collapse Prediction and Contingency Analysis. *J. Electr. Eng. Technol.* **2009**, *4*, 438–442. [CrossRef]
6. Adegoke, S.A.; Sun, Y. Power System Optimization Approach to Mitigate Voltage Instability Issues: A Review. *Cogent Eng.* **2023**, *10*, 2153416. [CrossRef]
7. Zha, Z.; Wang, B.; Fan, H.; Liu, L. An Improved Reinforcement Learning for Security-Constrained Economic Dispatch of Battery Energy Storage in Microgrids. In Proceedings of the Neural Computing for Advanced Applications, Second International Conference, NCAA 2021, Guangzhou, China, 27–30 August 2021; Zhang, H., Yang, Z., Zhang, Z., Wu, Z., Hao, T., Eds.; Springer: Singapore, 2021; pp. 303–318.
8. Mu, B.; Zhang, X.; Mao, X.; Li, Z. An Optimization Method to Boost the Resilience of Power Networks with High Penetration of Renewable Energies. In Proceedings of the Neural Computing for Advanced Applications, Second International Conference, NCAA 2021, Guangzhou, China, 27–30 August 2021; Zhang, H., Yang, Z., Zhang, Z., Wu, Z., Hao, T., Eds.; Springer: Singapore, 2021; pp. 3–16.
9. Ratra, S.; Tiwari, R.; Niazi, K.R. Voltage Stability Assessment in Power Systems Using Line Voltage Stability Index. *Comput. Electr. Eng.* **2018**, *70*, 199–211. [CrossRef]
10. Pérez-Londoño, S.; Rodríguez, L.F.; Olivar, G. A Simplified Voltage Stability Index (SVSI). *Int. J. Electr. Power Energy Syst.* **2014**, *63*, 806–813. [CrossRef]
11. Kessel, P.; Glavitsch, H. Estimating the Voltage Stability of a Power System. *IEEE Trans. Power Deliv.* **1986**, *1*, 346–354. [CrossRef]
12. Sakthivel, S.; Mary, D.; Ezhilan, C. Global Voltage Stability Limit Improvement by Real and Reactive Power Optimization through Evolutionary Programming Algorithm. *Int. J. Adv. Sci. Technol. Res.* **2012**, *1*, 88–102.
13. Sajan, K.S.; Kumar, V.; Tyagi, B. Genetic Algorithm Based Support Vector Machine for On-Line Voltage Stability Monitoring. *Int. J. Electr. Power Energy Syst.* **2015**, *73*, 200–208. [CrossRef]
14. Hamid, Z.A.; Musirin, I.; Rahim, M.N.A.; Kamari, N.A.M. Application of Electricity Tracing Theory and Hybrid Ant Colony Algorithm for Ranking Bus Priority in Power System. *Int. J. Electr. Power Energy Syst.* **2012**, *43*, 1427–1434. [CrossRef]
15. Yang, D.S.; Sun, Y.H.; Zhou, B.W.; Gao, X.T.; Zhang, H.G. Critical Nodes Identification of Complex Power Systems Based on Electric Cactus Structure. *IEEE Syst. J.* **2020**, *14*, 4477–4488. [CrossRef]
16. Adebayo, I.; Jimoh, A.A.; Yusuff, A. Voltage Stability Assessment and Identification of Important Nodes in Power Transmission Network through Network Response Structural Characteristics. *IET Gener. Transm. Distrib.* **2017**, *11*, 1398–1408. [CrossRef]
17. Adegoke, S.A.; Sun, Y. Optimum Reactive Power Dispatch Solution Using Hybrid Particle Swarm Optimization and Pathfinder Algorithm. *Int. J. Comput.* **2022**, *21*, 403–410. [CrossRef]
18. Suresh, V.; Senthil Kumar, S. Research on Hybrid Modified Pathfinder Algorithm for Optimal Reactive Power Dispatch. *Bull. Polish Acad. Sci. Tech. Sci.* **2021**, *69*, 137733. [CrossRef]

19. Yapici, H. Solution of Optimal Reactive Power Dispatch Problem Using Pathfinder Algorithm. *Eng. Optim.* **2021**, *53*, 1946–1963. [CrossRef]
20. Mukherjee, A.; Mukherjee, V. Chaotic Krill Herd Algorithm for Optimal Reactive Power Dispatch Considering FACTS Devices. *Appl. Soft Comput. J.* **2016**, *44*, 163–190. [CrossRef]
21. Mouassa, S.; Bouktir, T.; Salhi, A. Ant Lion Optimizer for Solving Optimal Reactive Power Dispatch Problem in Power Systems. *Eng. Sci. Technol. Int. J.* **2017**, *20*, 885–895. [CrossRef]
22. Üney, M.Ş.; Çetinkaya, N. New Metaheuristic Algorithms for Reactive Power Optimization. *Teh. Vjesn.* **2019**, *26*, 1427–1433. [CrossRef]
23. Adegoke, S.A.; Sun, Y. Diminishing Active Power Loss and Improving Voltage Profile Using an Improved Pathfinder Algorithm Based on Inertia Weight. *Energies* **2023**, *16*, 1270. [CrossRef]
24. Harish Kiran, S.; Dash, S.S.; Subramani, C. Performance of Two Modified Optimization Techniques for Power System Voltage Stability Problems. *Alex. Eng. J.* **2016**, *55*, 2525–2530. [CrossRef]
25. Jaramillo, M.D.; Carrión, D.F.; Muñoz, J.P. A Novel Methodology for Strengthening Stability in Electrical Power Systems by Considering Fast Voltage Stability Index under N—1 Scenarios. *Energies* **2023**, *16*, 3396. [CrossRef]
26. Adebayo, I.G.; Sun, Y. Voltage Stability Based on a Novel Critical Bus Identification Index. In Proceedings of the 2019 14th IEEE Conference on Industrial Electronics and Applications (ICIEA), Xi'an, China, 19–21 June 2019; pp. 1777–1782. [CrossRef]
27. Adebayo, I.G.; Sun, Y. A Comparison of Voltage Stability Assessment Techniques in a Power System. 2018. Available online: https://core.ac.uk/download/pdf/187150311.pdf (accessed on 5 July 2023).
28. Alam, M.S.; De, M. Optimal Reactive Power Dispatch Using Hybrid Loop-Genetic Based Algorithm. In Proceedings of the 2016 National Power Systems Conference (NPSC) 2016, Bhubaneswar, India, 19–21 December 2016; pp. 1–6. [CrossRef]
29. Vishnu, M.; Sunil Kumar, T.K. An Improved Solution for Reactive Power Dispatch Problem Using Diversity-Enhanced Particle Swarm Optimization. *Energies* **2020**, *13*, 2862. [CrossRef]
30. Samuel, I.A.; Katende, J.; Awosope, C.O.A.; Awelewa, A.A. Prediction of Voltage Collapse in Electrical Power System Networks Using a New Voltage Stability Index. *Int. J. Appl. Eng. Res.* **2017**, *12*, 190–199.
31. Chaturvedi, K.T.; Pandit, M.; Srivastava, L. Particle Swarm Optimization with Time Varying Acceleration Coefficients for Non-Convex Economic Power Dispatch. *Int. J. Electr. Power Energy Syst.* **2009**, *31*, 249–257. [CrossRef]
32. Roy Ghatak, S.; Sannigrahi, S.; Acharjee, P. Comparative Performance Analysis of DG and DSTATCOM Using Improved Pso Based on Success Rate for Deregulated Environment. *IEEE Syst. J.* **2018**, *12*, 2791–2802. [CrossRef]
33. Musiri, I.; Abdul Rahman, T.K. On-Line Voltage Stability Based Contingency Ranking Using Fast Voltage Stability Index (FVSI). In Proceedings of the IEEE/PES Transmission and Distribution Conference and Exhibition, Yokohama, Japan, 6–10 October 2002; Volume 2, pp. 1118–1123. [CrossRef]
34. Moghavvemi, M.; Faruque, M.O. Power System Security and Voltage Collapse: A Line Outage Based Indicator for Prediction. *Int. J. Electr. Power Energy Syst.* **1999**, *21*, 455–461. [CrossRef]
35. Kennedy, J.; Eberhart, R. Particle Swarm Optimization. In Proceedings of the ICNN'95-International Conference on Neural Networks, Perth, WA, Australia, 27 November–1 December 1995; pp. 1942–1948. [CrossRef]
36. Poli, R.; Kennedy, J.; Blackwell, T.; Freitas, A. Particle Swarms: The Second Decade. *J. Artif. Evol. Appl.* **2008**, *2008*, 108972. [CrossRef]
37. Vinodh Kumar, E.; Raaja, G.S.; Jerome, J. Adaptive PSO for Optimal LQR Tracking Control of 2 DoF Laboratory Helicopter. *Appl. Soft Comput. J.* **2016**, *41*, 77–90. [CrossRef]
38. Neyestani, M.; Farsangi, M.M.; Nezamabadipour, H.; Lee, K.Y. A Modified Particle Swarm Optimization for Economic Dispatch with Nonsmooth Cost Functions. *IFAC Proc. Vol.* **2009**, *42*, 267–272. [CrossRef]
39. Ratnaweera, A.; Halgamuge, S.K.; Watson, H.C. Self-Organizing Hierarchical Particle Swarm Optimizer with Time-Varying Acceleration Coefficients. *IEEE Trans. Evol. Comput.* **2004**, *8*, 240–255. [CrossRef]
40. Cao, S.; Ding, X.; Wang, Q.; Chen, B. Opposition-Based Improved Pso for Optimal Reactive Power Dispatch and Voltage Control. *Math. Probl. Eng.* **2015**, *2015*, 754582. [CrossRef]
41. Asija, D.; Choudekar, P.; Soni, K.M.; Sinha, S.K. Power Flow Study and Contingency Status of WSCC 9 Bus Test System Using MATLAB. In Proceedings of the 2015 International Conference on Recent Developments in Control, Automation and Power Engineering (RDCAPE), Noida, India, 12–13 March 2015; pp. 338–342.
42. Parmar, R.; Tandon, A.; Nawaz, S. Comparison of Different Techniques to Identify the Best Location of SVC to Enhance the Voltage Profile. *ICIC Express Lett.* **2020**, *14*, 81–87. [CrossRef]
43. Sriram, C.; Kishore, M.N.R. Teaching Distance Relay Protection and Circuit Breaker Co-Ordination of an IEEE 9 Bus System Using MATLAB/SIMULINK. In Proceedings of the Innovations in Electrical and Electronics Engineering: Proceedings of the 4th ICIEEE 2019, Telangana, India, 26–27 July 2019; Saini, H.S., Srinivas, T., Vinod Kumar, D.M., Chandragupta Mauryan, K.S., Eds.; Springer: Singapore, 2020; pp. 439–447.
44. Modha, H.; Patel, V. Minimization of Active Power Loss for Optimum Reactive Power Dispatch Using PSO. In Proceedings of the 2021 Emerging Trends in Industry 4.0 (ETI 4.0), Raigarh, India, 19–21 May 2021; pp. 1–5. [CrossRef]
45. Khan, I.; Li, Z.; Xu, Y.; Gu, W. Distributed Control Algorithm for Optimal Reactive Power Control in Power Grids. *Int. J. Electr. Power Energy Syst.* **2016**, *83*, 505–513. [CrossRef]

46. Suresh, V.; Kumar, S.S. Optimal Reactive Power Dispatch for Minimization of Real Power Loss Using SBDE and DE-Strategy Algorithm. *J. Ambient Intell. Humaniz. Comput.* **2020**, 1–15. [CrossRef]
47. Barakat, A.F.; El-Sehiemy, R.A.; Elsayd, M.I.; Osman, E. Solving Reactive Power Dispatch Problem by Using JAYA Optimization Algorithm. *Int. J. Eng. Res. Afr.* **2018**, *36*, 12–24. [CrossRef]

Disclaimer/Publisher's Note: The statements, opinions and data contained in all publications are solely those of the individual author(s) and contributor(s) and not of MDPI and/or the editor(s). MDPI and/or the editor(s) disclaim responsibility for any injury to people or property resulting from any ideas, methods, instructions or products referred to in the content.

Article

Research on Multi-AGV Task Allocation in Train Unit Maintenance Workshop

Nan Zhao [1] and Chun Feng [1,2,*]

[1] School of Transportation and Logistics, Southwest Jiaotong University, Chengdu 611756, China
[2] National United Engineering Laboratory of Integrated and Intelligent Transportation, Southwest Jiaotong University, Chengdu 611756, China
* Correspondence: ifengchun@swjtu.edu.cn

Abstract: In the context of the continuous development and maturity of intelligent manufacturing and intelligent logistics, it has been observed that the majority of vehicle maintenance in EMU trains still relies on traditional methods, which are characterized by excessive manual intervention and low efficiency. To address these deficiencies, the present study proposes the integration of Automatic Guided Vehicles (AGVs) to improve the traditional maintenance processes, thereby enhancing the efficiency and quality of vehicle maintenance. Specifically, this research focuses on the scenario of the maintenance workshop in EMU trains and investigates the task allocation problem for multiple AGVs. Taking into consideration factors such as the maximum load capacity of AGVs, remaining battery power, and task execution time, a mathematical model is formulated with the objective of minimizing the total distance and time required to complete all tasks. A multi-population genetic algorithm is designed to solve the model. The effectiveness of the proposed model and algorithm is validated through simulation experiments, considering both small-scale and large-scale scenarios. The results indicate that the multi-population genetic algorithm outperforms the particle swarm algorithm and the genetic algorithm in terms of stability, optimization performance, and convergence. This research provides scientific guidance and practical insights for enterprises adopting task allocation strategies using multiple AGVs.

Keywords: automated guided vehicle; task allocation; multi-population genetic algorithm; particle swarm optimization; genetic algorithm

MSC: 65D99; 90B06

1. Introduction

Intelligent manufacturing has emerged as a primary means of enhancing a nation's industrial competitiveness [1]. Within the framework of "Industry 4.0" and intelligent manufacturing, intelligent logistics is considered a fundamental and crucial component in achieving intelligent manufacturing objectives [2]. In this context, Automated Guided Vehicles (AGVs) are extensively utilized as indispensable material handling equipment to fulfill the objectives of intelligent logistics. Regarding intelligent manufacturing, China has witnessed a continuous elevation in its railway equipment capabilities. Over the span of ten years, from 2012 to 2021, the nationwide inventory of railway passenger cars has increased from 57,700 to 78,000 units, while the number of high-speed train sets has escalated from 825 to 4153 sets [3]. With the ongoing growth in high-speed train sets, a corresponding surge in equipment maintenance has also been observed. The maintenance of high-speed train sets constitutes a critical link in ensuring their seamless operation. The train unit maintenance workshop possesses several significant characteristics that have a crucial impact on its operations and efficiency. Firstly, the workshop is equipped with advanced equipment and technology specifically designed to meet the maintenance needs

Citation: Zhao, N.; Feng, C. Research on Multi-AGV Task Allocation in Train Unit Maintenance Workshop. *Mathematics* **2023**, *11*, 3509. https://doi.org/10.3390/math11163509

Academic Editors: Mingbo Zhao, Haijun Zhang and Zhou Wu

Received: 19 July 2023
Revised: 9 August 2023
Accepted: 10 August 2023
Published: 14 August 2023

Copyright: © 2023 by the authors. Licensee MDPI, Basel, Switzerland. This article is an open access article distributed under the terms and conditions of the Creative Commons Attribution (CC BY) license (https://creativecommons.org/licenses/by/4.0/).

of high-speed train sets. These technologies cover mechanical, electrical, and electronic systems, enabling comprehensive and efficient repair tasks. Secondly, the workshop faces diverse maintenance tasks that encompass various fields such as mechanical, electrical, and electronic repairs. These tasks require specialized skills and expertise to ensure the effective and reliable operation of the train sets. Thirdly, due to the critical importance of maintenance for ensuring safe operations, the workshop operates under strict time constraints. Timely completion of repair tasks is essential to ensuring the prompt return of train sets to operation. Fourthly, the workshop needs to manage a large number of train sets, which involves effective vehicle allocation, scheduling, and maintenance planning to handle multiple train set repairs simultaneously. Fifthly, the workshop must meet the power demands of train sets and maintenance equipment. A stable and reliable power supply is essential to guaranteeing continuous operation. Sixthly, vehicle scheduling and transportation present significant challenges for the workshop. Proper vehicle scheduling and route planning are crucial for the timely delivery of train sets and transportation to the workshop. Seventhly, safety and quality control are paramount concerns for the workshop. Strict adherence to safety protocols and reinforcement of quality control measures are essential for ensuring operational safety and reliability.

In summary, the train unit maintenance workshop is a complex and efficient system that requires specialized skills and effective management to ensure the safe and reliable maintenance of high-speed train sets. This study explores the multi-AGV task allocation problem in the workshop, addressing challenges related to vehicle management, scheduling, and task assignment, thus improving the operational efficiency and maintenance quality of the workshop. As a result, this research optimizes the workshop's operations and enhances the overall performance of the maintenance system.

2. Literature Review

The multi-AGV task allocation problem refers to the allocation of tasks to multiple AGVs and scheduling the execution order of tasks, with the objective of maximizing the efficiency and quality of task completion. Due to its complexity and intractability, the multi-AGV task allocation problem is a typical NP-hard problem [4]. In the domain of task allocation models, there are primarily single-objective and multi-objective planning models. Single-objective planning models, such as Lu et al. [5], aim to minimize the total completion time as the objective function to optimize the task allocation and sequencing of mobile robots. Zhuang et al. [6] focus on minimizing the number of shelf transportation operations as the objective, considering handling conflicts in the task allocation model for mobile robots. Li et al. [7] consider minimizing the maximum travel time of AGVs and propose an AGV task allocation algorithm based on shelf priority. Multi-objective planning models, like Li Teng et al. [8], establish a two-level task allocation model, minimizing the total cost at the upper level and minimizing the number of idle robots at the lower level. To mitigate uncertainties and discrepancies between the model and actual operational conditions, a robust optimization model was further developed. Zou et al. [9] design a greedy algorithm to construct a multi-objective task allocation model, optimizing the total energy consumption of AGVs, the number of AGVs used, and the task timeliness that affects customer satisfaction. Li et al. [10] have developed a dual-objective, energy-saving single-load AGV planning model for multiple transportation tasks, aiming to minimize transportation distance and energy consumption. Mousavi et al. [11], considering the battery level of AGVs, optimize AGV task scheduling with the objectives of minimizing completion time and the number of AGVs. Regarding algorithm design, most current studies employ metaheuristic algorithms [12–16] for solving the task allocation problem. In recent years, with the advancement of machine learning and deep learning [17–21], these methods have gradually found applications in addressing task allocation problems. Zou et al. [22] proposed the Discrete Artificial Bee Colony algorithm (DABC) and other novel advanced techniques for task allocation problem-solving. Tang et al. [23] designed a two-layer genetic algorithm, with the inner layer optimizing the task scheduling sequence of AGVs and picking stations and the results being fed back to the outer layer model to optimize equipment configuration and sorting station layout. Yue et al. [24] introduced an enhanced hybrid genetic algorithm and particle swarm optimization algorithm (PSO-GA) to establish multi-AGV task allocation models. Liu et al. [25] proposed an improved particle swarm optimization algorithm to solve multi-objective task allocation models, exhibiting enhancements in population convergence speed and algorithm performance. Tang et al. [26] presented a novel approach based on classical soft Actor-Critic and hierarchical reinforcement learning algorithms, namely the layered soft Actor-Critic algorithm, to address dynamic scheduling problems in order picking. Yang Wei et al. [27] proposed a variable neighborhood simulated annealing algorithm to solve the job scheduling problem of mobile robots in warehousing systems. They designed three types of neighborhood perturbation operations, including insertion, swap, and "2-opt", to systematically transform the search space and improve the algorithm's search ability and scope. Yang Zhifei et al. [28] extracted the advantages of different algorithms and proposed an adaptive multi-objective genetic-differential evolution algorithm to address robot dispatching tasks. They introduced a new multi-stage real-number coding rule and incorporated elite and adaptive strategies to enhance the algorithm's convergence speed. Song Wei et al. [29] applied an ant colony algorithm to process task sequences and then used a genetic algorithm to allocate subsets of tasks for task chaining. Xu Liyun et al. [30] improved the encoding method and genetic operators of the cultural genetic algorithm and demonstrated through simulation experiments that the improved algorithm achieved faster convergence. In terms of applying these algorithms to other research domains, Chen et al. [31] introduced a multi-agent control structure model to solve complex distributed resource planning problems by leveraging the advantages of multi-agent systems. Kler et al. [32] utilized data analysis to optimize inventory and supply chain networks in meat and poultry farms, aiming to achieve the goals of a green supply chain. Ntawuzumunsi et al. [21] proposed an energy-efficient algorithm based on data aggregation technology for communication between intelligent beekeeping devices. Joshi et al. [20] investigated how machine learning techniques can be used to predict phishing attacks in blockchain networks.

Existing research has demonstrated the wide applicability and potential of various intelligent algorithms in different domains, contributing to improved efficiency, resource utilization, and problem-solving capabilities. Regarding the AGV task allocation research, the focus has mainly been on the allocation of only one task per AGV within a certain period. Researchers have constructed single-objective and multi-objective models and made improvements to the original algorithms to enhance their convergence and solution performance. However, some of the improved algorithms have resulted in increased complexity in the theoretical derivation steps and higher computational requirements. In the case of AGVs operating in a single-task mode, system optimization is constrained, and as task volume escalates, task backlog issues can emerge. Increasing the number of AGVs for task execution may exert pressure on traffic, thereby impeding overall system efficiency improvements. Furthermore, existing research has primarily concentrated on algorithmic enhancements while neglecting optimization pertaining to research scenarios and model characteristics. Hence, this paper aims to address these gaps by focusing on the research scenario of a high-speed train maintenance workshop. The objective is to minimize the total distance and time required to complete all tasks while considering constraints such as the AGV's maximum load capacity, remaining battery level, and time. Multiple population-based genetic algorithms are designed to solve the task allocation model. Theoretical contributions are made to the field of multi-AGV task allocation, and practical implications are expected to enhance the overall efficiency of the logistics system in the high-speed train maintenance workshop.

3. Problem Description and Hypotheses

In the logistics system of a high-speed train maintenance workshop, Automated Guided Vehicles (AGVs) are responsible for the transportation of all raw materials within the workshop. Their primary task involves delivering raw materials from the storage points to the designated maintenance workstation points. Considering the specific characteristics of the high-speed train maintenance workshop, it is worth noting that different systems can undergo maintenance simultaneously at the same workstation. In other words, when repairing a specific section of a train car, there is a unique target maintenance workstation. In a given time period, the high-speed train maintenance workshop generates a set of n delivery tasks, denoted as $N = \{1, 2, \ldots .n\}$. These tasks can be grouped as $G_k = \{i, j \ldots \mid i, j \in N\}$. The workshop has a total of m AGVs available for task execution, forming the set $K = \{1, 2, \ldots .m\}$. As the AGVs purchased for the workshop are of the same model, each AGV shares the same maximum load capacity and travel distance when fully charged. To closely resemble real-world scenarios, this study considers the delivery tasks performed by AGVs at non-saturated battery levels. With respect to the discharge characteristics of lithium batteries, the remaining travel distance decreases rapidly as battery usage increases. To align with the maintenance rhythm, each task i should be assigned in such a manner that the AGV's arrival time is no earlier than the task generation time a_i, and the task completion time falls within the task deadline b_i. Given these conditions, how can the task grouping and allocation problem be formulated to maximize the overall system efficiency? Specifically, the optimization objectives are to minimize the total travel distance under the task grouping and to minimize the AGV task completion time. Constraints such as the AGV's maximum load capacity, remaining battery level, and time availability are taken into consideration. By establishing a mathematical model, an optimal task grouping, and allocation scheme can be derived.

In order to account for the discrepancies between the model's solution and the actual operational scenario, the following assumptions should be met:

(1) The maintenance task represents the comprehensive system of the first section of a train car.
(2) The inventory of raw materials at the storage points adequately meets the requirements of the delivery tasks.
(3) AGV travel paths can be reliably and consistently planned without encountering conflicts.
(4) The consideration of raw material volumes and the loading/unloading times of AGVs is omitted.
(5) Under normal circumstances, all AGVs maintain a uniform speed during travel.
(6) When executing a task group, each required storage point for a task can be traversed by an AGV only once.
(7) AGVs start their operations by uniformly parking at a designated location, known as the starting point, with Task 1 assigned as the initial task.
(8) Upon completion of all tasks within a task group, AGVs park at the target maintenance workstation, referred to as the endpoint, with Task n designated as the final task.

4. Model Establishment

Based on the problem description above, the model parameters and definitions of decision variables are as follows:

Model Parameters:
W: represents the maximum load capacity of each AGV;
w_i: represents the weight of raw materials required for task i;
e_k: represents the remaining battery level of AGV k;
f: represents the safety battery level expressed as a percentage;
L: represents the function that relates the percentage of battery consumption to the remaining travel distance for each AGV;
a_i: represents the generation time of task i;
b_i: represents the deadline time of task i;
v: represents the travel speed of each AGV;
$d_{i,j,k}$: represents the shortest distance from task i to task j for AGV k;

$D_{G_k,k}$: represents the shortest total distance for AGV k to complete task group G_k;
$t_{i,j,k}$: represents the minimum time from task i to task j for AGV k;
$t'_{i,k}$: represents the time required for AGV k to complete task i;
$T_{G_k,k}$: represents the minimum total time for AGV k to complete task group G_k.

Decision Variables:

$$x_{i,j,k} = \begin{cases} 1, AGV\ k\ travels\ from\ task\ i\ to\ task\ j \\ 0, others \end{cases} \quad (1)$$

$$y_{i,k} = \begin{cases} 1, task\ i\ is\ delivered\ by\ AGV\ k \\ 0, others \end{cases} \quad (2)$$

Objective function:

$$Z = \min\{D_{G_k,k} + (\max T_{G_k,k})\} \quad (3)$$

Constraint function:

$$D_{G_k,k} = \sum_{i=1}^{n}\sum_{j=1}^{n}\sum_{k=1}^{m} x_{i,j,k} d_{i,j,k} \quad (4)$$

$$T_{G_k,k} = \sum_{i=1}^{n}\sum_{j=1}^{n}\sum_{k=1}^{m} x_{i,j,k} t_{i,j,k} \quad (5)$$

$$t_{i,j,k} = \frac{d_{i,j,k}}{v}, \forall i,j \in N, k \in K \quad (6)$$

$$\sum_{k=1}^{m} y_{i,k} = 1, \forall i \in N \quad (7)$$

$$\sum_{i=1}^{n} x_{i,j,k} = y_{j,k}, \forall j \in N, k \in K \quad (8)$$

$$\sum_{j=1}^{n} x_{i,j,k} = y_{i,k}, \forall i \in N, k \in K \quad (9)$$

$$\sum_{k=1}^{m} w_i y_{i,k} \leq W, \forall i \in N \quad (10)$$

$$x_{i,j,k}(t'_{i,k} + t_{i,j,k} - a_j) \leq 0, \forall i,j \in N(i,j \neq 1,n), k \in K \quad (11)$$

$$\sum_{k=1}^{m} x_{i,j,k}(t'_{i,k} + t_{i,j,k} + t'_{j,k}) - b_i \leq 0, \forall i,j \in N(i,j \neq 1,n) \quad (12)$$

$$L(x) = ax^2 + bx + c \quad (13)$$

$$\sum_{i=1}^{n}\sum_{j=1}^{n}\sum_{k=1}^{m} x_{i,j,k} d_{i,j,k} \leq L(1-e_k) - L(1-f) \quad (14)$$

$$\sum_{j=2}^{n-1} x_{1,j,k} = 1, \forall k \in K \quad (15)$$

$$\sum_{i=2}^{n-1} x_{i,n,k} = 1, \forall k \in K \quad (16)$$

$$\begin{aligned} x_{i,j,k} &\in (0,1), \forall i,j \in N, k \in K \\ y_{i,k} &\in (0,1), \forall i \in N, k \in K \end{aligned} \quad (17)$$

In the aforementioned model, $x_{i,j,k}$ and $y_{i,j,k}$ are binary decision variables taking values of 0 or 1. Equation (3) represents the objective function, which aims to minimize the total distance and time required to complete all tasks. Equations (4) and (5) are utilized to calculate the total distance and total time, respectively, for completing all tasks within each task group. Equation (6) computes the completion time between two tasks based on speed and distance. Constraint (7) ensures that each task is assigned to an AGV. Constraints (8) and (9) guarantee that tasks within the same task group are exclusively assigned to a single AGV. Constraint (10) ensures that the weight of each task group does not exceed the maximum load capacity of the AGV. Constraint (11) guarantees that an AGV, which sequentially performs tasks i and j, arrives at the storage point of task j no earlier than the task generation time of task j after completing task i. Constraint (12) ensures that the total completion time of the task group does not exceed the deadline time of each individual task. Equation (13) expresses the relationship between the AGV's battery consumption curve and the remaining travel distance [33]. Constraint (14) ensures that each AGV operates within its battery constraint range, with a safety battery level reserved for returning to the charging area. Equation (15) states that each AGV must pass through task 1 and can do so only once. Equation (16) states that each AGV must pass through task n and can do so only once.

5. Algorithm Design

The multi-population genetic algorithm [34–37] is an optimization algorithm based on the genetic algorithm that enhances search capability and global optimization performance by introducing multiple independent populations. Each population functions as an independent subsystem of the genetic algorithm, possessing its own set of individuals and evolutionary process. Below is a detailed introduction to the main characteristics of the Multi-Population Genetic Algorithm (MGA) and the algorithm design process in this paper, as shown in Figure 1.

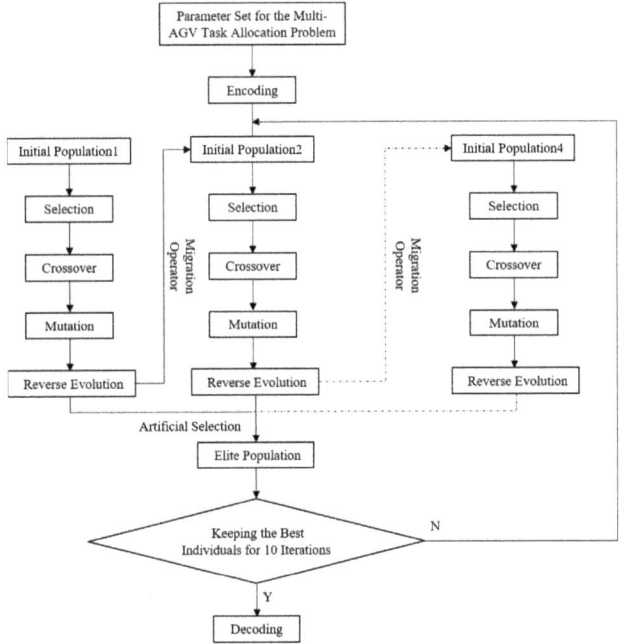

Figure 1. Flowchart of the Design Process for the Multi-Population Genetic Algorithm in this Study.

5.1. Main Characteristics of the Algorithm

(1) Multiple Independent Populations: The multi-population genetic algorithm consists of several independent populations, each with its own unique set of individuals and evolutionary process. Each population can be configured with distinct parameters and operational strategies.

(2) Population Interaction: Information and individuals are shared among multiple populations through exchange strategies, facilitating global search capability. Exchange strategies may include periodic individual migration, sharing of optimal solutions, and exchange operations.

(3) Parallel Computation: The ability for multiple populations to undergo parallel evolution endows the multi-population genetic algorithm with high computational efficiency and search capability.

5.2. Algorithm Design Process

(1) Encoding: The encoding process involves generating a sequence of mutually distinct natural numbers from 1 to n, where n represents the number of delivery tasks. This sequence constructs a permutation representing a combination of delivery tasks, with each number denoting a specific task. Each permutation corresponds to a potential task allocation scheme. Adhering to the given constraints, the elements of the solution are systematically assigned to the delivery routes of the respective AGVs. To elaborate, consider the example solution 123456. The first element of the solution represents the first target point for the delivery route of the first AGV. It is then checked whether this allocation adheres to the imposed constraints, including the AGV's maximum load capacity, remaining battery level, and time requirements. If the constraints are met, the second element of the solution is assigned as the second task point for the first AGV. In cases where the constraints are not satisfied, indicating that the task cannot be assigned to the first AGV, it is then assigned as the first task point for the second AGV, and this process continues iteratively.

(2) Initializing Populations: In this study, four populations are created, each comprising 20 individuals (solutions). To generate these individuals, 20 randomly generated non-repeating sequences between 1 and n, where n represents the number of delivery tasks, are utilized. Each individual within a population represents a distinct task allocation solution. To promote diversity and facilitate thorough exploration of the search space, unique crossover and mutation probabilities are randomly assigned to each population. The crossover probability ranges from 0.7 to 0.9, while the mutation probability ranges from 0.001 to 0.05. Both probabilities are generated using random number distributions.

(3) Selection, Crossover, and Mutation: Firstly, fitness evaluation is conducted for each individual within the population, with the fitness function value being the reciprocal of the objective function value. By computing the total distance and time of the corresponding task allocation solution for each individual, their respective fitness values are derived. Lower fitness values indicate more superior task allocation solutions, increasing the likelihood of individuals being selected as parents to produce the next generation. Subsequently, these individuals are randomly paired for information exchange through the crossover operation. This process introduces diversity among individuals within the population, facilitating exploration of a broader solution space. Lastly, following the crossover operation, the genes of the offspring individuals are subjected to mutation with a certain probability. The mutation operation introduces new gene combinations within individuals, further enhancing population diversity and avoiding being trapped in local optima.

(4) Reverse Evolution: In order to enhance the local search capability of the genetic algorithm, a reverse evolution operation is introduced after the selection, crossover, and mutation operations. The reverse evolution operation randomly selects a gene segment from the parent and performs a reverse order operation on that segment.

Subsequently, the fitness value of the parent after the reverse operation is calculated to determine whether to accept the parent with the reverse operation. The reverse operation is only effective if the fitness of the parent improves after the reverse operation, in which case it is included in the next generation of individuals. Otherwise, the reverse operation is considered ineffective.

(5) Migration Operator: To facilitate information exchange among populations, a strategy of periodically introducing the best individual from one population into another population is employed. Specifically, the best individual from one population is selected to replace the worst individual in another population. Through this information exchange mechanism, the flow and sharing of information among populations are encouraged. Introducing the best individual allows beneficial genetic information to be transmitted to other populations, thereby enhancing their overall fitness. Simultaneously, replacing the worst individual helps prevent populations from prematurely converging to local optima and increases the diversity of the populations.

(6) Elite Population: To enhance information exchange and sharing among populations, a strategy of selecting the best individuals from other populations and placing them into a special elite population for preservation is adopted. The elite population can be viewed as a collection of the best solutions from each population. By regularly selecting the best individuals from other populations and adding them to the elite population, excellent solutions from various populations can be accumulated and shared with other populations for evolution.

(7) Termination Criteria: To further enhance the stability and convergence of the algorithm, the best individual in the elite population is required to maintain its status as the best solution for a consecutive number of generations equal to or greater than 10. In other words, when the best individual in the elite population remains unchanged for 10 or more consecutive generations, it can be considered that the algorithm has reached a relatively stable state, and the iteration process can be terminated.

6. Simulation Experiments and Analysis

To verify the correctness of the mathematical model and the effectiveness of the Multi-population Genetic Algorithm (MGA), comparative experiments were conducted in this study. The experiments were designed and implemented using Matlab. The results obtained from Particle Swarm Optimization (PSO) and the Genetic Algorithm (GA) were compared and analyzed against the results of the Multi-Population Genetic Algorithm. Through this comparative analysis, the solving capabilities and performance of each algorithm can be evaluated, confirming the correctness of the mathematical model, and validating the effectiveness of the Multi-Population Genetic Algorithm in problem-solving.

In this study, an 80×80 maintenance workshop for high-speed trains was established, with the starting point of tasks set at (1, 1) and the destination point at (80, 80). Randomly generated obstacle distributions were introduced to represent walls, shelves, and other objects within the maintenance workshop. These obstacles contribute to creating a more realistic map of the maintenance workshop, thereby enhancing the authenticity and reliability of the experiments. By incorporating randomly generated obstacle distributions, various constraints and challenges present in real-world scenarios can be considered during the simulation experiments. Consequently, this approach allows for a more comprehensive evaluation and optimization of the operational efficiency within the maintenance workshop.

6.1. Small-Scale Simulation Experiment

Assuming the maintenance workshop is equipped with five Automatic Guided Vehicles (AGVs) capable of executing distribution tasks. Each AGV has a full battery range of 200 km. To ensure the safe operation of AGVs, a safety battery level of 10% of the total battery capacity is set, allowing AGVs to maintain sufficient charge to return to the charging area during their journeys. The remaining battery percentages for each AGV are shown in

Table 1. Additionally, each AGV has a maximum load capacity of 100 kg and a travel speed of 20 km/h. For further investigation of the performance of distribution tasks, 20 sets of distribution tasks were randomly selected through code. The locations of these tasks are between the starting point and the destination point, with random coordinates assigned to each task. The dataset includes the coordinates of the task points, task generation times, task completion deadlines, and the weight of the materials, as presented in Table 2.

Table 1. Remaining Battery Levels of AGVs.

AGV No.	Remaining Battery Percentage
1	67
2	88
3	96
4	78
5	76

Table 2. Task Information.

Task No.	Task Points X	Task Points Y	Material Weight (kg)	Task Generation Time (s)	Task Deadline Time (s)
1	1	1	/	/	/
2	40	48	11	160	170
3	35	16	6	49	59
4	45	55	12	14	114
5	20	55	19	50	160
6	14	29	27	35	45
7	23	30	12	98	108
8	21	51	4	80	90
9	11	44	12	95	105
10	55	60	17	97	107
11	30	60	17	13	133
12	20	60	12	67	77
13	50	35	20	65	74
14	30	25	24	159	169
15	15	10	19	32	42
16	30	5	7	61	71
17	10	20	19	75	85
18	5	30	3	157	167
19	20	40	12	87	97
20	15	55	17	76	86
21	40	60	9	26	136
22	80	80	/	/	/

The algorithm was implemented in Matlab2021b with the following parameter settings: Population size $n^p = 20$ Maximum iteration count $I_{max} = 50$. For the Particle Swarm Algorithm (PSO): Inertia weight $w = 0.01$, Learning factors $c_1 = c_2 = 1$. For the Genetic Algorithm (GA), the crossover probability $p_1 = 0.85$ Mutation probability $p_2 = 0.1$. For the proposed Multi-population Genetic Algorithm (MGA), the number of populations is set to $m^p = 4$. The simulation results of the three algorithms for the multi-AGV task allocation problem in the maintenance workshop are presented in Figure 2.

In Figure 2, the horizontal axis represents the number of iterations, and the vertical axis represents the fitness value, which corresponds to the objective function in our model, i.e., the total sum of AGV's running distance and delivery time under the given task allocation. From Figure 2, it can be observed that as the number of iterations increases, the fitness value continuously decreases until it reaches a stable state. Eventually, the optimal task allocation result that minimizes the objective function is obtained. To eliminate the impact of randomness on the experimental results, the algorithm parameters and experimental scenarios were kept unchanged, and the experiment was repeated 50 times. The average optimal results and the number of iterations obtained from the statistical analysis are shown in Table 3.

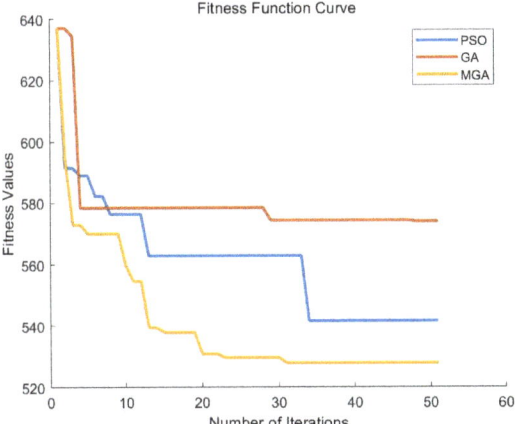

Figure 2. The fitness function curves for the three algorithms on the small-scale test case.

Table 3. The average optimal results obtained from the algorithms.

Algorithm	Average Optimal Results	Average Number of Iterations
PSO	542	34
GA	574	48
MGA	528	31

According to Table 3, the Particle Swarm Optimization (PSO) algorithm found the average optimal result of 542 in the 34th iteration, the Genetic Algorithm (GA) found the average optimal result of 574 in the 48th iteration, and the Multi-population Genetic Algorithm (MGA) found the average optimal result of 528 in the 31st iteration. Moreover, the MGA achieved a better optimal result than the other two algorithms, indicating that the proposed mathematical model is correct and effective and that the MGA exhibits superior performance in terms of solving ability and efficiency.

From the above 50 experiments, the optimal results obtained from the three algorithms are used for the multi-AGV task allocation search to obtain the task execution sequences, as shown in Table 4. In Table 4, Task ID 1 represents the starting point, and Task ID 22 represents the endpoint. When the AGV task execution sequence is 1, it indicates that the corresponding AGV vehicle was not assigned. From the contents of Table 4, it can be observed that by using the multi-population genetic algorithm for the multi-AGV task allocation model, three automatic guided vehicles (AGV1, AGV4, and AGV5) can complete the 20 sets of delivery tasks, achieving dynamic optimality in matching the delivery of raw materials with AGV vehicles.

Based on the multi-AGV task allocation results obtained from the three algorithms, corresponding route maps were generated, denoted as Figure 3a–c, respectively. In the figures, black dots represent randomly generated obstacles. From Figure 3c, it can be observed that the route generated by the multi-population genetic algorithm successfully avoids all obstacles and delivers all target points from the starting point to the endpoint. This visually demonstrates the effectiveness of the multi-population genetic algorithm in optimizing the task allocation order and path selection for the delivery tasks.

Table 4. The optimized task combinations for the three algorithms.

Algorithm	AGV No.	The Task Execution Sequence
PSO	1	1
	2	1-17-7-5-8-9-19-10-22
	3	1
	4	1-6-11-21-4-13-2-22
	5	1-15-16-3-14-18-20-12-22
GA	1	1-17-6-9-20-5-8-22
	2	1
	3	1-15-16-12-11-21-10-4-22
	4	1
	5	1-3-13-2-14-18-19-7-22
MGA	1	1-17-7-14-18-2-10-22
	2	1
	3	1
	4	1-16-3-13-19-9-11-21-4-22
	5	1-15-6-5-12-20-8-22

6.2. Large-Scale Simulation Experiment

To further investigate the algorithm's generalization, we increase the number of AGVs to 4 and add 20 additional randomly generated delivery tasks based on the small-scale case. The parameters for the additional AGVs and the information for the new tasks are presented in Table 5 and Table 6, respectively. The other AGV parameters remain unchanged.

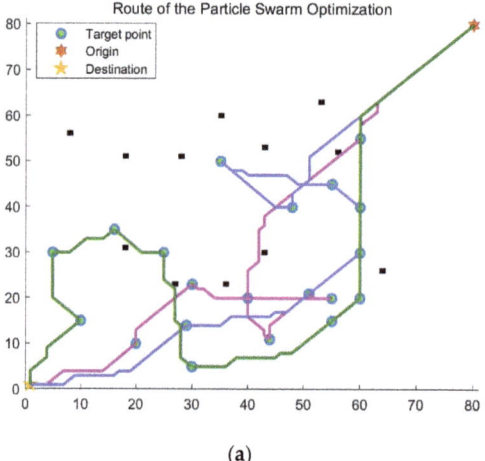

(a)

Figure 3. *Cont.*

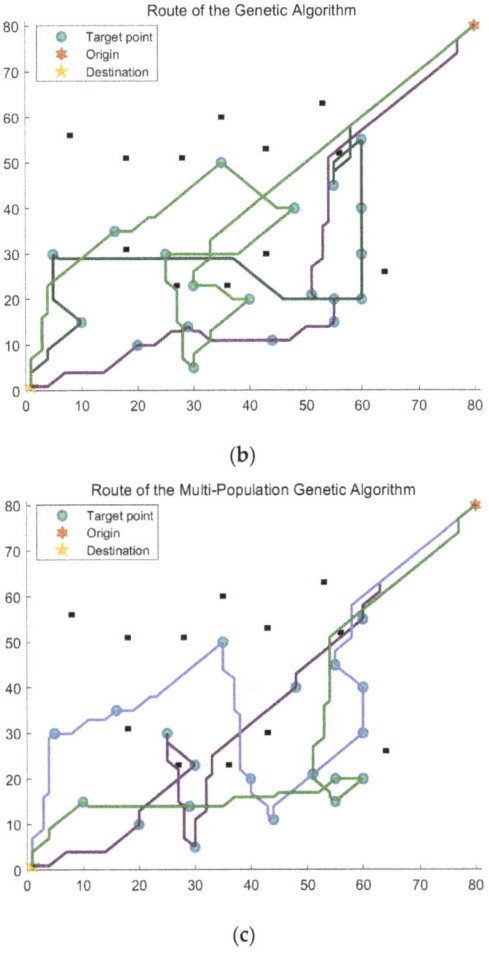

Figure 3. (**a**) The route generated by the Particle Swarm Optimization (PSO) algorithm for the small-scale case; (**b**) The route generated by the Genetic Algorithm (GA) for the small-scale case; (**c**) The route generated by the Multi-Population Genetic Algorithm (MGA) for the small-scale case. (The black dots in the figure represent randomly generated obstacles.).

Table 5. Additional AGV Battery Residual Capacity.

AGV No.	Remaining Battery Percentage
6	71
7	95
8	88
9	87

The algorithm in this study was implemented using Matlab2021b. To ensure consistency between the small-scale and large-scale experiments, the algorithm parameters were kept unchanged as specified in Section 5.1. The algorithm was run, and the iterative convergence plot of the best solution was obtained, as shown in Figure 4. Additionally, the optimal solutions and optimized task assignments were compiled and presented in Table 7.

Table 6. Additional Task Information.

Task No.	Task Points X	Task Points Y	Material Weight (kg)	Task Generation Time (s)	Task Deadline Time (s)
1	1	1	/	/	/
22	45	20	21	7	107
23	45	10	5	62	72
24	55	5	9	68	78
25	65	35	5	3	163
26	65	20	16	172	182
27	45	30	16	132	142
28	35	40	14	37	47
29	41	37	9	39	49
30	64	42	10	63	73
31	10	30	3	71	81
32	5	15	5	111	121
33	24	55	7	36	56
34	35	25	23	55	65
35	13	35	12	45	55
36	40	35	5	8	128
37	40	25	7	4	14
38	25	25	9	56	66
39	30	15	9	48	58
40	30	20	7	88	98
41	5	20	12	43	53
42	80	80	/	/	/

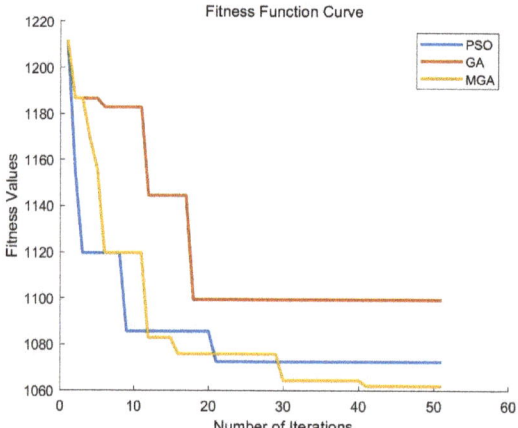

Figure 4. The fitness function curves for the three algorithms on the large-scale test case.

In the case of large-scale instances, the Particle Swarm Optimization (PSO) algorithm converges to the optimal solution around the 21st iteration, while the Genetic Algorithm (GA) finds the optimal solution around the 18th iteration. On the other hand, the proposed Multi-Group Genetic Algorithm (MGA) obtains the optimal solution around the 41st iteration. In terms of computational efficiency, PSO takes approximately 1.974 s, GA takes about 1.802 s, and MGA requires 6.886 s. Despite MGA's longer computational time due to its complex structure, it achieves significantly superior optimal results within a reasonable computational time. This demonstrates the enhanced computational performance of MGA, enabling it to generate superior task allocation solutions within a relatively short time. MGA is suitable for multi AGV task allocation problems because it efficiently generates feasible task allocation solutions. Although its computational time is slightly longer than other algorithms, it can attain significantly better results within the same computational time. This validates the effectiveness and practicality of the proposed Multi-Group Genetic Algorithm in solving multi-AGV task allocation problems.

Table 7. Optimal Results and Optimized Task Assignments for Three Algorithms in Large-Scale Experiment.

Algorithm	Optimal Result	AGV No.	The Task Execution Sequence
PSO	1073	1	1-16-40-32-18-14-2-10-42
		2	1-17-6-31-9-12-11-33-42
		3	1-41-35-5-28-36-22-25-30-42
		4	1-15-3-23-24-27-26-42
		5	1-38-39-7-19-8-20-42
		6	1
		7	1
		8	1
		9	1-37-34-29-4-21-13-42
GA	1099	1	1
		2	1-6-31-17-32-18-14-27-42
		3	1
		4	1-34-24-26-10-42
		5	1-38-40-7-16-39-23-3-13-42
		6	1
		7	1-22-36-29-28-12-20-33-2-42
		8	1-15-41-35-9-19-8-5-21-42
		9	1-37-4-11-30-25-42
MGA	1062	1	1-25-30-10-8-20-11-21-4-42
		2	1-6-17-32-18-9-2-26-42
		3	1-16-3-34-22-13-24-23-39-42
		4	1
		5	1
		6	1
		7	1-15-41-38-7-40-14-27-42
		8	1-37-36-29-28-5-12-33-19-35-31-42
		9	1

Based on the results from Table 7, it can be concluded that the multi-population genetic algorithm effectively solves the multi-AGV task allocation problem. Compared to the other two algorithms, the multi-population genetic algorithm reduces the number of deployed AGV vehicles, increases the utilization rate of each AGV, and lowers the total cost of the logistics system. This, in turn, enhances the overall efficiency of the dynamic train maintenance workshop's logistics system.

Figure 5a–c illustrate the route maps for the three algorithms. In the large-scale scenario, from the route map of the multi-population genetic algorithm, it can be observed that the system successfully avoids all obstacles and completes the delivery of all task groups. This further demonstrates the effectiveness of the multi-population genetic algorithm in improving the system's operational efficiency.

In conclusion, the multi-population genetic algorithm exhibits excellent optimization, convergence, and stability performance in both large-scale and small-scale scenarios. As the problem size increases, the algorithm produces solutions of higher quality compared to the other two algorithms. Although there is a certain difference in running time, it is within an acceptable range with the improvement of computer performance. Therefore, it can be concluded that the proposed multi-population genetic algorithm is effective in solving the multi-AGV task allocation problem. Specifically, Unique Probability Mechanism: The unique probability mechanism is a crucial component in the multi-population genetic algorithm, aiming to maintain population diversity and avoid premature convergence to local optima. This mechanism assigns a unique probability value to each individual in the population based on its fitness evaluation, where the fitness function value is the objective function value. Individuals with lower fitness values (corresponding to better task allocation solutions) are assigned higher probabilities being selected as parents for reproduction in the next generation. By doing so, the algorithm ensures a balance between exploration and exploitation, allowing the population to thoroughly explore the solution space and prevent getting stuck in suboptimal solutions. Local Search Strategy: The local search strategy is another key element introduced in the multi-population genetic algorithm to enhance its local search capabilities. After performing crossover, the offspring individuals undergo a local search process to fine-tune their solutions within a local neighborhood. This process involves exploring the surrounding solutions and adjusting the genes in a probabilistic manner. The local search strategy promotes intensification around promising regions of the solution space, enabling the algorithm to converge more quickly to good-quality solutions. It effectively improves the exploitation ability of the algorithm and further refines the task allocation solutions. Information Exchange Methods: Information exchange is a significant aspect of the multi-population genetic algorithm, which encourages inter-population cooperation and knowledge sharing. Individuals from different populations are randomly paired for information exchange through crossover, facilitating the integration of diverse genetic information and promoting the global search ability of the algorithm. Additionally, information is also exchanged among individuals within the same population through mutation, which introduces new gene combinations and maintains population diversity. This comprehensive information exchange mechanism ensures that valuable genetic information is propagated effectively throughout the entire population, contributing to a more thorough exploration of the solution space.

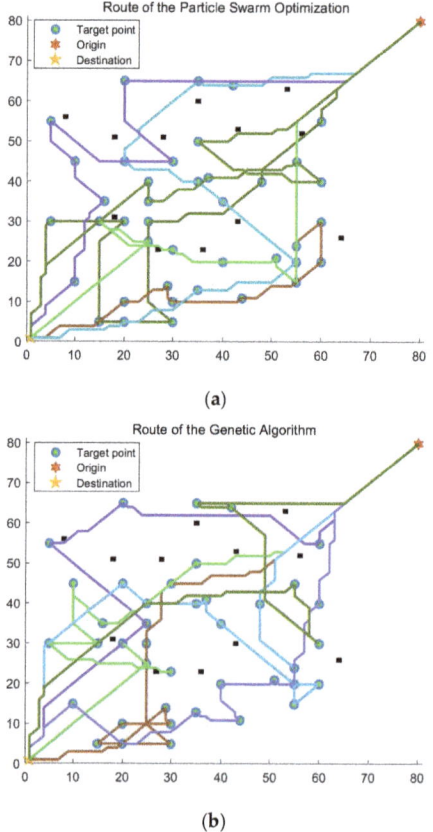

Figure 5. *Cont.*

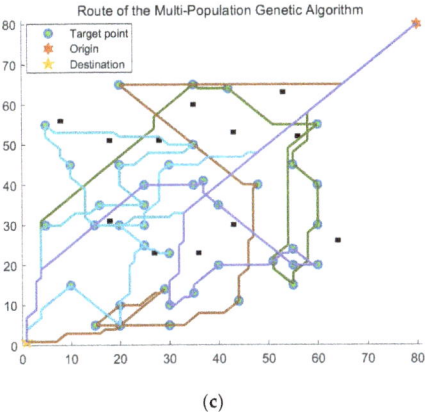

(c)

Figure 5. (**a**) The route generated by the Particle Swarm Optimization (PSO) algorithm for the large-scale case; (**b**) The route generated by the Genetic Algorithm (GA) for the large-scale case; (**c**) The route generated by the Multi-Population Genetic Algorithm (MGA) for the large-scale case. (The black dots in the figure represent randomly generated obstacles).

In summary, the unique probability mechanism, local search strategy, and information exchange methods synergistically enhance the performance of the multi-population genetic algorithm. The unique probability mechanism maintains population diversity, the local search strategy refines solutions around local optima, and the information exchange methods foster global search and knowledge sharing. The experimental results demonstrate that the multi-population genetic algorithm outperforms other algorithms, such as Particle Swarm Optimization (PSO) and Genetic Algorithm (GA), in terms of stability, optimization performance, and convergence speed, making it a powerful and effective approach to tackle the multi-AGV task allocation problem.

7. Conclusions

The aim of this research is to address the multi-AGV task allocation problem in real maintenance workshops and optimize task assignment using the Multi-population Genetic Algorithm (MGA). Our study primarily focuses on maximizing production efficiency and resource utilization in the workshop, aiming to enhance operational efficiency and reduce costs. Throughout the research process, we developed a comprehensive AGV allocation model that considers constraints such as the AGV's maximum load capacity, remaining battery power, and time availability to ensure reasonable task distribution and path planning.

The main contribution of this research lies in the introduction of the MGA algorithm, which takes into account factors like task priority, distance between tasks, and proximity to maintenance workstations, resulting in more rational and efficient task allocation. Comparative experiments with traditional Particle Swarm Optimization (PSO) and the Genetic Algorithm (GA) demonstrated that MGA exhibited faster convergence and superior optimal solutions for large-scale instances, highlighting its competitive advantage in multi-AGV task allocation. However, our research also has certain limitations. The algorithm may require longer computation times when dealing with more complex and dynamic operating environments, necessitating further optimization of algorithm parameters and structures to improve efficiency. Additionally, some assumptions made in the algorithm may not entirely align with real workshop conditions, calling for the consideration of additional real-world factors to enhance the model's practical applicability. Future improvements could involve incorporating factors such as loading and unloading times and raw material volumes to more accurately reflect real workshop scenarios. Further optimization of local search and information exchange methods within the algorithm could enhance convergence and optimization performance. Additionally, exploring the combination of the MGA algorithm with other intelligent techniques could address more complex and diverse industrial scenarios.

Overall, this research offers an efficient and optimized solution for AGV task allocation in practical maintenance workshops and provides valuable references for related research and applications. Continual refinement and optimization will allow these findings to have a greater impact in a broader range of industrial settings, driving advancements in intelligent manufacturing and logistics. We believe that the outcomes of this research will provide robust support in tackling challenges faced in actual maintenance operations and offer new insights and directions for future improvements and adaptations in this field.

Author Contributions: Conceptualization, C.F.; methodology, N.Z.; software, N.Z.; validation, N.Z.; formal analysis, N.Z.; investigation, N.Z.; resources, N.Z.; data curation, N.Z.; writing—original draft preparation, N.Z.; writing—review and editing, N.Z.; visualization, N.Z.; supervision, N.Z. All authors have read and agreed to the published version of the manuscript.

Funding: This research received no external funding.

Data Availability Statement: The labeled dataset used to support the findings of this study is available from the first author upon request.

Conflicts of Interest: The authors declare no conflict of interest.

References

1. Javed, M.A.; Muram, F.U.; Punnekkat, S.; Hansson, H. Safe and secure platooning of Automated Guided Vehicles in Industry 4.0. *J. Syst. Archit.* **2021**, *121*, 102309. [CrossRef]
2. Ghobakhloo, M. The future of manufacturing industry: A strategic roadmap toward Industry 4.0. *J. Manuf. Technol. Manag.* **2018**, *29*, 910–936. [CrossRef]
3. Lu, B. Building a Strong Transportation Country with Railways Leading the Way: Promoting the High-Quality Development of Railways. *China Business News*, 31 October 2022. [CrossRef]
4. Wang, K.; Hu, T.; Wang, Z.; Xiang, Y.; Shao, J.; Xiang, X. Performance evaluation of a robotic mobile fulfillment system with multiple picking stations under zoning policy. *Comput. Ind. Eng.* **2022**, *169*, 108229. [CrossRef]
5. Lu, J.; Ren, C.; Shao, Y.; Zhu, J.; Lu, X. An automated guided vehicle conflict-free scheduling approach considering assignment rules in a robotic mobile fulfillment system. *Comput. Ind. Eng.* **2023**, *176*, 108932. [CrossRef]
6. Zhuang, Y.; Zhou, Y.; Yuan, Y.; Hu, X.; Hassini, E. Order picking optimization with rack-moving mobile robots and multiple workstations. *Eur. J. Oper. Res.* **2022**, *300*, 527–544. [CrossRef]
7. Li, K.; Liu, T.; He, B.; Xu, D. Research on AGV Path Planning and Scheduling in "Goods-to-Person" Picking System. *Chin. J. Manag. Sci.* **2022**, *30*, 240–251. [CrossRef]
8. Li, T.; Feng, S.; Song, J.; Liu, J. Robust Bilevel Planning Model for Robot Task Allocation in "Goods-to-Person" Picking System. *Oper. Res. Manag. Sci.* **2019**, *28*, 10.
9. Zou, W.Q.; Pan, Q.K.; Wang, L.; Miao, Z.H.; Peng, C. Efficient multi objective optimization for an AGV energy-efficient scheduling problem with release time. *Knowl. -Based Syst.* **2022**, *242*, 108334. [CrossRef]
10. Li, J.; Zhang, Z.; Wu, L.; Wu, Z. Research on Energy-saving Single-load AGV Path Planning for Multi-Transport Tasks. *Manuf. Technol. Mach. Tool* **2022**, *3*, 6.
11. Mousavi, M.; Yap, H.J.; Musa, S.N.; Tahriri, F.; Md Dawal, S.Z. Multi-objective AGV scheduling in an FMS using a hybrid of genetic algorithm and particle swarm optimization. *PLoS ONE* **2017**, *12*, e0169817. [CrossRef]
12. Nishi, T.; Matsushita, S.; Hisano, T.; Morikawa, M. A practical model of routing problems for automated guided vehicles with acceleration and deceleration. *J. Adv. Mech. Des. Syst. Manuf.* **2014**, *8*, JAMDSM0067. [CrossRef]
13. Kirkpatrick, S.; Gelatt, C.D.; Vecchi, M.P. Optimization by simulated annealing. *Science* **1983**, *220*, 671–680. [CrossRef] [PubMed]
14. Zhang, Q.; Li, H. MOEA/D: A multi-objective evolutionary algorithm based on decomposition. *IEEE Trans. Evol. Comput.* **2007**, *11*, 712–731. [CrossRef]
15. Liang, J.J.; Qin, A.K.; Suganthan, P.N.; Baskar, S. Comprehensive learning particle swarm optimizer for global optimization of multimodal functions. *IEEE Trans. Evol. Comput.* **2006**, *10*, 281–295. [CrossRef]
16. Dorigo, M.; Maniezzo, V.; Colorni, A. Ant system: Optimization by a colony of cooperating agents. *IEEE Trans. Syst. Man Cybern. Part B* **1996**, *26*, 29–41. [CrossRef]
17. Lee, D.; Lee, S.; Masoud, N.; Krishnan, M.S.; Li, V.C. Digital twin-driven deep reinforcement learning for adaptive task allocation in robotic construction. *Adv. Eng. Inform.* **2022**, *53*, 101710. [CrossRef]
18. Sarker, I.H. Machine Learning: Algorithms, Real-World Applications and Research Directions. *SN Comput. Sci.* **2021**, *2*, 160. [CrossRef]

19. Sarker, I.H. Deep Learning: A Comprehensive Overview on Techniques, Taxonomy, Applications and Research Directions. *SN Comput. Sci.* **2021**, *2*, 420. [CrossRef] [PubMed]
20. Joshi, K.; Bhatt, C.; Shah, K.; Parmar, D.; Corchado, J.M.; Bruno, A.; Mazzeo, P.L. Machine-learning techniques for predicting phishing attacks in blockchain networks: A comparative study. *Algorithms* **2023**, *16*, 366. [CrossRef]
21. Ntawuzumunsi, E.; Kumaran, S.; Sibomana, L.; Mtonga, K. Design and development of energy efficient algorithm for smart beekeeping device to device communication based on data aggregation techniques. *Algorithms* **2023**, *16*, 367. [CrossRef]
22. Zou, W.Q.; Pan, Q.K.; Meng, T.; Gao, L.; Wang, Y.L. An effective discrete artificial bee colony algorithm for multi-AGVs dispatching problem in a matrix manufacturing workshop. *Expert Syst. Appl.* **2020**, *161*, 113675. [CrossRef]
23. Tang, H.; Cheng, X.; Jiang, W.; Chen, S. Research on equipment configuration optimization of AGV unmanned warehouse. *IEEE Access* **2021**, *9*, 47946–47959.
24. Yue, X.; Xu, X.; Wang, X. Research on Multi-AGV Scheduling Algorithm for FMS Based on Improved Hybrid PSO-GA. *Comput. Sci.* **2018**, *45*, 5.
25. Liu, X.F.; Fang, Y.; Zhan, Z.H.; Zhang, J. Strength Learning Particle Swarm Optimization for Multi objective Multirobot Task Scheduling. *IEEE Trans. Syst. Man Cybern. Syst.* **2023**, *53*, 4052–4063. [CrossRef]
26. Tang, H.; Wang, A.; Xue, F.; Yang, J.; Cao, Y. A novel hierarchical soft actor-critic algorithm for multi-logistics robots task allocation. *IEEE Access* **2021**, *9*, 42568–42582. [CrossRef]
27. Yang, W.; Li, R.; Zhang, K. Task Allocation Optimization of Multi-AGVs Based on Variable Neighborhood Simulated Annealing Algorithm. *Comput. Appl.* **2021**, *41*, 3056–3062.
28. Yang, Z.; Su, C.; Hu, X.; Chen, D. Multi-objective Scheduling Optimization of Multi-AGV System for Intelligent Production Workshop. *J. Southeast Univ.* **2019**, *49*, 1033–1040.
29. Song, W.; Gao, Y.; Shen, L.; Zhang, Y. A Multi-Robot Task Allocation Algorithm Based on Near-field Subset Partitioning. *Robot.* **2021**, *43*, 629–640.
30. Xu, L.; Chen, Y.; Gao, X.; Li, A. Scheduling Optimization of Mixed-flow Flexible Manufacturing Unit's Automated Guided Vehicles. *J. Tongji Univ.* **2017**, *45*, 1839–1858.
31. Chen, M.; Sharma, A.; Bhola, J.; Nguyen TV, T.; Truong, C.V. Multi-agent task planning and resource apportionment in a smart grid. *Int. J. Syst. Assur. Eng. Manag.* **2022**, *13*, 444–455. [CrossRef]
32. Kler, R.; Gangurde, R.; Elmirzaev, S.; Hossain, M.S.; Vo, N.V.; Nguyen, T.V.; Kumar, P.N. Optimization of meat and poultry farm inventory stock using data analytics for green supply chain network. *Discret. Dyn. Nat. Soc.* **2022**, *2022*, 8970549. [CrossRef]
33. Fu, Z.; Hu, Z.; Zong, K. Scheduling Optimization of AGVs at Container Terminal under Non-Saturated State of Battery. *J. Dalian Marit. Univ.* **2017**, *43*, 5.
34. Tong, W.; Tao, B.; Jin, X.; Li, Z. Design Optimization of Multipole Galatea Trap Coils by Multiple Population Genetic Algorithm. *IEEE Trans. Plasma Sci.* **2016**, *44*, 1018–1024. [CrossRef]
35. Zhou, Y.; Zhou, L.; Wang, Y.; Yang, Z.; Wu, J. Application of Multiple-Population Genetic Algorithm in Optimizing the Train-Set Circulation Plan Problem. *Complexity* **2017**, *2017*, 3717654. [CrossRef]
36. Jiao, Y.L.; Xing, X.C.; Zhang, P.; Xu, L.C.; Liu, X.R. Multi-objective storage location allocation optimization and simulation analysis of automated warehouse based on multi-population genetic algorithm. *Concurr. Eng.* **2018**, *26*, 367–377. [CrossRef]
37. Wang, L.; Wang, X.; Liu, D.; Hu, H. Path Optimization Method for Unmanned Autonomous Vehicle Delivery under Intelligent Connected Vehicles. *J. Syst. Sci. Math. Sci.* **2020**, *40*, 15.

Disclaimer/Publisher's Note: The statements, opinions and data contained in all publications are solely those of the individual author(s) and contributor(s) and not of MDPI and/or the editor(s). MDPI and/or the editor(s) disclaim responsibility for any injury to people or property resulting from any ideas, methods, instructions or products referred to in the content.

Article

Analysis of Psychological Factors Influencing Mathematical Achievement and Machine Learning Classification

Juhyung Park [1], Sungtae Kim [2] and Beakcheol Jang [1,*]

[1] Graduate School of Information, Yonsei University, Seoul 03722, Republic of Korea; winderland@yonsei.ac.kr
[2] Able Edutech Inc., Seoul 04081, Republic of Korea; iforyou76@yonsei.ac.kr
* Correspondence: bjang@yonsei.ac.kr

Abstract: This study analyzed the psychological factors that influence mathematical achievement in order to classify students' mathematical achievement. Here, we employed linear regression to investigate the variables that contribute to mathematical achievement, and we found that self-efficacy, math-efficacy, learning approach motivation, and reliance on academies affect mathematical achievement. These variables are derived from the Test of Learning Psychology (TLP), a psychological test developed by Able Edutech Inc. specifically to measure students' learning psychology in the mathematics field. We then conducted machine learning classification with the identified variables. As a result, the random forest model demonstrated the best performance, achieving accuracy values of 73% (Test 1) and 81% (Test 2), with F1-scores of 79% (Test 1) and 82% (Test 2). Finally, students' skills were classified according to the TLP items. The results demonstrated that students' academic abilities could be identified using a psychological test in the field of mathematics. Thus, the TLP results can serve as a valuable resource to develop personalized learning programs and enhance students' mathematical skills.

Keywords: machine learning; linear regression; psychological test; mathematical achievement

MSC: 68T01

Citation: Park, J.; Kim, S.; Jang, B. Analysis of Psychological Factors Influencing Mathematical Achievement and Machine Learning Classification. *Mathematics* **2023**, *11*, 3380. https://doi.org/10.3390/math11153380

Academic Editors: Mingbo Zhao, Haijun Zhang and Zhou Wu

Received: 18 June 2023
Revised: 25 July 2023
Accepted: 31 July 2023
Published: 2 August 2023

Copyright: © 2023 by the authors. Licensee MDPI, Basel, Switzerland. This article is an open access article distributed under the terms and conditions of the Creative Commons Attribution (CC BY) license (https://creativecommons.org/licenses/by/4.0/).

1. Introduction

The EdTech market has been growing steadily with new value created by integrating information technologies, e.g., big data and artificial intelligence (AI), with education [1]. In particular, AI is becoming increasingly influential, especially in the field of mathematics education, because it enables students to develop and improve their mathematical skills [2,3]. MATHia, which was developed by researchers at Carnegie Mellon University, utilizes AI technology to provide feedback and customize learning programs by identifying students' weaknesses. In addition, Woongjin ThinkBig, a South Korean education group, has developed an AI application to teach mathematics and analyze each student's individual learning abilities based on big data and AI to provide personalized learning materials that are appropriate for each student.

Similarly, there is an active movement to provide personalized content recommendations in the mathematics education field, which promotes the need for research on identifying student skills and the factors that affect mathematical achievement. To develop such a personalized learning system, it is important to understand students' psychology because the student's abilities must be assessed to realize personalized learning, and individual psychological factors, e.g., self-confidence and anxiety, can influence the student's abilities [4,5].

Previous studies have shown that psychological factors are significant contributors to academic achievements [4–12]; however, these studies primarily focused on general psychological factors and did not specifically explore the field of mathematical psychology in predicting student abilities. In addition, most mathematics education institutions have traditionally relied solely on grades as the primary indicator of students' skills, thereby overlooking the potential insights that can be acquired through a more comprehensive approach.

Given these gaps in the existing research, the purpose of this study is to analyze mathematics-related psychological factors that impact students' mathematical achievement. By examining these factors, we seek to gain a deeper understanding of their influence on students' mathematics performance. In addition, our objective is to go beyond the analysis of these mathematics-related psychological factors and advance toward a more proactive approach. In doing so, we intend to uncover prediction models that can classify students' mathematical abilities effectively. To achieve this goal, we employed machine learning classification techniques based on the identified psychological factors. By adopting this methodology, we aim to identify the key psychological factors and harness their potential predictive power. Ultimately, this study aims to contribute to the field by bridging the gap between mathematics and psychology and shed light on the relationship between relevant psychological factors and mathematical achievement.

2. Related Work

Related studies can be broadly categorized into those that reveal psychological factors affecting academic achievement and those that classify or predict students' grades. In terms of identifying the psychological factors that affect academic achievement, a previous study stated that personal traits, e.g., self-confidence, are among the most crucial variables that determine a student's mathematical achievement [4]. Another study proved that Anxiety and depression have been shown to disrupt concentration and reduce academic achievement in high school students [5]. According to one study [6], students' self-efficacy, engagement, and mathematical achievement are positively associated. In addition, a negative relationship between anxiety (from multiple psychological test items) and mathematical achievement has been reported [7]. Students with self-efficacy tend to have more positive emotions, thereby resulting in better academic performance [8].

A previous study that analyzed the aspects of learning motivation reported that intrinsic motivation affects the behaviors and achievement of learners [9]. Another study [10] reported that burnout increases the probability of experiencing psychological and physical disengagement from academic pursuits, which in turn can result in a decline in academic achievement. It has also been found that higher levels of academic self-efficacy were positively associated with greater academic achievement and resilience, thereby indicating a direct relationship between these variables [11]. In addition, a previous study [12] found that various costs, including emotion, effort, opportunity, and ego costs, play a crucial role in predicting mathematical achievement.

In studies on the classification of student grades [13–16], student performance has been classified using machine learning technologies. The classification and regression tree (CART) algorithm and k-nearest neighbors (KNN) techniques have been used to classify the skills of college students attending web-based lectures based on data related to their homework assignments and quizzes [13]. In addition, the average grades of Bulgarian university students were classified according to their admission scores using KNN and decision tree techniques [14]. Another study employed a support vector machine (SVM) to classify college students' academic performances based on Internet usage data [15], and one study [16] employed the random forest to predict the final grades of Malaysia Polytechnics students based on their previous semester's final examination results.

Studies have also investigated grade prediction using machine learning techniques [17–19]. For example, one study performed linear regression to predict academic achievement based on students' backgrounds and past academic scores from the Institute of Aeronautical Engineering in India [17]. In addition, the random forest method has been employed to predict the grade point averages of master students in computer science at ETH Zurich based on their bachelor's grade point averages [18]. In addition, a machine learning–based recommendation system considered the grades of students at the Ho Chi Minh City University of Technology in Vietnam to predict students' future grades [19].

Previous studies have analyzed various variables that influence academic performance; however, there is an identifiable research gap when it comes to psychological factors specifically related to mathematics. To address this gap, this study focuses on the field of mathematics and utilizes a psychological test to identify the factors that influence mathematical achievement.

Furthermore, to the best of our knowledge, no prior study has focused on predicting academic achievements primarily based on psychological factors. Thus, in this study, we employed machine learning techniques to classify students' abilities based on the identified psychological variables. Through these techniques, we aim to provide insights into how psychological factors can be utilized to predict and understand mathematical achievement.

3. Materials and Methods

3.1. Data Description

In this study, we considered 1880 elementary, middle, and high school students who were learning mathematics at Able Edutech Inc., a mathematics EdTech company, from August 2016 to April 2022. Table 1 shows the variables, i.e., the ID (each student's unique number), mathematical achievement (Test 1 and Test 2 scores, which are diagnostic tests), and the Test of Learning Psychology (TLP) scores of each student. To facilitate our research, Able Edutech Inc. coded the students' personal data into a unique ID number to anonymize the data. The TLP is a psychological test about mathematics learning developed by the Korea Learning Psychometric Research Institute and the Yonsei University Cognitive Science Research Center. The TLP results were collected when students first enrolled in the company, and the mathematical achievements were obtained through two tests after attending courses. Regarding the TLP items used in this study, some were difficult to analyze due to limited or missing data on student responses; thus, these items were excluded from the analysis. The five selected psychological test factors were self-efficacy, math-efficacy, learning approach motivation, performance approach motivation, and reliance on academies.

Table 1. Variables considered in this study.

Variables	Description	Range	Count
ID	Student's unique number	1–1880	1880
Mathematical achievement	Test 1 and Test 2 Scores	0–100	2
TLP items (self-efficacy, math-efficacy, learning approach motivation, performance approach motivation, reliance on academies)	Scores of psychological test items	0–100	5

Self-efficacy refers to the belief and confidence in one's ability and the degree of belief one possesses in their ability to perform a certain task. Math-efficacy, similar to self-efficacy, refers to the belief and confidence students have in their mathematical abilities. Learning approach motivation represents the extent to which a student enjoys seeking knowledge and the extent to which they study to obtain knowledge. Reliance on academies measures students' dependence on academies and their awareness of the importance of academies in supporting their studies.

3.2. Data Visualization

Based on the collected data, the number of students sorted by grade level is shown in Figure 1. Most students were fifth-graders (in elementary schools), first-graders (in middle schools), and first-graders (in high schools). However, in the original data, in terms of a grade-wise analysis, the data for only 464 students were linked to relevant variables, e.g., elementary/middle/high school grades, TLP test results, and mathematics scores. In contrast, the data for 1880 students contained TLP test and mathematics scores when grade information was excluded. Thus, in this study, rather than analyzing the students by grade, we analyzed the data and classified the abilities of all 1880 students using machine learning.

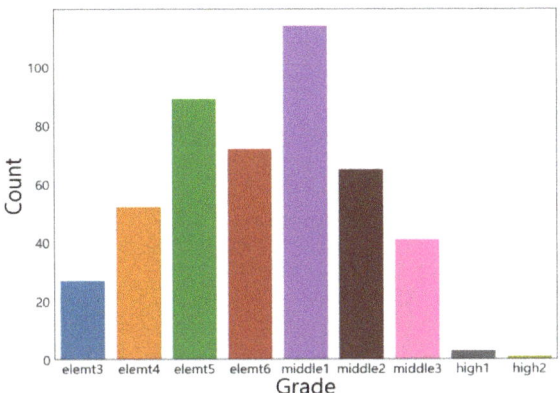

Figure 1. Number of students by grade.

The data on the mathematical achievement comprised the scores for Test 1 and Test 2, which are diagnostic tests for learning mathematics. The Test 1 scores are shown in Figure 2. The results revealed that 202 students were in the 0–10 points range, followed by 65, 53, 45, 32, 30, 18, 13, 5, and 1 students in the 30–40, 20–30, 10–20, 40–50, 50–60, 60–70, 70–80, 90–100, and 80–90 points range, respectively.

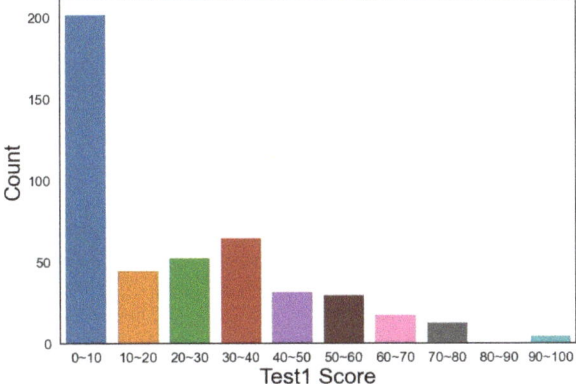

Figure 2. Distribution of Test 1 scores.

The results of Test 2 are shown in Figure 3. Here, 218 students scored in the 0–10-point range. For the remaining scores, 75, 61, 59, 17, 16, 14, 3, 1, and 0 students scored in the 10–20, 20–30, 30–40, 70–80, 40–50, 60–70, 50–60, 90–100, and 80–90.

Then, the number of students was analyzed according to their TLP scores, as shown in Figure 4. The histograms of self-efficacy, math-efficacy, and learning approach motivation exhibit a left-skewed distribution, and their medians are greater than the means. Performance approach motivation and reliance on academies have a symmetric tendency, which is similar to a normal distribution.

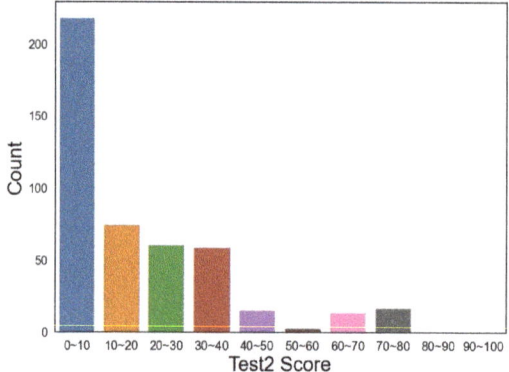

Figure 3. Distribution of Test 2 scores.

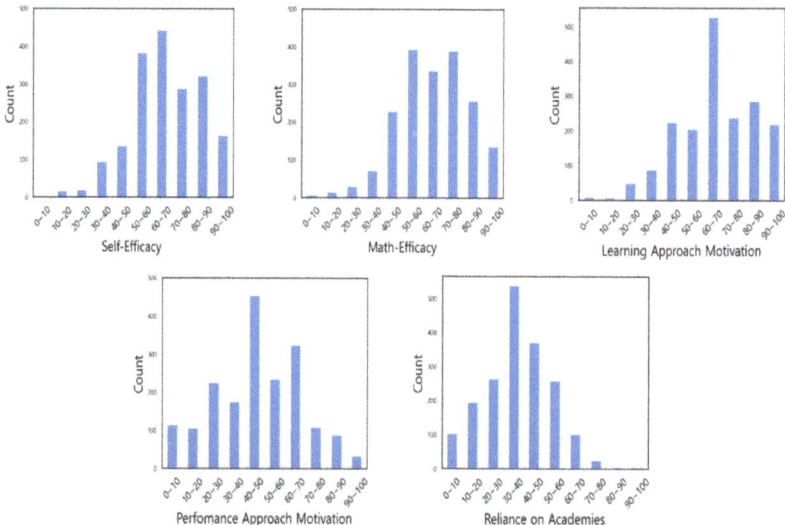

Figure 4. Number of students by TLP.

Specifically, regarding the point ranges of students according to their self-efficacy, 444 students scored in the 60–70-point range. Then, 384, 324, 289, 165, 137, 95, 21, 18, and 3 students scored in the 50–60, 80–90, 70–80, 0–100, 40–50, 30–40, 20–30, 10–20, and 0–10 point ranges, respectively. In terms of math-efficacy, the largest number of students was 395, with a score range of 50–60. Then, 391, 339, 258, 230, 137, 73, 32, 17, and 8 students scored in the 70–80, 60–70, 80–90, 40–50, 90–100, 30–40, 20–30, 10–20, and 0–10 point ranges, respectively. Regarding learning approach motivation, 529 students scored in the 60–70 point range. Then 287, 240, 226, 221, 207, 89, 50, 23, and 8 students scored in the 80–90, 70–80, 40–50, 90–100, 50–60, 30–40, 20–30, 0–10, and 10–20 point ranges, respectively. For performance approach motivation, 455 students scored in the 40–50 point range. Then, 326, 236, 226, 176, 118, 110, 107, 90, and 36 students scored in the 60–70, 50–60, 20–30, 30–40, 0–10, 70–80, 10–20, 80–90, and 90–100 point ranges, respectively. Regarding reliance on academies, most students (n = 539) scored in the 30–40 range. Then, 373, 266, 260, 196, 105, 103, 26, and 6 students scored in the 40–50, 20–30, 50–60, 10–20, 0–10, 60–70, 70–80, and both 80–90 and 90–100 point ranges, respectively.

4. Method

The overall workflow of this study is illustrated in Figure 5. In this study, we attempted to identify TLP items that impact mathematical achievement and classify the students' abilities accordingly.

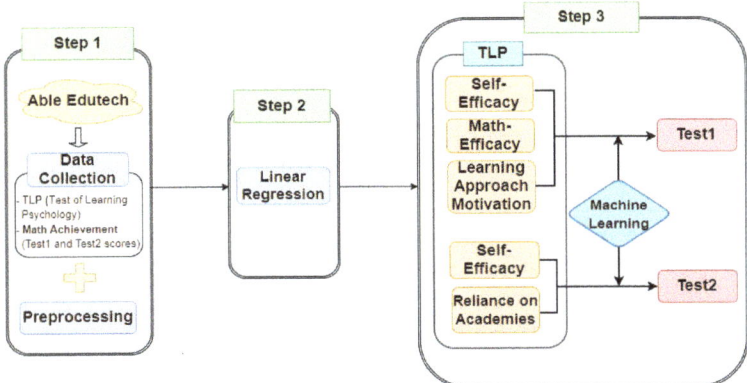

Figure 5. Workflow.

In the first step, we collected and preprocessed the data (TLP items and Test 1/Test 2 scores) provided by Able Edutech, and we selected the variables required for analysis. In the preprocessing stage, we removed missing values. In addition, outliers were observed in the mathematical achievement variable, and according to an agreement with Able Edutech, we replaced these outliers with the maximum value. The dependent variable for machine learning, i.e., mathematical achievement (Test 1 and Test 2), was categorized into high and low levels based on the grades. However, there was a significant data imbalance in all tests; thus, oversampling techniques were utilized to balance the data. The results are shown in Tables 2 and 3.

Table 2. Count of Test 1 classes after oversampling.

Test 1 Classes	Count	Oversampled Count
High level	276	1604
Low level	1604	1604

Table 3. Count of Test 2 classes after oversampling.

Test 2 Classes	Count	Oversampled Count
High level	126	1754
Low level	1754	1754

In the second step, linear regression analysis was conducted to identify the TLP items that have a statistically significant influence on students' mathematical achievement and select relevant variables for machine learning classification.

In the final step, we classified students' mathematical achievements according to these variables using machine learning techniques. Here, we employed various algorithms, i.e., the logistic regression, K-nearest neighbors (KNN), random forest, decision tree, Support vector machine (SVM), gradient boosting machine (GBM), light gradient boosting machine (LGBM), and extreme gradient boosting (XGBoost) algorithms. These algorithms are described in the following.

4.1. Used Algorithms

4.1.1. Linear Regression

Linear regression is a regression analysis technique that models the linear correlation between the dependent variable y and the independent variable x. A linear relationship implies that the independent variable x affects the dependent variable y according to y = ax + b, where the slope a and y-intercept b are obtained from the training data. For such a linear relationship, the value of y for the dependent variable can be predicted when a new variable, x, is given. Linear regression results can be easily interpreted and modeled quickly.

4.1.2. Machine Learning Classification Algorithms

Logistic regression is a representative supervised machine learning algorithm used for binary classification tasks. Using a sigmoid function with a value between 0–1, classification is performed based on the probability that an item belongs to a particular category. The sigmoid function is expressed in Equation (1), where e, i.e., Euler's number, is (2.718281...).

$$\text{Sigmoid Function} = \frac{1}{(1+e^{-x})} \tag{1}$$

Here, if the input value x is a large negative number, it is set to 0, and if x is a large positive number, it is set to 1. Thus, classification is performed by predicting a probability value between 0–1.

A support vector machine (SVM) is a supervised machine learning algorithm and a powerful classification model [20]. Support vectors are the nearest data points to the decision boundary. The decision boundary is selected in a way that maximizes the distance between them. The objective of the SVM is to find an optimal decision boundary, which can be expressed as follows:

$$w^T x + b = 0. \tag{2}$$

Here, w represents the normal vector to the decision boundary, and b is the intercept. In addition, w^T denotes the transpose of w. The goal of the SVM is to maximize the distance between the support vectors and the decision boundary. Therefore, the SVM can be formulated as the following optimization problem:

$$\text{minimize } \frac{1}{2}\|w\|^2, \text{ subject to } y_i\left(w^T x_i + b\right) \geq 1 \text{ (for all data points)}. \tag{3}$$

Here, $\|w\|^2$ represents the norm of w, and y_i represents the class of the data point. The SVM can find the optimal decision boundary by solving this optimization problem. SVM is a model that classifies which side of the boundary the input data belongs to through the decision boundary.

The K-nearest neighbors (KNN) technique is a simple supervised classification algorithm that works to identify classes with a set number of k data that are near to new data among the existing data and classify the new data into a class that has more existing data. The distance calculation is performed based on the Euclidean distance metric:

$$\text{Euclidean distance} = \sum_{i=1}^{n}(x_i - y_i)^2 \tag{4}$$

Here, x represents a new data point, and y represents all data points in the dataset. Compared with other models, the KNN algorithm is advantageous because it is relatively easier to understand.

A random forest is a type of ensemble learning method wherein results are obtained by collecting the classification results from multiple decision trees constructed during the training process. Random forests are used to solve various problems, e.g., classification and regression tasks. The random forest model was developed according to Breiman's method [21]. Note that random forest predictions are based on the results of many randomly generated decision trees; thus, overfitting is reduced, and good generalization performance is demonstrated. Therefore, the random forest algorithm is a fast technique that provides highly accurate results.

A decision tree is a supervised machine learning algorithm that classifies data using classification criteria based on the attributes of each data item. In other words, the decision tree method classifies data by branching based on whether specific criteria are satisfied. The results of decision trees are easy to interpret and understand. Regarding other techniques, regularization or variable creation/removal is required in some cases, whereas decision trees rarely require data processing. Additionally, the decision tree model is rarely affected by outliers, exhibits good stability, and can be applied to both numerical and categorical data.

The gradient boosting machine (GBM), developed by Friedman [22], is a supervised machine learning technique used for regression or classification tasks that reduces residuals through gradient descent and incorporates boosting techniques. Here, boosting refers to combining weak learners to reduce errors and create a strong learner. In other words, a strong prediction model is constructed using an ensemble of weak prediction models, and the subsequent classifier is trained based on the prediction error of the previous weak classifier to compensate for its error. Generally, the GBM method outperforms the random forests method.

The extreme gradient boosting (XGBoost) algorithm, developed by Chen [23] at the University of Washington, improves and extends gradient boosting algorithms to support parallel learning. The XGBoost method comprises a Classification and Regression Tree (CART) model, which is expressed as follows.

$$\hat{y}_i = \sum_{k=1}^{K} f_k(x_i), f_k \in F \tag{5}$$

Here, $\hat{y}_i$ represents the predicted value of data point x_i, K denotes the number of CARTs used, and f represents the CART models. The objective function for training the CART model is expressed as follows.

$$Obj = \sum_{i=1}^{n} l(y_i, \hat{y}_i) + \sum_{k=1}^{K} \Omega(f_k) \tag{6}$$

Here, $l(y_i, \hat{y}_i)$ represents the objective function computed from the true answer y_i and the predicted value $\hat{y}_i$, and Ω is the regularization function of the model used to prevent overfitting. This algorithm executes faster than the gradient boosting method and provides excellent performance in classification and regression tasks. Additionally, it includes an overfitting regulation function; thus, it exhibits strong durability.

The light gradient boosting machine (LGBM) algorithm was developed by Microsoft. This algorithm performs ranking and classification based on the decision tree algorithm and overcomes the shortcoming of existing models that require a long computation time. This process is achieved by deepening the tree in a leaf-wise manner as opposed to gradient boosting-type trees, which are generally level-wise methods, thereby reducing both time and memory costs.

4.1.3. Machine Learning Evaluation Metrics

In this study, various evaluation metrics were utilized to assess the performance of the machine learning classification algorithms. Accuracy measures the proportion of correctly predicted samples out of the total samples. It represents how well the model classifies the data correctly. Precision is the proportion of true positive predictions (correctly predicted positive samples) to the total positive predictions made by the model. It assesses the accuracy of positive predictions. Recall measures the proportion of true positive predictions to the total actual positive samples. It evaluates the model's ability to find all positive samples. The F1-score is the harmonic mean of Precision and Recall, providing a balance between the two metrics. It is useful when both Precision and Recall are important, and a higher F1-score indicates a better model performance. The evaluation metrics were calculated as follows:

$$\text{Accuracy} = \frac{TP + TN}{TP + FN + FP + TN}$$
$$\text{Precision} = \frac{TP}{TP + FP}$$
$$\text{Recall} = \frac{TP}{TP + FN}$$
$$F1 - \text{Score} = 2 \times \frac{\text{Precision} \cdot \text{Recall}}{\text{Precision} \cdot \text{Recall}}$$

True Positive = TP, True Negative = TN, False Positives = FP, False Negatives = FN.

ROC-AUC is a widely used evaluation metric for binary classification models. It evaluates the model's performance by plotting the True Positive Rate (Recall) against the False Positive Rate and calculating the area under the ROC curve (AUC). A higher AUC value, ranging from 0 to 1, indicates better model performance.

5. Results

5.1. Linear Regression

Data processing for regression analysis was performed using the statsmodels Python package. Table 4 shows the results of the linear regression analysis with the results of the TLP items as independent variables and the Test 1 and Test 2 scores (mathematical achievement) as dependent variables. The variables are statistically significant ($p < 0.05$).

Table 4. Variables considered in the study.

Dependent Variables	Independent Variables	Coefficient	T-Value	P-Value	Prob (F-Statistics)
Test 1	Self-Efficacy	0.160 ***	3.579	0.000	0.000
	Math-Efficacy	0.190 ***	4.102	0.000	0.000
	Learning Approach Motivation	0.119 **	2.846	0.004	0.004
Test 2	Self-Efficacy	0.074 *	2.216	0.027	0.027
	Reliance on Academies	−0.079 *	−2.214	0.027	0.027

***: $p < 0.001$, **: $p < 0.01$, *: $p < 0.05$.

Table 4 shows that Prob (F-statistics) verifies the significance of the models (<0.05). The significance of the *p*-value for each dependent variable was confirmed. Here, self-efficacy, math-efficacy, and learning approach motivation had a statistically significant effect on Test 1, with math-efficacy having a relatively greater influence than the other factors. In Test 2, self-efficacy and reliance on academies were identified as statistically significant variables, and reliance on academies exhibited a relatively greater influence than self-efficacy.

5.2. Performance Evaluation of Machine Learning Classification Models

In the linear regression results, we confirmed which TLP variables affect mathematical achievement. Additionally, to classify mathematical achievement, we applied machine learning techniques that enable the classification of students' mathematical achievements using the identified variables.

We considered the logistic regression, KNN, random forest, decision tree, SVM, GBM, LGBM, and XGBoost, which are machine learning classification models implemented in Python. Using these models, machine learning classification was performed with self-efficacy, math-efficacy, and learning approach motivation as the independent variables for the dependent variable Test 1 and self-efficacy and reliance on academies as the independent variables for Test 2. The training and test data were split at a ratio of 8:2, and the evaluation results of all machine learning application models were performed with five-fold cross-validation. The evaluation results of the machine learning-based classification of the dependent variable scores (i.e., Test 1 and Test 2) into high and low ranks are shown in Table 5.

Table 5. Evaluation results.

	Model	Accuracy	Precision	Recall	F1-Score	AUC
Test 1	Logistic regression	0.58	0.59	0.58	0.58	0.59
	KNN	0.58	0.57	0.62	0.60	0.60
	Random forest	0.73	0.70	0.74	0.79	0.78
	Decision tree	0.69	0.68	0.77	0.71	0.70
	SVM	0.60	0.62	0.51	0.56	0.63
	GBM	0.65	0.65	0.69	0.67	0.68
	LGBM	0.66	0.65	0.69	0.67	0.70
	XGBoost	0.70	0.68	0.76	0.71	0.74
Test 2	Logistic regression	0.57	0.57	0.55	0.56	0.60
	KNN	0.65	0.62	0.78	0.69	0.67
	Random forest	0.81	0.76	0.88	0.82	0.88
	Decision tree	0.77	0.73	0.87	0.79	0.79
	SVM	0.59	0.57	0.66	0.61	0.62
	GBM	0.68	0.65	0.76	0.70	0.70
	LGBM	0.69	0.66	0.75	0.70	0.73
	XGBoost	0.77	0.73	0.86	0.79	0.80

Machine learning-based classification was performed with the Test 1 score as the dependent variable. The best accuracy obtained by the random forest model was 73%. Then, accuracy values of 70, 69, 66, 65, 60, and 58% were obtained by the XGBoost, decision tree, LGBM, GBM, SVM, and both KNN and logistic regression methods, respectively. The precision of the random forest method was the highest at 70%. Then, 68, 65, 62, 59, and 57%, respectively, for decision tree and XGBoost, GBM and LGBM, SVM, logistic regression, and KNN. The decision tree method obtained the highest recall score of 77%, followed by the XGBoost, random forest, GBM and LGBM, KNN, logistic regression, and SVM with 76, 74, 69, 62, 58, and 51%, respectively. The highest F1-score of 79% was obtained by the random forest method, followed by the decision tree and XGBoost, GBM and LGBM, KNN, logistic regression, and SVM methods with 71, 67, 60, 58, and 56%, respectively.

Then, machine learning–based classification was performed with the Test 2 scores as the dependent variable. The results showed that the best accuracy of 81% was obtained by the random forest model, followed by the decision tree and XGBoost, LGBM, GBM, KNN, SVM, and logistic regression methods with 77, 69, 68, 65, 59, and 57%, respectively. The random forest method obtained the best precision of 76%, followed by the decision tree and XGBoost, LGBM, GBM, KNN, and both logistic regression and SVM methods with 73, 66, 65, 62, and 57%, respectively. The recall of the random forest method was the highest at 88%, followed by the decision tree, XGBoost, KNN, GBM, LGBM, SVM, and logistic regression methods, which obtained recall values of 87, 86, 78, 76, 75, 66, and 55%, respectively. The highest F1-score of 82% was obtained by the random forest method. The F1-scores of the decision tree and XGBoost, GBM and LGBM, KNN, SVM, and logistic regression methods were 79, 70, 69, 61, and 56%, respectively. In terms of the AUC, both Test 1 and Test 2 demonstrated that the random forest method obtained the highest value (Test 1: 0.78, Test 2:

0.88), and the logistic regression method obtained the lowest value (Test 1: 0.59, Test 2: 0.60). Comprehensively, we found that the random forest method obtained the best performance in terms of Test 1 and Test 2 across most of the performance metrics. Thus, we classified the students' abilities by TLP items, resulting in high evaluation values.

6. Discussion

In this study, we identified the psychological factors that influence mathematical achievement and classified students' abilities based on the identified variables. As a result, the following academic implications arise from this research: By introducing the TLP, which is a psychological assessment test specifically designed to measure students' learning psychology in the mathematics field, we investigated the relationship between psychological factors and mathematical achievement. We believe that our findings have significant academic value because they effectively fill an identified gap in previous studies by focusing on a mathematics-centric psychological test. Furthermore, we discovered the influence of new variables, e.g., math-efficacy, learning approach motivation, and reliance on academies, on the mathematical achievements of students. These findings establish a foundation to utilize these relevant variables in predicting mathematical achievement.

The practical implications of this study are summarized as follows. We have identified variables that influence students' abilities and identified machine learning classification algorithms that can be applied in the mathematics education field. Previously, educational institutions, particularly academies, have relied solely on grades to assess students' abilities. However, through our findings, we have demonstrated the ability to predict students' abilities using mathematics-related psychological factors and identified psychological elements that may be lacking in students' mathematical proficiency. Ultimately, we expect that this will enable educational institutions to design effective personalized learning programs to improve students' academic performance by positively transforming their deficient psychological factors in addition to the existing grade-based management system.

7. Conclusions

In this study, we utilized the TLP items to identify their impact on students' mathematical test scores and employed machine learning techniques to classify students' mathematical skills. We believe that our research findings provide two significant insights.

First, the linear regression analysis results indicated that self-efficacy, math-efficacy, and learning approach motivation influenced mathematical achievement in Test 1. In Test 2, self-efficacy and reliance on academies affected mathematical test scores, which measured mathematical achievement. Overall, we have confirmed the influence of self-efficacy on mathematical achievement and demonstrated that the psychological test of mathematical learning can measure these achievements effectively.

Second, by applying several machine learning techniques, we achieved high performance in all performance evaluation indicators (accuracy, precision, recall, and F1-Score), and students' skills were successfully classified based on the TLP items.

These results have practical implications for both educators and psychologists seeking to understand the psychological factors that influence students' mathematical learning. In addition, the results can support the development of personalized study programs based on each student's skills and enhance their mathematical achievements.

In future research, it would be beneficial to obtain psychological test results on mathematical learning from a larger sample of students and collect mathematics scores over a more extended period compared to the data used in the current study. In terms of the TLP items employed in this study, some items had limited or no data on student responses, thereby making it challenging to analyze these items effectively. Thus, these items were excluded; however, by acquiring additional data on these psychological variables, future studies could explore their impact further. Similarly, it would be beneficial to examine the effects of additional variables, e.g., age, gender, grade, and study hours, on mathematical achievement. This expanded analysis is expected to realize more accurate predictions of students' mathematical skills and provide a more comprehensive understanding of the factors that influence student performance. Furthermore, our findings can be utilized to develop a personalized learning system that incorporates the classification of students' skills. Such a system could recommend relevant mathematics content tailored to individual students' abilities, thereby offering a promising method to improve mathematical learning outcomes.

Author Contributions: J.P.: Conceptualization, writing original draft, review and editing, data curation and analysis, methodology, visualization, project administration. S.K.: Resources, project administration. B.J.: Conceptualization, supervision, funding acquisition. All authors have read and agreed to the published version of the manuscript.

Funding: This work was supported by the Ministry of SMEs and Startups grant funded by the Korean government (No. S3246571) and the Yonsei University Research Fund (No. 2023-22-0104).

Data Availability Statement: Data for this study was collected from Able Edutech Corporation. For further assistance, please contact the author.

Conflicts of Interest: The funders had no role in the design of the study; in the collection, analyses, or interpretation of data; in the writing of the manuscript; or in the decision to publish the results.

References

1. Luan, H.; Geczy, P.; Lai, H.; Gobert, J.; Yang, S.J.H.; Ogata, H.; Baltes, J.; Guerra, R.; Li, P.; Tsai, C.C. Challenges and future directions of big data and artificial intelligence in education. *Front. Psychol.* **2020**, *11*, 580820. [CrossRef] [PubMed]
2. Hwang, G.-J.; Tu, Y.-F. Roles and research trends of artificial intelligence in mathematics education: A bibliometric mapping analysis and systematic review. *Mathematics* **2021**, *9*, 584. [CrossRef]
3. Bin Mohamed, M.Z.; Hidayat, R.; binti Suhaizi, N.N.; bin Mahmud, M.K.H.; binti Baharuddin, S.N. Artificial intelligence in mathematics education: A systematic literature review. *Int. Electron. J. Math. Educ.* **2022**, *17*, em0694. [CrossRef]
4. Çiftçi, S.K.; Yildiz, P. The Effect of Self-Confidence on Mathematics Achievement: The Metaanalysis of Trends in International Mathematics and Science Study (TIMSS). *Int. J. Instr.* **2019**, *12*, 683–694. [CrossRef]
5. Khesht-Masjedi, M.F.; Shokrgozar, S.; Abdollahi, E.; Habibi, B.; Asghari, T.; Ofoghi, R.S.; Pazhooman, S. The relationship between gender, age, anxiety, depression, and academic achievement among teenagers. *J. Fam. Med. Prim. Care* **2019**, *8*, 799–804. [CrossRef]
6. Olivier, E.; Archambault, I.; De Clercq, M.; Galand, B. Student self-efficacy, classroom engagement, and academic achievement: Comparing three theoretical frameworks. *J. Youth Adolesc.* **2019**, *48*, 326–340. [CrossRef] [PubMed]
7. Abu-Hilal, M.M. A structural model for predicting mathematics achievement: Its relation with anxiety and self-concept in mathematics. *Psychol. Rep.* **2000**, *86*, 835–847. [CrossRef] [PubMed]
8. Hayat, A.A.; Shateri, K.; Amini, M.; Shokrpour, N. Relationships between academic self-efficacy, learning-related emotions, and metacognitive learning strategies with academic performance in medical students: A structural equation model. *BMC Med. Educ.* **2020**, *20*, 76. [CrossRef]
9. Tokan, M.K.; Imakulata, M.M. The effect of motivation and learning behaviour on student achievement. *S. Afr. J. Educ.* **2019**, *39*, 1–8. [CrossRef]
10. Madigan, D.J.; Curran, T. Does burnout affect academic achievement? A meta-analysis of over 100,000 students. *Educ. Psychol. Rev.* **2021**, *33*, 387–405. [CrossRef]
11. León Hernández, A.; González Escobar, S.; Arratia López Fuentes NI, G.; Barcelata Eguiarte, B.E. Stress, self-efficacy, academic achievement and resilience in emerging adults. *Electron. J. Res. Educ. Psychol.* **2019**, *17*, 129–148.
12. Jiang, Y.; Rosenzweig, E.Q.; Gaspard, H. An expectancy-value-cost approach in predicting adolescent students' academic motivation and achievement. *Contemp. Educ. Psychol.* **2018**, *54*, 139–152. [CrossRef]
13. Romero, C.; Ventura, S.; Espejo, P.G.; Hervás, C. Data mining algorithms to classify students. In Proceedings of the First International Conference on Educational Data Mining (EDM 2008), Montreal, QC, Canada, 20–21 June 2008; pp. 8–17.
14. Kabakchieva, D. Student performance prediction by using data mining classification algorithms. *Int. J. Comput. Sci. Manag. Res.* **2012**, *1*, 686–690.
15. Xu, X.; Wang, J.; Peng, H.; Wu, R. Prediction of academic performance associated with internet usage behaviors using machine learning algorithms. *Comput. Hum. Behav.* **2019**, *98*, 166–173. [CrossRef]
16. BujangSelamat, A.; Ibrahim, R.; Krejcar, O.; Herrera-Viedma, E.; Fujita, H.; Ghani, N.A.M. Multiclass prediction model for student grade prediction using machine learning. *IEEE Access* **2021**, *9*, 95608–95621.
17. Sravani, B.; Bala, M.M. Prediction of student performance using linear regression. In Proceedings of the International Conference for Emerging Technology (INCET), Belgaum, India, 5–7 June 2020; pp. 1–5. [CrossRef]
18. Zimmermann, J.; Brodersen, K.H.; Pellet, J.-P.; August, E.; Buhmann, J.M. Predicting graduate-level performance from undergraduate achievement. In Proceedings of the 4th International Conference on Educational Data Mining, Eindhoven, The Netherlands, 6–8 July 2011; pp. 357–358.

19. Le Mai, T.; Do, P.T.; Chung, M.T.; Thoai, N. Adapting the score prediction to characteristics of undergraduate student data. In Proceedings of the International Conference on Advanced Computing and Applications (ACOMP), Nha Trang, Vietnam, 26–28 November 2019; pp. 70–77. [CrossRef]
20. Cortes, C.; Vapnik, V. Support-vector networks. *Mach. Learn.* **1995**, *20*, 273–297. [CrossRef]
21. Breiman, L. Random forests. *Mach. Learn.* **2001**, *45*, 5–32. [CrossRef]
22. Friedman, J.H. Greedy function approximation: A gradient boosting machine. *Ann. Statist.* **2001**, *29*, 1189–1232. Available online: http://www.jstor.org/stable/2699986 (accessed on 17 June 2023). [CrossRef]
23. Chen, T.; Guestrin, C. Xgboost: A scalable tree boosting system. In Proceedings of the 22nd ACM SIGKDD International Conference on Knowledge Discovery and Data Mining, San Francisco, CA, USA, 13–17 August 2016; pp. 785–794. [CrossRef]

Disclaimer/Publisher's Note: The statements, opinions and data contained in all publications are solely those of the individual author(s) and contributor(s) and not of MDPI and/or the editor(s). MDPI and/or the editor(s) disclaim responsibility for any injury to people or property resulting from any ideas, methods, instructions or products referred to in the content.

Article

A Moth–Flame Optimized Echo State Network and Triplet Feature Extractor for Epilepsy Electro-Encephalography Signals

Xue-song Tang, Luchao Jiang, Kuangrong Hao *, Tong Wang and Xiaoyan Liu

Faculty of Information Science, Donghua University, Shanghai 201620, China
* Correspondence: krhao@dhu.edu.cn

Abstract: The analysis of epilepsy electro-encephalography (EEG) signals is of great significance for the diagnosis of epilepsy, which is one of the common neurological diseases of all age groups. With the developments of machine learning, many data-driven models have achieved great performance in EEG signals classification. However, it is difficult to select appropriate hyperparameters for the models to file a specific task. In this paper, an evolutionary algorithm enhanced model is proposed, which optimizes the fixed weights of the reservoir layer of the echo state network (ESN) according to the specific task. As evaluating a feature extractor relies heavily on the classifiers, a new feature distribution evaluation function (FDEF) using the label information of EEG signals is defined as the fitness function, which is an objective way to evaluate the performance of a feature extractor that not only focuses on the degree of dispersion, but also considers the relation amongst triplets. The performance of the proposed method is verified on the Bonn University dataset with an accuracy of 98.16% and on the CHB-MIT dataset with the highest sensitivity of 96.14%. The proposed method outperforms the previous EEG methods, as it can automatically optimize the hyperparameters of ESN to adjust the structure and initial parameters for a specific classification task. Furthermore, the optimization direction by using FDEF as the fitness of MFO no longer relies on the performance of the classifier but on the relative separability amongst classes.

Keywords: epilepsy detection; moth–flame optimization; echo state network; feature extraction; EEG signals

MSC: 68W50

1. Introduction

As a chronic non-communicable brain disease, epilepsy can occur in people of any age. It is one of the most common neurological diseases with about 50 million patients, and about 5 million people are diagnosed each year around the world [1]. Electro-encephalography (EEG) is a commonly used auxiliary diagnostic method in the discovery and treatment of brain diseases [2], but there are certain limitations in traditional EEG methods. On the one hand, traditional EEG diagnosis based on visual assessments requires experienced specialists for correct judgments, which is subject to their professional experience. Further, as the frequency of using EEG equipment in outpatients and inpatients increases, it usually takes several hours or days to record the EEG data, analyze and diagnose. On the other hand, patients with epilepsy can register as completely normal when undergoing an outpatient EEG examination, because the brain of an epilepsy patient usually does not consistently trigger seizures. Recording EEG for longer periods can capture abnormal EEG signals, but it is expensive and time-consuming for both patients and doctors.

EEG signals are nonlinear and nonstationary [3]. Figure 1 displays a group of normal, inter-ictal, and seizure EEG signals collected by Bonn University that are difficult to be interpreted visually. Moreover, the inter-ictal signals, which are important for the diagnosis and treatment of patients, cannot be easily distinguished from normal signals.

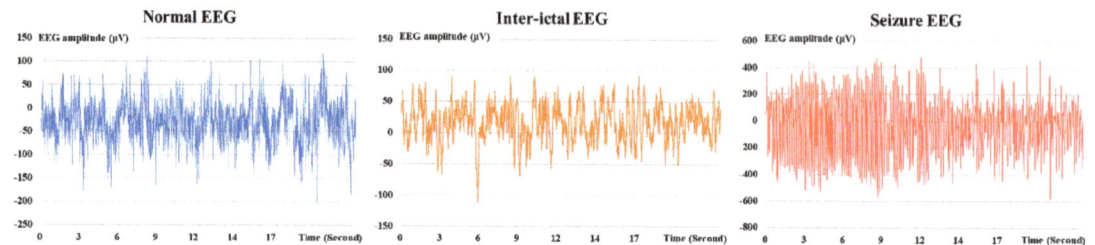

Figure 1. Samples of normal, interictal, and seizure EEG signals from the Bonn University data set.

With the development of computer technologies, a variety of algorithms have been designed with excellent results in the automatic classification of EEG signals [4]. EEG signal classification consists of two parts: feature extraction, which is the most important part, and classification. Methods based on time–frequency domain, such as the AR model [5], fast Fourier transform method [6], and Hilbert Huang method [7], have been applied to extract the features of EEG signals with trivial information loss. However, these methods are generally based on linear models, so the non-linear characteristics of EEG signals that are essential in EEG signals processing can be ignored.

In recent years, machine learning and deep learning models have been applied to capture the features of EEG signals. Zhou et al. [8] used CNN to extract features for EEG signals and applied the model to a seizure detection task. Although CNN can effectively focus on local features, it cannot directly capture the long-term relationships in the EEG signals. To solve this problem, Mishra et al. [9] combined CNN and RNN models to solve the sleep stage classification problem based on the EEG signals. RNN contains connections between nodes to form a directed graph sequence. This structure allows RNN to naturally handle the time dynamic behavior of time series. However, it also causes the problem of gradient vanishing [10], which makes the training of RNN very difficult and time-consuming. Sun et al. [11] proposed an ESN feature extractor model, which is an unsupervised self-encoding model based on an ESN. The model can extract EEG signal features and achieves good performance in the classification of the epileptic EEG signals. ESN is a special network model that provides a new structure of the recurrent neural network and a new criterion of supervised training [12]. Compared to RNN, most parameters of ESN are randomly generated, except for the readout layer that needs training, so the model is very fast and does not suffer from the problem of gradient vanishing. ESN can achieve excellent performance on a variety of chaotic time series prediction tasks and complex industrial time series problems. However, the performance of ESN largely depends on the choice of hyperparameters that requires massive experimental cost for achieving a good configuration [13].

Evolutionary algorithms, which are inspired by biological evolution, are effective in optimizing the hyperparameters of the model. Wang et al. [14] chose the genetic algorithm (GA) to optimize the hyperparameters of ESN and applied ESN to ECG signal prediction tasks, which achieves better results compared to the original ESN model. Moth–flame optimization (MFO) [15] is an extended version of the swarm intelligence algorithm, which simulates the special navigation method of moths flying around flames and provides a new heuristic search paradigm in the optimization field, called spiral search. The new search paradigm enables the MFO algorithm to search near the candidate optimal solutions. Mei et al. [16] applied MFO in ORPD problems to obtain the best combination of control variables. The MFO algorithm has good performances in various fields and the advantages of simplicity and rapid searching over other optimization algorithms [17]. In this paper, we propose a new model named MFO-ESN that applies the MFO algorithm to automatically search for better hyperparameters of an ESN feature extractor.

An essential problem of combining MFO and ESN is to define the fitness function, which can evaluate the performance of the feature extractors and determine the optimization direction. For classification tasks, the most intuitive way is to use the accuracy of a classifier. However, the method relies significantly on the choice of classifiers, which is not objective and may lead to overfitting problems. The basic idea behind a good feature extraction for classification tasks is to find a way to map the raw data onto a feature space, which draws the feature vectors from the same class closer than those from the different ones. We propose a new feature distribution evaluation function to fit the MFO-ESN, named FDEF. FDEF is based on the idea of triplet loss [18] and can evaluate the performance of a feature extractor without using a specific classifier.

Triplet loss is a metric that concerns the relation of the triplet. For classification tasks, a triplet consists of the observed sample: the corresponding positive sample whose class is the same as the observed sample, and the corresponding negative sample whose class is different from the observed sample. Triplet loss is a detailed and objective way to judge how easy the sample can be classified, which not only focuses on the degree of dispersion, but also considers the relation amongst triplets.

The main contributions of this work can be summarized as follows:

(1) A novel feature extraction called moth–flame optimized echo state network (MFO-ESN) is developed, which uses MFO to optimize the hyperparameters of ESN for fitting the specific tasks.
(2) A new function based on the triplet is introduced to evaluate the distribution of features extracted by MFO-ESN without relying on specific classifiers.
(3) MFO-ESN is verified on the real-world single-channel EEG signals classification task with an accuracy of 98.16%. The results also show that MFO-ESN with FDEF can promote the performances of many classifiers.
(4) We also conduct experiments on the multi-channel EEG signals classification task with the highest specificity of both the patient specific and the cross-patient task. The cross-patient task simulates the real diagnosis situation with high specificity, proving the strong generalization ability of MFO-ESN.

The remainder of this paper is organized as follows. In Section 2, a review of related works is given, including the ESN algorithm and the MFO algorithm. In Section 3, a new feature evaluation function (FDEF) fitting MFO-ESN is presented. A detailed description of the feature extractor combining ESN and MFO named MFO-ESN is also proposed. The experiment process and results of the single-channel and multi-channel epilepsy EEG signals classification task are described in Sections 4 and 5, respectively. In Section 6, we conclude this paper and propose a future study direction.

2. Related Works

2.1. Echo State Network (ESN)

The echo state network (ESN) is a particular RNN and a typical representative of reservoir computing (RC) [12]. The canonical ESN model is a neural network with a three-layer structure, including an input layer, a reservoir layer, and an output layer. ESN simulates the connection of neurons in the cerebral cortex and constructs a huge and sparse neuron reservoir layer. The neurons in the reservoir layer are randomly initialized and do not need training. The reservoir layer that imitates the sparsely connected structure of brain neurons replaces the hidden layer of the traditional feedforward neural networks for the function of information processing and storage [19]. Therefore, the reservoir layer is the most important part of a canonical echo state network, whose architecture is shown in Figure 2.

Focusing on the architecture details of the canonical ESN, we denote the number of neurons for the input layer, reservoir layer, and output layer as K, P, and L, respectively. The input unit, reservoir state, and output unit at time t can be represented as follows:

$$u(t) = (u_1(t), \ldots, u_K(t))^T \tag{1}$$

$$x(t) = (x_1(t), \ldots, x_M(t))^T \qquad (2)$$

$$y(t) = (y_1(t), \ldots, y_L(t))^T \qquad (3)$$

The weights from the input layer to the reservoir layer amongst the internal neurons in the reservoir layer, and from the reservoir layer to the output layer, are denoted as W_{in}, W_{res} and W_{out}, respectively.

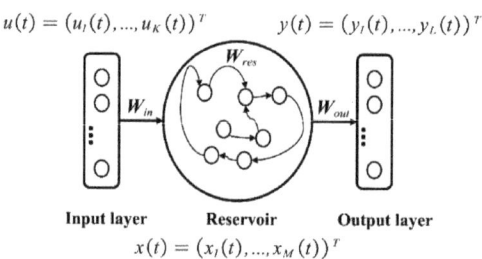

Figure 2. The ESN architecture.

The activation states of the reservoir neurons $x(t+1)$ and the output layer $y(t+1)$ at time $t+1$ can be updated through the following equations [20]:

$$x(t+1) = f(W_{in}u(t+1) + W_{res}x(t)) \qquad (4)$$

$$y(t+1) = W_{out}x(t+1) \qquad (5)$$

where f presents the activation function of the neurons in the reservoir layer. We use *tanh* function as the activation function.

In the canonical ESN model, W_{in} and W_{res} are initialized randomly and fixed, and the readout matrix W_{out} is trained by using the certain supervised learning algorithm [19]. This is called "free training", and enables the ESN model to be a fast-training model. The purpose of the training process is to minimize the error between the desired output ($y_{desired}$) and the real output of the ESN model ($y(t)$) [21].

Furthermore, we apply the ridge regression algorithm to calculate the weights of the readout matrix W_{out} as follows [22]:

$$W_{out} = \left(X^T X + \lambda^2 I\right)^{-1} X^T y_{desired} \qquad (6)$$

where $X = (x(t), u(t))^T$, I is the identity matrix, and $\lambda > 0$ is a regularization coefficient.

The hyperparameters of ESN include the number of neurons in the reserve pool (M), the spectral radius (SR), the connection density (CD), and the input scaling coefficient (IS). ESN has the advantage in training because most parameters of ESN are "free-training". ESN is a simple and effective model but suffers from the problem that the effectiveness of ESN relies heavily on the selection of hyperparameters [23]. Therefore, hyperparameter configuration is an urgent problem to be solved. In the following, we will briefly introduce these hyperparameters and explain their importance.

(1) *The number of neurons in the reservoir layer* (P): P is the most important hyperparameter, which determines the complexity of ESN and directly affects its performance in various tasks. Generally, increasing P can increase the memory capacity of ESN [24] that is of significance to handling complex tasks. However, excessively increasing P will lead to overfitting.

(2) *Spectral radius* (SR): SR is the maximum achievable value of the characteristic value of the reservoir matrix W_{res}. To guarantee the echo state principle (ESP) of ESN, the value of SR should be less than 1 [25].

(3) *Connection density (CD)*: CD indicates the number of neurons in the reservoir layer that participate in random connections. The selection range of CD is usually between 0.01 and 0.2 [26]. In addition, a range of interesting initial structures is proposed to select proper CD, such as distance-based [13], small-world [27], or scale-free [28,29].
(4) *Input scaling coefficient (IS)*: It is important to choose an appropriate IS that can scale the input data to a proper range, so that the neurons of ESN can be well activated and fully take advantage of the non-linearity of the activation function [30].

2.2. Moth–Flame Optimization (MFO)

Moth–flame optimization (MFO) is an extension of the swarm intelligence algorithm [15]. It imitates the behavior of a moth flying spirally around the flame and, finally, reaching the flame.

MFO assumes that both moths and flames are candidate solutions to the problem. The sets of moths and flames are denoted as matrices $M = (N, \dim)$ and $F = (N, \dim)$, respectively, where N is the max numbers of moths and flames, and dim is the dimension of the solution. Moths represent real searching individuals in the solution space searching around the flame in a spiral motion. Flames denote the historical optimal solution reached by the moths spiraling around the closest flame. The positions of the individual moths and flames can be updated while the moths are flying [15] and have the following characteristics:

(1) The moths can only fly within a limited search range.
(2) The initialized positions of the moths are the starting points of the spiral flight.
(3) The endpoints of the spiral flight are the positions of the flames.
(4) The positions of the flames are adjusted during the process of searching.

The position of each moth can be updated by Equation (7), which simulates the flight mode of the moth.

$$M_i = D_i \cdot e^{bt} \cdot \cos(2\pi t) + F_j \tag{7}$$

where M_i denotes the ith moth, and F_j denotes the jth flame that is the closest flame to M_i. D_i is the Euclidean distance between M_i and F_j, which denotes the closest distance amongst M_i and flames. The shape of the spiral flight is controlled by the parameter b that is generally set to 1. The coefficient t is used to control the distance between the moth and the flame during the spiral flight and can be calculated by Equation (8).

$$t = \left(-\frac{l+L}{L} - 1\right) \times rand + 1 \tag{8}$$

where l is the current iterations and L is the maximum iterations. $rand$ is a uniformly distributed random number. For a certain iteration, the coefficient t calculated by Equation (8) is used to update the positions of all moths using Equation (7).

Equation (9) is used to decrease the number of flames ($flame_{no}$) during each iteration. L and l denote the maximum iterations and the current iterations, separately. N demotes the max number of flames.

With the number of flames decreasing in a linear way, the local search capacity of the moths is improved.

$$flame_{no} = round\left(N - l \times \frac{N-1}{L}\right) \tag{9}$$

3. Methodology

The previous introduction shows that the reservoir layer constructed by random initialization is the most important part of ESN. However, many researchers have proposed various methods to initialize ESN. For example, Strauss et al. [31] presented the design strategy of ESN, such as ensuring the echo state property (ESP) and reducing the influence of noise during the training process. Bianchi et al. [32] studied the dynamic characteristics of ESN through a recursive analysis, which contributes to further understanding and constructing the optimal reservoir layer. However, it is difficult to consider multiple parameters of a reservoir layer simultaneously, such as *M*, *SR*, *CD*, and *IS*. Therefore, tuning the hyperparameters is usually time-consuming and difficult, particularly for complex tasks.

To improve the above shortcomings, moth–flame optimization is used to select the hyperparameters of ESN, named MFO-ESN. Meanwhile, a novel evaluation function (FDEF), which can evaluate the performance of the feature extractor in a detailed and more objective way, is proposed as the fitness function of MFO-ESN.

3.1. Feature Distribution Evaluation Function (FDEF)

Features are the most important factor in machine learning projects where learning is easy if many independent features can be acquired and each correlate well with the class [33]. The quality of the features extracted from the original EEG signal has a great impact on the classification of the subsequent classifier. An excellent feature extractor should be able to produce obvious differences in the extracted features from different classes of EEG signals in distribution. For the extracted features of the same class, the similarities will be retained, while the differences that we are not concerned about will be ignored. Therefore, we propose a novel feature distribution evaluation function (FDEF), which is calculated as Equation (10).

$$\text{FDEF} = \sum \frac{D(I_i^o, I_i^p)}{D(I_i^o, I_i^n)}$$

$$\text{s.t.} \begin{cases} D(I_i^o, I_i^p) < D(I_i^o, I_i^n) \\ I_i^o \in I \end{cases} \quad (10)$$

where I is the feature set containing all features extracted from raw data, while I_i^o is the feature point we observed.

For every observed feature point I_i^o, we construct a triplet $I_i = <I_i^o, I_i^p, I_i^n>$, including the positive point I_i^p and the negative point I_i^n. I_i^p is the center of the feature points whose class is the same as I_i^o, and I_i^n is the center of the feature points whose class is different from I_i^o. $D(I_i^o, I_i^p)$ and $D(I_i^o, I_i^n)$ denote the distance amongst I_i^o, I_i^p, and I_i^n, as measured by the L_2-norm, respectively.

$D(I_i^o, I_i^p)$ is the positive distance that is the smaller the better, and $D(I_i^o, I_i^n)$ is the negative distance that should be larger than $D(I_i^o, I_i^p)$. FDEF can evaluate the ratio between positive distance and negative distance, which is different from another direct metric using subtraction, such as Equation (11):

$$\text{Loss}(I^o, I^p, I^n) = \sum \left(D(I_i^o, I_i^p) - D(I_i^o, I_i^n) + m \right)_+ \quad (11)$$

where *m* is a margin that is enforced between a positive pair and a negative pair. The purpose of minimizing Equation (11) is to make the distance between the positive pair smaller than the distance between the negative pairs by more than *m*.

Equation (11) is a direct way to describe the difference between positive distance and negative distance. It has been applied in FaceNet [18] as a loss function that achieved state-of-the-art performances in the person re-ID tasks. However, compared to Equation (11), Equation (10) has two advantages:

(1) FDEF is robust to the mean value of features. The mean values of the features extracted through different ESN feature extractors are different. Further, features with a bigger mean value always obtain a better result using Equation (11) without considering the distribution of features.

(2) FDEF is not sensitive to the dimension of the feature. The number of neurons in the reservoir layer (P) is a key parameter that needs to be adjusted. The feature dimension is the same as P, which means the feature dimension changes during the training

process of MFO-ESN. Equation (11) is sensitive to the varying feature dimensions that force the model to reduce P.

Therefore, compared to Equation (11), FDEF using the ratio description pays more attention to the distribution state of the aggregation and dispersion of the samples in the sample space, rather than the specific distance value and the difference in feature dimensions.

For Equation (10), the positive distance should be smaller than the negative distance, which promises that the observed feature point is closer to the center of the corresponding class—in other words, it is more centralized. Therefore, penalty items are added to those points that do not meet the constraint. The new form of FDEF is shown in the following:

$$\text{FDEF} = \sum \left(\frac{D(I_i^o, I_i^p)}{D(I_i^o, I_i^n)} + \alpha \cdot \text{Relu}\left(\frac{D(I_i^o, I_i^p)}{D(I_i^o, I_i^n)} - 1 \right) \right) \quad (12)$$

where $\alpha > 0$ is the punishment coefficient and $\text{Relu}(x)$ is the rectified linear unit. The parameter α is similar to the parameter m in Equation (11) that needs to be modified carefully to ensure the convergence of the model.

Regarding multiple classes, we follow the strictest method, which is to choose the smallest negative distance as the negative distance in the FDEF formula. This choice forces the spacing between classes to be more obvious. Of course, since all calculations are based on the L2 normalization, when the number of classes or points become larger, the issue of convergence should be considered.

3.2. Moth–Flame Optimized ESN

As mentioned above, most parameters of ESN are initialized randomly and fixed, and the initialization of ESN largely depends on the selection of the hyperparameters. The selection and adjustment of hyperparameters are crucial to the ESN model. Unfortunately, because the relations amongst these hyperparameters of ESN are not clear, choosing appropriate hyperparameters for the specific tasks is difficult and usually not sufficient. In response to this situation, the MFO-ESN model is proposed, and its structure is shown in Figure 3. In MFO-ESN, MFO is used to optimize the hyperparameters of ESN, so that the ESN feature extractor can better extract the features of the input EEG signal fitting EEG classification tasks.

The number of neurons in the reservoir layer (P), spectral radius (SR), connection density (CD), and input scaling coefficient (IS) are selected as the hyperparameters to be adjusted. Therefore, we set the dimension of moth and flame as 4 to represent these hyperparameters.

The features of the EEG signals are extracted using an ESN feature extractor [9] whose architecture is the same as ESN. The ESN feature extractor is an unsupervised model that applies the idea of the autoencoder to extract features from the EEG signals. It utilizes a readout matrix W_{out} as the hidden layer, as well as the extracted feature. MFO-ESN uses the label information to optimize the effectiveness of ESN by selecting appropriate hyperparameters. Different from the usual optimization ways, MFO-ESN does not use the classification accuracy of the classification task that may be influenced by classifiers as a fitness function; rather, it uses FDEF to evaluate the distribution of features extracted by ESN.

To evaluate the fitness of the moth, the corresponding hyperparameters are used to initialize ESN for extracting features from the raw EEG signals. Then, the fitness is calculated according to Equation (12). With the positions of moths updated according to Equation (7), their fitness changes. Flames denote the historical optimal solution reached by the moths that spiral around the closest flame.

Considering the calculation cost and the suggestion of initializing the ESN model in [31], P is set within the range of [5, 100], SR is within the range of [0.1, 1], CD is within the range of [0.1, 1], and IS is within the range of [0.1, 5].

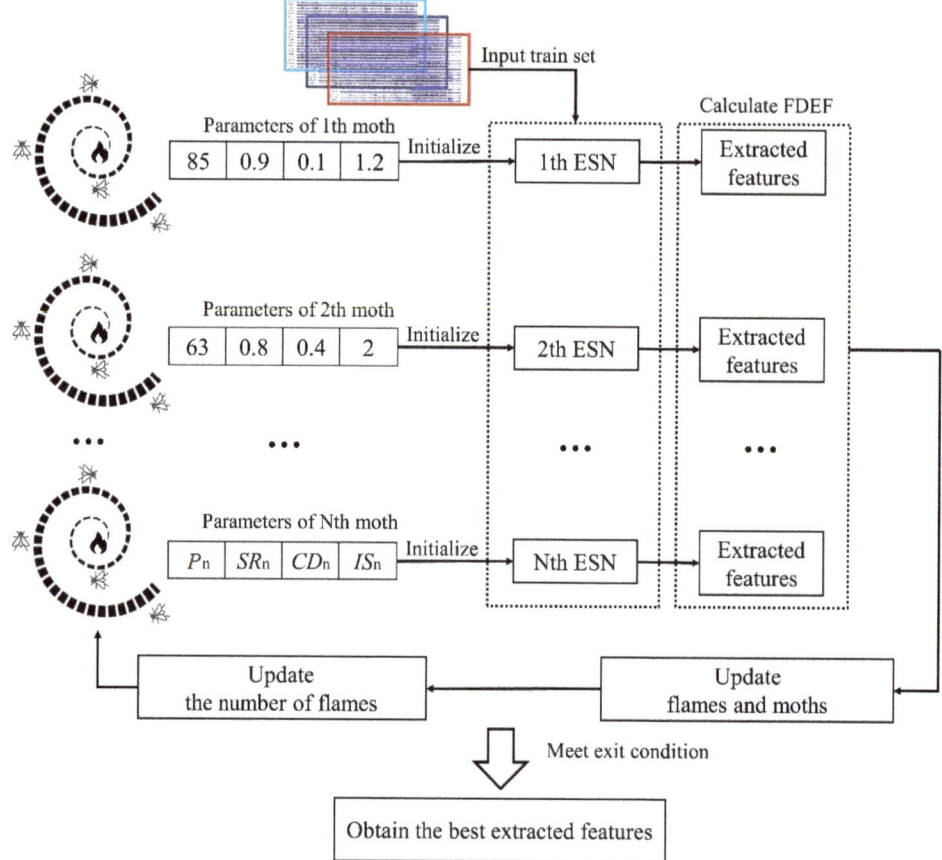

Figure 3. The structure of MFO-ESN.

MFO requires multiple moths to search around multiple flames. Since the search path of the moth is spiral, it converges slowly in the latter part of the iteration, while the local search capability decreases. Therefore, the number of moths cannot be too small. We set 20 as the population of moths as well as flames and set the maximum iterations as 100. The running process of the MFO-ESN algorithm is shown in Algorithm 1.

Algorithm 1 MFO-ESN

Input: the population number (N), the maximum times of iteration (T)
Output: the best hyperparameters of ESN
Steps:
(a) Set the population number and maximum number of iterations.
(b) Initialize the moth population.
(c) Initialize the ESN using hyperparameters represented by moths.
(d) Extract features using initialized ESN.
(e) Calculate fitness values of moths according to Equation (12) and sort fitness values.
(f) Update the moth position based on Equation (7).
(g) Update the flame position to determine the current optimal solution.
(h) Determine the number of moths and flames based on Equation (9).
(i) Repeat step (c) to step (h) until the constraint is met.
(j) The process ends.

4. Experiments on the Bonn University EEG Data Set

4.1. A Brief Description of the Data Set

We used the epileptic seizure events data from the Bonn University EEG data set that were provided by Andrzejak et al. in 2001 [34]. The complete data set consists of five subsets denoted from A to E, and each subset contains 100 single-channel EEG signals of 23.6-s duration (4097 time steps). These EEG signals are cut and selected from continuous multi-channel EEG records and after artificial artifact removal that mainly removes myoelectric artifacts and ocular artifacts. The electrode position adopts the international 10–20 system. The sampling frequency is 173.61 Hz and the filter bandwidth is 0.53–40 Hz (12 db/oct). Subsets A and B are taken from five healthy volunteers with eyes open and closed separately. Subsets C, D, and E are recorded from patients with epilepsy. Subsets C and D store the EEG signals during seizure-free intervals. The difference in C and D lies in the zone in which they are recorded. Set D is recorded within the epileptogenic zone, while set C is from the hippocampal formation of the opposite part of the brain. Each EEG segment in set E contains data related to at least one seizure activity.

4.2. Feature Extraction of Epileptic Seizure EEG Signals

To evaluate the performance of the MFO-ESN feature extraction model and compare this study with other similar studies, this paper divides the five groups of EEG signals into three classes (AB/CD/E), representing normal EEG signals, EEG signals from patients without seizures, and EEG signals from patients with epilepsy seizures.

We separated the training set and testing set using a random division whose division ratio is 8:2, and the MFO-ESN was trained with the training set. During each iteration of MFO-ESN, we recorded the fitness function FDEF and hyperparameters of the best extractor in the training set. Figure 4 shows the change of FDEF as the number of iterations increases.

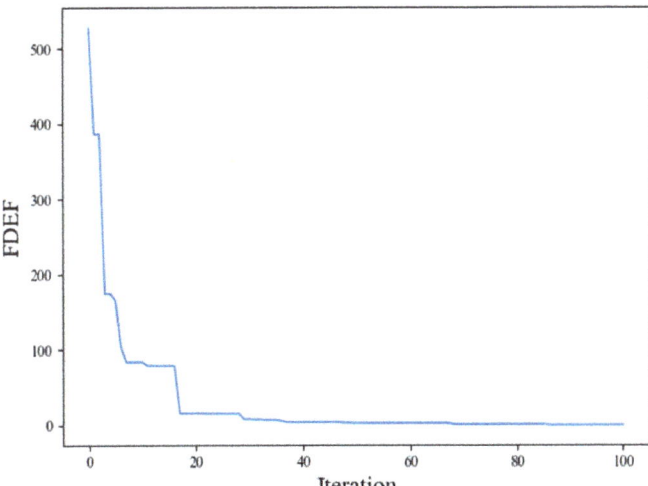

Figure 4. FDEF after 100 iterations by MFO-ESN.

To visualize the distribution of the extracted features, two dimensions of the extracted features are shown in Figure 5. It can be observed that the distribution of the three classes of the extracted features is regional. The first dimension of the class of A/B and the class of C/D is close because the EEG of two classes is not in the epileptic period. The second dimension is obviously different, which reflects the difference of two classes, i.e., the class of A/B is from healthy people, while the class of C/D is the inter-ictal EEG.

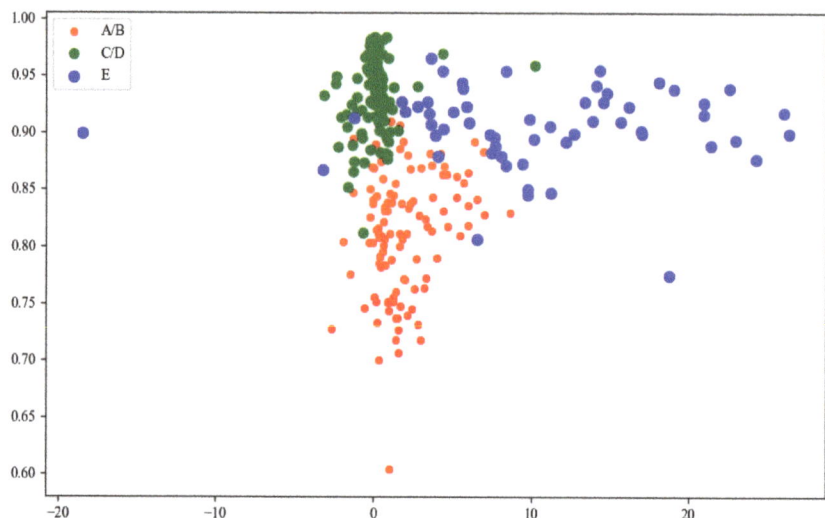

Figure 5. The distribution of extracted features in two dimensions.

4.3. Epileptic EEG Signal Classification

To compare the performance of MFO-ESN with other works, we applied the MFO-ESN combined with SVM to solve the epileptic classification task. SVM is a type of supervised learning method whose target is to find the maximum-margin hyperplane of the learning samples. The performance of SVM is widely verified by various applications [35,36]. The division of the data set is the same as in Section 4.2. In detail, we repeated the experiment 20 times and took the average value as the results for the MFO-ESN combining SVM.

Table 1 shows the results achieved by the MFO-ESN combining SVM and that of other methods. It is reasonable that the performance of MFO-ESN is better than the ESN feature extractor because the MFO-ESN can optimize the hyperparameters of the ESN feature extractor. Therefore, MFO-ESN combined with SVM obtained the highest accuracy of 98.16%. Moreover, to prove the effectiveness of FDEF, MFO-ESN without FDEF is proposed as the ablation experiment that uses the accuracy of SVM in the data set as the fitness function of MFO. However, MFO-ESN without FDEF achieves an accuracy of 93.19%, which is lower than the ESN feature extractor because of the problem of overfitting. As the direction of optimization is not to promote the accuracy for a specific classifier in the training set but to maximize the relative separability between classes, the MFO-ESN can achieve a more robust extractor. The ablation study shows that the FDEF plays an essential role in the MFO-ESN, which is also the main contribution of this research.

Table 1. Comparison of MFO-ESN + SVM with other methods.

Methods	Feature Extractor	Classifier	Accuracy
Guler et al. (2005) [37]	Lyapunov Exponents + RNN	Logistic regression	0.9697
Guo et al. (2011) [38]	Genetic Programming	KNN	0.9350
Shoeibi et al. (2018) [39]	CNN	Logistic regression	0.8870
Tuncer et al. (2019) [40]	LSP + NCA	SVM	0.9650
Raghu et al. (2019) [41]	Matrix Determinant	MLP	0.9652
Sema et al. (2020) [42]	5 BPFs + TFEBE	SVM	0.9488
this paper	ESN feature extractor	SVM	0.9592
this paper	MFO-ESN without FDEF	SVM	0.9319
this paper	MFO-ESN	SVM	**0.9816**

We aimed to evaluate the effectiveness of the features extracted by the MFO-ESN with other classifiers in the epilepsy classification task. We trained a variety of different classifiers using the training set data and evaluated them in the testing set. We compared the results with the original models and display the results in Table 2. It can be seen from the results that the proposed method can also outperform most of the previous research. It can be observed that compared with the original feature extraction models, the MFO-ESN feature extraction improves the classification accuracy of the classifier to varying degrees, which proves the effectiveness of MFO-ESN.

Table 2. The results of different classifiers using MFO-ESN.

Methods	Feature Extractors	Classifier	Accuracy
Guler et al. (2005) [37]	Lyapunov Exponents + RNN	Logistic	0.9697
this paper	MFO-ESN	regression	**0.9713**
Guo et al. (2011) [38]	Genetic Programming	KNN	0.9350
this paper	MFO-ESN		**0.9760**
Raghu et al. (2019) [41]	Matrix Determinant	MLP	0.9652
this paper	MFO-ESN		**0.9793**
Shoeibi et al. (2018) [39]	CNN	Logistic	0.8870
this paper	MFO-ESN	regression	**0.9426**
this paper	ESN feature extractor	SVM	0.9392
this paper	MFO-ESN		**0.9816**

5. Experiments on the CHB-MIT EEG Data Set

ESN can be effectively used to process multi-channel time series data, while all the EEG signals in the Bonn University data set are in single-channel form. To demonstrate that MFO-ESN is also suitable for multi-channel EEG tasks and to evaluate the performance of MFO-ESN with SVM in a further step, we conducted experiments on epilepsy classification by using the CHB-MIT EEG dataset.

5.1. A Brief Description of the Data Set

This dataset collected by Boston Children's Hospital (CHB) and the Massachusetts Institute of Technology (MIT) consists of 916 h of continuous scalp EEG recordings grouped into 24 cases. This dataset is available to download online [43] and is described in detail in [44]. The EEG signals of each case recorded in the international 10–20 electrode system, with a sampling rate of 256 Hz, are saved in several EDF format files, and most of them contain 23 channels (24 or 26 channels in a few cases). Most files contain exactly one hour of EEG signals, while some files belonging to case 10 are two hours long, and those belonging to cases 4, case 6, case 7, case 9, and case 23 are four hours long.

A total of 198 seizures are manually annotated by medical specialists (pointing out the start time and end time) in 916 h. There are 45 s of seizure activity recordings on average that are too small compared to the normal EEG signals. To increase the sample number of seizure class and balance the data set, the data used in the experiments are converted into a series of segments using a sliding window whose size is 5 s, and every segment contains 23 channels as case 1. Segments belonging to a normal class do not include seizure EEG signals annotated by the experts; meanwhile, segments belonging to a seizure class do not include normal EEG signals. Figure 6 shows a period of EEG signals of case 5 and, according to the doctor's annotations, the seizure begins in 2348 seconds and ends in 2465 seconds. The five-seconds-long window slides on the EEG signals without overlapping. In more detail, for a 117-seconds-long seizure process, we can obtain 23 segments of 5 seconds in length.

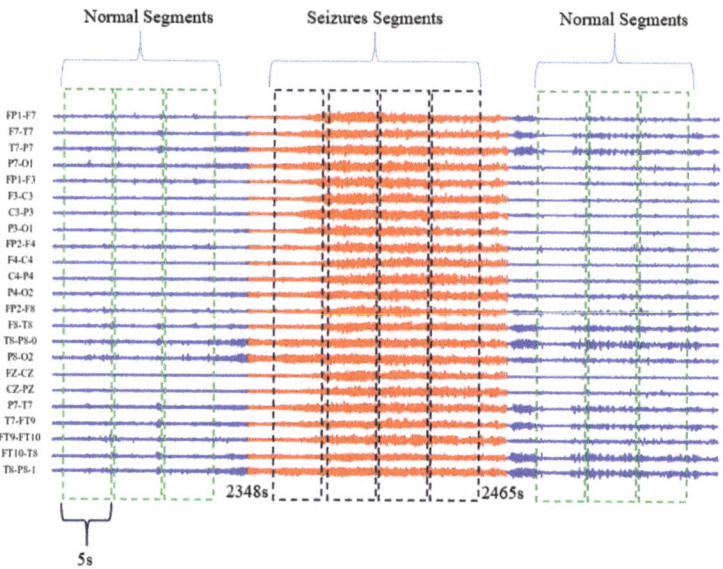

Figure 6. The division of the CHB-MIT data set.

This experiment consists of two parts: patient-specific and cross-patient. Patient specific denotes that the training set and testing set are both from the same case. We randomly chose a 20% segment of the seizure class; we chose the same number of segments from the seizure class for training and the rest of the segments for testing. Cross-patient denotes that the data from different cases are used to train and test. In more detail, the data from case 1, whose EEG signals are collected from an 11-year-old female, and case 2 from an 11-year-old male, are not involved in training but are only used for testing. The data from the other 22 cases are divided into the training set and the testing set. This setting, where case 1 and case 2 do not participate in training, can better simulate epilepsy diagnosis where the data from new patients cannot be trained.

5.2. Results and Discussion of the Multi-Channel Classification

To better evaluate the performance of the model and compare it to other works, three statistical indicators are used for evaluation:

$$Sensitivity = \frac{TP}{TP + FN} \tag{13}$$

$$Specificity = \frac{TN}{TN + FP} \tag{14}$$

$$Accuracy = \frac{TP + TN}{TP + TN + FP + FN} \tag{15}$$

where TP, TN, FN, and TP are shown in Table 3.

Table 3. Confusion matrix.

		Predict Class	
		Seizure Class	Normal Class
Actual class	Seizure class	TP	FN
	Normal class	FP	TN

The quantity of the seizure class is far lower than the normal class, which heavily affects the accuracy. Therefore, of greater concern to us is the sensitivity, which evaluates how many seizure segments are classified correctly, and the specificity, which represents the ability of the model to accurately classify normal segments.

Table 4 shows the results of the patient-specific and cross-patient experiments. The patient-specific experiment can be considered as a private custom system where the training set and testing set are from the same case. The overall performance achieves a specificity of 92.56%, a sensitivity of 96.79%, and an accuracy of 92.75%. Out of all cases, case 7 obtains the highest accuracy of 99.97%, with a specificity of 100% and a sensitivity of 99.96%. As we can see, the accuracy is much closer to the specificity because the number of normal segments in the testing set is far greater than seizure segments. For an epilepsy diagnosis, sensitivity is more important than either accuracy or specificity, as high sensitivity can ensure that any suspicious patients will be further judged by the doctor in time.

Table 4. Results of patient-specific and cross-patient experiments.

Case	Patient-Specific				Cross-Patient			
	Sen. (%)	Spec. (%)	Acc. (%)	F1 (%)	Sen. (%)	Spec. (%)	Acc. (%)	F1 (%)
1	95.76	97.05	97.09	97.07	94.26	93.64	95.36	94.49
2	99.46	100.00	99.51	99.75	99.03	97.54	98.65	98.09
3	100.00	84.28	84.63	84.45	100.00	81.22	82.39	81.80
4	94.52	97.51	98.06	97.78	94.74	95.73	97.19	96.45
5	98.36	87.65	88.48	88.06	97.12	87.99	88.46	88.22
6	100.00	83.26	83.64	83.45	97.81	82.91	83.01	82.96
7	99.96	100.00	99.97	99.98	98.73	99.09	99.52	99.30
8	96.25	83.44	83.52	83.48	93.59	81.98	82.86	82.42
9	94.71	75.53	75.59	75.56	94.56	73.04	74.21	73.62
10	93.45	100.00	99.32	99.66	94.36	99.43	99.52	99.47
11	96.25	100.00	99.45	99.72	94.69	99.88	99.01	98.94
12	99.46	81.53	81.77	81.65	96.68	78.74	79.33	79.03
13	97.72	99.10	98.16	98.63	95.30	98.23	98.29	98.26
14	99.75	89.49	89.64	89.56	100.00	87.19	88.03	87.61
15	97.54	88.13	88.43	88.28	93.69	85.22	86.83	86.02
16	96.35	98.69	99.52	99.10	96.35	97.54	99.46	98.49
17	90.13	93.24	93.63	93.43	90.13	93.91	95.42	94.66
18	98.96	86.36	86.37	86.36	95.29	86.51	87.07	86.79
19	100.00	99.46	99.61	99.53	96.24	98.54	98.16	98.35
20	95.80	98.36	99.10	98.73	96.72	96.76	98.15	97.45
21	98.05	88.83	88.86	88.84	96.81	86.69	87.25	86.97
22	96.38	99.58	99.84	99.71	100.00	98.46	99.41	98.93
23	90.25	94.66	94.67	94.66	97.16	91.59	92.21	91.90
24	93.83	95.30	95.98	95.64	94.00	93.67	95.06	94.36
Ave.	96.79	92.56	92.75	92.63	96.14	91.02	91.92	91.44

Sen. = sensitivity, Spec. = specificity, Acc. = accuracy.

Compared to the patient-specific experiment, the cross-patient experiment achieves an average specificity of 91.02%, a sensitivity of 96.14%, and an accuracy of 91.92%. With the increase in the training segments and test samples, the performance of the model is not significantly different from the patient-specific experiment. More importantly, the performance of case 1 and case 2, which have not been trained before, is still good enough. The results prove that our model not only performs well on existing patient data, but also on other unseen patients.

As shown in Table 5, we compared the studies that use the CHB-MIT data set. Most of these studies use complex deep models such as CNNs, RNNs, and their variants. Li et al. [45] obtained the highest accuracy of 95.96% and highest sensitivity of 96.05% for the patient-specific experiment. Chen et al. [46] obtained the highest accuracy of 92.30% and highest sensitivity of 92.89% for the cross-patient experiment. This is probably because ESN is a simple fast-training model whose ability to handle complex tasks is inferior to complex deep learning models. However, we achieved the highest sensitivity—which is more significant for diagnosis—of 96.79% in the patient-specific and 96.14% in cross-patient experiments. This may be one reason why minimizing FDEF can be regarded as a new way to maximize the difference between classes, so that our model can more effectively detect seizure segments.

Table 5. Comparisons of results between MFO-ESN + SVM and other methods.

Methods	Detector Type	Sen. (%)	Spec. (%)	Acc. (%)	F1 (%)
MIDS + CNN [47]	Patient-specific	74.08	92.46	83.27	87.62
Data argument + CNN [47]	Patient-specific	72.11	95.89	84.00	89.55
LMD + Bi-LSTM [48]	Patient-specific	93.61	91.85	92.66	92.25
CE-stSENet [45]	Patient-specific	92.41	**96.05**	**95.96**	**96.00**
KNN [49]	Cross-patient	88.00	88.00	88.00	88.00
Dyadic WT + SVM [46]	Cross-patient	91.71	**92.89**	**92.30**	**92.59**
MFO-ESN + SVM	Patient-specific	**96.79**	92.56	92.75	92.65
MFO-ESN + SVM	Cross-patient	**96.14**	91.02	91.92	91.47

6. Conclusions

In this paper, the proposed MFO-ESN model uses MFO to optimize the hyperparameters of ESN. Further, a new feature distribution evaluation function, FDEF, is proposed as the fitness function of MFO-ESN by using the label information of the EEG signals. Without using specific classifiers, MFO-ESN can extract more suitable features for the classification tasks. Combined with the SVM model, the effectiveness of the extracted features is verified on the Bonn EEG multi-classification data set and obtains an average accuracy of 98.16%. It is also found that the features extracted by the MFO-ESN model improve the performance of multiple classifiers, which means that MFO-ESN is an effective preprocessing method for EEG signal classification tasks. Furthermore, we apply MFO-ESN with SVM in the multi-channel EEG signals classification task of CHB-MIT and obtain the highest sensitivity of 96.79% in patient-specific and 96.14% in cross-patient experiments with good specificity and accuracy.

Apart from its higher performance, MFO-ESN with FDEF has two additional advantages compared with the previous EEG feature extraction methods: (1) it can automatically optimize the hyperparameters of ESN to adjust the architecture and initial parameters for the specific classification task; (2) using FDEF as the fitness of MFO decouples the optimization of the feature extractor from the classifier, which means the optimization direction no longer relies on the performance of the classifier but on the relative separability amongst classes. These advantages mean that the proposed MFO-ESN model can achieve efficient feature extraction and demonstrate that it has a better generalization ability.

In the future, this method can be further studied with respect to the following considerations. From the perspective of practical applications, the efficiency of MFO-ESN can be further evaluated on other EEG signal classification tasks. Given that the hyperparameters of ESN are searched in the set parameter space, how to improve the efficiency of the search and stop functions in the proper time are also key problems. In the theoretical direction, we can further improve the current ESN method. For example, the relationships amongst channels can be well described by the positioned EEG electrodes where epileptic seizures in different brain regions have different manifestations and treatments. By designing the structure of ESN to combine both the spatial information represented by the channels and the temporal information existing in the EEG time series, a better feature extraction result is promising.

Author Contributions: Methodology, X.-s.T.; Investigation, L.J.; Data curation, X.L.; Supervision, K.H. and T.W. All authors have read and agreed to the published version of the manuscript.

Funding: This work was supported in part by the Fundamental Research Funds for the Central Universities (2232021D-37), the National Natural Science Foundation of China (nos. 61806051, 62176052), and the Natural Science Foundation of Shanghai (21ZR1401700, 20ZR1400400).

Data Availability Statement: The data can be acquired via emails of the first author and corresponding author.

Conflicts of Interest: The authors declare no conflict of interest.

References

1. Megiddo, I.; Colson, A.; Chisholm, D.; Dua, T.; Nandi, A.; Laxminarayan, R. Health and economic benefits of public financing of epilepsy treatment in India: An agent-based simulation model. *Epilepsia* **2016**, *57*, 464–474. [CrossRef] [PubMed]
2. Liu, Q.; Ganzetti, M.; Wenderoth, N.; Mantini, D. Detecting Large-Scale Brain Networks Using EEG: Impact of Electrode Density, Head Modeling and Source Localization. *Front. Neuroinform.* **2018**, *12*, 4. [CrossRef] [PubMed]
3. Lehnertz, K. Epilepsy and Nonlinear Dynamics. *J. Biol. Phys.* **2008**, *34*, 253–266. [CrossRef] [PubMed]
4. Chan, H.-L.; Kuo, P.-C.; Cheng, C.-Y.; Chen, Y.-S. Challenges and Future Perspectives on Electroencephalogram-Based Biometrics in Person Recognition. *Front. Neuroinform.* **2018**, *12*, 66. [CrossRef] [PubMed]
5. Vijayan, A.E.; Sen, D.; Sudheer, A. EEG-Based Emotion Recognition Using Statistical Measures and Auto-Regressive Modeling. In Proceedings of the 2015 IEEE International Conference on Computational Intelligence & Communication Technology, IEEE, Ghaziabad, India, 13–14 February 2015; pp. 587–591. [CrossRef]
6. Farihah, S.N.; Lee, K.Y.; Mansor, W.; Mohamad, N.B.; Mahmoodin, Z.; Saidi, S.A. EEG average FFT index for dyslexic children with writing disorder. In Proceedings of the 2015 IEEE Student Symposium in Biomedical Engineering & Sciences (ISSBES), IEEE, Shah Alam, Malaysia, 4 November 2015; pp. 118–121. [CrossRef]
7. Yuyi, Z.; Surui, L.; Lijuan, S.; Zhenxin, L.; Bingchao, D. Motor imagery eeg discrimination using hilbert-huang entropy. *Biomed. Res.* **2017**, *28*, 727–733.
8. Zhou, M.; Tian, C.; Cao, R.; Wang, B.; Niu, Y.; Hu, T.; Guo, H.; Xiang, J. Epileptic Seizure Detection Based on EEG Signals and CNN. *Front. Neuroinform.* **2018**, *12*, 95. [CrossRef]
9. Mishra, S.; Birok, R. Sleep Classification using CNN and RNN on Raw EEG Single-Channel. In Proceedings of the 2020 International Conference on Computational Performance Evaluation (ComPE), IEEE, Shillong, India, 2–4 July 2020; pp. 232–237. [CrossRef]
10. Hochreiter, S. The Vanishing Gradient Problem During Learning Recurrent Neural Nets and Problem Solutions. *Int. J. Uncertain. Fuzziness Knowl.-Based Syst.* **1998**, *6*, 107–116. [CrossRef]
11. Sun, L.; Jin, B.; Yang, H.; Tong, J.; Liu, C.; Xiong, H. Unsupervised EEG feature extraction based on echo state network. *Inf. Sci.* **2019**, *475*, 1–17. [CrossRef]
12. Jaeger, H. Echo state network. *Scholarpedia* **2007**, *2*, 2330. [CrossRef]
13. Jarvis, S.; Rotter, S.; Egert, U. Extending stability through hierarchical clusters in Echo State Networks. *Front. Neuroinform.* **2010**, *4*, 11. [CrossRef]
14. Wang, L.; Hu, H.; Ai, X.-Y.; Liu, H. Effective electricity energy consumption forecasting using echo state network improved by differential evolution algorithm. *Energy* **2018**, *153*, 801–815. [CrossRef]
15. Mirjalili, S. Moth-flame optimization algorithm: A novel nature-inspired heuristic paradigm. *Knowl. Based Syst.* **2015**, *89*, 228–249. [CrossRef]
16. Mei, R.N.S.; Sulaiman, M.H.; Mustaffa, Z.; Daniyal, H. Optimal reactive power dispatch solution by loss minimization using moth-flame optimization technique. *Appl. Soft Comput.* **2017**, *59*, 210–222. [CrossRef]
17. Shehab, M.; Abualigah, L.; Al Hamad, H.; Alabool, H.; Alshinwan, M.; Khasawneh, A.M. Moth–flame optimization algorithm: Variants and applications. *Neural Comput. Appl.* **2020**, *32*, 9859–9884. [CrossRef]
18. Schroff, F.; Kalenichenko, D.; Philbin, J. Facenet: A unified embedding for face recognition and clustering. In Proceedings of the IEEE Conference on Computer Vision and Pattern Recognition, Boston, MA, USA, 7–12 June 2015; pp. 815–823.
19. Jaeger, H. *Tutorial on Training Recurrent Neural Networks, Covering BPPT, RTRL, EKF and the "Echo State Network" Approach*; GMD-Forschungszentrum Informationstechnik: Bonn, Germany, 2002.
20. Bo, Y.-C.; Zhang, X. Online adaptive dynamic programming based on echo state networks for dissolved oxygen control. *Appl. Soft Comput.* **2018**, *62*, 830–839. [CrossRef]
21. Wang, X.; Jin, Y.; Hao, K. Evolving Local Plasticity Rules for Synergistic Learning in Echo State Networks. *IEEE Trans. Neural Netw. Learn. Syst.* **2019**, *31*, 1363–1374. [CrossRef]
22. Wyffels, F.; Schrauwen, B.; Stroobandt, D. Stable Output Feedback in Reservoir Computing Using Ridge Regression. In *International Conference on Artificial Neural Networks*; Springer: Berlin/Heidelberg, Germany, 2008; pp. 808–817. [CrossRef]
23. Chouikhi, N.; Ammar, B.; Rokbani, N.; Alimi, A.M. PSO-based analysis of Echo State Network parameters for time series forecasting. *Appl. Soft Comput.* **2017**, *55*, 211–225. [CrossRef]

24. Lukoševičius, M.; Jaeger, H. Reservoir computing approaches to recurrent neural network training. *Comput. Sci. Rev.* **2009**, *3*, 127–149. [CrossRef]
25. Jaeger, H.; Maass, W.; Principe, J. Special issue on echo state networks and liquid state machines. *Neural Netw.* **2007**, *20*, 287–289. [CrossRef]
26. Song, Q.; Feng, Z. Effects of connectivity structure of complex echo state network on its prediction performance for nonlinear time series. *Neurocomputing* **2010**, *73*, 2177–2185. [CrossRef]
27. Watts, D.J.; Strogatz, S.H. Collective dynamics of 'small-world'network. *Nature* **1998**, *393*, 440–442. [CrossRef] [PubMed]
28. Deng, Z.; Zhang, Y. Collective Behavior of a Small-World Recurrent Neural System With Scale-Free Distribution. *IEEE Trans. Neural Netw.* **2007**, *18*, 1364–1375. [CrossRef] [PubMed]
29. Barabási, A.-L.; Albert, R. Emergence of scaling in random networks. *Science* **1999**, *286*, 509–512. [CrossRef] [PubMed]
30. Jaeger, H.; Haas, H. Harnessing Nonlinearity: Predicting Chaotic Systems and Saving Energy in Wireless Communication. *Science* **2004**, *304*, 78–80. [CrossRef]
31. Strauss, T.; Wustlich, W.; Labahn, R. Design Strategies for Weight Matrices of Echo State Networks. *Neural Comput.* **2012**, *24*, 3246–3276. [CrossRef]
32. Bianchi, F.M.; Livi, L.; Alippi, C. Investigating Echo-State Networks Dynamics by Means of Recurrence Analysis. *IEEE Trans. Neural Netw. Learn. Syst.* **2016**, *29*, 427–439. [CrossRef]
33. Domingos, P. A Few Useful Things to Know about Machine Learning. *Commun. ACM* **2012**, *55*, 78–87. [CrossRef]
34. Andrzejak, R.G.; Lehnertz, K.; Mormann, F.; Rieke, C.; David, P.; Elger, C.E. Indications of nonlinear deterministic and finite-dimensional structures in time series of brain electrical activity: Dependence on recording region and brain state. *Phys. Rev. E* **2001**, *64*, 061907. [CrossRef]
35. Chauhan, V.K.; Dahiya, K.; Sharma, A. Problem formulations and solvers in linear SVM: A review. *Artif. Intell. Rev.* **2019**, *52*, 803–855. [CrossRef]
36. Raj, S.; Ray, K.C. ECG Signal Analysis Using DCT-Based DOST and PSO Optimized SVM. *IEEE Trans. Instrum. Meas.* **2017**, *66*, 470–478. [CrossRef]
37. Güler, N.F.; Übeyli, E.D.; Güler, I. Recurrent neural networks employing Lyapunov exponents for EEG signals classification. *Expert Syst. Appl.* **2005**, *29*, 506–514. [CrossRef]
38. Guo, L.; Rivero, D.; Dorado, J.; Munteanu, C.R.; Pazos, A. Automatic feature extraction using genetic programming: An application to epileptic EEG classification. *Expert Syst. Appl.* **2011**, *38*, 10425–10436. [CrossRef]
39. Shoeibi, A.; Ghassemi, N.; Alizadehsani, R.; Rouhani, M.; Hosseini-Nejad, H.; Khosravi, A.; Panahiazar, M.; Nahavandi, S. A comprehensive comparison of handcrafted features and convolutional autoencoders for epileptic seizures detection in EEG signals. *Expert Syst. Appl.* **2020**, *163*, 113788. [CrossRef]
40. Tuncer, T.; Dogan, S.; Akbal, E. A novel local senary pattern based epilepsy diagnosis system using EEG signals. *Australas. Phys. Eng. Sci. Med.* **2019**, *42*, 939–948. [CrossRef]
41. Raghu, S.; Sriraam, N.; Hegde, A.S.; Kubben, P.L. A novel approach for classification of epileptic seizures using matrix determinant. *Expert Syst. Appl.* **2019**, *127*, 323–341. [CrossRef]
42. de la O Serna, J.A.; Paternina, M.R.A.; Zamora-Mendez, A.; Tripathy, R.K.; Pachori, R.B. EEG-Rhythm Specific Taylor–Fourier Filter Bank Implemented With O-Splines for the Detection of Epilepsy Using EEG Signals. *IEEE Sens. J.* **2020**, *20*, 6542–6551. [CrossRef]
43. Goldberger, A.; Amaral, L.; Glass, L.; Hausdorff, J.; Ivanov, P.C.; Mark, R.; Mietus, J.; Moody, G.; Peng, C.; Stanley, H. Components of a new research resource for complex physiologic signals, PhysioBank, PhysioToolkit, and Physionet. *Circulation* **2000**, *101*, e215–e220. [CrossRef]
44. Shoeb, A.H. Application of Machine Learning to Epileptic Seizure Onset Detection and Treatment. Ph.D. Thesis, Massachusetts Institute of Technology, Cambridge, MA, USA, 2009. Available online: https://dspace.mit.edu/handle/1721.1/7582 (accessed on 3 March 2023).
45. Li, Y.; Liu, Y.; Cui, W.-G.; Guo, Y.-Z.; Huang, H.; Hu, Z.-Y. Epileptic Seizure Detection in EEG Signals Using a Unified Temporal-Spectral Squeeze-and-Excitation Network. *IEEE Trans. Neural Syst. Rehabil. Eng.* **2020**, *28*, 782–794. [CrossRef]
46. Chen, D.; Wan, S.; Xiang, J.; Bao, F.S. A high-performance seizure detection algorithm based on Discrete Wavelet Transform (DWT) and EEG. *PLoS ONE* **2017**, *12*, e0173138. [CrossRef]
47. Wei, Z.; Zou, J.; Zhang, J.; Xu, J. Automatic epileptic EEG detection using convolutional neural network with improvements in time-domain. *Biomed. Signal Process. Control.* **2019**, *53*, 101551. [CrossRef]
48. Hu, X.; Yuan, S.; Xu, F.; Leng, Y.; Yuan, K.; Yuan, Q. Scalp EEG classification using deep Bi-LSTM network for seizure detection. *Comput. Biol. Med.* **2020**, *124*, 103919. [CrossRef] [PubMed]
49. Fergus, P.; Hussain, A.; Hignett, D.; Al-Jumeily, D.; Abdel-Aziz, K.; Hamdan, H. A machine learning system for automated whole-brain seizure detection. *Appl. Comput. Inform.* **2016**, *12*, 70–89. [CrossRef]

Disclaimer/Publisher's Note: The statements, opinions and data contained in all publications are solely those of the individual author(s) and contributor(s) and not of MDPI and/or the editor(s). MDPI and/or the editor(s) disclaim responsibility for any injury to people or property resulting from any ideas, methods, instructions or products referred to in the content.

Review

Sustainable Rail/Road Unimodal Transportation of Bulk Cargo in Zambia: A Review of Algorithm-Based Optimization Techniques

Fines Miyoba [1], Egbert Mujuni [2], Musa Ndiaye [1], Hastings M. Libati [1] and Adnan M. Abu-Mahfouz [3,4,*]

[1] Department of Electrical Engineering, Copperbelt University, Kitwe 10101, Zambia; fines.miyoba@cbu.ac.zm (F.M.); musa.ndiaye@cbu.ac.zm (M.N.); libati@cbu.ac.zm (H.M.L.)
[2] Department of Mathematics, University of Dar-es-Salaam, Dar-es-Salaam 16101, Tanzania; emujuni@udsm.ac.tz
[3] Council for Scientific and Industrial Research, Pretoria 0083, South Africa
[4] Department of Electrical and Electronic Engineering Science, University of Johannesburg, Johannesburg 2006, South Africa
* Correspondence: a.abumahfouz@ieee.org

Abstract: Modern rail/road transportation systems are critical to global travel and commercial transportation. The improvement of transport systems that are needed for efficient cargo movements possesses further challenges. For instance, diesel-powered trucks and goods trains are widely used in long-haul unimodal transportation of heavy cargo in most landlocked and developing countries, a situation that leads to concerns of greenhouse gases (GHGs) such as carbon dioxide coming from diesel fuel combustion. In this context, it is critical to understand aspects such as the use of some parameters, variables and constraints in the formulation of mathematical models, optimization techniques and algorithms that directly contribute to sustainable transportation solutions. In seeking sustainable solutions to the bulk cargo long-haul transportation problems in Zambia, we conduct a systematic review of various transportation modes and related mathematical models, and optimization approaches. In this paper, we provide an updated survey of various transport models for bulk cargo and their associated optimized combinations. We identify key research challenges and notable issues to be considered for further studies in transport system optimization, especially when dealing with long-haul unimodal or single-mode heavy cargo movement in countries that are yet to implement intermodal and multimodal systems.

Keywords: greenhouse gases; intermodal; mathematical optimization; multimodal; rail/road transportation; sustainable transport; unimodal

MSC: 35Q49

1. Introduction

In the last few years, there has been growth in the use of mathematical optimization in finding optimal routes for the planning of transportation systems (rail, road, water and air transportation). These optimization techniques have mostly been aimed at reducing carbon dioxide emissions and related costs [1]. Consequently, the reduction of CO_2 emissions in transportation has been the focus of what could be determined as sustainable transportation. However, sustainable transportation is more than just emission reduction as defined by Litman [2]. Litman mentions that sustainability encompasses economic, social and environmental concerns from long-term impacts of transportation. Despite agreeing with most researchers seeking sustainable transportation modes, Litman further gives guidance to the fact that desired values can be obtained by understanding the presumed assumptions and effects of different types of experiments.

Figure 1 illustrates three major issues that mathematical models and algorithms seek to address under sustainable transportation mechanisms.

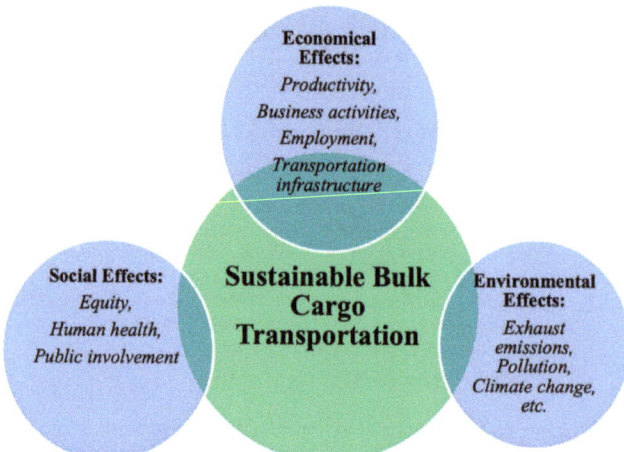

Figure 1. Direct and indirect effects of transportation [2].

Landlocked countries such as Zambia have seen an increase in the transportation of bulk mining cargo by either road or rail without consideration of long-term transportation sustainability. Countries like Indonesia [3] with over 31% rail freight of the total transport freight share have researchers working on the optimization of the rail transport sector to improve its operations. China is equally yet to fully develop it's freight carbon dioxide emission optimization models at a provincial level [4]. This level of research based on modal optimization for sustainable transportation still remains a niche in developing countries such as Zambia. As Zambia is poised to increase its annual copper production from the current annual production of eight hundred thousand (800,000) to three million (3,000,000) tons [5], a need arises to develop local monitoring mechanics as bulk cargo is being transported on the existing two main rail/road networks. For Zambia, being one of the major producers of copper concentrates and copper cathodes, it's transportation routes to the ports of Dar es salaam, Walvis Bay and Durban are mainly by rail and road networks and this compelled the government of Zambia to introduce a law forcing transporters to divert 30% [6] of bulk mining cargo towards the rail network without prior study.

This work focuses on the local and regional impacts of the transportation of bulk cargo and specifically bulk mining cargo. For our study, we have picked Zambia as our locality of reference because of it being a major copper producer with a unimodal transport system. Further pushes by the local government to move mining cargo to rail has motivated us to conduct this study. We feel the local transport variations would have a ripple effect on the regional and global movement of bulk cargo as most copper shipments in Zambia are destined for Asia via several regional countries. In this regard, this paper highlights the opportunities available for mathematical optimization in bulk cargo transport programming with the aim of ensuring long-term sustainability. This particularly for a country like Zambia that relies on a unimodal mechanism of transportation (either road, rail or a combination).

This study further explores various intervention mechanisms carried out across different continents towards the sustainable transportation of cargo. Generally, sustainable transportation goals can be achieved through good planning and the proper use of mathematical optimization techniques. There have been several papers on the performance of multimodal and intermodal transport systems along with proposals of associated optimization techniques aimed at transport sustainability. However, this paper focuses on single-mode (unimodal) transport system optimization techniques that may be valuable for application in landlocked countries like Zambia that rely mainly on unimodal transportation.

As part of the survey, we conducted an exhaustive search of scholarly articles to identify papers published in the area of optimization and sustainable freight transportation. The keywords were intermodal, multimodal, unimodal, optimization and sustainability. No study has been conducted in a situation where rail and road systems are independently used for long-haul bulk mining cargo transportation towards the same destinations under a real driving environment, a position that has created a problem in national bulk cargo freight emission policy regulation formulation. This calls for more research to be conducted for the optimization of unimodal transportation systems in situations where there are disparities in rail/road cargo share where each transport mechanism wants a larger share of the bulk cargo while ignoring the emission concerns.

In summary, this paper makes the following key contributions:

1. We present an up-to-date review of the application of mathematical optimization in sustainable transportation of cargo with a focus on unimodal transport systems suitable for landlocked countries.
2. For the reviewed transport models, we identify the key challenges in implementation suitability for a developed country like Zambia.
3. We provide potential solutions for adaptation of these optimization models to suit the Zambian transport system for bulk mining cargo and ultimately enable the drive towards sustainability.

The rest of the paper is laid out as follows: Section 2 discusses work related to the focus of this survey paper while highlighting the unique contributions of this work and Section 3 discusses the available mathematical optimization models for sustainable transport. Section 3 is segmented to discuss three transportation modes, namely intermodal, multimodal and unimodal which is the focus of this work. In Section 4, we shift focus to the effect of cargo overloading, an aspect that affects rail/road sustainability. Here, we try to highlight how cargo weight plays an important role in the mathematical optimization model for sustainable transport. Section 5 discusses the lessons learnt in this review and it is in this section that implementation and research challenges are discussed. The paper is then concluded in Section 6 with potential solutions and future works discussed therein.

2. Related Work

This section presents several works in the area of long-term sustainability for the transportation of cargo based on mathematical optimization approaches. The work in this paper draws attention to the Zambian long-haul freight system which is similar to most developing countries. Zambia's rail/road long-haul routes are well defined and not prone to any obstructions like buildings because the Zambian government has assigned some independent deviations in some high-density areas. An illustration of a single-mode long-haul freight system being practiced in Zambia is shown in Figure 2. Loading bays are mining companies' warehouses whilst the offloading points are the exit ports of Dar es Salaam (Tanzania), Walvis-bay (Namibia) and Durban [7].

Before we can streamline efforts towards sustainable transports in Zambia, it is essential to look at related applications from the research. For example, Diaz-Parra et al. [8] present an algorithm that solves the planning, routing and scheduling problems presented under land transportation to minimize transportation costs and transit time. In their work, a school bus routing solution using a mixed integer or non-linear mixed integer programming model is used to minimize operational and cost-related problems where the number of buses is regarded as the variable. The authors Wu et al. [9] agree with Diaz-Parra et al. [8] on the importance of routing planning in transportation. However, Wu et al. [9] developed a Non-Dominated Sorting Genetic Algorithm II (NSGA-II) to solve the localized problem of route planning during the transportation of hazardous materials across the city of Guangzhou, China where the authors endeavor to reduce the costs and risks as a result of the transportation of hazardous materials.

Figure 2. Illustration of single-mode road/rail long-haul transportation to Dar es Salaam.

Despite Wu et al. [9] and Diaz-Parra et al. [8] having contributed to the solution of transportation problems in network routing where transit time and distance between the sources and destinations are considered in the development of solution models, parameters related to emissions are not considered.

On the other hand, Archetti et al. [10] looked at long-haul freight as an integral transport system of road, sea and rail. The authors propose similar modal shifts as a requirement for the reduction of emissions and other costs while recommending unimodal transportation as a preference when transportation distance increases. This has also been supported in several works including [10–15].

While there is a mention of emission reduction in [10], there is no mention of emission reduction in [8]. In agreement to [10] on the reduction of emissions in transportation, the authors Fan et al. [16] conducted a search on publications that concern topics on transportation and carbon emissions using the bibliometric method for the period 1997 to 2023. The authors present that the major contributor to carbon dioxide emissions during transportation is the energy use (fuel consumption). Despite researchers [10] proposing modal shift as a solution towards transportation emissions reduction, the authors in [16] still argue that more emission collection methods still need to be improved to obtain more usable emissions data. The demand for sustainable transportation in the area of greenhouse gases (GHGs) has recently increased prompting [17] to develop a model to calculate road traffic emissions on German transport networks. Two major situations were considered in the development of the model, namely the free and regulated modes. Under the free mode, the tests were conducted without any controls or constraints while the regulated mode meant the tests were under certain conditions such as emission limits. Though their findings showed a reduction of nitric oxide by 32% and 13% particulate matter under the regulated mode compared to the free mode, their study left out the critical greenhouse contributor carbon dioxide in their analysis [18]. The authors recommended the use of the developed model outside Germany; however, the exclusion of carbon dioxide emissions may not be very useful for developing countries. CO_2 emission analysis is critical in developing countries due to the presence of old, disposed-of vehicles imported from developed nations.

Further, Praveen et al. [19] present a survey on several optimization algorithms to help in identifying those that would provide optimal vehicle routing values and reduce on environmental emissions when they are all subjected to similar conditions and parameters.

They conducted studies on several algorithms that include Simulated Annealing, Genetic Algorithm, Anty Colony Optimization [20], Discrete and Improved Bat Algorithm (DaIBA), Evolutionary Simulated Annealing [21], BAT Algorithm and Firefly Algorithm (FA). Results in their work showed that the Discrete and Improved Bat Algorithm (DaIBA) provided a better optimal solution when compared to other algorithms.

However, without infrastructure planning, transportation routing studies cannot be conclusive. To resolve these existing challenges in transportation infrastructure planning and maintenance, studies were conducted to develop optimization techniques that could be used to easily resolve the challenges in road network infrastructure restoration. The existing needs and transit time were used as part of the parameters in developing the bi-objective bi-level optimization model by [22]. Although the impact on the environment was not directly mentioned in their study, the development of optimization models for infrastructure improvement affects the transit time, consequently affecting emission of greenhouse gases.

Apart from the route selection algorithms, Ref. [23] believed that when people share transport facilities with cargo, this would reduce the adverse effects on the environment and traffic congestion. A survey on various studies on shared mobility were conducted with a consideration of model parameters and constraints such as routing, time, loading capacity, cost, and synchronization. The objective functions in this study were grouped into operational and quality-oriented categories. It was assumed that when people park their vehicles to use one car during travel, traffic jams occur due to the increase of vehicles on the road. The reviewed literature was grouped according to problem variations such as dynamic ride sharing (DARP) and solution methods of either exact or heuristic approaches. Mourad et al. [23] further proposed more research to be conducted to develop new models on the shared mobility of people and cargo transportation so that environmental matters can also be addressed. However, the environmental concerns have been brought to the attention of other authors such as Gandhi et al. [12] and Heinold et al. [24].

Heinold et al. [24] reviewed emission estimation models using the methodologies for estimating air pollutant emissions from transport that give real outputs of the emitted greenhouse gases from rail transportation, while other surveys conducted in the area of railway systems concern the improvement of train time scheduling and management. Han [25] conducted a survey study on works solving vehicle routing problems to identify gaps and make necessary proposals that would improve the optimization models and algorithms that were earlier developed. The notable constraints seen in the study were the time and distance (route). System dynamic modelling was performed by [26] to scrutinize the improvements made to the earlier system dynamic mathematical models. Despite Han [25] modelling time and distance problems, Prabowo [3] had earlier considered cost and efficiency as the major problems that needed to solved in Indonesia by considering modal shifts of rail and road systems. The study assumed that it is cheaper to transport goods by road when the transportation route is up to 350 km but expensive beyond that. The motivation for the optimization of the railway transport systems was derived from the lack of innovation by the main railway company and the discovery that cargo customers preferred transportation of their goods by road (trucks) to transportation via railways.

Prabowo's study [3] follows an earlier study by [27] that reviewed optimization models and algorithms to distinguish parameters used in the development of the routing models and algorithms in multimodal transportation.

Table 1 provides a summary of the related works covered in this section in comparison with what is covered in this work.

Table 1. Summary of related work and solution approaches.

Ref.	Title	Solution Approach Parameters				
		Transport System (Modal)	Transportation Cost per Ton-Kilometers and Road/Rail Maintenance	Exhaust Emissions (Kilograms/Ton-Kilometers) under Real Driving Conditions (RDC)	Time (h)	Distance (km)
[10]	Optimization in multimodal freight transportation problems: A Survey	Multimodal	✓	×	×	✓
[8]	A Survey of Transportation Problems	Multimodal	✓	×	✓	×
[25]	A Survey for Vehicle Routing Problems and Its Derivatives.	Multimodal	×	×	✓	✓
[28]	A review of online dynamic models and algorithms for railway traffic management.	Multimodal	×	×	✓	✓
[23]	A survey of models and algorithms for optimizing shared mobility	Multimodal/Intermodal	✓	×	×	✓
[19]	A Survey on Various Optimization Algorithms to Solve Vehicle Routing Problem	General	×	×	✓	✓
[9]	Multi-class hazmat distribution network design with inventory and superimposed risks	General	×	×	✓	✓
[16]	A review of transportation carbon emissions research using bibliometric analyses	General	×	✓	×	✓
This Survey	Sustainable Rail/Road Transportation of Bulk Cargo: A Review of Algorithm-Based Optimization Techniques	Unimodal	✓	✓	✓	✓

3. Transport Optimization Models for Cargo Movement

3.1. Intermodal Transport Optimization

Intermodal transportation is the movement of a single cargo from one transport system to a different transport system but under different transfer contracts [29]. Sörensen et al. [30] proposed the improvement to the mathematical modelling of the intermodal transport system by considering various parameters and constraints in the transportation problem formulation. The proposed problem parameters with symbols from the general transportation problem formulation are considered as follows:

All customers to be considered (set notation, I),

Proposed locations (set notation, K),

Goods to be transported from i to j (notation, q_{ij}),

Cost of transportation through route ij (notation, C_{ij})

Transportation cost if part of the goods from route ij are transported via terminals k and m (notation, C_{ij}^{km}),

Loading capacity of terminal k (notation, C_k),

Building cost (fixed) of terminal k (notation, F_k).

As is always the case when formulating a mathematical model, the following variables were considered in the model improvement:

y_k: considered as a binary variable where the binary is 1 when k is a terminal and 0 when not,

w_{ij}: when part of q_{ij} is transported from i to j without diverting,

x_{ij}^{km}: When part of q_{ij} is transported from i to j through terminals k and m

The main objective of the authors [30], was to reduce costs and the following objective function was developed:

$$\text{Min}, \sum_{i,j \in I} \sum_{k,m \in K} c_{ij}^{km} x_{ij}^{km} + \sum_{i,j \in I} c_{ij} w_{ij} + \sum_{k \in K} F_k y_k \text{ (Objective function)}$$

The constraints considered in their study are as follows:

(1) $x_{ij}^{km} \leq q_{ij} y_k \ \forall k, m \in K, \forall i, j \in I,$

(2) $x_{ij}^{km} \leq q_{ij} y_m \ \forall k, m \in K, \forall i, j \in I,$

(3) $\sum_{k, m \in K} x_{ij}^{km} + w_{ij} = q_{ij} \ \forall i, j \in I,$

(4) $\sum_{i,j \in I} \sum_{m \in K} x_{ij}^{km} + \sum_{i,j \in I} \sum_{m \in K} x_{ij}^{mk} \leq C_k w_{ij}, \forall k \in K,$

(5) $w_{ij} \geq 0, x_{ij}^{km} \geq 0, x_{ij}^{kk} \geq 0, \forall i, j \in I, \forall k, m \in K,$

(6) The value of $y_k \in \{0,1\} \ \forall k \in K.$

The objective function reduces the sum of the associated costs with unimodal and intermodal transportation modes including the cost of terminal opening. If the terminal k is open, the products must be transported through it due to restrictions (1) and (2). Constraint or restriction (3) guarantees that the total supplies routed both directly and through terminals matches the demand related to each origin/destination pair. Restriction (4) addresses the terminals' limited capacity. Two distinct terminals are needed to satisfy constraints number (5). Furthermore, restrictions (6) ensure that y_k can only take the values 0 or 1 and that the quantities of items carried by road via terminals are not negative. The developed program is a linear one where binary and real variables exit.

Liu et al. [31] developed a cost analysis and route selection logistics optimization model named Geospatial Intermodal Freight Transportation (GIFT) to optimize the containerized soybeans freight flow nationally. The GIFT model optimized supply, demand sharing, routing methods, intermodal cargo transport mode switching and flow distribution with infrastructure capacity as the constraint. However, this study does not consider the cost related to infrastructure maintenance and emission constraints resulting from the bulk transportation of soya beans on road and rail systems.

Wiegmans and Konings [32] cited road transport as a major contributor to congestion, air pollution, increases in accidents and noise as a motivation to develop a model to analyze and compare the transport costs of intermodal inland waterway transport to that of the road system. This was performed to ascertain the variance (fixed and variable) between intermodal and unimodal road transport systems, though the findings were not conclusive because of so many cost factors (fuel, equipment maintenance, labor, cargo handling charges, etc.) that required consideration in their study. Their study, however, did not consider the sustainability of both transport systems in terms of tonnage per kilometer maintenance of the multi-transport networks (rail, road and waterway). However, ref. [33] proposed other cost models for terminal location analysis and operational activities. Mostert et al. [34] hoped to bridge the gap that exists in the research between cargo transportation modes and human external costs as a result of goods haulage at the transport mode selection level by developing an intermodal allocation model in Belgium that would lead to the reduction of operational and other indirect costs (pollution affects medical expenses).

During studies to analyze the preferences between road and rail/road intermodal transport systems in terms of freight costs, Christian Bierwirth [35] used a mixed integer programming model (MIP) to model freight costs from the factories. This followed similar research for Indian Railways under rail–truck intermodal transportation where a mathematical model was developed for pricing and terminal location optimization purposes to ease solutions of optimal freight rates and the matching intermodal terminal sites in Delhi and Mumbai transport routes [36]. However, both studies still lacked vital information on the emission costs emanating from transportation systems that would be helpful in future searches for environmentally friendly transportation.

Another aspect is the use of mixed integer algorithms meant to solve intermodal transportation risks and apportion containers to various transport modes in Turkey by using the fuzzy-based method [37]. The risk factors considered during the evaluation process included human accidents and deaths, emission values and noise levels leading to the conclusion that their method produced a transportation system that was more economical and environmentally acceptable. Their study, however, also had a bias toward intermodal transportation than long-haul unimodal transportation without considering emissions and optimal cargo tonnage in the mathematical model development.

Several research papers reviewed under this section focused on costs, routing and cargo freight timing on mixed rail/road transport systems without much consideration of a single long haul of bulk cargo on unimodal rail/road transportation systems existing in many landlocked countries. The time effect and emissions do not seem to be the main factor in modal choice planning. This drawback encourages researchers to conduct more studies on time-dependent long-haul road or rail freight systems.

The articles cited in this section are summarized in Table 2. The summary gives a clear glance at the direction taken by the researchers in trying to resolve the challenges in intermodal transportation systems.

Table 2. Summary of different approaches highlighted under Intermodal Transport Research.

Ref.	Transportation Mode	Method of Analysis	Parameters and Constraints Considered					
			Infrastructure Maintenance Costs and Investment	Transportation Cost (Handling and Movement)	Emissions (Environmental and Social Effects/Costs	Fuel Costs (L/ton-km)	Time (h)	Distance
[31]	Intermodal	(Geospatial Intermodal Freight Transportation) GIFT model and GAMS software.	x	√	x	x	x	√
[32]	Intermodal	Intermodal transport problems and analyses model	√	x	x	x	√	√
[33]	Intermodal	General Optimization	√	√	x	x	x	x
[34]	Intermodal	Intermodal allocation model	√	√	√	x	x	x
[35]	Intermodal	Intermodal Transportation Problem (ITP) model- ILOG Cplex 12.1	x	√	x	x	x	√
[36]	Intermodal	Non-linear trucker shipping cost minimization function	x	√	x	x	√	√
[37]	Intermodal	Mixed Integer Programming and Fuzzy methods	x	√	√	x	x	√

3.2. Multimodal Transport Optimization

Multimodal transportation is the movement of cargo from one transport system to another using the same contract or under one logistics company [29]. This section looks at a few techniques towards the solutions of transportation problems. Sun et al. [1] optimizes the freight route selection problem to lower transport costs during goods movement through the multimodal transport networks. Optimization objectives such as emission costs have been presented using fuzzy time windows [38] though both techniques do not consider tonnage under real-driving conditions when considering emission costs.

Despite the routing problem being dominant, researchers in Turkey [39] further optimized travelling time to solve the routing problem in the city of Izmir using round-based transit optimizer routers, transit mode routing and contraction hierarchies on transportation graphs as their first path-finding algorithm. In coming up with the model for optimal multimodal transportation route selection, Huynh et al. [40] used an analytical hierarchy process (AHP) and zero one-goal programs (ZOGP). The multi-objective optimization technique resulted in the solution of an optimal route selection problem in the affected region. However, the cargo weight per fuel distance cost relationship was not properly defined in this research.

Shen and Wang [41] introduced a binary logic and a regression model for the transportation of some grain crops using mixed rail/road transport systems using from United States of America Freight Analysis Framework (FAF2.2) databases. Other information used came from US highway networks and TransCAD. Their study approach, however, did not include the variables in terms of exhaust emissions per tonnage transported in solving their multimodal transportation problem.

The economic and travel desire behavioral changes that accompany transportation infrastructure developments prompted Moeckel et al. [42] to develop a nested multinomial logic mode selection model with the consideration of travel-related costs, distance, transit stations access, transport service frequency, number of transfers and parking costs. The transit station choice model was conducted with consideration of the increase in fuel prices and the corresponding bus services. The authors support investment in long-distance travel infrastructure bearing in mind that the investments to be made would come with other effects such as environmental, social and economic changes.

However, environmental effects on transportation systems changes call for further models to be developed using real-life measured parameters, especially concerning unimodal long-distance bulk cargo hauling and led Kraft and Stanislav [43] to present a model to predict long-distance traffic flows with a focus on road transport in the Czech Republic. The use of data collected from the existing road traffic flows in the development of the model and distance–decay function makes it easier to predict future traffic flows on the highways to be constructed. The above-cited method has a very good intention in landscape planning. However, it is worth recommending that the model should have included bulk cargo capacity tests during planning for future road developments as this determines the life span of the roads. Further, the environmental impacts of the emissions coming from the vehicles involved in long-haul transportation should be considered. Various approaches taken in trying to solve transportation problems under a multimodal system are summarized in Table 3.

Table 3. Summary of different approaches highlighted under Multimodal Transport Research.

Ref.	Transportation Mode	Method of Analysis	Parameters and Constraints Considered					
			Infrastructure Maintenance Costs and Investment	Transportation Cost (Handling and Movement)	Emissions (Environmental and Social Effects/Costs)	Fuel Costs (L/Ton-km)	Time (h)	Distance [44]
[27]	Multimodal	Various (Review)	x	✓	✓	x	✓	x
[39]	Multimodal	Dijkstra's Algorithm	x	x	✓	x	✓	✓
[40]	Multimodal	Analytic hierarchy process (AHP) and Zero-one goal programming (ZOGP)	x	✓	x	x	✓	✓
[41]	Multimodal	Binary Logit Model and Geographical Information System [45]	x	✓	x	✓	✓	✓
[3]	Multimodal	Explorative and Comparable descriptive Methods	✓	✓	x	x	x	✓
[42]	Multimodal	Multinomial logit mode-choice	✓	✓	x	✓	x	✓
[43]	Multimodal	Statistical program	✓	x	x	x	x	✓
[10]	Multimodal	General (Unimodal/Intermodal/Multimodal)	✓	✓	✓	x	x	✓

3.3. Unimodal Transport Systems

Problems involving rail and road long-haul single-mode transportation have rarely been explored, especially the use of parameters such as tonnage, transit time, emissions and fuel consumption to solve real-world and real driving problems towards sustainable transportation [46]. Unimodal transportation is receiving less attention from researchers in preference to the multimodal systems as the latter is considered to not be viable when considering intercontinental cargo shipping as highlighted in the literature survey by [10]. The researchers do not consider the unimodal freight system, especially transportation by road, to be a very optimal solution to the transportation problems. They encourage a shift from unimodal to a combination of unimodal and multimodal systems. Despite unimodal transportation being considered a lesser solution to transportation problems, the system still exists in many landlocked countries with no option for alternative transport modes.

Despite many researchers calling for a shift from unimodal transport systems to other modes (multimodal and intermodal), there is a need to do more in terms of real-life challenges because of bulk cargo transportation so that overall sustainable freight service is achieved. This calls for more proactive research activities to optimize this transportation system to develop optimal solutions to social, economic and environmental problems that arise as a result of overwhelming bulk cargo either by road or rail networks.

According to Singh et al. [47], the traditional transportation problem comprises of 'm' sources each creating a limited accessible unit of a specific item and 'n' demand points each having limited interest of that commodity. The particular bulk transportation problems (BTPs) considered by researchers are the single-mode, multi-standards, multi-file and non-raised transportation problems. The single-mode approach involves the reduction of either cost or total time taken during transportation while the multi bulk transportation problem considers more objectives such as minimizing cost, time and damage of goods during transportation. When there are more indices such as source, destination, make of goods, transport modes and usable resources, then a multi-index method is utilized. In this regard, we present the mathematical model approaches provided by Singh et al. [47].

3.3.1. Single Function Formulation

Minimizing cost objective function;

Minimize, $C = \sum_{i=1}^{m} \sum_{j=1}^{n} c_{ij} x_{ij}$.

The objective function is subjected to the following constraints;

(1) $\sum_{j=1}^{n} b_j x_{ij} \leq a_i \quad (i = 1, 2, \ldots, m)$

(2) $\sum_{i=1}^{m} x_{ij} = 1 \quad (j = 1, 2, \ldots, n)$

(3) The value $x_{ij} = 0$ or $1 (i = 1, 2, \ldots, m; j = 1, 2, \ldots, n)$. x_{ij} are the decision variables such that;

The quantity of units of the available item is given by $a_i (i = 1, 2, 3 \ldots, m)$ based at source location i, whereas $b_j (j = 1, 2, 3, \ldots, n)$ is the unit of the items wanted at destination j. The cost of bulk transportation of a particular item from source i to end point j is given by parameter $c_{ij}(i = 1, 2, \ldots, n)$ and $x_{ij}(i = 1, 2, \ldots, m; j = 1, 2, \ldots, n)$ is the variable of the assumption whether the requirement is fulfilled or not at the demand or destination point j coming from source point i. For this mathematical formulation, $a_i's$, $b_j's$ and $c_{ij}'s$ are all considered as positive real values. C denotes the overall cost of the bulk transportation.

Minimizing time objective function;

To develop the time objective function, the following is considered,

Minimize, $T = max \{t_{ij} : x_{ij} = 1\}$,

Subject to;

(1) $\sum_{j=1}^{n} b_j x_{ij} \leq a_i \quad (i = 1, 2, \ldots, m)$,

(2) $\sum_{i=1}^{m} x_{ij} = 1 \quad (i = 1, 2, \ldots, n)$,

(3) The value of $x_{ij} = 0 \, or \, 1 \quad (i = 1, 2, \ldots, m; j = 1, 2, \ldots, n)$.

T is the overall time taken to transport the bulk cargo from i to j. x_{ij} are the decision variables such that there is 1 if the cargo is transported and if not, there is 0. $t_{ij}(i = 1, 2, \ldots, m; j = 1, 2, \ldots, n)$ is the bulk cargo movement time from the origin i to destination j. $a_i's$, $b_j's$ and $t_{ij}'s$ are positive real figures.

3.3.2. Two-Dimensional Function Assignment

According to [47], the general mathematical model objective functions for both time and cost assignment problems are expressed in the following equations;

For cost minimization;

Minimize, $C = \sum_{i=1}^{m} \sum_{j=1}^{n} c_{ij} x_{ij}$

For time minimization

Minimize, $T = max\{t_{ij} x_{ij} : i = 1, 2, \ldots, m; j = 1, 2, \ldots, n\}$.

The letters C and T represent the Cost and Time functions during bulk cargo transportation.

The two equations (cost and time functions) are subjected to the following listed restrictions;

(1) $\sum_{j=1}^{n} b_j x_{ij} \leq a_i$ $(i = 1, 2, \ldots, m)$,

(2) $\sum_{i=1}^{m} x_{ij} = 1$ $(j = 1, 2, \ldots, n)$,

(3) The value of $x_{ij} = 0$ or 1 $(i = 1, 2, \ldots, m; j = 1, 2, \ldots, n)$.

The letters m and n represent the origins and destinations of the respective bulk cargo being transported. The quantity of the commodity present at source i is represented by $a_i (i = 1, 2, 3 \ldots, m)$ and the demand value at destination j is $b_j (j = 1, 2, 3, \ldots, n)$. The value of $c_{ij} (i = 1, 2, \ldots, m; j = 1, 2, \ldots, n)$ is the cost of transportation from i to j and the time taken during transportation is $t_{ij} (i = 1, 2, \ldots, m; j = 1, 2, \ldots, n)$. The decision variables describing whether the conditions of destination j are met by the source i are represented by $x_{ij} (i = 1, 2, \ldots, m; j = 1, 2, \ldots, n)$ where the variable is 1 if the condition is met and 0 when not. $a_i's$, $b_j's$, $c_{ij}'s$ and $t_{ij}'s$ parameters are considered to be positive real figures.

Logistic companies would love to transport the cargo of the customers at a lower cost to make some profit. In another development, the cargo owners would love to have their goods transported to the customers or other need areas with fewer costs.

From the literature survey conducted in [10], a source–truck–train–truck–destination cost analysis mathematical model was presented where the authors looked at costs related to network design for long-haul rail services. The objective function of minimizing linear costs in terms of development of infrastructure and associated facilities was presented where N represented origins/destinations and A for a set of connections or routes connecting the origins and demand (destination) points. Parameters considered in the mathematical are listed as follows:

$\bar{c_{ij}}$ standing for costs for construction of fixed network (i, j),

c_{ij}^k for transportation cost of cargo k along route (i, j),

u_{ij} representing the transportation capacity of network (i, j),

d_i^k being the demand of item k at destination k.

The variables considered in the model are given by the following expressions:

$y_{ij} (i, j) \in A$. These parameters are used to model abstract design decisions using integer variables,

Decision variables are such that $y \in \{0, 1\}$ when action is limited to a certain route and $y \in N_+$ represents the number of facilities constructions that include the service capability, f_{ij}^k, $(i, j) \in A, k \in K$ represents the traffic passing through route (i, j) carrying cargo k.

When y_{ij} decision variables are considered to be binary numbers, the objective function is developed as follows:

Minimize, $\sum_{(i,j) \in A} \bar{c_{ij}} y_{ij} + \sum_{(i,j) \in A, k \in K} c_{ij}^k f_{ij}^k$

This objective function is subjected to the following restrictions or constraints:

(1) $\sum_{j \in N} f_{ij}^k - \sum_{j \in N} f_{ji}^k = d_i^k$ $i \in N, k \in K$,

(2) $\sum_{k \in K} f_{ij}^k \leq u_{ij} y_{ij}, \quad (i,j) \in A,$

(3) $f_{ij}^k \geq 0, \quad (i,j) \in A, k \in K,$

(4) $y_{ij} \in \{0,1\}, \quad (i,j) \in A$

Constraint (1) is there to satisfy the destination demand requirement from the source on a specific route. The route restriction in terms of capacity was fulfilled by constraint (2). The ultimate goal of the research on train/road transportation was to optimize costs related to the movement of goods from the source to the destination via the road and train networks with consideration for the costs of the route and facilities construction. However, constraints in terms of emission levels during transit were not considered during the study.

Problems tackled by researchers in the field of unimodal transportation are not often inspired by real case applications of real size data in order to find solutions that can be effectively used in practice. The majority of the studies analyze the problem without making use of real data and relying mostly on simulated instances.

4. Overview on the Impact of Overloading Cargo on Transport Sustainability

Simulation models have been developed to improve transport systems policy formulation for sustainable bulk cargo transportation and this led to a system dynamic technique. The techniques can be used to determine the possible and the negative situations on parameters like operational costs, social impact costs, accidents and pavement maintenance when roads are subjected to weights beyond stipulated tonnage during stone transportation. Simulation results in studies have shown that with reduced tonnage, there is a corresponding reduction in operational costs [48].

According to [45], an excellent loading policy is relative to the economic and social costs involved. To this effect, Ghisolfi et al. [45] presented a generalized cost function that depended on the vehicle make, road condition, travelling distance, transit time and fixed costs such as toll fees and other related expenses. The general cost function was presented as follows:

$$GC_{v,r,p} = \beta_1 \cdot (T_{v,r,p} \cdot CT_{v,r,p}) + \beta_2 \cdot (L_{r,p} \cdot CL_{v,r,p}) + \beta_3 \cdot (CT_v) + \beta_4 \cdot (CF_v) \quad (1)$$

Equation (1) parameters are explained below:

$GC_{v,r,p}$: This represents the general cost as a result of transportation using vehicle v along route (r,p) where r is the terrain type and p is the condition status of the pavement,

$T_{v,r,p}$: Travel time by vehicle v through route type (r,p),

$CT_{v,r,p}$: Cost per travel time using vehicle v via link (r,p),

$L_{r,p}$: Length of route (r,p),

$CL_{v,r,p}$: Cost per unit distance using vehicle v along route (r,p),

CT_v: Toll fee chargeable on vehicle v along a selected route,

CF_v: Represents the fine imposed on overloaded vehicle v and

β_1, β_2, β_3 and β_4 represent perceived values.

Some researchers had earlier utilized a system dynamic model in China to get rid of overloading and to achieve a sustainable means of intercity cargo transportation [49]. The researchers looked at the impacts that arise because of the predominant two types of road freight systems which include the ordinary and express highways. Transporters using the faster road network are subjected to higher tariffs than those that opt for the ordinary route leading to most freight participants shunning the faster routes. This study seeks to assess the results of modal shift efforts and related policies to identify the useful ones that provide sustainable intercity freight systems. This study discovered that there was compliance during the day because of random inspections by route patrol police officers but the situation changes at night as more overloaded vehicles avoid the toll fees along the faster route.

According to Liu et al. [49], there is congestion on ordinary road routes because drivers with overloaded vehicles avoid higher charges at night resulting in unsustainable effects like accidents and road damage. In Nigeria, highway pavement damage has been a source of concern leading to studies to resolve the problem where some of the parameters such as time, handling costs and costs incurred by the government, such as accident compensation and environmental protection activities costs, have been considered [50]. Sustainability in bulk cargo transportation is very important to resolve the overloading on unimodal transport networks, especially the road network in most landlocked countries. It is also proper to appreciate the study conducted in seeking sustainable transport systems modal shifts to reduce truck overloading negative impacts in [48].

Table 4 gives us a further indication that much concern is on infrastructure degradation without equal consideration on the emission rates.

Table 4. Summary of literature related to overloading.

Ref.	Transportation Mode	Method of Analysis	Parameters and Constraints Considered					
			Infrastructure Maintenance Costs	Transportation Cost per ton-km	Emissions (kgs/ton-km)	Fuel Costs (L/ton-km)	Time (h)	Distance
[50]	Unimodal (road)	Weigh-in-motion (WIM) system	✓	x	x	x	✓	✓
[45]	Unimodal (road)	System Dynamics (SD) Model	✓	✓	x	x	x	x
[48]	General (Uni-modal/Intermodal/Multimodal)	System Dynamics (SD) Model	✓	x	x	✓	✓	x
[49]	Intermodal and Multimodal	System Dynamics (SD) Model	✓	✓	✓	x	x	✓

5. Research Challenges and Lessons Learnt

From the reviewed literature, route selection, modal shift controls, transportation time and distance reduction seemed to have been the main cause for transport systems optimization. The research has exposed various approaches and studies hinging on intermodal and multimodal systems and luck of some practical parameter scientific data. However, the summary provided in Table 4 gives a picture that unimodal transportation is much considered in the studies looking at the mitigation of overloading, especially on truck transportation and the cost of transportation encored by transporters.

The second transportation problem receiving much attention is the reduction of transportation distances. Emissions arising from vehicles, trains and other systems have not received much attention in the studies of modal shifts and routing and this can be confirmed by the strategy for low-emission mobility [11] where the European commission sought the intervention of several consultants in coming up with modern techniques and technologies in the optimization of transportation systems. Further proposals were made to improve the emission measurement methods on automotive vehicles by developing more 'real driving' emission measurement tools. In its Regulation (EU) 2019/1242, the European Union and Council of 2019 proposed a new technique of finding out the levels of exhaust emissions for heavy-duty vehicles to simulate quantities of emissions and fuel consumption to determine the impact of fuel consumption and emission levels [51]. All these efforts by the European Union prove that the exhaust emission factor or parameter is paramount in the optimization and determination of a sustainable transportation system, especially when dealing with the transportation of heavy cargo.

The European Union has agreed on strategies to improve on activities to reduce carbon dioxide (CO_2) emissions by introducing efficient vehicle models leading to zero greenhouse gas emissions. These activities of research carried out by the European Union are commendable because carbon dioxide is believed to be the main contributor to the production of greenhouse gases harmful to the environment. Exhaust emission parameters under real driving conditions is very important in the development of optimization techniques, hence the need for efficient equipment to measure it. However, the literature reviewed does not provide overwhelming approaches and data usable for the development of a universal optimization model for bulk transportation control.

6. Conclusions and Future Work

Most of the papers reviewed so far have dealt with the problem of reducing costs related to transportation and distance studies. Unimodal long-haul distance studies have not received much attention as most researchers focus on the improvement of intermodal and multimodal transportation systems. It is worth noting that there is a considerable research gap in bulk cargo rail/road transportation systems emissions and tonnage in landlocked Zambia and other low-income countries where long-haul single-mode rail/road transport system is still the only means of cargo transportation. Additionally, there is an absence of exhaustive, current rail/road emission statistics for Zambia in the scientific literature, and the development of mathematical models of transportation under a real driving environment (RDE) and related parameters like emissions, tonnage, fuel consumption and transit time. All this, while taking into account stipulated government regulations.

Author Contributions: Conceptualization, F.M., M.N., H.M.L. and A.M.A.-M.; methodology, F.M., E.M., M.N. and A.M.A.-M.; writing—original draft preparation, F.M. and E.M.; writing—review and editing, M.N., H.M.L. and A.M.A.-M.; supervision, M.N., H.M.L. and A.M.A.-M. All authors have read and agreed to the published version of the manuscript.

Funding: This research was funded by CBU Centre for Excellence for Sustainable Mining, grant number IDA 58030 and the APC was funded by CSIR, Pretoria, South Africa.

Data Availability Statement: No new data were created or analyzed in this study. Data sharing is not applicable to this article.

Conflicts of Interest: The authors declare no conflict of interest.

References

1. Sun, Y.; Lang, M. Modeling the multicommodity multimodal routing problem with schedule-based services and carbon dioxide emission costs. *Math. Probl. Eng.* **2015**, *201*, 406218. [CrossRef]
2. Litman, T. Developing Indicators for Comprehensive and Sustainable Transport Planning-Todd Litman, 2007. *J. Transp. Res. Board* **2007**, *2017*, 10–15. [CrossRef]
3. Prabowo, R. The Optimization of Railway Transportation Modes to Reduce Costs and Support Logistics Activities. In Proceedings of the Conference on Global Research on Sustainable Transport (GROST 2017), Jakarta, Indonesia, 22–23 November 2017; Atlantis Press: Amsterdam, The Netherlands, 2017; pp. 480–490. Available online: https://doi.org/10.2991/grost-17.2018.41 (accessed on 10 November 2023).
4. Chen, R.; Zhang, Y. Freight transport structure evaluation and optimization toward sustainable development: New evidence from the SBM-DEA model with undesirable outputs. *Environ. Dev. Sustain.* **2023**, *25*, 1–24. [CrossRef]
5. Baskaran, G.; Pearson, W. Tripling Zambia's Copper Production: A Way Out of Debt Crisis. Available online: https://www.brookings.edu/articles/tripling-zambias-copper-production-a-way-out-of-the-debt-crisis/ (accessed on 24 October 2023).
6. Ng'andwe, T. *2018 Statutory Instrument on Rail Transport*; Zambia Chamber of Mines: Lusaka, Zambia, 2018.
7. Masson, R.; Trentini, A.; Lehuédé, F.; Malhéné, N.; Péton, O.; Tlahig, H. The creation and application of a national freight flow model for South Africa. *EURO J. Transp. Logistics* **2017**, *6*, 81–109. [CrossRef]
8. Díaz-Parra, O.; Ruiz-Vanoye, J.A.; Bernábe Loranca, B.; Fuentes-Penna, A.; Barrera-Cámara, R.A. A Survey of Transportation Problems. *J. Appl. Math.* **2014**, *2014*, 848129. [CrossRef]
9. Wu, W.; Ma, J.; Liu, R.; Jin, W. Multi-class hazmat distribution network design with inventory and superimposed risks. *Transp. Res. Part E Logist. Transp. Rev.* **2022**, *161*, 102693. [CrossRef]
10. Archetti, C.; Peirano, L.; Speranza, M.G. Optimization in multimodal freight transportation problems: A Survey. *Eur. J. Oper. Res.* **2022**, *299*, 1–20. [CrossRef]
11. A European Strategy for Low-Emission Mobility. 2016. Available online: https://www.politico.eu/wp-content/uploads/2016/07/Transport-Paper.pdf (accessed on 25 October 2023).
12. Gandhi, N.; Kant, R.; Thakkar, J. A systematic scientometric review of sustainable rail freight transportation. *Environ. Sci. Pollut. Res.* **2022**, *29*, 70746–70771. [CrossRef]
13. Halim, R.A. Boosting intermodal rail for decarbonizing freight transport on Java, Indonesia: A model-based policy impact assessment. *Res. Transp. Bus. Manag.* **2023**, *48*, 100909. [CrossRef]
14. Kallab, C.; Haddad, S.; El-Zakhem, I.; Sayah, J.; Chakroun, M.; Turkey, N.; Charafeddine, J.; Hamdan, H.; Shakir, W. Generic Tabu Search. *J. Softw. Eng. Appl.* **2022**, *15*, 262–273. [CrossRef]
15. Mohri, S.S.; Mohammadi, M.; Gendreau, M.; Pirayesh, A.; Ghasemaghaei, A.; Salehi, V. Hazardous material transportation problems: A comprehensive overview of models and solution approaches. *Eur. J. Oper. Res.* **2022**, *302*, 1–38. [CrossRef]

16. Fan, J.; Meng, X.; Tian, J.; Xing, C.; Wang, C.; Wood, J. A review of transportation carbon emissions research using bibliometric analyses. *J. Traffic Transp. Eng.* **2023**, *10*, 878–899. [CrossRef]
17. Matthias, V.; Bieser, J.; Mocanu, T.; Pregger, T.; Quante, M.; Ramacher, M.O.P.; Seum, S.; Winkler, C. Modelling road transport emissions in Germany–Current day situation and scenarios for 2040. *Transp. Res. Part D Transp. Environ.* **2020**, *87*, 102536. [CrossRef]
18. EPA. Global Greenhouse Gas Emissions Data. Available online: https://www.epa.gov/ghgemissions/global-greenhouse-gas-emissions-data (accessed on 21 August 2023).
19. Praveen, V.; Keerthika, P.; Sarankumar, A.; Sivapriya, G. A Survey on Various Optimization Algorithms to Solve Vehicle Routing Problem. In Proceedings of the 2019 5th International Conference on Advanced Computing & Communication Systems (ICACCS), Coimbatore, India, 15–16 March 2019; pp. 134–137.
20. Henderson, D.; Jacobson, S.; Johnson, A. *The Theory and Practice of Simulated Annealing*; Springer: Berlin/Heidelberg, Germany, 2006; pp. 287–319. [CrossRef]
21. Alonso, G.; del Valle, E.; Ramirez, J.R. Optimization methods. In *Desalination in Nuclear Power Plants*; Elsevier: Amsterdam, The Netherlands, 2020; pp. 67–76. [CrossRef]
22. Zhao, T.; Zhang, Y. Transportation infrastructure restoration optimization considering mobility and accessibility in resilience measures. *Transp. Res. Part C Emerg. Technol.* **2020**, *117*, 102700. [CrossRef]
23. Mourad, A.; Puchinger, J.; Chu, C. A survey of models and algorithms for optimizing shared mobility. *Transp. Res. Part B Methodol.* **2019**, *123*, 323–346. [CrossRef]
24. Heinold, A. Comparing emission estimation models for rail freight transportation. *Transp. Res. Part D Transp. Environ.* **2020**, *86*, 102468. [CrossRef]
25. Han, M. A Survey for Vehicle Routing Problems and Its derivatives. *IOP Conf. Ser. Mater. Sci. Eng.* **2018**, *452*, 042024. [CrossRef]
26. Currie, D.J.; Smith, C.; Jagals, P. The application of system dynamics modelling to environmental health decision-making and policy—A scoping review. *BMC Public Health* **2018**, *18*, 402. [CrossRef]
27. Sun, Y.; Lang, M.; Wang, D. Optimization Models and Solution Algorithms for Freight Routing Planning Problem in the Multi-Modal Transportation Networks—A Review of the State of the Art. *Open Civ. Eng. J.* **2015**, *9*, 714–723. Available online: https://opencivilengineeringjournal.com/contents/volumes/V9/TOCIEJ-9-714/TOCIEJ-9-714.pdf (accessed on 12 November 2023).
28. Corman, F.; Meng, L. A review of online dynamic models and algorithms for railway traffic management. *IEEE Trans. Intell. Transp. Syst.* **2014**, *16*, 1274–1284. [CrossRef]
29. Manaadiar, H. Understanding the Difference between Intermodal and Multimodal Transport. Available online: https://www.shippingandfreightresource.com/difference-between-intermodal-and-multimodal-transport/ (accessed on 20 May 2021).
30. Sörensen, K.; Vanovermeire, C.; Busschaert, S. Efficient metaheuristics to solve the intermodal terminal location problem. *Comput. Oper. Res.* **2012**, *39*, 2079–2090. [CrossRef]
31. Liu, X.; Bai, Y.; Chen, J. An intermodal transportation geospatial network modeling for containerized soybean shipping. *J. Ocean Eng. Sci.* **2017**, *2*, 143–153. [CrossRef]
32. Wiegmans, B.; Konings, R. Intermodal Inland Waterway Transport: Modelling Conditions Influencing Its Cost Competitiveness. *Asian J. Shipp. Logist.* **2015**, *31*, 273–294. [CrossRef]
33. Wiegmans, B.; Behdani, B. A review and analysis of the investment in, and cost structure of, intermodal rail terminals. *Transp. Rev.* **2017**, *38*, 33–51. [CrossRef]
34. Mostert, M.; Caris, A.; Limbourg, S. Road and intermodal transport performance: The impact of operational costs and air pollution external costs. *Res. Transp. Bus. Manag.* **2017**, *23*, 75–85. [CrossRef]
35. Bierwirth, C.; Kirschstein, T.; Meisel, F. On Transport Service Selection in Intermodal RailRoad Distribution Networks. *Ger. Acad. Assoc. Bus. Res. (VHB)* **2012**, *5*, 198–219.
36. Dandotiya, R.; Nath Banerjee, R.; Ghodrati, B.; Parida, A. Optimal pricing and terminal location for a rail–truck intermodal service—A case study. *Int. J. Logist. Res. Appl.* **2011**, *14*, 335–349. [CrossRef]
37. Göçmen, E.; Erol, R. The Problem of Sustainable Intermodal Transportation: A Case Study of an International Logistics Company, Turkey. *Sustainability* **2018**, *10*, 4268. [CrossRef]
38. Sun, Y. Green and Reliable Freight Routing Problem in the Road-Rail Intermodal Transportation Network with Uncertain Parameters: A Fuzzy Goal Programming Approach. *J. Adv. Transp.* **2020**, *2020*, 7570686. [CrossRef]
39. Dalkılıç, F.; Doğan, Y.; Birant, D.; Kut, R.A.; Yılmaz, R. A Gradual Approach for Multimodel Journey Planning: A Case Study in Izmir, Turkey. *J. Adv. Transp.* **2017**, *2017*, 5656323. [CrossRef]
40. Huynh, V.-N.; Ammarapala, V.; Kaewfak, K. Multi-objective Optimization of Freight Route Choices in Multimodal Transportation. *Int. J. Comput. Intell. Syst.* **2021**, *14*, 794–807. [CrossRef]
41. Shen, G.; Wang, J. A Freight Mode Choice Analysis Using a Binary Logit Model and GIS: The Case of Cereal Grains Transportation in the United States. *J. Transp. Technol.* **2012**, *2*, 175–188. [CrossRef]
42. Moeckel, R.; Fussell, R.; Donnelly, R. Mode choice modeling for long-distance travel. *Transp. Lett.* **2015**, *7*, 35–46. [CrossRef]
43. Halás, M.; Kraft, S. Modeling and Prediction of Long-Distance Traffic Flows Through the Example of Road Transport in the Czech Republic. *Scott. Geogr. J.* **2016**, *132*, 103–117. [CrossRef]

44. Hickman, A.J.; Hassel, D.; Joumard, R.; Samaras, Z.; Sorenson, S.C. *Methodology for Calculating Transport Emissions*; TRL: Crowthorne, UK, 1999. Available online: https://trimis.ec.europa.eu/system/files/project/documents/meet.pdf (accessed on 18 January 2024).
45. Ghisolfi, V.; Ribeiro, G.M.; Chaves, G.d.L.D.; Orrico Filho, R.D.; Hoffmann, I.C.S.; Perim, L.R. Evaluating Impacts of Overweight in Road Freight Transportation: A Case Study in Brazil with System Dynamics. *Sustainability* **2019**, *11*, 3128. [CrossRef]
46. Mittal, H.; Tripathi, A.; Pandey, A.C.; Pal, R. Gravitational search algorithm: A comprehensive analysis of recent variants. *Multimed. Tools Appl.* **2021**, *80*, 7581–7608. [CrossRef]
47. Singh, S.; Chauhan, S.; Tanwar, K. A Survey on Bulk Transportation Problem. *Int. J. Adv. Res.* **2017**, *5*, 1240–1245. [CrossRef]
48. Shepherd, S.P. A Review of System Dynamics Models Applied in Transportation. *Transp. B Transp. Dyn.* **2014**, *2*, 83–105. [CrossRef]
49. Liu, P.; Mu, D.; Gong, D. Eliminating Overload Trucking via a Modal Shift to Achieve Intercity Freight Sustainability:A System Dynamics Approach. *Sustainability* **2017**, *9*, 398. [CrossRef]
50. Jacob, O.O.; Chukwudi, I.C.; Thaddeus, E.O.; Agwu, E.E. Estimation of the Impact of the Overloaded Truck on the Service Life of Pavement Structures in Nigeria. *Int. J. Traffic Transp. Eng.* **2020**, *9*, 41–47.
51. European Commission. Regulation (eu) 2019/1242 of the european parliament and of the council of 20 june 2019 setting co2 emission performance standards for new heavy-duty vehicles and amending regulations (ec) no 595/2009 and (eu) 2018/956 of the european parliament and of the council and council directive 96/53/ec. *Off. J. Eur. Union* **2019**, *50*, 202–240.

Disclaimer/Publisher's Note: The statements, opinions and data contained in all publications are solely those of the individual author(s) and contributor(s) and not of MDPI and/or the editor(s). MDPI and/or the editor(s) disclaim responsibility for any injury to people or property resulting from any ideas, methods, instructions or products referred to in the content.

MDPI AG
Grosspeteranlage 5
4052 Basel
Switzerland
Tel.: +41 61 683 77 34

Mathematics Editorial Office
E-mail: mathematics@mdpi.com
www.mdpi.com/journal/mathematics

Disclaimer/Publisher's Note: The statements, opinions and data contained in all publications are solely those of the individual author(s) and contributor(s) and not of MDPI and/or the editor(s). MDPI and/or the editor(s) disclaim responsibility for any injury to people or property resulting from any ideas, methods, instructions or products referred to in the content.

www.ingramcontent.com/pod-product-compliance
Lightning Source LLC
LaVergne TN
LVHW070456100526
838202LV00014B/1736